JUST BACKDATED

Melody Maker:
Seven Years in The Seventies

BY THE SAME AUTHOR

David Bowie Profile
David Bowie Black Book (co-author)
The Who: The Illustrated Biography
The A-Z Of Rock Guitarists
Pete Townshend: A Career Biography
Cat Stevens: A Career Biography
Deep Purple: The Visual Biography
Slade: Feel The Noize!
The Complete Guide To The Music of The Who
The Complete Guide To The Music of Paul Simon
Rock Stars At Home (contributor)
Tommy At 50 (co-author)
Caught In A Trap: The Kidnapping of Elvis

JUST BACKDATED

Melody Maker:
Seven Years in The Seventies

Chris Charlesworth

Spenwood Books
Manchester, UK

First published in Great Britain 2024
by Spenwood Books Ltd
2 College Street, Higham Ferrers, NN10 8DZ

A CIP record for this book is available from the British Library.

ISBN 978-1-915858-22-1 (hardback)
ISBN 978-1-915858-25-2 (paperback)

Hardback printed and bound in the Czech Republic by Akcent Media

Jacket design by Olivia Charlesworth

Layout and design: Bruce Graham
Front & rear cover images: Bob Gruen (The picture of the author on the cover
was taken by Bob Gruen at the 'War Is Over' concert in New York's Central Park
on May 11, 1975. This event is referenced on pages 240-241.)
All other image copyrights: Chris Charlesworth, unless captioned otherwise

PREFACE

Just Backdated: Seven Years In The Seventies is a memoir focusing primarily on the period between midsummer 1970 and the early months of 1977 when I was a staff writer for *Melody Maker*, the weekly music paper published in London. In among the reminiscences that follow are extracts from material I wrote for *MM* during that time, cunningly edited into one long narrative. I chose the title, a line from The Who's song 'Substitute', for a music blog I launched in 2014, partially motivated by those seven years during which I interviewed, reviewed or simply wrote about rock stars and the music they created. It was a dream job and now, looking back after so long and seeing the shape of today's music industry, what I did seems unfathomable.

Melody Maker no longer exists. First published in 1926 and once the UK's best-selling music weekly, it perished just as we entered the third millennium, its circulation a fraction of what it once was. Indeed, the UK's entire weekly music press no longer exists but I continue to believe it is held in great affection by its millions of readers. Staggering as it might seem today, in their heyday, when *MM* was top of the heap selling almost 200,000 copies a week, *New Musical Express* wasn't that far behind, on 180,000, *Sounds* was third with 100,000 and two others, *Disc & Music Echo* and *Record Mirror*, managed 50,000 each. That's 580,000 music papers sold every week in this little island of ours, over 30 million a year, and you can be sure that they were read by many more than that as they were passed around in schools, colleges, offices, clubs, pubs, maybe even doctors' waiting rooms.

This mega-circulation era began around 1972, when *MM* was in its pomp, so much so that its publisher IPC Business Press was prepared to stump up for a staff member to live in New York, in an apartment rented by them, inclusive of all utility and phone bills plus a living allowance exclusive of salary, and report back on what was happening in rock in America, an expense that would cause bean-counters apoplexy today. Three of us got that wondrous gig, Roy Hollingworth, Michael Watts and myself. I did it for almost four years, far longer than my two predecessors. It was the best job in the world.

By the time the US posting ended, in early 1977, *MM*'s crown had slipped and *NME* was top dog, deservedly so under the editorship of Nick Logan with Charles Shaar Murray, Nick Kent, Ian MacDonald and others carrying the torch that I like to think we had lit earlier in the decade. Nevertheless, the combined circulation of the music weeklies, now joined by *Kerrang!*, was still around half a million a week. (Any rivalry was strictly corporate. We were on friendly terms with the writers from other papers and one *NME* writer and I were an item for a while.) Moreover, this culture of weekly music press was exclusive to the UK; no other country had anything like it. There were no national music weeklies to cater to fans in the US, only Lisa Robinson's breathless New York weekly *Rock Scene* and dry music business publications like *Billboard* and *Cashbox*. The nearest thing was *Rolling Stone*, founded by Jann Wenner after a visit to *MM*'s office in 1967 to see how it was done, but that came out fortnightly and covered subjects other than music. Elsewhere in Europe some countries boasted a single weekly or monthly paper, and in Australia there was *Go-Set* which syndicated articles from *MM*, as did one in Sweden. Only the UK boasted this thriving weekly music press, and the competition between the titles was what kept us on our toes.

It was an era long before computers or even commercial radio. Televised pop consisted only of *Top Of The Pops*, *The Old Grey Whistle Test* and occasional *In Concert* programmes. The popular national press was more interested in rock stars' drug busts and girlfriends than the music they produced. Some acts had fan clubs that circulated newsletters but the only way to find out what your favourite act was up to, if they were going to release a new record or go out on tour, or if they were splitting up or changing personnel, was to read the music press, the only source of reliable information about what was happening in the rock world. Certain acts deemed "underground" demurred from appearing on TV or using photographs of themselves on their album sleeves, so the only way to find out what they actually looked like was to go and see them, not always an option, or look at their photographs in the music press.

The acts of the day needed the music press as much as we needed them. As a result, they were open to our needs, invariably willing to welcome us into their midst, whether or not they were promoting a new record or forthcoming tour. To my mind, this close relationship between musicians and journalists benefited both parties equally. No one vetted what questions were asked of interviewees and, for the most part, their answers were candid and honest. We saw the superstars at work, rest and play. Unlike today, when rock stars are insulated by several layers of retainers who keep the press at arm's length, access for us was virtually unlimited. We were all on the same side, at least until *NME* called Freddie Mercury a prat.

Now, in 2024, that golden era of the weekly music press is a fading memory. *NME*, the last to die, ceased publication in 2018, though it still has a presence on the internet, the same internet directly responsible for its and every other weekly music paper's demise. The loss of *NME* on top of all the rest was the final nail in the coffin of a vibrant culture that I mourn deeply, not least because I was lucky enough to play a small role in it.

I was also lucky in the cards I was dealt at birth. Anyone looking for an angst-ridden memoir that celebrates triumph over adversity will not find it in the pages that follow. I was born in 1947 into a comfortable, middle-class, loving family. My father was the branch manager of a national insurance company, my mother a housewife and charity worker whose life was cushioned by revenues from an iron foundry run by her two uncles. Long since sold off and demolished, our branch of the family did not benefit from its disposal but funds from the foundry paid for me to attend two fee-paying private schools, the second of which I loathed so much it still makes me shudder. On a happier note, neither of my parents were burdened by religion; in view of the confusion that worshipping a deity can inflict on impressionable lives, I remain forever grateful for that.

Like most of *Melody Maker*'s staff and its readers, I was a baby boomer, born shortly after the end of the Second World War into a country whose culture we would alter radically. We were the first generation to look to the future instead of the past, the first with a will of our own, the first to throw off the shackles of deadly conformity, the first to question the wisdom of our elders, the first to invent our own culture, the first to live our lives as we wanted and not follow those constrained by a sense of duty to illusory, outdated traditional values. We chucked all that on the fire and loved who we wanted, dressed how we wanted and styled our hair how we wanted. For me, the key expression of this individuality was in music and this is what this memoir is all about: *Seven Years In The Seventies*, my *Melody Maker* years.

My infatuation with pop music came out of nowhere, creeping up on me from the age of ten, perhaps as a way out of the conventional future expected of me, perhaps because it offered excitement absent from the Yorkshire market town where I was raised, perhaps, like many boys who pick up a guitar, as a way to meet girls.

All three turned out to be true.

INTRODUCTION

"The Beatles are on in Bradford. Would you like me to get tickets?"
My mum, November 1963.

It is December 1963 and I am 16. It is the height of Beatlemania, *With The Beatles*, the group's second LP, has just been released and I am about five rows back, on Paul's side, when the curtains open. The auditorium explodes. Pandemonium. Compere Rolf Harris dashes off and they begin to play, John, Paul, George and Ringo, the princes of pop in their shiny suits and Cuban-heeled boots, squinting beneath their fringes, jiggling their guitars and trying to sing above the shrieking from 2,000 teenage girls. I look on in wonder.

My dad is with me because Bradford is a 45-minute car journey away from where we live in Skipton, in what was then the West Riding of Yorkshire. He likes pop music and seems to like The Beatles, though not with the same passion as myself. I think he is just curious to see what all the fuss is about, and in 1963 in Britain you had to be deaf, dumb and blind not to notice the fuss that surrounds The Beatles.

Mum had obtained tickets because she'd been to many shows at the Gaumont, including an annual pilgrimage to the Christmas pantomime when my sister and I were younger, so she was on the theatre's advance mailing list. She mentioned it across the breakfast table when she opened a letter from the theatre a month or two before. "Oh, Chris… The Beatles are on in Bradford. Would you like me to get tickets?"

There aren't many boys in the audience, only hysterical girls and the sense of anticipation is insane. Dad and I have sat through all the other acts, among them Cilla Black, who performed two or three songs each. These preliminaries now concluded, all around me girls are quivering with excitement, clutching their heads, breathless, sobbing. Rolf Harris comes on to kill time just before The Beatles, because unlike everybody else on the bill they use their own drums and amplifiers that have to be set up behind the curtains. Rolf is destroyed by the screams, a calamity of his own making; the sketches of the four Beatles' faces he draws on his charcoal pad: John has a cheeky grin, Paul has big eyes, George looks curious and Ringo has a huge nose.

When The Beatles come on the screaming doesn't let up from beginning to end, not for a second, a constant drone, like the screeching of tyres on a

Formula One circuit. First George sings 'Roll Over Beethoven', sharing Paul's microphone a few feet away from us, his big round Gretsch guitar all but hiding his upper body, then he steps back to let Paul sing 'All My Loving' for which the three Beatles at the front join in on the chorus, their hair flopping about. Paul shakes the long neck of his unusually shaped bass guitar as he sings. Then it is John's turn to lower the tempo for 'This Boy', a slower number with an intense, scream-inducing middle section, followed by Ringo's spotlight, 'I Wanna Be Your Man', during which all hell breaks loose and the stewards have to hold back girls who rush out of their seats to the front. The shrieking intensifies during 'She Loves You', that summer's smash single, and for Paul's unhurried ballad 'Till There Was You'. Over at the other side of the stage, John, legs apart and staring into the middle distance, his Rickenbacker guitar high up on his chest, leads the sprint finish, 'I Want To Hold Your Hand', the new single, 'Money (That's What I Want)' from the new LP, and ending, as usual, with 'Twist And Shout', its ascending chorus a rallying cry for a decade about to swing. Then they dash off, without a word. The screaming turns to wailing, teenage girls crying their eyes out because The Beatles have left the stage, left the theatre, left Bradford too probably.

I barely heard a note they played or a lyric they sang but the excitement The Beatles inspired that December night is with me still. I wasn't to know it but it probably set me on the path to a career as a music writer, a profession that sustained me until retirement.

*

During the last week of my father's life, in January of 1997, I sat in vigil outside his room at a care home in the village of Cross Hills, about 20 miles from Skipton. It was the same week that Colonel Tom Parker, Elvis Presley's manager, died. Sitting outside Dad's room, I read Parker's obituary in the *Guardian* and thought how different their lives had been. They were born a year and a half apart, Parker in Holland, Dad in Harrogate, and would die within a few days of one another.

Each lunch time for five straight days that week I drove to the nearby Dog & Gun, the pub opposite the grounds of Malsis Hall, a stately home converted into a private boarding school where I was educated between the ages of eight and 13. It was in a classroom at Malsis where I first discovered rock 'n' roll: Little Richard singing 'Tutti Frutti' on a 78rpm record played on a wind-up gramophone that belonged to another Malsis boy. In quick succession I also heard 'Diana' by Paul Anka, 'Last Train To San Fernando' by Johnny Duncan

& The Blue Grass Boys, and two early Elvis recordings, 'Hound Dog' and 'Blue Suede Shoes'. I soon became absolutely infatuated with this stuff, and from that age the acquisition of rock 'n' roll records (and knowledge about those who performed them) became an all-consuming interest that exposure to The Beatles in 1963 tipped over into a lifelong passion.

Of course, it's far too simplistic – and probably also a great exaggeration – to suggest that the course my life would follow was decided for me at the age of ten by whomsoever it was that brought his wind-up record player and a brown and silver London American Little Richard 78rpm recording back to school with him. If I hadn't discovered rock 'n' roll at Malsis, I would probably have discovered it elsewhere, probably heard it on the radio, and still become hooked – but to this day I can recall with absolute clarity not just the actual room where I heard Little Richard singing 'Tutti Frutti' but also where the wind-up gramophone was located and even where I was standing in relation to it.

One day that week on my way to the Dog & Gun I drove up the winding drive to Malsis, past the playing fields where I once juggled rugby balls, past the lake that was out of bounds lest boys fall in and drown, and past the trees where we hid from one another in games of hide and seek. The old mansion was deserted. I parked my car in front of the portico and wandered round the back along a concrete path where I once roller-skated. I looked in the window of that same classroom and contemplated for a moment about how what had happened in there had impacted on my life. Then I went back to the care home and tried to tell Dad where I'd been and why. I might as well have tried to explain the lyrics to 'Tutti Frutti'.

I don't think I was ever able to convey to my dad my love of rock 'n' roll. But he accepted it. He never told me to "get a proper job", though I think he was forever bemused that his only son had managed to make a reasonable living from writing about what he always called "a bit of rhythm".

1

"A vague haze of delirium creeps up on me."
Pete Townshend, *Tommy,* May 1969

I've always loved newspapers. Back in Skipton when I was young my mum read the *Daily Mirror* and my dad the *Yorkshire Post,* and in the evenings the *Telegraph &* *Argus*, published in Bradford. I loved the Andy Capp cartoons in the *Mirror* and a writer who went by the pen name of Cassandra whose columns could be witty yet at the same time expose injustice and hypocrisy. Even today, aged 76, I feel somehow deprived if I don't spend an hour a day with my *Guardian*.

It was Mum who encouraged me to read, drawing my attention to the columns by Cassandra when I was old enough to understand them. By the age of 12 I'd devoured Sherlock Holmes and moved on to her historical romances by Anya Seton, the Hilary Mantel of her day. Mum was a member of the Brontë Society and she took me to Haworth, the home of sisters Charlotte, Emily and Anne, and out onto the moors where Heathcliff courted Cathy Earnshaw. On my bookshelves are Mum's pre-war editions of *Wuthering Heights* and *Jane Eyre,* tiny hardbacks bound in red cloth and printed on paper as flimsy as tissue, and others from the period, Galsworthy's *Forsyte Saga, The Little Mermaid* by Hans Christian Andersen, dated 1926 in her neat handwriting, and a collection of poems by Rupert Brooke, printed in 1917.

I also liked American pop music. My introduction came from Uncle Jack, my dad's eldest brother, who'd spent time hitching around America looking for casual work. On his travels he'd picked up a ukulele and taught himself to play some American folk songs, among them Woody Guthrie's 'This Land Is Your Land', which he sang to me at the flat in Scarborough where he lived with my paternal grandparents. Another was Woody's 'Grand Coulee Dam' and a third, by Burl Ives, was called 'Big Rock Candy Mountain' and had lyrics about cigarette trees and lemonade fountains. I'd have been about five or six when he played these songs to me, the first American music I'd ever heard, probably the very first music of any kind outside of nursery rhymes and hymns sung in school, and it made a deep impression. I never forgot the melody and lyrics to these songs and, when I was older, I sought them out on record.

Next there was Elvis. He looked and sounded like someone from another world. As a boy of 12 I cut out photographs of him from magazines and stuck them on my bedroom wall. I bought or was given ten of his first 12 LP records, four EPs and half a dozen singles. At the bottom of the road where we lived, on the corner before it merged with Skipton High Street, was a coffee bar and from the age of 12 I spent hours in there, sipping coffee or Coca-Cola and listening to records played on its juke-box. That coffee shop was where I discovered music beyond Elvis – mostly Chuck Berry, The Everly Brothers and Buddy Holly. 'Sweet Little Sixteen', 'Claudette' and 'Rave On' cost me many threepenny bits but I didn't just like rock 'n' roll. I loved the emotional plea of 'Will You Love Me Tomorrow' by The Shirelles, and the way 'To Know Him Is To Love Him' by The Teddy Bears was recorded, a haunting quality that accentuated the love-struck singer's palpable sincerity, and how the middle-eight ramped up the emotion, that soaring high note, and how it resolved into the verse via a tidy descending run.

I don't think it occurred to me at the time that all my favourite records came from America, the spiritual home of rock 'n' roll. Those records that I actually owned I would study assiduously, reading the information on the labels and noting down the names of the writers. I also cleaned them a lot and was mortified should any become scratched. Like the skinny, bespectacled nerd I was becoming, I decorated the plain white inner sleeves of my LPs with photographs cut out from *New Musical Express*. After much pleading I was given a guitar for Christmas 1962, a hollow-bodied acoustic, and I split my finger ends just as The Beatles released 'Please Please Me', impeccable timing.

*

At boarding school in York, the only subject in which I progressed was English and by the time I was 16 – the year my dad took me to see The Beatles in Bradford – I'd decided I wanted to be a newspaper reporter. To my immense relief, I left York a year later, pushed out by a headmaster who thought that playing the guitar and listening to The Beatles and Rolling Stones marked me down as disruptive and unlikely to pass any A-levels. He was probably right.

I applied for a job on the local weekly paper, Skipton's *Craven Herald & Pioneer*, went for an interview and started work there in September 1964, spending the next three and a half years as a cub reporter. I made many friends locally, some of them still friends today. Until I discovered the pleasures of the pub, I sat in the coffee bar and continued to play the jukebox. I snogged girls, some of whom welcomed exploratory forays into the mysteries of their underwear. I did a stint as a DJ at a local bar. I lived at home, walked to work at the *CH&P* offices every morning, and most days Mum had lunch waiting for me after the ten-minute walk to our house.

Meanwhile, I swopped the acoustic guitar for a solid electric, a red Futurama

III, and played in two local groups, The Pandas, formed by myself and three Skipton friends, and Sandra & The Montanas, a slightly more professional outfit based in Cross Hills that played throughout the West Riding, often in working men's clubs. Both covered songs from the Beat Boom, but neither aspired to progress beyond the local circuit, let alone write their own material. When The Montanas opted to replace me with a keyboard player who owned his own PA system I accepted my fate and swopped my Futurama for a Hofner violin bass like Paul McCartney's for no good reason other than that I fancied owning a guitar like one played by a Beatle and this was the cheapest.

It was to come in handy. The climax to my casual career as a musician came when I was asked to dep for the absent bass player in The Black Sheep, by common consent Skipton's top band, a six-piece that specialised in soul and R&B with a few Stones songs like 'Jumpin' Jack Flash' thrown in for good measure. Their speciality was a note-for-note reproduction of Geno Washington & The Ram Jam Band's *Hand Clappin' Foot Stompin' Funky-Butt Live!* LP, a record I still own, and a slew of Stax and Atlantic hits like 'Knock On Wood' and 'In The Midnight Hour'. First of all, though, I needed to learn The Black Sheep's repertoire and to this end spent an afternoon in the company of Richard Preston, esteemed not only as the best guitarist in Skipton but the owner of the best guitar in town, an orange Gretsch Tennessean, which he brought to our house. He taught me the bass lines to the songs and I practised them for hours.

The gig was the joint 21st birthday party of two acquaintances of mine, and took place in a marquee at one of their homes up the Dales in Grassington. What made it all the more motivating was that many of my local friends would be there, among them girls I wanted to impress. I did, too, and one of them stepped out with me for a while afterwards.

Nevertheless, I was coming to the realisation that for all my enthusiasm I didn't have what it took to become a real musician. I could learn the guitar chords to songs, lead parts, fills and even bass lines by rote but that was all. I couldn't improvise. I was tone deaf and couldn't sing for toffee. I didn't have a musical ear, which I believe is in the genes and cannot come simply from practice. But none of this has ever stopped from me loving guitars, treating them as special, objects of desire, and, back in 1968, dreaming of the day when I could afford a Fender or a Gibson.

*

Every Friday I went on a day-release course at Bradford Technical College to learn the tradecraft of journalism, how to subedit copy quickly, how to reduce 500 words of copy to 200 and not lose its meaning, how to interview, how to enliven dull press releases, how copyright, criminal courts and government worked. I learned to proof read, write shorthand and type, and there was an English course that took me past A-level standard, the set text *Catcher In The Rye*, so I absorbed alienation and anguish. It was drilled into me that the pinnacle of journalism was to work on Fleet Street in London.

I reported from Skipton Magistrates' Court where miscreants were fined for shoplifting, fighting or driving carelessly, and I made passing acquaintance with the town's ne'er-do-wells and the lawyers who defended them. I visited the police station each morning and took down details of crimes committed in the last 24 hours, thefts of cars, break-ins and sheep rustling. I reported on council meetings where decisions were made to grant planning permissions, repair roads or relocate bus stops. I reported on the diamond wedding celebrations of elderly couples who were photographed holding their telegrams from the Queen. Little knowing what the future held, I reported on a concert in nearby Ilkley by the classical guitarist John Williams, my first ever music review.

I also reported on potholing tragedies in which young men died underground when unexpected rainfall flooded the caverns they were exploring. These headline-grabbing stories attracted the attention of the national press which brought me into contact with reporters from national daily newspapers, usually from offices in Manchester, who arrived in the Dales wearing suits and ties and shiny shoes most unsuitable for trudging over the soggy moors where the Cave Rescue Organisation, among them friends of mine, did their work. In my wellies, sweater and anorak, I sniggered at these daily reporters. It was my first indication that I didn't want to join them.

Like everyone else on the course, I sailed through my journalism exams – there was a 90 per cent pass rate so if you failed you were in the wrong job – and graduated to the *Telegraph & Argus*, the evening paper read by my dad, published in Bradford, commuting daily from Skipton by car, a Ford Escort I was bought on my 19th birthday. This was a big step up, a far more serious platform for my calling. The reporters' room reeked of cigarette smoke, cheap perfume and deadline anxiety. At its centre was a large table at which we sat facing one another, manual typewriters clicking away amid piles of copy paper, carbon and overflowing ashtrays. Alongside one wall were phone booths to make calls away from the noise of the typewriters and people shouting. Downstairs in the basement, huge printing presses started rumbling around noon and continued until late afternoon. It was exciting, at first anyway, a living thing, even if today's paper wrapped tomorrow's fish and chips.

I worked shifts, sometimes late into the evening, calling the police, fire and ambulance on the hour until 2am and, when necessary, heading out into the night with a photographer to cover an accident or a fire. Once I had to knock on a door and request a photograph of a motorcycle crash victim from a grieving family; perhaps in shock, perhaps needing company, they welcomed me into their home and spoke at length about the teenage son who lay in a mortuary.

All the while, humming away in the background, my first love was pop music, by 1968 morphing into rock. I had never missed *Ready Steady Go!* on TV. I switched from *NME* to *Melody Maker*. I saw Steampacket at the Troutbeck in Ilkley, little knowing that their back-up singer, Rod Stewart, would one day become a star. Margaret, my first real girlfriend, whose dad was a Skipton publican, and I danced to 'Eve Of Destruction' at the Cow And Calf, up the road from the Troutbeck, where ultra violet lighting illuminated her white bra. On Saturday nights we went to Leeds Locarno or the Penny Farthing disco in Bradford where we danced to Tamla Motown records, our favourites 'Walk Away Renee' by The Four Tops and 'It Takes Two' by Marvin Gaye and Kim Weston.

Not many of my *T&A* colleagues shared my fondness for pop and I didn't talk about it much at work, but through a chance conversation I discovered that the chief subeditor, Leon Hickman, was a music lover too. Together we approached the editor of the paper and suggested that the *T&A* might attract younger readers if half a page a week was devoted to a pop column, perhaps a review of a Bradford concert by a noted group, maybe some record reviews, or news of a local band's tilt at success. To our delight he agreed. We called it 'The Swing Section' and I began to write about music regularly for the first time.

The first pop star I ever met was Sandie Shaw. In January 1969, Sandie and her then husband, the clothes designer Jeff Banks, produced a fashion line for Grattan, a big mail order company whose warehouse was in Bradford, and when Sandie visited to promote the clothes I was sent along to write about her, along with a photographer and Sally Brown, another reporter whose knowledge of dress design was no doubt greater than mine. After Sally talked to Sandie about clothes, I cleared up the issue of her singing barefoot. "I do wear shoes most of the time," she told me. "I just don't sing in them." The story I wrote was simply used to caption a photograph of her with some of the local girls who worked in the warehouse. Sandie was very tall and slim with legs that went on forever,

and she wore a minidress that exposed far more than was usually on display
in Bradford. I thought she was a very exotic creature indeed, like a gazelle or big
cat. I was besotted.

I wrote off to record companies in London requesting review copies of
records but the response was patchy. The first LP I ever reviewed was *Shine On
Brightly* by Procol Harum. I reviewed local shows by Marmalade, Joe Cocker
and The Move, speaking briefly to Roy Wood. On the phone from one of those
booths in the reporters' room I interviewed the guitarist Jimmy Page who told
me about a new group he'd formed called Led Zeppelin, and John Paul Jones,
the bass player, came on the line too. Jimmy told me they wouldn't release singles
or appear on TV. "We're not like Herman's Hermits," he said. I wrote about
how big groups often ignored Bradford when they toured the UK. I organised
a beat group contest at the Penny Farthing disco and the winners were given an
audition by Polydor Records. It wasn't much but it was a start.

*

Towards the end of August, 1968, I took my fortnight's holiday from the *T&A*
to spend one week in London, then drove down to Devon for a second week,
staying near Salcombe where Chris Whincup, the friend who accompanied me,
knew someone with a boat. Before we went chasing mackerel in the Kingsbridge
Estuary, however, we had an errand to run in London, to observe a group
rehearsing and report back to a Yorkshireman who'd invested in them. John
Roberts, who lived in Settle, north of Skipton, was a wealthy paper manufacturer
considerably older than us who took a keen interest in jazz and rock. He'd
invested £500 – about £9,000 in today's money – in a group formed by Jon
Anderson who, before he travelled south had sang with The Warriors, a band
from Accrington that John Roberts had befriended.

The group, of course, was Yes. Chris and I watched them rehearse in a
basement beneath the Lucky Horseshoe restaurant on Shaftesbury Avenue
where, as friends of their investor, Jon welcomed us and introduced us to the
others. The music we heard was a far cry from what I was used to playing in my
bands in Yorkshire, very complex and skilful, and the songs seemed to go on for
far longer than anything I'd heard before. It was all very professional and when
we returned to Yorkshire, we were able to report back to John Roberts that his
money was probably safe.

In London we stayed in a B&B on Sussex Gardens and because John
Roberts was friendly with Jack Barrie, its manager, we gained entry to La Chasse

Club on Wardour Street, a watering hole for the music industry. We were, of course, on the prowl for girls but our attempts at chatting up fell on stony ground with young women who preferred the company of long-haired musicians to country bumpkins like us. Still, this was all very exciting, my first brush with the pop world, a far cry from magistrates' courts and councils, and it made an indelible impression on me.

I went back to Yorkshire, wrote more for 'The Swing Section' in the *T&A* and was even persuaded by the news editor to go undercover to report, not particularly successfully, on the use of illegal drugs in Bradford's pubs and clubs. Then, early in 1969, the younger members of the staff on the paper were informed that its owner, Westminster Press, was launching a new evening newspaper in Slough and that anyone who wanted to work on it would be given relocation expenses and a pay rise. The first edition would be published on May 1.

Three of us from the *T&A* took up the offer, on my part because I fancied living away from home, though I didn't feel any desperate need to leave my parents. The only row I ever had with my dad was over a pair of shoes he bought me that I hated but I knew that the clothes I wore to go out in the evenings, usually blue jeans, a black polo neck and corduroy jacket, in emulation of the groups I saw on *Ready Steady Go!*, did not sit well with him. Still, there was no one incident that heralded a dramatic departure. It was simply that I felt stifled and needed a change, and Slough was close to London where live music was plentiful. Though Dad was encouraging, Mum wasn't and on the day I left, a sunny Easter Sunday, she became teary, as did I. But I was 22, well old enough to flee the nest.

For a month I lived above a pub on Eton High Street, watching snotty schoolboys in their drape jackets and starched white collars, who in a better world wouldn't rule over us when they came of age. Then I found a flat in Slough above a hairdressing salon, sharing with two girls, one a reporter from the paper, the other the pretty editorial secretary whose ambition was to become one. As soon as I was settled, I drove up to Yorkshire to retrieve my records and brown Dansette auto-change.

The work was much the same as it was in Bradford, courts, councils and committees, but there were two established weekly newspapers covering the same beat, the *Slough Observer* and *Windsor & Eton Express*, and their reporters didn't appreciate us muscling in on their territory. There wasn't any overt unpleasantness, just a sense that we weren't really welcome. Also, aside from a massive upturn in my sex life – I was soon sharing my bed with the editorial secretary, whose name was Jackie – I didn't much like Slough. The circulation area took in Windsor and Maidenhead, both lovely Thameside towns, but John Betjeman was right: Slough itself was a dump, epitomised by the trading estate across the road from our flat. Also, there wasn't much opportunity for writing about music and no one on the paper's hierarchy seemed inclined to remedy this.

One weekend that summer I took my new girlfriend Jackie up to Yorkshire and showed her the Dales. My mum was in hospital at the time with a recurrent back problem but she met my dad and Skipton friends of mine whose beer consumption noticeably alarmed her. Born and bred a southerner, Jackie was a bit of a fish out of water in Skipton, admired for her looks but still an *offcumden*, as many of my pals called anyone born south of Sheffield. I don't think she enjoyed the experience.

Meanwhile, although I'd always been a Beatles and Stones man, another group was creeping up on me and in May they gave us *Tommy*. I'd admired The Who since I first saw them in 1965 on *RSG!* and I'd already bought some of their singles and the LPs *Sell Out* and *Direct Hits*, but this new LP, with its gatefold sleeve and dreamlike blue artwork, was something else again. To Jackie's mortification I played it endlessly on the Dansette. Among other things, *Tommy* told me I needed a proper stereo.

After the first flush of romance with Jackie, I began to realise I'd leapt into a comfy domestic situation without really thinking, from one extreme to the other after the relative celibacy of living at home. She didn't share my enthusiasm for rock music and I was quietly relieved when she was offered a job in journalism on a paper in her home town of Harrow, which enabled us to drift gently apart. I left the place we'd shared in Slough and went to live at Englefield Green, near Egham, in a mansion in its own grounds that had been converted into funky flats. Here I shared space with a photographer, a draughtsman who worked on a Taylor Woodrow building site and a Jack-The-Lad travelling salesman who played the drums and somehow juggled two girlfriends, each ignorant of the other. My friend Chris, who'd seen Yes rehearse with me and infiltrated La Chasse Club in London, now worked for Shell at their Egham laboratory, and he moved in too.

When I wasn't working, usually covering much the same stories and events as I'd done for five years now, I was playing records and scheming. I went into London and bought myself a new guitar, a Gretsch Country Gentleman, my second Beatle guitar, and a Dynatron stereo, two speakers at last. Each week I read *Melody Maker*. I befriended a guy who turned me on to Led Zeppelin and The Doors. I smoked my first joint. I went to a party in London where The Beatles' "White Album" was playing and was given some acid, not realising until too late. I still don't know how I drove home.

Gradually, the vague haze of delirium was creeping up on me.

*

In the second week of August, 1969, I saw The Who for the first time at Plumpton Racecourse, the National Jazz & Blues Festival near Lewes. My friend Chris somehow landed a weekend job working on one of the bars, and he got me onto the site on the premise that I'd help washing glasses. I probably did too, but not on the Saturday night when The Who were playing.

By today's standards, the festival at Plumpton was small time, perhaps 25,000 attending at the most, which made it fairly easy to push my way down towards the front, to the right of the stage where Pete Townshend stood. I knew The Who's songs and the *Tommy* cycle well by now so watching them perform at last, a matter of yards from where I was craning my neck, was a rite of passage I'll not forget; their drive, their fluency, the deafening volume, far louder than any group I'd heard before; that hypnotic sight of The Who in full flight, tearing up a stage in an era when their energy knew no bounds.

As I watched, spellbound, never for a moment taking my eyes off them, Townshend in particular as he leapt into the air, pirouetted and spun his arm around like a Catherine wheel, it occurred to me that my fellow festival-goers, whooping, singing and yelling alongside me, strangers all yet crushed together like football fans behind the goal before all-seater stadiums, were the kind of people I wanted as friends. How was I to know it could be as good as this? At the climax of *Tommy*, as The Who sang about listening to us and getting the music, as the yelling around me grew even louder, I knew I wanted to be a part of it.

The Monday after the Plumpton festival, back in the *Evening Mail* offices in Slough, I was somewhere else inside my head. How could I explain to the people in this office how I'd felt on Saturday night? All too briefly I had been where I wanted to be, but now I was back where I was before. I'd begun to hate wearing a suit and tie, and I didn't like getting my hair cut – both prerequisites for newspaper reporters who were supposed to look like bank tellers. A week or two later, on a hot day after a liquid lunch, I fell asleep in the Slough courtroom, snored lightly and was ordered out by the magistrate. It got back to the editor and I was carpeted. In September I spent a week in France with an old friend, the drummer in my first Skipton band, driving south and staying in a log cabin on a campsite near Cannes. Drunk one night on cheap red wine, I told him how conflicted I was. "It'll be OK," he said. "Something will turn up."

He was right but I'd have to wait. It was October when I spotted the advert in *MM*'s back pages for the job on their editorial staff. Eureka! Why hadn't I thought of this before? I somehow got an afternoon off and caught the train into London, to *MM*'s offices on Fleet Street, for an interview with the paper's editor, Jack Hutton. He asked me to name my favourite group. I didn't hesitate. The Who.

Jack smiled. "Good choice," he replied.

I told him, no doubt prattling on like an idiot, how much I'd enjoyed seeing them at Plumpton, and he wrote something down on a pad on his desk. "There have been lots of replies to the advert," he told me as I left. I'll bet there has, I thought. Half of them were at Plumpton.

A week or two later, Jack's secretary called to tell me I hadn't got the job. But there was hope. I was on the short list, she told me. There might be another vacancy soon. I kept all this to myself, and to soothe my disappointment I exchanged my Ford Escort for a used MGB, red, open top, very flash.

About one weekend in four, I would drive back up to Yorkshire to see my friends there and reconnect with my mum, dad and sister Anne. For many years now, my mother had suffered from an agonising, chronic back condition, perhaps a legacy of her role in World War 2 when, as an Auxiliary Territorial Service chauffeuse to top military brass stationed around York, she'd driven poorly sprung jeeps over rough ground regularly for the duration. Treatment after treatment on her spine had failed, and for weeks that summer she was immobile, in a plaster cast from her neck to her knees after yet more fruitless surgery at Leeds Infirmary. Finally freed from the cast, one evening in late November Mum waited until Dad left her alone for a couple of hours and took her own life. Somehow holding his emotions in check, Dad called me in Englefield Green the following morning. Reeling, I drove up to Skipton and wept at her funeral.

Christmas 1969 was an awful, miserable time for the three of us. Dad tried desperately hard to put on a brave face, taking Anne and I out on Christmas day for a meal in a restaurant, the first and last time we ever did this. Nevertheless, in a peculiar way, the shock of it all, the sudden, unexpected loss of the parent who had encouraged my reading all those years ago, was a final loosening of any apron strings that tied me to my past in Skipton. It was as if I could now do something different with my life without the need for her approval, free to do precisely what I wanted, but whatever it was it hadn't happened, not yet.

In January I was back at the Slough *Evening Mail*, desperate for a change. One thing was certain: I couldn't go back north. In the flat in Englefield Green, I listened to my records on earphones, The Who now joined by Jimi Hendrix, Cream and The Beach Boys' *Pet Sounds*. I reinvestigated Dylan, the '65/'66 albums, and discovered Arlo Guthrie's *Alice's Restaurant* which I could soon recite parrot fashion. My LP collection was growing, Elvis, Buddy and the Everlys from way back, lots of Beatles and Stones soon to be joined by The Who's *Live At Leeds* and a dozen or more others. One day I arrived for work in an open-necked shirt and was sent home to put on a tie. We got word that John Lennon had bought a house at Ascot, just within our circulation area, and a photographer and I were dispatched to investigate. We got no further than the gates of Tittenhurst Park. Although it was a thrill to think I was so close to a Beatle, I couldn't help but think that had I not been wearing a suit and tie I might have crossed the divide.

By March I was in no doubt that this reporters' life wasn't for me. But what to do about it? It was all I was trained for but the thought of another day at the magistrates' court or council meeting was soul-destroying. I was drinking a lot at the Fox & Hounds, our local in Englefield Green, where I sometimes helped behind the bar. Perhaps out of frustration, I seduced Lorraine, the girlfriend of the mate who had turned me on to Zep and The Doors, and didn't feel as bad about it as I ought to have done. It happened in the passenger seat of my MGB, not the easiest manoeuvre, when I was giving her a ride home from the pub. She was more than willing.

Then, out of the blue, came the lifeline I was waiting for and everything changed. *Melody Maker* had just appointed a new editor, Ray Coleman, whose secretary called to say there was another vacancy on the paper and the letter I wrote in response to the ad the previous October was still on file. Was I still interested? Do bears shit in the woods? Of course, I was. I went for a second interview, this time with Ray, who also asked me to name my favourite group and when I told him it was The Who he too replied "good choice". This time I didn't prattle on and I was offered the job on the spot.

I worked my notice on the paper in Slough during April and when I told my colleagues there that I was going to work on *Melody Maker* they looked askance, as if I was jumping off a precipice. My dad didn't comment much. He knew I was out of his hands now. I have no idea what Mum would have thought, probably hated the idea. It didn't matter. Nothing did now. On April 27, I saw The Who for the second time, taking Lorraine to the Civic Hall in Dunstable where they played *Tommy* again and Pete Townshend smashed a guitar.

So it was that at the end of May 1970, I left regular journalism for good and became a full-time music writer. When I rolled up for work in *MM*'s offices for the first time, I'd reached Fleet Street but on my own terms.

It really was the first day of the rest of my life.

2

"No one comes in on Tuesdays."
Max Jones, June, 1970

It was the middle of June, 1970. I drove to Egham station and caught a train to Waterloo and a bus to Fleet Street. For this auspicious occasion, I dressed in black flared trousers, a grey hounds-tooth jacket with wide lapels and a yellow shirt. Foolishly, I put on a kipper tie, not the sort of tie I would have worn for the newspaper office in Slough but a tie nonetheless, perhaps out of habit, perhaps because the only member of the staff I'd met thus far, editor Ray Coleman, wore a kipper tie when he interviewed me. I soon realised the folly of this and never wore a tie again for work at *Melody Maker*, but I resisted the temptation to nip into the loo and remove it, feeling that would make me look even more foolish.

MM's offices at the time were at 161 Fleet Street, on the second floor of a large, institutional, six-storey building on the north side whose doors, back and front, were manned by overweight security men in uniforms and peaked caps. Discomfited by the manner of his dress, one of these uniformed custodians had in 1962 denied entry to Bob Dylan, on his way to meet Max Jones, the revered jazz critic. Many other periodicals published by IPC Business Press occupied the same premises, among them several football and farming magazines, as well as such fascinating titles as *Laundry & Dry-Cleaning News, Psychic News* and *Cage Birds Weekly*, whose bow-tie-wearing editor we affectionately referred to as Joey. Next to *Melody Maker* was *Cycling Monthly* and two doors along was *Disc & Music Echo*.

Considering that *Melody Maker* was about to enter its golden age, when the circulation would rise to almost 200,000 a week, the offices were fairly underwhelming. Cigarette smoke hung in the air, as it did in every newspaper office where I'd worked, and there was a litter-strewn flat roof outside, accessed by a door in the corner. It was dimly lit with a scuffed parquet floor, dented bottle-green filing cabinets on two sides, old wooden desks, rickety chairs and black manual typewriters that looked to have seen service for a decade or more. The phones were also black and made from heavy Bakelite and the walls were covered in a random assortment of torn and faded posters. Periodically a lady with an urn on a trolley would stop by to offer us tea or coffee.

Richard Williams, the tall and quietly dignified assistant editor, had written out some Dylan lyrics and stuck them to the walls. I sat opposite a sign that read "you don't need a weatherman to know which way the wind blows" and on a pillar to my right were the words "don't follow leaders, watch the parking meters". Behind Richard's chair were pictures of Italian footballers, and next to him sat Alan Lewis, the bearded chief sub-editor, whose humour was dryer than the Sahara.

The vacant desk that I assumed was next to one occupied by features editor Chris Welch, a cheerful, curly-haired fellow whose *Melody Maker* features and idiosyncratic singles reviews I had been reading for years. Next to him, in a suit and tie, was the urbane, middle-aged Laurie Henshaw, the news editor, a veteran of the swing era, and reputedly something of a ladies' man. In the corner opposite Laurie sat the venerable Max Jones, who always wore a dark blue beret and spent much of his day at El Vino's, the wine bar on the opposite side of Fleet Street. Max was forever complaining about something or other, a problem with his expenses, the lack of parking facilities or how a "ped" – his word for pedestrian – had somehow inconvenienced him on his drive to work. A conscientious objector during World War 2 who'd once had a fling with Billie Holiday, Max's speciality was jazz but he liked rock music too, at least some of it, and could discuss it intelligently. For this reason, he was the first member of my parents' generation that I met – and one of the very few that I would ever meet – with whom I could relate as if he was a member of my own generation.

There were several empty desks which suggested to me that *MM* was not operating at a full complement that June day, and I soon learnt that my arrival coincided with a period of acute editorial instability brought about by the abrupt departure of editor Jack Hutton, who had interviewed me the previous October. Hutton had quit at the end of April to launch *Sounds*, a rival rock weekly, and somehow persuaded a good proportion of *MM's* editors and writers to join him there, along with Peter Wilkinson, the head of the ad department, and two top brass from the business end of IPC's Specialist & Professional Press. The new editor, Ray Coleman, had joined *MM* from the *Manchester Evening News* in 1960 and stayed for five years, rising to deputy editor under Hutton before being appointed editor of *Disc & Music Echo*. Ray transferred back to *MM* at the beginning of May but within three weeks of taking over the editorship most of his staff had quit. It wasn't quite the *Marie Celeste* but the ship was certainly undermanned and entering choppy waters too.

"The mass defection to what would be *Sounds* happened very quickly," says Richard Williams, who had opted to remain. "He took five writers and his secretary, and also made offers to Chris Welch and me, telling me that he was going to start 'a left-wing *Melody Maker*', which I suppose he thought would appeal. I declined because I'd come to London six months earlier to work for the *MM*, and that's what I wanted to carry on doing. We coped with the defections by working extremely hard, churning out copy."

"It was chaotic, exhausting and confusing," confirms Chris Welch. "Jack Hutton telephoned me at my Catford home one Sunday afternoon. His first words were: 'Hi Chris, are you standing up? You'd better sit down.' He told me he was leaving *MM*, starting a new weekly magazine and asked if I'd like to join their editorial team. Well, I was stunned and did sit down. I had to think about it. But my first instinct was not to leave the paper I loved and plunge into the unknown."

Back at the office on Monday morning, Chris was confronted by Ray who by then had discovered what was going on. "He looked at me suspiciously, wanting to know what I planned to do. He must have been under terrible stress with all his former colleagues, including Jack, seemingly engaged in some kind of plot and betrayal. I assured Ray I hadn't planned to leave. Then during the morning came an offer of a pay rise if I elected to stay. Well that was nice. However, there must have been secret negotiations behind the scenes with management, because come midday I had another offer of a higher amount. Then in the afternoon, I had my third pay rise in one day. It all made it much easier simply to say, 'Yes, I'm staying!' Then I had to tell Jack my decision and he didn't speak to me again for some years."

Up to the May 30 issue of *MM* seven writers were listed as Staffmen on the masthead but by June 6 this had been reduced to two, Max and Chris Hayes, whom I had yet to meet, while the various editors listed above were either leaving or switching roles on a weekly basis. My name first appeared in the June 20 issue, bringing the Staffmen total to three. Meanwhile, Ray was busy recruiting new writers, me amongst them, young journalists from provincial newspapers with backgrounds similar to my own. In the coming weeks many other newcomers would arrive, among them Michael Watts, Roy Hollingworth, Mark Plummer, folk writer Andrew Means and sub editor Neil Roberts, a derisive New Zealander with whom I would play snooker at lunchtimes in the community hall adjoining nearby St Bride's Church. By the end of July *MM* had a full complement again.

All this was in the past or the future as I set to work that first Monday. It was very busy, it being news day, the day when the magazine's news pages were filled. Under the supervision of Laurie Henshaw, I was assigned to write various short news stories, some of them re-written from press hand-outs, others from information garnered on the telephone. I spoke to Ginger Baker about personnel changes in his group Air Force. Chris Welch was busy putting together the Raver column, *MM*'s gossip page, which often featured the adventures and opinions of Jiving K Boots, a fictitious rock star from his home territory of Catford.

The contents of the Raver were fairly random. "Anyone got anything for the Raver?" Chris might ask. "I saw Georgie Fame backstage at..." someone might say. Chris got to work. "Georgie Fame seen digging...".

At various times during the day, I felt like pinching myself to make sure I wasn't dreaming. Here I was, on the staff of *Melody Maker*, Britain's most distinguished rock and pop paper, the magazine that I'd read religiously for three years. I'm not quite sure how I expected the offices of *MM* to be, but it certainly wasn't like this. This was too ordinary, the offices too drab, the staff too matter-of-fact, the situation too mundane.

I wasn't quite sure at what time the staff downed tools but when I noticed others leaving, around six, I opted to do the same, though I asked Laurie if he needed anything more from me. He didn't and I was duly dismissed. It was a far from inspirational introduction to my life on *MM* but a good deal less onerous than working for the Slough *Evening Mail*. On the train from Waterloo back to Egham, daydreaming as I passed Battersea Power Station, I was idly wondering whether it had all been a dream, whether I might I wake up tomorrow and be back at Slough Magistrates Court, once again reporting on the justice meted out to those who drove carelessly on the M4.

*

My second day at *Melody Maker*, a Tuesday, was even less inspiring. When I arrived at the office at the appointed time of 10am no-one else was there apart from Jeff Starrs, a young lad with long curly hair who compiled the charts and filed away press cuttings, and a man of sombre yet benign disposition who arrived just after me but was absent the previous day. This was Chris Hayes and he seemed to me to be much older than his 54 years, resembling nothing less than a relic from a bygone age. He was very tall and unusually slim, his thinning black hair styled in what today would be called a combover, and dressed formally in dark grey, a double-breasted jacket with matching trousers, a cream shirt and dark tie. With the bleak countenance of someone who'd just returned from the funeral of a dearly-loved relative, Chris was a man of lugubrious, melancholy, detached temperament, any levity reserved only for special occasions that seldom occurred. In 2003, in a *Guardian* obituary, Richard Williams would describe him as "a remote figure, resembling an insurance salesman from an early Graham Greene novel." I thought he might be distantly related to the Addams Family.

I subsequently learned that Chris, who had worked for *MM* since 1934, was, like Laurie Henshaw, another throwback to the era of big bands, *MM*'s staple until Elvis changed everything. He commuted to London once a week from Saltdean, a coastal village east of Brighton, and was employed now on a part-time basis solely to produce the 'Any Questions' column, to which readers would write to inquire about which brands of equipment were favoured by the stars. As befitting a reporter of so much experience, he was unusually fastidious in this mission, meticulously chronicling who preferred Fenders to Gibsons, Gretsches to Rickenbackers, Voxes to Marshalls, Watkins Copicats to Binson echo boxes.

After arranging his papers on the vacant desk behind me, Chris picked up the phone to get his answers. With absolutely nothing else to do I sat and listened to his end of the conversation.

"Tell me Eric old boy [Chris always, but always, called everybody 'old boy'], there's a reader from Leicester here... writes in and wants to know what sort of guitar you use these days?"

I was not so much bemused by the fact that Chris was evidently talking to Eric Clapton (at 10.30 in the morning), as much as the casual manner in which he addressed him.

"Fender Stratocaster, old boy? How do you spell that? S... T... R... A ...T... O... C... A... S... T... E... R. Thanks. And what sort of amp do you use these days? Marshall? Does that have two Ls?"

Another call. "Pete, old boy, there's a reader from Brighton wants to know what sort of wah-wah you use." (This to Pete Townshend.) "What, you don't use a wah-wah? But how do you spell wah-wah anyway? W... A... H. W... A... H. Sounds bloody silly to me, old boy. Best of luck with all that *Tommy* business."

And so it went on, with Chris talking on the phone to the great and not so great. He became quite exasperated when a PR person refused to immediately connect him with the rock star to whom he wished to speak – "Well, can't you wake him up?" – though the depth of his telephone book largely precluded the need for PRs anyway.

Occasionally his conversations would stray off the point and I came to realise that he was a chronic hypochondriac, and that an innocent "How are you?" could solicit from Chris a detailed account of all illnesses, aches, pains and minor accidents he'd suffered during the previous 12 months or, if you were really unlucky, a deeply pessimistic forecast of his health prospects for the foreseeable future.

At one point in the day, I thought it appropriate to introduce myself. He scrutinised me closely, peering down at me from a great height, and there may have been a glimmer of a smile, a slight movement of the lips. "Hello old boy, another Chris, what? Welcome to *Melody Maker* old boy."

I hardly ever spoke to him again.

It was verging on the surreal. For almost three hours the office was occupied solely by Chris Hayes, myself and the office lad, still busy cutting up copies of *MM* and filing them away. Since there was no one there to tell me what to do, I did absolutely nothing but listen to Chris on the phone and look at back issues of the paper that I'd read before anyway. The phone on my desk never rang, so I just sat there, feeling a bit self-conscious, redundant, completely ignorant of what, if anything, was expected of me.

Eventually, around lunchtime, Max Jones rolled up. "Couldn't park my bloody car anywhere," he said to no one in particular. "What are you doing here?"

"I started work here yesterday."

"Yes, I know, but no one comes in on Tuesdays."

"No one told me that."

Before heading off to El Vino's Max explained that Tuesday was press day. Editor Ray Coleman, chief sub-editor Alan Lewis and Laurie Henshaw all spent Tuesdays at QB Press, a print works in Colchester where *MM* was printed. Sometimes Richard Williams might join them but first thing in the morning on Tuesdays he was on the phone from his home, dictating a review of whoever had opened up for the week at Ronnie Scott's Club the night before and also, possibly, the 100 Club. The rest of the staff stayed at home "doing research", which meant listening to records or reviewing them, or simply catching up on sleep.

I went out for lunch, on my own, to the Golden Egg next door, then returned to the office where, for want of anything better to do, I asked Jeff Starrs to let me look at *MM*'s Who cuttings file and spent a pleasant hour rummaging through their past. I headed off to Waterloo around 4pm feeling a bit guilty about how idle I'd been.

*

After the purposeless Tuesday, the staff reassembled in the office on Wednesday morning. Copies of that week's paper, hot off the press from Colchester, awaited us and were scrutinised eagerly. I was probably the first to arrive, not yet realising that the 10am start was, in fact, hypothetical, and that *MM* writers came and went as required, not as dictated by a clock. I would soon understand that in joining *MM*, I had converted to a timetable far removed from the daily grind of everyday workforces and, in this respect, it set the tone of my existence for the next decade and sometime beyond.

At noon we all went up in the elevator to a higher floor where, in the IPC boardroom, we took our places around a big rectangular table for the weekly editorial conference, chaired by our editor. Ray was a decade older than me, having turned 33 on June 15, the Monday I joined the paper, but his vigorous domination of *MM* made him appear much older. He was an erudite, rather intense figure, bespectacled with a high forehead, and had he worn a dog collar could easily have passed himself off as an energetic, reformist cleric. I would come to learn that he was a schoolboy chess champion, a newspaperman at heart and, like Chris Hayes, a raging hypochondriac who sent staff home if they so much as cleared their throat in his presence.

Present at the editorial meeting were all the staff I met on Monday, now joined by the magazine's chief photographer, the denim-clad, rake-thin and rather impish Barrie Wentzell. Ray brought the meeting to order and there followed an intense discussion, lasting approximately one hour, about what to include in the following week's paper. As the new boy, I kept my own counsel. But this was more like it, I thought.

Chris Welch, as ever, was assigned the singles reviews, and there was a conversation about who might take part in 'Blind Date', a regular feature in which a musician was played singles "blind" and had to guess who'd recorded them and comment. Someone – it might have been me – was delegated to expedite this. The charts were scrutinised for newcomers. Potential interviews were discussed, along with the impending arrival of foreign, usually American, musicians and the benefits of interviewing them. Max informed us all how he intended to fill the jazz and blues pages.

Ideas were solicited for more general features – subjects like The Future Of Festivals, The Musicians' Union and Rock or Jazz At The Crossroads (a perennial favourite) – that might require several interviews, or "thought pieces" where some member of the staff had a bone to pick on some aspect of music, or broadcasting, or the price of records or tickets for gigs. The year I joined I wrote a feature on the growth of bootleg records and about fans' buying habits by spending a day working behind the counters of record shops in Notting Hill and Shepherd's Bush.

Alan Lewis, as chief sub, ran down any items held over from the previous week that could be included, and made a regular entreaty to everyone to hand in their features promptly. It invariably fell on deaf ears.

Ray or Richard Williams dispensed concert tickets to those delegated to review certain shows, an occasionally vexed issue should there occur a particularly attractive prospect that several members of the staff wished to attend. On the matter of album reviews, Richard supervised the distribution of LPs and kept a tally in a small exercise book, every so often chasing us up if we'd hung on to one for what he considered too long yet failed to submit a review. This was never an issue with major acts, of course, but it happened all the time with B-listers.

The meeting concluded, we dispersed to the *MM* pub, the Red Lion in Red Lion Alley, that was run by a huge gay fellow called Wally who wore a black Russian tunic. Lunches were long and liquid, unless they were taken upstairs where, oddly, there was a small Chinese restaurant. My new friend Barrie Wentzell invariably ordered a "glass of dry white wine and a small piece of cheese".

After lunch everyone returned to the office and began making phone calls, following up whatever had been decided at the meeting. Only on Wednesday afternoons and Mondays was the office as occupied and active as this.

When I left at the end of the day, on my way to Waterloo, I noticed that the first issue of *MM* with my name on its staff list was on sale at newsstands on the Aldwych, alongside the *Evening Standard* and *Evening News*. It wouldn't hit newsagents' shops until the following morning so these were the earliest on sale anywhere in the country, and *MM*'s presence alongside the big selling London evening papers seemed to me to reflect not just its status as an arbiter of taste but the huge importance of rock and pop in modern culture. It also communicated to me that I'd done the right thing in joining its staff. Onwards and upwards…

3

"Keith here, Keith Moon of The Who."
Keith Moon, August, 1970

At first, I felt like an imposter at *MM*. Although my collection of about 25 LPs was expanding rapidly – and would soon increase at a hitherto unimaginable rate as promo records rained down on me from every label under the sun – I hadn't attended that many rock concerts, largely because until now I'd never lived in a big city where shows took place regularly, but it didn't seem to matter because the new team of reporters had similar backgrounds and experience to my own: Michael Watts had written a pop column for the *Wolverhampton Express & Star*, and Roy Hollingworth for the *Derby Evening Telegraph*, while Richard Williams had done the same thing at the *Nottingham Evening Post* before arriving at *MM* a year before us. Chris Welch, a relative veteran, had started work at the *Kentish Times*. What's more, Michael shared my fondness for Sherlock Holmes and together we joined the London Sherlock Society, attending meetings in a building on Whitehall alongside lawyers, bookkeepers and civil service mandarins who wouldn't know John Lennon from Mick Jagger.

My arrival at *Melody Maker* coincided with 'All Right Now' becoming a huge hit and Free breaking big time. I loved the springiness of their style, the economy of Paul Kossoff's guitar playing and elasticity of Andy Fraser's bass, and went twice to see them play in their stomping ground, the North East. This had the additional benefit of introducing me to Island Records' PR David Sandison, who opened his cupboard of promotional LPs and told me to help myself whenever I visited Island's HQ on Basing Street in Notting Hill.

My first interview with Free appeared in the issue of *MM* published the week after I joined the paper. I met Paul Rodgers in his poky little flat in a big old redbrick block in Clerkenwell and we chatted in a nearby greasy spoon café. The same issue featured my interview with Don Everly, done in his suite at the Inn On The Park, and after I left him, my head spinning at meeting an old hero, I found myself sharing an elevator with Dustin Hoffman. Because his toe-curling single 'Goodbye Sam, Hello Samantha' was number 11 in the charts, I was assigned to interview Cliff Richard on the phone, which was difficult because he spoke very fast, and I also reported on John Evan joining Jethro Tull. 'Thank Evan – Tull's Got A Pianist' was Alan Lewis' punning headline.

I also reviewed shows of Pete Brown's Piblokto – "too long and a bit boring" – and Status Quo, the latter enabled by PR Max Clifford who in time would make a name for himself as the middle man between red-top tabloids and those who sought to benefit by selling them sordid tales of deceit between the sheets. Max was working for top music PR Les Perrin at the time and Quo, then undergoing a major image change from modish psychedelic matchstick men to denim-clad purveyors of no-nonsense boogie, were among his clients. Spotting a new name on the *MM* staff list, Max was quick off the mark, inviting me to see Quo at a college in Twickenham. I wasn't particularly keen on the idea and when I demurred, he said, and I kid you not, "I'll bring a bird for you."

I was momentarily speechless. Perhaps he thought I imagined that Status Quo would stump up for a chicken dinner after the show. More likely he realised I was new to the job and a bit wet behind the ears. So, he clarified his offer. "I'll bring a girl for you for the night."

Totally inexperienced in the ways by which unscrupulous PRs might snare the likes of me, I simply didn't know how to respond or whether or not this was the norm in the world of pop into which I had so recklessly thrown myself. "Er, that's not necessary," I stammered. "I'll come anyway."

My name had been left on the door at the college in Twickenham and, mindful of what might lie ahead, I turned up with my friend Chris Whincup just in case the "bird" was waiting for me anyway. She wasn't but Clifford was surprised that I'd turned up with my mate. Indeed, he seemed more than surprised, scrutinising me like I was mad, or maybe gay. Why on earth, he reasoned, would anyone turn down a "bird" – it was left unsaid what the provision of a "bird" would lead to, but it doesn't take much to figure out – in exchange for something as simple as a favourable *MM* review for Status Quo? As it was, I gave them a favourable review anyway and never encountered Max Clifford again.

Far more exciting was driving to Sunderland the following weekend to see Free. "Beatlemania type Free-fever grips Britain," read the headline. "The epidemic will spread," I reported. "It's very infectious."

I spent the night at my dad's house in Skipton, then drove south to Shepton Mallet for the biggest rock assignment I covered during my first summer on *MM*, the Bath Festival over the last weekend of June. Compared to the National Jazz & Blues Festival at Plumpton where I'd seen The Who the previous year, this was huge; perhaps as many as 150,000 people way up on a gentle slope, almost as far as the eye could see. They'd come to see Led Zeppelin, taking pride of place in the line-up on Sunday, the final day. It was their biggest show yet in the UK, an important step in the upward momentum their career was taking, and the first of many Zep concerts I would catch over the next six years.

I got snarled up in traffic and didn't arrive until quite late on the Saturday afternoon, my portable typewriter in the boot of my MGB, all set to report on this major event like the trusty reporter I'd trained to be. I parked backstage, hooked up with Chris Welch and Barrie Wentzell, then wandered around, two weeks into the job and feeling unusually privileged to be patrolling the inner sanctum at a major festival. The weather was fine, though it wouldn't stay that way, and for longer than seemed necessary I was entertained by a chap with a guitar called Joe Jammer, evidently someone's roadie, who was filling in while Frank Zappa readied himself to face the crowd. I also watched It's A Beautiful Day whose singer Patti Santos had made an altogether pleasing impression on me earlier in the week when I'd collared her for *MM*'s 'Blind Date' feature.

The highlight of the evening, though, was Pink Floyd, setting their controls for the heart of the moon and playing until the early hours of Sunday morning. I listened to them in wonderment and awe, then retired for the night, driving to Bath and a nice warm bed in a B&B, unlike those who slept beneath the stars.

The next day I drove back to the site around midday and was astonished by the scenes in the village of Shepton Mallet. There was a phone box with a queue that stretched for almost 100 yards. I calculated that if there were three people in the queue for each two yards, there were 150 people waiting, and that if each call lasted ten minutes, the last person in the line would wait for 25 hours before reaching the front. There were similar queues for toilets and food on the site; indeed, the contrast between the conditions endured by the fans and those enjoyed backstage by the artists and their guests brought a sharp intake of breath. Huge tepees had been erected as private quarters for artists while a marquee served as a dining room in which waitresses dressed in traditional black dresses with white aprons served three course meals and a selection of fine wines.

In the adjoining bar I met the members of Led Zeppelin for the first time, introduced by my new friend Chris Welch. Jimmy Page was dressed as a yokel in his grandad's old coat and a scarecrow hat, John Bonham was wrapped up in a leather coat with fur trim and John Paul Jones, who arrived by helicopter, kept his thoughts to himself, as he always would. Robert Plant, bare chested, bearded, hair aglow and by far the most affable, autographed a pink backstage pass for me, and later in the day I passed this memento on to my friend Lorraine, a big Zep fan, who was in the crowd.[1] I actually got DJ John Peel to make an announcement from the stage: "Would Lorraine meet Chris by the backstage gate in 15 minutes."

It was my introduction to Led Zeppelin as a live force. They appeared 30 minutes after an American group called The Flock and – though I didn't know it at the time – Led Zep's crew, led by their formidable manager Peter Grant, had hustled them off the stage with undue haste in order that Jimmy and his men could perform just as the sun was setting behind the stage. Mighty impressive they were too, even though my view was restricted by being so close to the high stage that I had to crane my neck to see what was going on up there. I couldn't see Bonzo at all, and if the other three stepped back they too were out of my sight line. But I could certainly hear them. Good grief!

They opened their set with the hitherto unreleased 'Immigrant Song' which they attacked with all the ferocity of the marauding Vikings Robert was singing about. Drums and bass reverberated like cannon fire, and Jimmy Page's guitar cut through the twilight like a broadsword. Every other band on the bill sounded decidedly limp dick compared to this onslaught. The reception was phenomenal, song after song greeted with wild applause, and they returned to the stage for multiple encores. It was a coming of age for them, their first really huge British show, a triumph, and there I was lapping it all up. Serious competition for my beloved Who, I remember thinking.

Aside from the mighty Zeppelin, Sunday's stars also included Country Joe and Jefferson Airplane whose set was aborted amid pouring rain due to fear of electrocution. When I saw them boarding a coach to make a hasty getaway I jumped on and grabbed a word with Grace Slick. "It's too wet out there," she told me. "We can't play. We feel we'll just get electrocuted."

There was a long delay before The Byrds played a truly delightful all-acoustic set, and, closing the show early next day, Dr John who tripped the night away as it turned to daybreak. Sunday's music at Bath that year started at midday and finished at about 6am on Monday morning. I saw it all and in the misty dawn light drove straight back to London, parked my MGB behind Fleet Street, rode the elevator to the *MM* office and wrote about the most exciting weekend of my life thus far.

---

1 *I hadn't been on MM long enough yet to realise it was dreadfully uncool for rock writers to ask for an autograph. Now I wish I'd asked them all, all the many I eventually met, for their autographs.*

It wouldn't be the last night without sleep that I willingly endured in seven years' service on *Melody Maker*.

*

I couldn't keep away from Free and in the last week of July found myself undertaking my first ever trip abroad on an assignment for *MM*: three Dutch concerts by Island bands Traffic, Free and Bronco. Since I'd only been on the paper for just over a month this was a big deal, so much so that I called my dad and sister up in Yorkshire to let them know that this new job of mine involved foreign travel, a fairly exotic concept in those days. Truth to tell, it was only the second time I'd been in an aeroplane.

Stan Barr, the manager of another Island band, Quintessence, was also among the party. A big American rumoured to have served in Vietnam, Stan didn't get to sit with the rest of the party on the plane, and once we were airborne he came lurching down the central aisle to talk with us. He stayed there for some time, looking as if he intended to remain standing for the entire flight. Soon he was approached by a stewardess.

"Would you mind going back to your seat sir?" she asked politely. "It's dangerous to stand in the aisle."

Stan looked down on this diminutive stewardess from a great height. "Dangerous, lady?" he scoffed. "When you've flown over Vietnam in a plane with no seats that wasn't safe enough to take off in the first place, with a pilot who's drinking Jack Daniels straight from the bottle, when there's napalm going off all around you, when there's a hole in the side of the plane where the door should be and there's bullets flying in all directions, when the tops of the trees are brushing up against the fuselage and the din's so loud you can't talk to anyone or hear anyone... that's dangerous lady. This is a piece of cake."

This tirade promoted a cheer from all of us but the stewardess was unimpressed. "That's all very well sir, but you must sit down," she replied.

There were concerts in The Hague, Rotterdam and Amsterdam and a TV show somewhere out in the country, and on the way to the TV station the driver got lost in the midst of a forest with Steve Winwood and myself in the back of his Mercedes. I was supposed to be interviewing him during the drive but our whereabouts were his chief concern, and all I got out of the boy genius were a few quotes about his need to increase Traffic's line-up. Having spent the last five years of my life as a newspaper reporter I duly wrote up a story for *MM*'s news pages under the headline: WANTED: TWO TRAFFIC MEN.

"We want another two musicians in the group," Steve told me. "We want another keyboard man and a bass guitarist but we are looking for people who can play more than one instrument. I am doing too much work. It's very difficult playing bass and singing and playing lead organ in between. I could concentrate on singing better without playing bass as well."

Steve wasn't kidding about doing too much work. I watched three shows and came away in awe of his musicianship, the way he played bass on the pedals of his Hammond while he sang and held down the melody on the keys. I think that for one or two songs he even played an electric guitar, a white Strat, while sat at the organ, still playing bass on the pedals and singing, truly the performance of a maestro.

Free were still topping most UK charts with 'All Right Now' which seemed to have crossed the North Sea and was already familiar to Dutch audiences but none of the concerts were sold out, even with Traffic topping the bill. A group of us, including Paul Rodgers, were walking down a street in The Hague when we heard 'All Right Now' blasting out from the speakers outside a club called Tiffany's but when we tried to go inside the doorman refused us entry because Paul's hair was too long. "Can I have my record back?" he asked.

Back at our hotel a local covers band was entertaining guests and some of our party commandeered their instruments for a jam; Jim Capaldi on drums, Steve on a piano, Kevin Gammond and Robbie Blunt from Bronco on guitars and their singer Jess Roden on vocals. Boldly, I volunteered to play bass so long as our repertoire didn't extend beyond 12-bars in easy keys which it didn't, thankfully. In fact, we only managed two numbers before the local group demanded their instruments back. "It might have had something to do with volume switches being tampered with," I reported in *MM*.

It was at the Rotterdam show where Island's publishing chief Lionel Conway and myself befriended a couple of broadminded American girls who obligingly joined us in the hotel room we shared, another first for me insofar as all previous encounters of this nature had been conducted in private.

*

On July 25 I went to see The Who for the third time, my first as an *MM* writer, again at Dunstable where I'd seen them in April. It seems odd now that a group of the stature of The Who, stars of Woodstock no less, would play somewhere like Dunstable Civic Hall twice in four months, but in those days The Who played anywhere and everywhere, not least because they needed the money. They'd just returned from a US tour, and "almost lifted the roof off this architectural marvel as they pounded away for nearly two hours," I wrote in my review. The Who had begun to be billed as "the most exciting stage act in the world" around this time, and I said they "lived up to their name. The Who are unique in the excitement they manage to create – and this is almost entirely due to Pete Townshend's leaping and jumping as he treats guitar and amps with little or no respect...".

I had yet to meet any of The Who but after this show I made my way to the front and grabbed a chunk of wood from the guitar that Pete had smashed. I kept it for years but lost it in a house move somewhere down the line.

The following Friday, two days after my review appeared in *MM*, the phone rang on my desk.

"Hello."

"Is that Chris?"

"Yes."

"Keith here. Keith Moon. From The Who."

Indeed, I thought. Is there any other?

"I'm just ringing to say thanks for the nice review of the group you wrote."

"Er... it's a pleasure, Keith. I love The Who."

"So do I. We must have a drink sometime, dear boy."

"I'd love to."

"Meet me in La Chasse, or the Speakeasy. Come and say hello."

"I will, I promise. Bye."

I was flabbergasted. I only been at *MM* for six weeks and I'd written positively about a few other acts, yet none had called to thank me (and neither, in the future, would anyone else). Now here was Keith Moon, a member of a band that was far and away the most skilled and successful of all the bands I'd reviewed, calling up to thank me for a good review. Of course, The Who didn't actually need a good review to help their career at this stage – unlike some of the others – yet Keith saw fit to call. I was immensely impressed, and this certainly helped cement my love for this great group.

The first time we met, at La Chasse, Keith invited me to be his guest at a Who concert at the Hammersmith Palais, on October 29. From Track's offices on Old Compton Street, we were driven to Hammersmith in his lilac Rolls-Royce which pulled up outside the Palais' front doors in full view of fans waiting in line to get in. When Keith stepped out of the car the crowd parted like the Red Sea to allow him to walk through, cheering him as he went by. The security on the door – such as it was – stepped aside and saluted him. Keith acknowledged the ovation, grinning and waving. I was by his side. It was like walking into Old Trafford alongside Bobby Charlton.

That night was the first time I met the other three members of The Who. "In the dressing room," I wrote, "Pete was chatting about the price of singles, John was trying on a new snakeskin jacket and Roger was shaking hands with well-wishers. Keith smiled contentedly."

I watched The Who's set from a balcony above the stage. They played *Tommy* again, and at the end Pete threw his broken guitar into the crush at the front of the stage where fans fought over it. After about an hour I left with Keith. "Piles of speakers block the way out of the hall and everybody on the staff has a good word for Keith. Stewards young and old shake his hand as we leave and on the pavement a few girls want his autograph. A drunk gesticulates wildly as we climb into the car and slide smoothly away. A meal at the Speakeasy follows. The club is crowded with people who have come to see Stone The Crows but although it is full, Keith has no trouble getting a table."

*

The Speakeasy, on Margaret Street near Oxford Circus, was the best-known late-night watering hole for musicians in those days, immortalised in one of the spoof ads on *The Who Sell Out*: "Speak Easy, Drink Easy, Pull Easy." I would become a regular at the Speak over the next three years, and The Who weren't far off the truth with their ad.

It was midnight. I was drinking at the Speakeasy bar minding my own business when in walked a girl with whom I'd had a casual fling in the past. She was accompanied by a bloke who was holding her hand, so I assumed there wouldn't be any more flinging tonight. A few minutes later she sidled up to me at the bar, unaccompanied.

"Hi Chris, how are you?"

"Hi, I'm fine. Do you have a boyfriend now?"

"Yes, well, sort of. He's been taking me out a bit. He's a roadie for the Floyd. He's talking shop with some roadie mates of his over there." She indicated the other side of the bar. "It's so bloody boring. They're talking amplifiers and jack plugs and load ins at Sunderland Mecca or whatever."

I had just moved into a flat in Bayswater, just the other side of Edgware Road, not far from the Speak. My car was parked outside. There weren't as many traffic lights on Oxford Street in those days as there are now, so after midnight you could reach Marble Arch from the Speak in two minutes flat.

"Do you fancy nipping back to my flat?"

"Really?"

"Yes, we can be back here in half an hour."

"OK."

So off we went, buzzed off to Bayswater, had a quick fling and were back outside the Speak within 30 minutes, both of us giggling. She went in first, a bit sheepish, and I followed a couple of minutes later. I ordered another beer and stood by the bar minding my own business when she came over. "My bloke didn't even realise I'd been gone," she told me.

*

I'm getting ahead of myself. For the first few weeks on *MM*, I'd commuted from Egham every day but I soon realised this was hopelessly impractical as I had to catch a last train back, and that might mean leaving shows early. I needed a place in London, as close to the West End as possible, and close to a tube line that connected with Chancery Lane, the nearest station to Fleet Street. From the *Evening Standard* I found a flat share in Hyde Park Square, the posh end of Bayswater. My flatmates were a couple of estate agents and an accountant, all of whom found it entertaining to have a writer from a pop paper in their midst. We didn't socialise much but it didn't matter. I was in my own world in those days.

I moved into a room with a single bed, a wardrobe and a desk on which I placed my Dynatron record player and two speakers. Beneath it, LPs began to pile up like snow in winter. *Live At Leeds* seemed always to be on top of the pile.

4

"Ou se trouve la fille?"
Night porter at L'Opera Hotel, Paris, November 1970

There can be no question that life on *Melody Maker* in the early seventies was as good as it gets for a young journalist whose first love was rock music. The record industry was about to enter a boom period that was reflected in the largesse it doled out to us. There were endless supplies of free records and concert tickets, access to the best nightclubs, the opportunity to meet the stars of the day, parties thrown by record companies with free booze by the bucketload, and plenty of beautiful, free-spirited girls who weren't averse to stepping out on the arm of a *Melody Maker* writer even if they did see this as the first rung on the ladder to a night of passion with a rock god. It was a lifestyle far removed from the daily grind of everyday folk.

During my early weeks on *Melody Maker* everybody was finding their place and mine turned out to be News Editor. Ray Coleman evidently decided that of the new crop of *MM* writers he recruited in the summer of 1970, I was best suited to the more disciplined task of filling the first few pages with news stories than writing features. This was probably a good call as I'd spent five years nosing out news stories in the real world, but I can still recall my delight when I was promoted after just one month, and for the next three years I held down the News Editor's job.

This was an era in *Melody Maker*'s history when great emphasis was placed on news. The reason for this was the intense competition between ourselves and *New Musical Express* and the newcomer *Sounds*, and the consequent need to attract readers with bold, exclusive scoops. The front page of *MM* was dominated by a brash, headline-grabbing news story, often relating to the demise of a group, hitherto unforeseen personnel changes or an impending tour by a big-name act, either British or American.

It was the immediate post-Beatles era, of course, and stories about the activities of the group, collectively or individually, always made front page news. The most popular Beatles-related story was always a variation on the 'Beatles To Reform?' line, usually prompted by activity in a recording studio that involved a combination of two or more former Beatles working together, or a rash comment from one of them hinting vaguely that a reunion wasn't out of the question. Over the next few years, I was responsible for several 'Beatles To Reform?' stories, the first of which prompted Paul McCartney to write his famous letter to Mailbag, *MM*'s letters page, debunking the idea once and for all.

Paul's letter was in response to a question-and-answer session I did with Apple executive Peter Brown, once the personal assistant to Brian Epstein, now head honcho in the building in Savile Row where in January 1969 the four Beatles had performed together, on its roof, for the final time. Simply entering the building was a thrill but after I was shown into his office it was clear that Brown regarded me as a bit of a nuisance, asking all these questions about The Beatles he didn't want to answer. He confirmed there were no plans for them to record or perform together but when I asked him, "Are The Beatles finished as a group?" he was tactfully vague – "That is a question I cannot answer." – which meant the news story would be ongoing for many more years.

The following week *MM* published the letter from Paul in his own handwriting: "Dear Mailbag, In order to put out of its misery the limping dog of a news story which has been dragging itself across your pages for the past year, my answer to the question, will The Beatles get together again... is no." For many years that letter was displayed in a frame on the wall of Ray Coleman's office, and when it was sold at a prestigious auction room in the eighties no one was quite sure who was the vendor. It fetched £10,000 and rumour had it that Paul bought it back.

Meanwhile, back in the newsroom I also prematurely split a few groups and implied that several big US stars, including Elvis, were on their way to Britain for shows that never happened. Indeed, barring "Beatles To Reform", "Elvis To Visit Britain At Last?" – note the question mark – was the best of all news stories that never happened. In this regard, all a London concert promoter needed to do was to tell me he'd sent off a telegram to Colonel Tom Parker offering him half a million quid for an Elvis tour and it was front-page news, regardless of whether or not Parker had even bothered to reply.

Most of these speculative news stories resulted from intense pressure to come up with something dramatic when nothing dramatic was happening. Because of *Melody Maker*'s increasing status as the most widely read UK music weekly, those PRs who represented the top acts were anxious that their clients' tours should be front-page news and would barter "exclusives" with me. "If you can assure me of the front page, we won't tell *NME*," they would state. And, of course, I accepted the deal, even if sometimes their clients didn't make the front page. In any case, I always thought that a story about a band undertaking a tour was a bit like a story about a plumber mending a broken pipe.

Stories that generated "mania" were also popular with editor Ray. We'd watch the progress of singers and groups very carefully and if it seemed to us that a certain act was about to be promoted to Division One – the "toppermost of the poppermost", as John Lennon famously described it – we'd splash them on the front page alongside a story that said very little other than that they were becoming very popular indeed. Thus did we invent Freemania (when 'All Right Now' topped the charts) and Purplemania (when a Glasgow concert by Deep Purple turned into a riot). My colleague Michael Watts coined a neat variation in 'T. Rextasy'.

Another area made for headlines was the vexed question of bootlegging, then just coming into its own. By a happy coincidence it turned out that one of the biggest bootleg dealers in London ran a record shop in Chancery Lane, just around the corner from our offices. I became a regular customer and wrote about the ongoing availability of *Great White Wonder* by Bob Dylan, and newer boots like *The Beatles Live At Shea Stadium, LIVEr Than You'll Ever Be* by The Rolling Stones, *Wooden Nickel*, a live album by Crosby, Stills, Nash & Young, and *H-Bomb*, live Deep Purple. When I wrote a front-page story about the imminent release of *Live On Blueberry Hill*, a Led Zeppelin live double recorded in California, the wrath of Zep's brutal management descended on that little shop in Chancery Lane. I heard later that an axe was involved.

*

My first front page by-line in *MM* occurred in the August 8 issue. "DEEP PURPLE – KEEP IT COOL!" – a plea from drummer Ian Paice for festival-goers to behave themselves at the forthcoming Plumpton Festival which was in danger of being cancelled due to unruly fans misbehaving. In hindsight, it looks a bit like a confected story but it must have been gratifying for the new-look Deep Purple to find themselves on the front page after the personnel changes that brought in a new singer and bass player. The accompanying photograph was of Peter Green, who'd declined to rejoin Fleetwood Mac for the event.

I covered that Plumpton National Jazz & Blues Festival, where I'd been a year before to see The Who. It was a civilised affair, with seating provided for the folk acts during the afternoon, among them Cat Stevens whom I was seeing for the first time, alongside his guitar-playing sidekick Alun Davis. "He looked confident with a black pre-war Gibson that Sotheby's might be interested in," I wrote. "His quiet, pleasant and pretty songs drifted into the warm air with superb clarity, building up to 'Lady D'Arbanville', the song which, he said, had made him a pop star again."

Deep Purple failed to heed their own advice. They blazed through numbers from their just-released *In Rock* LP with instrumentals from earlier albums and, as had been their habit of late, a version of 'Paint It, Black', the Rolling Stones' song that was a drum spotlight for Ian Paice. At the end, guitarist Ritchie Blackmore instructed a roadie to pour petrol over his line of speaker cabinets and, with explosions going off all around the group, he set fire to them while wrecking a guitar and lobbing debris into the audience. The vandalism was partly motivated by ill-feeling towards Yes who were scheduled to perform before Deep Purple but turned up late to ensure they went on last. The festival hierarchy were not amused and neither, understandably, were Yes, who did follow after a considerable delay.

I would have a long association with both Deep Purple and Cat Stevens, two acts from differing ends of musical expression. I'd already seen Deep Purple in July, in the open air at Bedford Football Club where I was first entertained by Stan Webb and his ever-expanding guitar lead, then by Ritchie Blackmore, a guitarist "capable of sparking with the best", I wrote. A few days later I was invited to spend a day with three of them on a boat, *The Lady Roberta*, sailing down the Thames while I interviewed singer Ian Gillan, drummer Paice and bass player Roger Glover. I was hoping to renew my acquaintance with them after the NJF performance but they were nowhere to be seen. No doubt they'd felt it wise to beat a hasty retreat lest they be charged with arson.

Cat Stevens, bushy of beard and darkly handsome in the Mediterranean manner, had landed in the charts that week at number 21 with 'Lady D'Arbanville', and it was *MM*'s custom to publish stories on newcomers to the charts. Stevens, or Steve as he was known to his friends, was no newcomer of course, but he might as well have been since his new image was far removed from the foppish, velvet-suited Cat Stevens who'd graced the charts with 'Matthew And Son' and 'I Love My Dog' three years earlier. Steve and I met in the Red Lion pub behind our office where he ordered a large vodka and told me he was concentrating on LPs now after recovering from the TB that took him out of the limelight for almost two years. "It seems as I am making a comeback but I have never been away," he said. Early the following year I was invited to watch Steve's *In Concert* TV show being filmed and was offered a newly minted 50p piece in exchange for signing a piece of paper declaring I had no objection to my image appearing on screen.

In the fullness of time, I would write biographies of both Deep Purple and Cat Stevens.

*

In August I saw a newcomer called Elton John at the Krumlin Festival, near Halifax. *MM* asked me to cover the event because I could stay at my dad's house less than an hour's drive away, thus saving on a hotel bill. The organisers had advertised several famous groups, among them The Who and Pink Floyd, neither of whom showed up, and it was badly organised, not helped by atrocious weather; cold, wet and miserable, predictable for the moors at the northern edge of the Peak District.

Elton, dressed extravagantly, came on early on the Friday evening with his trio of Nigel Olsson on drums and Dee Murray on bass, and after three numbers he realised he needed to rock the place out to warm up the sparse crowd. To this end, he wisely chose to play something familiar, the Stones' 'Honky Tonk Women', demonstrating exuberance wholly at odds with the prevailing ambience, and towards the end of his set produced some bottles of brandy, doling it out to the audience in plastic cups. I was really taken with him. Here was a guy who was trying outrageously hard under extreme conditions – and succeeding too.

After his set I went backstage to find him. I was unfamiliar with the songs he performed though I knew 'Lady Samantha' and, of course, 'Honky Tonk Women'. Elton was in a caravan with Sandy Denny, getting changed and polishing off the brandy. I knocked on the door and someone answered. I said I was from *Melody Maker*. "Is this where Elton John is? I would just like a quick word with him." Elton overheard this and said that if this really was someone from *Melody Maker* then let him in. I was formally introduced and congratulated him on his set. "You did really well," I said.

"Thank you so much," he replied, offering me brandy. I asked him about his songs – 'Take Me To The Pilot', 'Border Song', 'Your Song' – and he clued me up on their titles. He was very friendly, humble even, overjoyed that someone from *MM* was showing an interest in his music. I didn't stay at the festival for long after his set, and drove back to my dad's house, returning to the festival the following day but it looked like it was going to be abandoned, so I drove back to London.

"Elton John made a festival debut he will not forget," I wrote in the following week's *MM*. "He went through his songs with the professionalism of a veteran. A man standing next to me commented, 'He's like a male, white Aretha Franklin.' He had the crowd cheering for more and had the whole field clapping to the Stones' 'Honky Tonk Women'. 'I hope this dispels the myth that I am Radio One Club and Tony Blackburn,' he quipped before coming back to a well-deserved encore. His bass player, Dee Murray, was playing chords on his bass guitar and drummer Nigel Olsson must have broken a dozen sticks. But it was worth it to hear the cheers echo over the Yorkshire hillside."

When the review came out the following week Elton's publicist Helen Walters called and thanked me. "Elton was really thrilled." Suddenly, within the next three months, it all started happening for Elton John. I had caught him just before he caught fire, and he never forgot this early support, at least while I wrote for *MM*.

At that time, Elton lived in an apartment building on Edgware Road called the Water Gardens, luxury flats near the beginning of the M40, and the shared flat I had just moved into was not that far away. One Saturday lunchtime I bumped into him in a dry-cleaners on Edgware Road. In those days he collected his own laundry.

*

My second trip abroad on behalf of *MM* occurred in early November, when Deep Purple's manager John Coletta invited me to Paris to see them perform at the Olympia. It was followed by an impromptu performance at a club called Gibus whose enterprising owner had somewhat cheekily advertised an appearance by Deep Purple that hadn't been agreed, let alone contracted.

The club's manager met with a furious Coletta backstage at the Olympia but Purple's manager, unwilling to disappoint scores of French fans who were likely to turn up, was backed into a corner. The group didn't seem to mind, though, and free food and drink was provided for the whole Purple entourage in exchange for a short set comprising old rock 'n' roll 12-bars, songs like 'Tutti Frutti', 'Long Tall Sally' and 'Lucille' that were simple to play. When Roger Glover couldn't be found it looked as if I might be conscripted to play bass – "We'll do them in G," Jon Lord told me, helpfully – but to my immense relief Roger turned up in time.

After helping ourselves to the free food and drink, Ritchie and I left Gibus to check out the Rock 'n' Roll Circus, the Paris rock club that would become notorious as the last place where Jim Morrison was seen alive. After a while I left with an agreeable French girl to whom I had become attached, leaving Ritchie there with her friend, but much to my frustration the night porter at L'Opera, the hotel where we were staying, refused to allow me to bring her up to my room. She was as disappointed as I was. We walked to a grassy area close to the Champs Elysee where she raised her skirt and we did it up against a tree.

Our relationship evidently over, she hopped into a passing taxi while I walked back to the hotel, only to bump into Ritchie who was about to enter with the other girl from the club.

Mindful of my own experience, I warned him that the night porter might not take kindly to his companion, which turned out to be case when he marched inside oblivious. Livid, he stormed back outside where, together, we hatched a plot to ensure that he would not spend the night alone. While he returned to the lobby and distracted the porter by asking for his room key, I was to sneak back inside with his girl and meet him on the first floor where he would reassume courtship. Unfortunately, the porter saw me and Ritchie's mademoiselle sprinting through the lobby and, although I met Ritchie as planned on the first floor and reunited them, a few minutes later the phone rang in my room. It was the night porter.

In vain did I deny having a girl there and he came up to look for himself, and when he couldn't find her, he demanded to know where she was. A confrontation ensued, not helped by my bad French.

"Ou se trouve la fille?" he yelled, looking under the bed and opening the wardrobe door.

"Quelle fille?" I responded, smirking.

"La juene fille qui arrive avec vous il ya quelques minutes," he replied, going into the bathroom.

"Il n'y a pas une fille ici," I said.

He looked like he was staying put until she emerged from somewhere or other, so as a last resort to get him out of my room I suggested he try Mr Coletta's room down the corridor. Unlike him, I knew full well that Mr Coletta had taken a girlfriend, a Playboy Bunny as I recall, over to Paris for the weekend and had, of course, booked a double room for he and her.

John wasn't best pleased to be disturbed in the middle of the night by the night porter, I gathered in the morning. Ritchie, whose girl remained undiscovered, was highly amused by the whole business and I earned his undying gratitude, or so I thought.

I was to regret this foolishness, however. A few days later, back in London, I felt decidedly uncomfortable while relieving myself and realised my French girl had left me with a souvenir of Paris. The clinic at St Mary's Hospital in Paddington sorted out the problem in no time with a penicillin shot in the backside but not before I came face to face with a social worker, a middle-aged lady of severe countenance, who demanded to know the name and address of the sexual partner responsible for my plight.

When I explained that I hadn't the foggiest idea, that it had occurred in Paris with a complete stranger, she glared at me as a judge might look upon a serial offender and delivered a stern lecture on the perils of promiscuity. "No sex or alcohol for a month," she pronounced, as if delivering a verdict from the bench. In the fullness of time, I would discover that three days abstinence is all that's necessary in these situations. Also, that at least one of the groups I befriended took a supply of penicillin on the road for just this eventuality.

5

"You can be the best fookin' band in the world but if nobody can see you, you might as well be the fookin' worst."
Chas Chandler, Amsterdam, July 1971

The remainder of 1970 passed by in a blur. There was Eric Clapton at the Lyceum, where Chris Welch introduced me to Kit Lambert, The Who's co-manager, who was so drunk he could barely stand. I shook his trembling hand and looked into his glassy eyes, surprised at how blotto he was and wondering how on earth he was going to get home. I would have one further memorable encounter with Kit in the years to come.

I was unfamiliar with most of the material that Eric played that night as he was debuting songs from his soon to be released *Layla* LP, and in order to establish their titles blagged my way backstage and knocked on his dressing room door. It was opened by someone who declined to help, sending me on my way rather abruptly in the light of my polite request, and as a result, aside from 'Let It Rain' from his earlier LP and Jimi Hendrix's 'Little Wing', I was unable to identify them in my otherwise positive review. "His effortless technique seems to produce the sound that all guitarists strive for."

In December The Who played a charity show at the Roundhouse in Camden Town where Elton was the support act. I saw him backstage and exchanged a few friendly words. He was overjoyed to be supporting The Who and playing to what he regarded as a large crowd. When The Who came on Pete Townshend announced that the night's performance of *Tommy* would be their last ever and dedicated it to, "Our support act. He's going to be very big."

Pete was wrong. The Who would play *Tommy* many more times into a distant future. But he was right about Elton. After five years of trying, he was suddenly an overnight success. Within weeks of this performance, Elton was one of the biggest names in the business, playing to crowds far larger than the Roundhouse.

My only other encounters of note as 1970 drew to a close were with Mott The Hoople and The Bee Gees, whose contrasting circumstances gave me pause for thought.

Mott taught me a lesson, albeit unintentionally. Before joining *MM*, I had naively assumed that any act worthy of coverage in the paper, who had released an album or two and could sell out concerts, would be living the Life of Riley, comfortably off and comfortably housed. In November I interviewed them at their communal flat in Earls Court where all bar Ian Hunter, who lived in Putney with his American wife Trudi, resided. Well, it was a pigsty, truly awful, worn carpets, dirty clothes strewn everywhere, a filthy kitchen and bathroom, and it was a shock to realise that far from living the Life of Riley, the members of Mott The Hoople were worse off than me, at least in terms of accommodation. They were lovely guys but as Ian Hunter's wonderful book *Diary Of A Rock 'n' Roll Star* later confirmed, life in a rock band was only really comfortable for those at the top of the tree. The rest, as that visit to the flat in Earls Court confirmed, had a tough time of it, even if they did get their mugs in *MM*.

In contrast, The Bee Gees were – or had been, and would be again – at the top of the tree. Barry Gibb occupied a palatial flat at the western end of Eton Square in snooty Belgravia, where Robin and Maurice joined him for the afternoon to tell me about how the three brothers had reunited after Robin's brief shot at a solo career. In an elegantly furnished lounge not much smaller than a tennis court, I was served tea by an attendant who doubled as a butler. "We reformed because we were tired of being on our own," said Barry, which was fair enough I suppose.

I'd had a weakness for The Bee Gees since I first heard 'Massachusetts' in 1967 and I would interview them twice more over the years. What I remember most is that on each occasion – hilariously – they simply argued with one another over how to answer my questions. Invariably Barry would say something positive and Robin would disagree, taking a negative line. Maurice, eternally patient, acted as the middle man, trying to keep the peace between them. They could be touchy, however. Letting slip anything that could be construed as the mildest suggestion of criticism or, heaven forbid, mockery could unite the three brothers in a vigorous defence of their position, as Clive Anderson would find out on his chat show in 1997.

*

In February I reported on how Frank Zappa was banned from the Royal Albert Hall where he'd hoped to perform his *200 Motels* soundtrack with the Royal Philharmonic Orchestra. Unfortunately, the RAH's authorities had decided the work was "obscene", perhaps because of the song 'Penis

Dimension', though they hadn't bothered to tell Frank in advance with the result that he turned up to rehearse, as did the orchestra, and chaos ensued. Frank, bad tempered but still loquacious, gave an impromptu press conference outside the RAH where singer Mark Volman told me: "This scene is just too stupid for words." Frank's manager Herb Cohen added: "I think the Albert Hall are more anti-groups than anti-lyrics."

The real purpose of Frank and The Mothers' UK visit was for them to spend a week at Pinewood making the film of *200 Motels* in which Ringo Starr had a role as Frank and Keith Moon as a nun. Keith, being Keith, invited me along, suggesting I meet him at the Castle Hotel in Windsor where he was staying with the rest of the cast.

As it happened, Keith's driver had inadvertently been given that day off, leaving Keith stranded at the hotel when an unexpected call came through to say he was required on set. He was in a bit of a panic when I arrived but I saved the day by driving him to Pinewood myself in the orange Mini I'd just swopped for the MGB because it was easier to drive in London. Fortunately, the Mini had an inbuilt cassette player and a copy of *The Beach Boys' Greatest Hits* in the glove compartment, so Keith wasn't too bothered at having to ride in a car somewhat less well-appointed than the Roller to which he was accustomed. He was a bit heavy on the volume, as I recall.

Half an hour later we pulled up at the celebrated film studio and I spent an agreeable afternoon watching him and assorted cast members doing their thing in a surreal movie that in many ways foreshadowed the rock videos that about ten years later would become essential for bands with chart ambitions. Keith introduced me to his friend Ringo, my first close encounter with a Beatle. Ringo didn't say much. I got the impression he didn't welcome chance meetings with music writers who might ask him Beatle-related questions he was loathe to answer. Still, one down and three to go on the Beatle front.

This occurred during a period when The Who were using the Young Vic theatre near Waterloo for rehearsals, some of which took place before an invited audience and which were to be filmed and recorded for Pete Townshend's unrealised *Lifehouse* project, and while I was with him at Pinewood that day Keith mentioned that The Who would be "rehearsing" there the following Sunday. Acting on this information, I went down to the Young Vic to see for myself, only to be greeted by Pete yelling, "What's the fucking *Melody Maker* doing here?" He wasn't best pleased at my appearance and pleaded with me not to write about what I saw lest the theatre become swamped by Who fans if the group's presence there became public knowledge. I was as good as my word, though I stayed to watch them running through songs that would appear on *Who's Next* later in the year, none of which I recognised. Nevertheless, I felt rather privileged to be watching The Who rehearse.

*

Like the other newcomers on the staff at *MM* I was drawn to Charisma Records, the independent label run by Tony Stratton Smith, a portly bon vivant who'd burrowed his way into the music business through befriending Brian Epstein, the manager of The Beatles. A former sports writer, Strat – as he was universally known – launched Charisma in 1969 after becoming dissatisfied with how other labels treated bands he managed. He and his staff were often to be found at La Chasse on Wardour Street, the music biz drinking club where I had now become a regular.

The Charisma crowd, among them label boss Gail Colson and her brother Glen, the company PR, a future flatmate of mine, were a friendly bunch, as was Strat who sat on a stool drinking large vodkas and coming up with enterprising ideas to promote the bands on his label. He liked left-field acts, not necessarily in line with commercial trends, and had a knack of spotting the odd act that defied fashion and slipped in through the back door. Such was the case with a Newcastle band of folk-rockers he'd signed called Lindisfarne, led by gifted songwriter Alan Hull, that sang songs about sickly sausage rolls, a mysterious Lady Eleanor and swinging together for defying the law. I saw them at the Marquee and loved them.

In February Strat invited me to join him and Lindisfarne on a visit to Northern Ireland, with college shows in both Belfast and Derry. "In the carnival atmosphere they created, it was easy to forget we were in the centre of a city on the brink of civil war," I wrote in *MM* of the Belfast show. "The grim reality came back to us while listening to records in a student's bedroom. Two explosions occurred within seconds of each other." The next day, after a short drive north, we reached Derry for a show at Magee University where roadies had to form a barrier at the front to prevent an inebriated audience from joining the band on stage. I would go on to spend many happy times in the company of Lindisfarne.

Back in London I volunteered to interview the flamboyant flamenco guitarist Manitas De Plata, in town to play the Royal Albert Hall. Born Ricardo Ballardo, he was less than forthcoming as an interviewee because he spoke not a word of English and we had to communicate through an interpreter, a French-speaking English girl hired for the day by his PR. Manitas used the opportunity to chat her up. In response to my first question, about long he'd been playing guitar, she replied, "He's just asked me to have dinner with him tonight." She didn't seem too keen on the idea, probably because he claimed to be 37 but looked considerably older. He also claimed that Picasso was his father, along with Salvador Dali. Or maybe they were his adopted fathers. He didn't like rock music and told me he thought electric guitars made a disgusting noise but he had at least one thing in common with rock's original electric guitar hero, Chuck Berry: he demanded cash and refused cheques. "If bank has no money, then you get no money," he said via our interpreter. "Cash mean something and cheque mean nothing."

*

Oblivious to the long-term consequences, The Rolling Stones were carelessly managed early in their career. Andrew Loog Oldham may have been a genius at promoting his charges as the flipside to the cuddly Beatles – would you let your daughter marry them? – but he fell under the charm of Allen Klein, the notorious American wheeler-dealer, who somehow ended up owning the rights to the songs they recorded for their first label, Decca. Not until the Stones launched their own label through Atlantic Records did they begin to make serious money from record sales.

Although I had the odd close encounter with various Stones, I never interviewed any of them at length for *MM* or travelled around with them as I did with The Who, Led Zeppelin and few others. Other writers got there first, most notably Chris Welch and Michael Watts, and this was fine by me. The first time I saw them was from the balcony of the Roundhouse in March, and I came away impressed, but eight nights later at the Marquee Club things were very different. This was an invitation-only affair at which they were being filmed for a US TV special *Live From London's Marquee*. I rolled up with my invitation and noted the envious crowds lining Wardour Street, and the large recording trucks parked outside, and took my place amongst a rather sparse crowd of guests in the Marquee's main stage area.

We were told to make a noise, as if we were a genuine audience, but there were endless delays and stops and starts which caused the cynics amongst us to smirk. During a break between numbers Keith Richards objected to a Marquee sign that hung over the stage and tore it down. Harold Pendleton, the Marquee's owner, remonstrated with him, insisting it be reinstated and in the ensuing argument Keith threatened to bash him over the head with a translucent Perspex guitar. I believe it was a delayed reaction to a number of grudges the errant Stone bore against Pendleton that stretched back to the days when the Marquee preferred trad jazz to the kind of music the Stones played.

Either way the incident soured an evening already in terminal decline. The Stones, who were often billed as "The Greatest Rock 'n' Roll Band in the World", seemed unable to perform competently or even finish a song without stopping. Time after time they came unstuck midway through and had to begin again. After an hour or so of this, many of those present sloped off to the bar, causing Mick Jagger to lose his rag and order everyone out. We all trooped outside to where the large crowd of fans had blocked Wardour Street and headed for nearby pubs. The official word was that the "audience was not showing sufficient enthusiasm" but it was a PR disaster on the eve of their self-imposed tax exile to France.

Just over two weeks later I was among a press contingent celebrating the launch of the Stones' own label, aligned with Ahmet Ertegun's New York-based Atlantic Records, and the imminent release of *Sticky Fingers*, the prologue to their masterpiece *Exile On Main St*, for my money the greatest album the Stones ever made. At Atlantic's expense, I and a dozen others flew on a private jet to Nice, attended a party with the Stones at a beachside restaurant in Cannes and spent the night in the swish Carlton Hotel. The host on this trip was former Beatles PR Derek Taylor, then the Special Projects Manager at WEA in London, who was in his element orchestrating a lavish knees-up like this.

"We've been there two hours and it's approaching midnight when a bustle at the door turns our heads," I reported for *MM*. "'Jagger's here,' someone says urgently and we look round. Mick strides in with his beautiful lady on one arm. He makes for the food table and 20 photographers gather round. He smiles and poses and the flashbulbs pop. A persistent cameraman annoys Mick. Mick covers him in wine. The photographers persist and Mick composes himself. This is what the party is for, anyway. Publicist Les Perrin and other Stones drag him to one side and talk. Then Perrin tells us Mick will be over to our table soon, just as soon as he's got a drink.

"But it's much, much later when he does and in the meantime the rest arrive; Mick Taylor in denims, Bill Wyman in stripes. Charlie arrives with an entourage that includes Stephen Stills and Ahmet Ertegun, boss of Atlantic Records. Flashbulbs pop in all directions now. I keep looking around and see that Jagger has started talking at the English-speaking table. I pick up the conversation midway through some chat about The Rolling Stones' new label. 'We can record what we want on it really,' Mick is saying. 'If we like a group we can put them on our label, and we may make solo albums, but there are no definite plans. I don't know what mine would be like, probably songs like 'Wild Horses', with Keith playing acoustic guitar or something.'

"Keith Richards arrives in a white silk jacket looking more like a gypsy than ever. Earrings hang from his ears, his spikey hair stands on end and his eyes look strangely dark. He lunges forward to greet Mick, who obviously wants to bring our little chat to an end. That's it. Mick's lady is tired of having no arm to cling on to and he wants to talk with Keith. The photographers persist until they get the whole group together, and then there's an enormous shot of the group with all the record label people, and with the Atlantic boss, and with all the Stones people, and with the girlfriends. It's rather like a wedding reception where the two sides – Stones and recording company – all want the various combinations of the active personnel pictured together, like the groom's family with the bride's family, not forgetting cousins, uncles and aunts. Well, the company does even if the Stones don't. Around two the party starts to break up. Mick says he's going to the Casino and breezes out."

At one point during this party Keith Richards nicked my gold-plated Ronson cigarette lighter, a 21st birthday present from my dad, which I was foolish enough to leave on the table where he was sat when I nipped off to the loo. Of course, I can't say for certain that he was the culprit but he was certainly sitting opposite my fag lighter when I left the table and he was sitting there when I came back and noticed the lighter had disappeared. Bearing in mind how Keith had dealt with Harold Pendleton at the Marquee, confronting him seemed unwise so I stayed silent. Never forgot though.

The next day the private jet took us to Geneva because Derek Taylor, bless him, wanted to visit a restaurant that overlooked the giant fountain that gushes upwards from the lake. Limousines ferried us into town and we ate lunch there, and a very nice lunch it was too, before we flew home. Looking back on the jaunt now, it seems to typify the ridiculous extravagance that was endemic in the record business in the early seventies. Still, I wasn't complaining.

*

The May 1 edition of *Melody Maker* contained the first of many interviews I would do with Noddy Holder, the frontman of Slade, a group I wrote about extensively. The first time I saw them on stage was at Samantha's, a club/ disco in central London, in early October 1970. There was hardly anyone there, and no one who was there looked like they had gone along to see Slade. It was more the kind of place where you'd find soul music played for dancing, where singles went to hook up and, hopefully, leave as one half of a couple.

Samantha's was down a flight of steps at 3 New Burlington Street, off Regent Street, very dark inside, and Slade were deafeningly loud in a small room that wasn't designed for 100-watt stacks. Chas Chandler, their imposing manager who'd played bass in The Animals and back in 1966 discovered Jimi Hendrix, had coerced me along. While Slade played, Chas bought me endless scotch and cokes and yelled into my ear about how they were a breath of fresh air, which he pronounced "eayer". After their set the four boys came over and introduced themselves, a weapons-grade charm offensive. They were well pleased to make the acquaintance of an *MM* writer, and I thought they were hilariously funny, like a four-man comedy act. Their thick Black Country brogue and Chas's strong Geordie exposed me to a bewildering variety of accents that night.

More importantly, I was struck by how good Slade were on stage, a tight, well-drilled rock 'n' roll band with a knockout singer, full of energy and confidence, casually proficient in the art of stagecraft. As I would soon learn, this degree of expertise had been honed during at least three years of gigging around pubs and dance halls in the Midlands, on a season in the Bahamas and even trips to Scotland, which meant they had the same familiarity with one another's skills as The Beatles had from their time in Liverpool and Hamburg, and The Who as The Detours in the clubs and pubs of West London. I still believe you can't beat this sort of experience in the real world of rock 'n' roll, the world where instead of appearing on a televised talent contest you gig regularly for at least a couple of years before seeing the inside of a recording studio.

The second time I saw Slade in action was an unadvertised gig Chas had booked for his boys at a posh ballroom in the City of London, the financial district, very late on a Saturday night/Sunday morning, for an audience of well-heeled debutantes and Hooray Henrys, all dressed to the nines, probably celebrating some Lord or Lady's 21st birthday. The attraction was a decent pay packet – Chas told me they got £400 (just over £5,000 today), a windfall in 1970 – and all the booze they could drink – beer, wine, champagne, spirits, the lot. They'd given me the address and told me to get there around midnight, and tell anyone who asked that I was "with the band", which I did.

When I arrived, the crew had already set up their gear and Chas and his boys were tackling a vast amount of booze in the dressing room, a daunting task they approached with characteristic enthusiasm. After they'd played, the dressing room was swamped with well-wishers, high-born girls in long, off-the-shoulder ballgowns with low necklines who talked to us in cut-glass voices, watched over by young men in bow-ties and dinner jackets who grinned uneasily as the booze flowed. Happily, no one disgraced themselves by making a lewd suggestion to any of them, not even Noddy who was the chief culprit when it came to this kind of thing, sometimes even from the stage. I watched it all in a spirit of intensifying euphoria and left hopelessly pissed at around 3am, staggering into the dark night of the City where cabs were few and far between at that time on a Sunday morning. I'd wandered down the Embankment and was approaching Blackfriars Bridge before I found one.

Come May 1971 Slade had just recorded a song called 'Get Down And Get With It' which reached number 14 in June, their first chart entry, and once they'd got their foot in the door there was no stopping them. With Chandler producing, bassist Jim Lea composing the music and Noddy the lyrics, a glorious run of stomping hit singles with calculatingly misspelt titles followed: 12 top ten placings between 1971 and 1974, including six number one singles and three number one LPs, which positions them statistically and unequivocally as the top UK chart act of the era.

In July Chas invited me to see them in Holland, and I travelled around the low country with him and his wife Lotte, squeezed into the rear of his wine-red Aston Martin DB5. There were shows in The Hague, Rotterdam and two in Amsterdam, one of which was in the Vondelpark where they performed on a bandstand in the centre of a small lake. Chas bristled because a tree obscured the sightline between the audience and the stage.

"Tell the promooter to get rid of that fookin' tree... mon," he growled in thick Geordie to an interpreter who scurried off with an anxious look on his face. The response, when it arrived, was negative.

"Then tell him if he doesn't cut down the fookin' tree I'll throw him in the fookin' lake and cut it down mysen'... mon."

Whereupon Chas despatched a roadie with an axe to attend to the problem. A little later, Slade having performed their usual raucous set to a wildly appreciative audience who could see them from all angles, Chas explained his management philosophy. "It's all about being seen," he said. "You can be the best fookin' band in the world but if nobody can see you, you might as well be the fookin' worst. You have to be seen... mon."

The other Amsterdam date was in the Paradiso, my only visit to that city's famed rock club. We stayed at Chas' favourite hotel, The 13 Balkans, where The Animals used to stay in Amsterdam. Unambiguously downmarket, it was located in the midst of the red-light district, from where, after we'd consumed far too much cheap brandy, Noddy and I ventured out on to the streets in search of the kind of fun and games that can be found in the centre in this magnificent city. We chanced our arm in a bordello, only to be shown the door for being too drunk, probably for the best.

When I got back, I headed to my room which I was sharing with Dave Hill, Slade's high-spirited guitarist, who'd found a friendly Dutch girl with whom to while away the time. I noted they were in the bed together and that a good deal of movement was occurring beneath the sheets. Not long after the culmination of their union, however, the girl tried to climb into bed with me but I demurred, whereupon she left the room naked, clutching her clothes. I was told the following morning that she'd spent the rest of the night in a room occupied by Slade's road crew.

6

"Nothing beats a blow job after eggs and bacon."
Roger Daltrey, Charlotte, North Carolina, November 1971

I covered two festivals in the summer of 1971, at Reading and Weeley, a village near Clacton-on-Sea. Retro rockers Sha Na Na were the stars at Reading, and the Faces and Lindisfarne at Weeley. T. Rex, fast becoming Marc Bolan's vehicle for long-awaited stardom, had the unenviable task of following Rod Stewart and his merry men, and was jeered for his trouble.

Rod was a favourite of all us at *MM*. I thought the first three solo LPs he'd released were superb, better in fact than those he recorded with the Faces. The group mined both in entertaining shows that veered between high-spirited exuberance and freewheeling musicianship bordering on disorderly if too much drink had been taken. Nevertheless, there was plenty of heart in the band, unlike T. Rex which Bolan had assembled hastily and so lacked stage experience. What's more, Bolan was viewed with some suspicion through having abandoned the underground credibility of Tyrannosaurus Rex in a flagrant bid to win over teenybop hearts and minds. He succeeded, too, but this did him no favours in the long term, or with festival crowds who demanded integrity.

I was able to compare the Faces with my beloved Who at London's Oval cricket ground in September when both bands appeared at a concert staged to benefit those suffering in Bangladesh, following on from George Harrison's New York Concert For Bangladesh in August. The Who donated their fee of £9,000 to the Bangladesh Relief Fund and the day's total contribution came to £15,000, though there was some doubt over whether the money actually reached the victims it was intended to help. The Who outsmarted the Faces by using a better quality, more powerful PA system on the day, causing Rod to leave halfway through their act in a bad temper, and back in the *MM* office afterwards Faces champion Roy Hollingworth and myself agreed to disagree on the merits of both bands.

By this time, I'd befriended Pete Rudge who was managing The Who in all but name after running a top-flight international act proved beyond the capabilities of Kit Lambert and Chris Stamp. He gave me a couple of on-stage passes and I took along my sister Anne who was visiting London from Yorkshire, her first ever rock concert, a pretty impressive start by anyone's standards. We were stood on John's side, just a few feet from where he would be standing himself when, moments before The Who came on stage, Anne told me she needed to use the loo. "No way," I said. "We'll never get back to this spot once the show has started." So, I had a word with one of The Who's roadies and Anne took care of matters behind John's speakers just as The Who appeared. She was a bit startled by the ovation.

It was a terrific show, superb sound and at one point Keith played his drums with a cricket bat. 'Naked Eye', a new song, was simply outstanding, and big spotlights were turned on the crowd at the end of the *Tommy* segment. What a sight: 30,000 fans enjoying the best live band in the world in their home town on a lovely autumn evening. There was a bit of smashing up, Pete pole-axed a Gibson and Keith walked through his kit at the end.

Afterwards we went for a meal with the group and Kit Lambert in South Kensington. Anne ended up sitting next to Pete at the restaurant and they talked together for a long time. Secretary to a hospital doctor, Anne was far removed from the music business and, although she enjoyed the show, she wasn't at all in awe of The Who, and treated Pete like any other bloke. Afterwards he told me how refreshing it had been to sit and talk with someone who wasn't fawning over him or trying to flirt. For years afterward, whenever I saw Pete, he'd ask after Anne and would ask me to pass on his regards. It seemed to me that, unlike many rock stars, Pete wanted to stay in touch with regular people to keep his feet on the ground.

A month later, on October 9, I saw The Who again, this time in the gymnasium at Surrey University in Guildford. Keith had invited me along to what thespians would call a dress rehearsal but I was sworn to secrecy. Entry was restricted to University students and advertised just 24 hours in advance because only 600 tickets were available, making this possibly the smallest venue The Who played during the seventies. The temporary stage in the gym was only a couple of feet off the ground, and those at the front were almost within touching distance of the band. John Sebastian, who with his wife Catherine was Keith's house guest at the time, came along and jammed on harmonica during the set. It was John's 27th birthday and their wives were present, so there was a merry mood on and off stage. They were on top form too, one of the very best Who shows I ever saw; a truly magic evening, but not without its downside for me.

Coverage of the show by Richard Green in *New Musical Express* the following week puzzled the band, their entourage and myself since Green hadn't been there, and it would be an understatement to say that I was angry. Robert Ellis, a photographer who had been there, had sold his pictures to *NME* without telling The Who and told Green who'd written a report as if he was there. By now I'd become *MM*'s unofficial Who correspondent, expected to know everything about the band, and I certainly wasn't supposed to be scooped by *NME*. I explained what had happened but Ray was mad as hell that I'd put the band's wishes before the magazine. It was very embarrassing for me.[2]

I would watch ten Who concerts in 1971, more than in any other year. In October I saw them in Southampton and travelled down with Keith in the back of his Rolls-Royce, Pete "Dougal" Butler at the wheel, and on the way back we called in at the home of Ric Lee, the drummer with Ten Years After, who lived somewhere between Southampton and Chertsey. Of course, we emptied his cocktail cabinet. Afterwards I spent the night at Keith's house where I'd left my car, far too drunk to drive back to London, and the sleeping pill he gave me knocked me out until well into the following afternoon.

In November The Who were the first band to play the Rainbow Theatre, formerly the Finsbury Park Astoria in North London, which opened as a regular rock venue, managed by John Morris, an American entrepreneur/promoter who'd been the stage manager at the Woodstock Festival. As a favour to Morris, the band agreed to open the Rainbow, playing for three straight nights, and to mark the occasion Pete wore a jump suit made from silver lamé material with the red Rainbow logo emblazoned across the back. After an opening address by Morris, a chorus line of dancing girls preceded The Who on to the stage. "Thanks for coming," Pete told the audience. "I suppose you had to come really, 'cos there's nowhere else to go, is there?"

I noted in *Melody Maker*: "Certainly Thursday night was an occasion in the history of British rock. They couldn't have chosen a better group than The Who to take the first steps on the Rainbow stage." After the show there was a party in the theatre's foyer at which Keith entertained the invitation-only guests with sketches from *Monty Python's Flying Circus*. At one of the other two Rainbow shows Keith arrived on stage not from the wings but by running down the aisle in the auditorium, and at another Roger was nowhere to be seen at showtime. Turns out he was on the roof, entertaining a young lady who took his entry entreaty to "feel me, touch me" quite literally.

Feeling that it was important for *Melody Maker* to get behind the

---

2 *About 25 years later, at a New Year's Eve dinner party with some friends of my wife in San Francisco, I actually found myself sitting next to someone who'd been in the audience at that show, one of the 600. She'd been a student there in 1971. An extraordinary coincidence!*

establishment of a dedicated rock venue in London, I interviewed John Morris about his hopes for the Rainbow and not long after it opened, he gave me a staff pass that admitted me to the theatre anytime. It was a passport to all the rock shows at the best gig in town.

*

As *MM*'s news editor I was the lucky recipient of a handwritten invitation to a party that Paul and Linda McCartney threw at the Empire Ballroom in Leicester Square that same month to announce the formation of Wings. It was full of rock musicians I'd encountered in the past 12 months, among them Faces, Elton, Purple, and Keith and John from The Who. I figured that since John was in the bass trade, he'd know Paul so I asked him to introduce me to him and sure enough he did. We managed to push past everyone and I had a brief chat, the second time I'd spoken to a real live Beatle. Paul was wearing a loud check suit, a bit wild and crazy, and his hair was shorter than usual.

Me: "Why the Empire Ballroom on a Monday night?"

Paul: "Why not?"

Linda: "We thought it would be a nice idea to invite a whole lot of our friends to a big party where they could bring their wives."

Paul: "EMI are paying for it."

Me: "When will we hear Wings live?"

Paul: "Well, it should be soon now. We want to start in a very small way, maybe do some unadvertised concerts or something."

As I would do two years later with John Lennon, I simply requested from Paul a more in-depth interview in the near future, and a meeting was fixed at Abbey Road Studios.

That evening was doubly eventful for me. For most of the year I'd been going out with Julie Webb, a reporter from *NME*, but we'd just broken up and it threw me a bit when she turned up at Paul's bash on the arm of my *MM* colleague Roy Hollingworth, dressed to kill and clinging to him like a limpet, but this was overshadowed by my second close encounter with a real live Beatle.

The next day in the office Roy looked a tad sheepish so the Julie issue was a bit of an elephant in the room. No matter. The day after saw my first ever visit to Abbey Road, and on the way I walked across the famous zebra crossing more than once before heading up the small flight of steps to the reception, thinking as I did how many famous feet had climbed these steps before me. I met Paul in the control room of Studio 2, the holiest of the holies, and my head swam a bit a bit as I looked down on the big studio floor where The Beatles made history, all those records that had given me and millions of others so much pleasure, but now here I was faced with Paul in a strop about John's song 'How Do You Sleep?' on his *Imagine* LP.

"John and Yoko are not cool in what they're doing," he said, a quote *MM* chose to trailer on page one – and it seemed to me I'd arrived too late and missed the party, as now John and Paul were sniping at each other like a divorced couple, a bit like me and Julie.

"I just want the four of us to get together somewhere and sign a piece of paper saying it's all over, and we want to divide the money four ways," Paul told me. "No one would be there, not even Linda or Yoko, or Allen Klein. We'd just sign the paper and hand it to the business people and let them sort it out. That's all I want now. But John won't do it. Everybody thinks I am the aggressor but I'm not you know, I just want out.

"John's whole image now is very honest and open. He's all right is John, I like his *Imagine* album but I didn't like the others... there was too much political stuff on the other albums. You know I only listen to them to see if there's something I can pinch."

Paul touched on the song 'How Do You Sleep?' "I think it's silly. So what if I live with straights? I like straights. I have straight babies... he says the only thing I did was 'Yesterday' and he knows that's wrong."

When I asked about The Beatles' live shows – or rather lack of them – Paul remarked: "I just wanted to get into a van and do an unadvertised Saturday night hop at Slough Town Hall or somewhere like that. We'd call ourselves Ricki & The Red Streaks or something and just get up and play."

This was the only substantial interview I ever did with Paul, although I would encounter him several times again over the years. It evidently touched a nerve with John who wrote a long letter to *MM* the following week, answering several points that Paul had made, which we published in full. During my time on the paper John wrote to us many times, usually typed letters with his handwriting scribbled in the margins, often with "LP Winner" at the bottom. This one ended with him writing: "Love and peace. Get it on and rip 'em off! John Lennon."

Still, it was now two down and two to go in my quest to meet all four Beatles.

*

In November of 1971 I flew to America for the first time, to New York to attend a party thrown by RCA Records to celebrate their signing The Kinks, but in the event I saw The Who yet again, on the opening night of a US tour that took them across the south and up into California.

I was deliriously excited to be visiting the US. There was a long queue for visas at the Embassy in Grosvenor Square where I handed over a letter from Ray that explained the purpose of my visit. I filled in a form declaring I had never been a member of the Communist Party and wouldn't seek to overthrow the Government of the United States during my stay. I was in a group of four, along with Rodney Burbeck, RCA's press officer, and writers from *NME* and the London *Evening Standard*. We flew on an early jumbo jet, a plane that had only come into service the previous year, and so great was the novelty of watching a film as I flew over the Atlantic that I can still remember it: *The Anderson Tapes*, in which Sean Connery starred as the leader of a gang of thieves who rob every apartment in a tall building in Manhattan – which just happened to be my destination.

We were met at JFK by the driver of a long black limousine, the first I'd ever seen, and driven ever so smoothly, a magic carpet ride into Manhattan. I was star-struck at the sights, sound and smell of America. The roads were called expressways or parkways or boulevards. There were huge green highway signs, toll booths, flashing neon lights, big American cars, yellow cabs, steam rising from the streets and buildings taller than any I'd ever seen before, row on row of enormous skyscrapers. Everyone seemed to be in a hurry.

We stayed at the swanky Plaza on the south east corner of Central Park, the same hotel where The Beatles had stayed on their first visit to NYC in 1964, and on our first night in New York our hosts took us to dinner and a Broadway musical. When my head hit the pillow my wristwatch, still in UK time, said it was 4.30am, and the following morning I awoke early in my Plaza bed with my first dose of jet lag. I ordered coffee and breakfast on room service, switched on the TV and discovered something about America I didn't like – the endless crass adverts. When the food arrived, the bellboy hung around waiting for his tip, but all I had were five $20 bills. I told him to come back later. I liked his crispy bacon and scrambled eggs though, and the coffee was the best I'd ever tasted.

That day RCA had laid on touristy things. We all went to the top of the Empire State Building and there was a boat trip around Manhattan, but I opted out and went off on my own, hailing my first yellow cab. "Bleecker Street," I told the driver, not knowing where it was, only that I wanted to walk in the freewheelin' footsteps of Bob Dylan. I went into a coffee shop in the Village and for the first time in my life ate a sandwich with multiple ingredients. If you ordered a ham and cheese sandwich in the UK, you'd have been asked which, ham *or* cheese. Here you could have both ham *and* cheese between two fat slices of bread pinned together with a cocktail stick to stop everything from falling out. What a stunning idea.

In the evening we went to The Kinks' party at the Playboy Club on East 59th Street. I guess no one worried too much in those days about waitresses with fluffy tails wearing corsets, bunny ears and a fixed smile. Ray Davies, brother Dave, Mick Avory and the rest were there, of course, and so – to my delight and surprise – were John and Keith from The Who, shepherded by tour boss John "Wiggy" Wolff. Turned out they had stopped off for a night or two in New York before a US tour.

Rivers of free booze were served by bunny girls, one of whom might have been Debbie Harry. Ray and some bigwig from RCA made short speeches. When the party wound down John, Keith and Wiggy invited me to share a cab downtown to visit Nobodys, the rock 'n' roll bar on Bleecker Street. I'd heard that Nobodys was the NY equivalent of the Speakeasy in London, very debauched and teeming with groupies, but I wasn't impressed. It was just one big room with a bar in the corner.

I was dog-tired and drunk by now, of course, but in the dim light over more brandies John and Keith told me about the imminent Who tour and suggested I join them. It sounded like a great idea but I was conflicted because this might not sit well with RCA and The Kinks, who'd paid for my trip to America. Diplomacy was required.

Over the past 24 hours I had repeatedly asked if I could interview Ray and Dave Davies but my requests were stalled. "We'll get back to you on it," I was told, but I heard nothing. I learned that on the last night of our stay The Kinks were playing a gig somewhere in upstate New York but no one from RCA or The Kinks' management seemed willing to take me there or even arrange transport. I thought this was absurd. I'd come all this way and was staying three nights in the Plaza at great expense, and all I could write about was a knees-up at the Playboy Club. *MM*'s circulation was now approaching 200,000 a week, and here was a fantastic opportunity for me to do a big piece on The Kinks, maybe focusing on their uneasy relationship with America, but the general indolence surrounding them made this impossible. No one could be bothered.

So I decided to hell with it – I'd write about The Who as well. Pete Rudge was handling their American tours from an office in NY on 57th Street that he shared with Vicki Wickham, once the booker for *Ready Steady Go!* and now the manager of LaBelle. The morning after the party, indecently hungover and still jetlagged, I walked there from the Plaza, past the Russian Tea Room and Carnegie Hall. Two days into my visit I was beginning to like walking the streets of New York, just observing everything and everyone around me. I decided I could learn to like this town. Six years later I would bump into Ray Davies on 57th Street and together we would mourn Elvis who had died the week before.

Pete Rudge wasn't around when I reached his office but Vicki was and she told me he would be at some lunchtime record company bash in a restaurant on the Upper East Side. We went together, and when I cornered Pete I explained my situation to him. Unsurprisingly, he didn't hesitate for a moment to arrange travel for me so I could report on the opening night of The Who's tour at Charlotte, North Carolina. When I got back to the Plaza, I re-booked my flight to London and told Rodney Burbeck I wouldn't be returning to the UK with everybody else the following day. He wasn't best pleased, but there was nothing he could do. I wasn't the most popular guest at an RCA dinner on that final night but all the while I couldn't help but contrast and compare the decisiveness of The Who's management with the lethargy of The Kinks'.

The next 24 hours were memorable to say the least. I met up with The Who at La Guardia, New York's domestic airport, and on the plane down the East Coast sat next to Pete Townshend. He told me about an impending visit to Myrtle Beach, the location of the world's biggest Meher Baba centre, and how on a recent visit to a wealthy friend's home in Florida a stunning girl in a bikini had propositioned him as he relaxed by a pool. This led to a discussion on the temptations faced by married rock stars but we were interrupted when the plane hit turbulence, and as we were tossed about in the sky Pete suddenly developed a nose bleed. It was a regular commercial flight, with two seats in each row. I was sat by the window with Pete in the aisle, so he twisted sideways in his seat and leant over backwards with his head in my lap looking up at me. I asked the stewardess for a damp cloth and applied it to his nose, well aware that I had unexpectedly become responsible for the most famous nose in rock. This was not part of the *MM* job description.

Charlotte was very different from New York but also very different from English provincial cities. The streets were wider and there was so much more space everywhere, lots more green and huge free parking lots. Everything just seemed bigger – the roads, the stores, the gas stations, the fast food restaurants. Back home everything seemed cramped in comparison, and messier too. I shared a limo with The Who from the airport to their hotel, a modest Holiday Inn, and waiting for them was a package freighted from MCA in Los Angeles containing advance copies of their hits LP *Meaty Beaty Big And Bouncy*. We all sat around in Pete Rudge's room admiring it. I still have the copy I was given that day.

Charlotte Coliseum was packed with 13,000 expectant fans for what was The Who's début in North Carolina. Pete Rudge gave me a backstage button, which I retained as a keepsake, and I was hanging around in the dressing room chatting with Keith before The Who went on stage. Ever impulsive, he proposed we go on a voyage of discovery and in a storage room along a winding corridor we discovered the perfect instrument of mischief, a man-sized hollow wooden egg on a four-wheeled cart used in parades. Keith concealed himself inside the egg and I towed him back towards the dressing room where he intended to leap out and surprise everyone. Indeed, he was hatching a plot to be wheeled on stage in this contraption. Unfortunately, en route to the dressing room there was a steeply sloping downhill curve, and I lost control, causing it to crash, the egg to topple over and Keith to come tumbling out head first. The noise alerted a security guard who arrived on the scene in a very bad temper. He failed to recognise The Who's drummer, and only our English accents saved us from being chucked out into the car park.

I watched the show from the side of the stage, a few rows up on Pete's side. I was pretty familiar with their set, but you could never take things for granted with The Who. By now I knew that anything could happen and I was never disappointed. They ran on stage and opened with 'I Can't Explain', reaching the familiar riff after a ragged jam, and then played 'Summertime Blues', a loosener before the more complex songs, five in all, from *Who's Next*. The stage wasn't too high off the ground and there were concerns the audience might rush to the front and try to climb up, but they calmed down once The Who got into their stride.

The concert took on added momentum during a reduced *Tommy* medley of five songs which, judging by the reaction, was what the crowd had come to hear. After its 'See Me, Feel Me' climax, they launched into 'Baby Don't You Do It', which became an extended jam, and closed with 'My Generation' morphing into 'Naked Eye', all delivered by what I believed was the best rock band in the world in full flight. That casual panache, that extraordinary blend of rashness and fluency, humour and sincerity, vigour and ease, that awe-inspiring experience of seeing The Who at the height of their powers, won over another American town in another American state right before my eyes. The only logical way to draw the proceedings to a close was for its guitarist to inflict damage to the speaker stacks behind him.

In the calm of the dressing room the four slurped drinks. As ever, they took it for granted what they'd just done. There was no preening, no back-slapping.

There never was. I was hoping, however, that there might be some fun and games back at the hotel. While Pete Rudge stayed behind with the promoter to count the proceeds, I left the venue in the back of a limousine with the four members of The Who and Wiggy sat in the front seat next to the driver. Trapped in traffic leaving the car park, John said, "You know you've made it when you get stuck in your own traffic jam." Pete laughed and said you'd only made it when you'd figured out how to avoid getting stuck in your own traffic jam.

Back at the hotel we all headed for the bar. Roger soon left, accompanied by a girl who smiled like she'd won the lottery, and before long Pete and John left too. When the bar shut I wound up in Keith's room with some Who crew, a local fan or two who'd discovered our whereabouts, maybe the odd intrepid girl, two bottles of champagne, some vodka and a mini-bar that was soon exhausted. Some of Keith's guests were watching a movie on a TV mounted on a bracket on the wall, but not Keith, who was telling jokes and laughing at them himself. "Did you hear the one about two nuns and a goat?"

Keith was talking too loud for those watching TV. Someone asked him to make less noise. "We're trying to watch a movie."

This was a catastrophic mistake. As calm as you like, our host strode over to the TV set and, without even bothering to unplug it, wrenched it from its mounting, carried it to the window and lobbed it through the glass. We were about eight floors up. There was a tremendous crash. "As I was saying…," continued Keith to his now speechless audience. "There were these two nuns and a goat…".

It took about three minutes for the night porter to arrive. Keith was ready for him, and before the hapless man could even open his mouth Keith hit his stride. "I don't know how I can possibly apologise for that terrible accident," he began in exaggerated Queen's English. "I can't tell you how sorry I am, dear boy. I was trying to move the television closer to the window so that more of my guests could watch it from the bed when it slipped from my grasp and, heaven forbid, fell through the window… just the most awful thing to happen, a really dreadful accident… I just hope no-one was beneath it. Where did it fall? In the car park? Oh dear, what a terrible thing to have happened. How much will it cost? I can pay you now…".

And it so it went on, with Keith never allowing the porter to get a word in edgeways until, finally, compensation having been agreed, the porter was about to leave and return with some material with which to affect a temporary repair on the window, which Keith had requested. Meanwhile, all of us had somehow managed to suppress our laughter. Finally, as a crowning gesture, Keith delivered the killer blow: "Er... if you're coming back would you be so kind as to bring two more bottles of chilled champagne and..." Keith hesitated for just the right number of seconds, "... another TV?"

The following morning, I went down for breakfast in the dining room, arriving just as Roger was polishing off the American equivalent of a full English. I was surprised to see him there. "Bit of trouble with Keith last night," he said as I took a seat at his table. I nodded, wondering how he knew. "Bloody typical. Bloody idiot."

I told Roger I hadn't expected to see him in the dining room. "Bird was still asleep," he said by way of an explanation. "A bit tired. Didn't 'ave the 'eart to wake her, so came down 'ere." He polished off his cup of coffee and stood up. "I will now though. Nothing beats a blow job after eggs and bacon."

And that was the last I saw of The Who, collectively at least, until August 17 the following year in Amsterdam. Aside from Roger, I didn't see any of them before I left their hotel. Pete was headed to Myrtle Beach on a day off. I checked out of the hotel, got a cab to the airport, then flew back to NY and on to London after an unforgettable introduction to America.

7

"The band thought I was dead."
Frank Zappa, *The Real Frank Zappa Book*, 1989

I returned from America with two LPs in my luggage, both of which I reviewed in the following week's *MM*. Of The Kinks' *Muswell Hillbillies*, their first for RCA, curiously pressed on ultra-thin bendy vinyl, I wrote: "Musically, there's nothing on the album to compete with 'Waterloo Sunset' but it's catchy stuff all the same. If the tunes don't appeal, listen to the words – they will." Turning to The Who's *Meaty, Beaty, Big And Bouncy*, I mentioned that the group's origins were reflected on the inside of the fold-out sleeve with its old poster of The Who appearing at the Railway Hotel in Harrow. On the back, however, there was a photograph of The Who with Keith in a tie-dyed t-shirt.

I didn't realise it at the time but this t-shirt was in my possession. Keith had given it to me when I stopped off at Tara House in Chertsey on the way to the Who concert at Guildford in October. It was probably given to him in 1970 when The Who were touring the US, by John Sebastian, who was famous for making and wearing his own tie-dyed clothing. He even made Pete some tie-dyed overalls. Evidently when he arrived at Tara House that day Sebastian had given Keith more tie-dyed clothing, which is why he gave this surplus t-shirt to me.

Of course, Keith didn't realise he was giving me that particular t-shirt at the time and neither did I, not that it would have made any difference as Keith treated clothes, especially t-shirts, like drumsticks, to be used and discarded at will. I wore it a few times during the seventies until it shrank and I got bigger. Thereafter it remained at the bottom of a drawer and then in a box in our attic. I never threw it out because of who gave it to me.

In 2005, having read reports of sales of rock stars' clothing fetching good money, I decided to put it up for auction at Christies, and it was then that another Who fan, a friend of mine, suggested it might be the same one that Keith wore on the cover of *MBB&B*. Well, I checked the album and, bugger me, it was. Since tie-dyed clothing can't be replicated exactly it was easy to prove and this naturally made a difference to the price.

It was a bit mouldy but we gave it a good wash and, lo and behold, after the sale I was able to buy a new car.

*

The same month I attended Chris Welch's wedding St Margaret's Church in Blackheath, a star-studded occasion at which Keith Emerson played the pipe organ. His bride was Marilyne Rangecroft, editor Ray Coleman's secretary, and they'd somehow kept their courtship secret from the rest of the staff, at least until a few weeks before the wedding. At the reception in a nearby church hall there was a jam session featuring ELP, Ginger Baker, Peter Frampton, Jon Hiseman, Marc Bolan and various members of Yes. The groom, a decent drummer, played along with them all. What I remember most about the whole shindig, however, was seeing Ginger smoking a huge joint while chatting with the vicar who'd conducted the service.

On December 10, a couple of months after the Rainbow had opened, Frank Zappa & The Mothers of Invention played the first of four scheduled shows there, twice a night over a Friday and Saturday. Because the pass that manager John Morris had given me enabled me to come and go as I pleased, I'd turned up for the end of the first concert, intending to have a beer or two in the backstage bar during the break between shows, maybe even grab a quick interview with one of the Mothers, before catching and reviewing the second show.

In the event, because I could roam anywhere, I'd wandered down towards the front on the right side and was leaning against the wall by an exit door watching Frank & The Mothers do their encore, a tongue-in-cheek cover of 'I Want To Hold Your Hand' during which a photo of The Beatles was beamed on to a backdrop. This was a tribute to the Fabs who, at the end of 1963 and start of 1964, had played a 16-night Christmas season at the theatre when it was known as the Finsbury Park Astoria. Frank and his band performed a note-for-note cover of this old Beatles' chestnut, the first of their singles to grab America by the throat. Singers Mark Volman and Howard Kaylan, late of The Turtles, were as good as it gets in the vocal department, clearly inspired by playing on a stage where JPG&R had once trod.

It happened in the blink of an eye, just as the song finished. Frank was acknowledging the applause when, from the front row, a man ran up the side stairs, onto the stage and gave him a hefty shove from the rear. Into the orchestra pit Frank went, guitar and all. The man rushed off stage but was grabbed by members of the audience who handed him over to Frank's road crew to deal with, no doubt harshly. Meanwhile, an ambulance was called and Frank was stretchered out the stage door.

I was in the perfect spot to witness all this – I actually climbed on stage after the incident – and was now in the perfect position to observe the aftermath. The audience was asked to leave, which they did in an orderly manner, but not before a rumour spread that Frank had been killed. The departing crowd, probably 3,000 plus, mingled with those outside waiting for the second show, another 3,000 plus, so there was a huge mass of people outside on Seven Sisters Road, most of whom believed Frank Zappa had been murdered by a crazed fan who, it later transpired, was jealous because his girlfriend was attracted to Frank.

"The band thought I was dead," Zappa recalled in his 1989 book *The Real Frank Zappa Book*. "My head was over on my shoulder, and my neck was bent like it was broken. I had a gash in my chin, a hole in the back of my head, a broken rib, and a fractured leg. One arm was paralysed."

Frank spent the best part of a year in a wheelchair. John Morris was mortified. In the story I wrote for the following week's *MM*, he told me that ten and a half thousand tickets were sold but not used. Not only had one of the world's most gifted and popular rock stars been savagely attacked in his theatre but the losses on the cancelled shows, all sell outs, were critical. Ticket money had to be returned and this might cause the theatre to close. It didn't but John told me it was touch and go for a while – he needed to sell out three shows a week just to break even – so I doubled my efforts to help in any way I could.

Frank's assailant, 24-year-old Trevor Howell, appeared in court the following March charged with assault. "I did it because my girlfriend said she loved Frank," he said before being sentenced to 12 months inside.

I saw Cat Stevens again that month, at the Drury Lane Theatre in Covent Garden, a prestigious affair at which he was accompanied by a small choir, miniature string ensemble and, for the song 'Rubylove', a quartet of Greek musicians playing bouzoukis. My date was Denise, a friend of one of my estate agent flatmates, quite posh and a huge fan, clearly besotted with him and rendered speechless when I introduced them at the post gig party. Constantly surrounded by the rich and fashionable, Steve operated in a different milieu, with an aura of suppressed elegance, to most musicians. He mixed not with the rough and tumble of the rock 'n' roll world but with society friends, introduced to him by his manager Barry Krost, a flamboyantly gay man, and his publicist, the ever-energetic Tony Brainsby. He was courted by artists and models, actors and actresses, debutantes, dress designers and fashion photographers.

What's more, the way my friend Denise reacted was no isolated occurrence. Almost every attractive girl I ever met in those days was infatuated with Cat Stevens, and that should he care to do so he could have the pick of them.

*

As ever, I spent Christmas in Skipton and in January suffered a shock to the system, appendicitis, diagnosed by the same doctor on Harley Street that I'd visited to handle an unwanted pregnancy, a girl called Lucy who worked for Charisma Records with whom I'd wound up in bed once or twice. I was pretty sure I wasn't her only admirer, and thus never quite sure whether I or someone else was responsible. The doctor removed my appendix and advised me to take two weeks off, so I headed up to Yorkshire again.

Back in London I was invited to lunch by Pat Meehan, the manager of Black Sabbath, with Ozzy Osbourne for company, during which arrangements were made for me to write a story about the group. Meehan was an entertaining character, albeit a bit slippery, with offices in Lisle Street between Leicester Square and Chinatown, and over mouthfuls of sweet and sour king prawn and special fried rice it was decided that a day or two later I would travel with Meehan to Manchester to see Black Sabbath at the Free Trade Hall, then journey on with them the following day to Newcastle for another show at the City Hall. Somewhere along the way I would be granted an interview.

Transport became an issue. Meehan owned three expensive cars, a Rolls-Royce Silver Shadow, an Aston Martin DBS and a Ferrari Dino, and his Aston was in the car park at Heathrow Airport's Terminal Three. His Ferrari, meanwhile, was being serviced and the Rolls-Royce was parked nearby. Because his wife required it that evening, his assistant would drive us in it to Heathrow, where Meehan would resume possession of the DBS in which he would drive us both to Manchester.

Alas, on arrival at Heathrow the Aston was found to have been stolen, or at least was not where Meehan thought it was. The only option was to rent a car from Hertz and he opted for a Jaguar XJ6, the most expensive vehicle the company offered but when he tried to do so he was informed he already had another Jaguar XJ6 out on rental. After some discussion with his assistant, he remembered that this Jag had been left in a car park at Dover some days before and abandoned after the employee driving it had embarked on a ferry for Calais. He apologised to the Hertz girl and informed her of its whereabouts, saying they could collect it at any time from this location, whereupon, as a valued customer, he was allowed to rent a second XJ6.

Thus equipped, we set off for Manchester at least an hour later than intended, heading towards the M1 from Heathrow via Watford. On the outskirts of Watford, however, disaster struck for the second time. A stone was thrown up against the Jaguar's windscreen, which shattered as a result. Meehan tried to drive on but couldn't, so he produced the car's jack from the boot and smashed the glass out entirely. It being a cold winter's night, it was impossible to drive without a windscreen. Trapped in Watford at tea-time, Meehan found a pay-phone, managed to locate another Hertz office and requested another Jaguar. All they could offer was a Ford Granada, which seriously displeased him. A man who owns a Rolls-Royce, a Ferrari and an Aston Martin and is by and large unimpressed by Jaguars was unlikely to look favourably on a humble Ford.

As we were both very hungry by now, we took tea in a nearby transport café while we waited for the beleaguered Jag to be exchanged for the Ford. Meehan, a man used to haute cuisine of a somewhat higher standard than was available at this eatery, was sanguine about the situation. "When you're up, you're up – when you're down, you're down," he said, biting into his bacon sandwich.

Darkness fell. We were now very late and in order to try and reach Manchester in time for the gig, Meehan thrashed the Granada mercilessly on the M1 and M6. It was well past show time when we screeched to a halt around the back of the Free Trade Hall. Yet even though we seemed to have reached the end of our wearisome journey, fate had a further trick up its sleeve.

In his haste to exit the car, Meehan accidentally locked it with the key inside, an action that necessitated breaking in so that he might extract some contracts relating to the evening's show. A Sabbath roadie was summoned and – as is the way with roadies – he had a jemmy to hand. He obliged his boss by wrenching open the driver's door, which henceforth refused to close. Having thus incapacitated the Granada, Meehan abandoned it in a side street, its unlockable door hanging open. We had now missed the entire concert.

An hour later, back at our hotel, Meehan was on the phone demanding yet *another* vehicle from Hertz's central Manchester office, only to be told that this was out of the question. An exchange of views followed. He now had *three* cars out on his Hertz credit card, all abandoned, two in states of disrepair. There are limits, I suppose.

The following day, somehow or other, Meehan did manage to obtain from Hertz a Ford Capri to drive to Newcastle for the next show on Sabbath's tour. I didn't accompany him on this journey, so I don't know what terrors he visited on the Capri. I suspect the worst. I travelled in a mini-coach with the group's tour manager and guitarist Tony Iommi, interviewing him along the way. Meehan abandoned the Capri in Newcastle and, the following morning, flew with me back to London, where we were met at Heathrow by his assistant in the blue Roller.

I would have a further encounter with Meehan and Black Sabbath in early 1974 but it didn't come as much of a surprise when some years down the line I heard on the rock grapevine that after Meehan and the group parted company there wasn't much cash left in the Sabbath kitty.

*

A few nights later I was at the Rainbow again to see Pink Floyd. I'd seen them at Bath and again at the Crystal Place Bowl in London the previous May, when a small lake intruded between them and their audience, from which there emerged an inflatable monster. Here at the Rainbow they performed an embryonic version of *Dark Side Of The Moon* a full 12 months before the LP was released, and I went back the next night because I enjoyed it so much or, at least, felt there was something significant about what I had heard. I managed two consecutive Floyd shows not through the good offices of the group, who were notoriously unwilling to accommodate music writers, but through the kindness of theatre manager John Morris.

It wasn't often that a lengthy piece of music, heard for the first time, made such an impact on me. Indeed, the only other time it had happened up to that point was with The Who's *Tommy*, but *Dark Side*, performed live and loud, sounded spectacular first time around. There was a continuity to the songs that seemed to me like an extension of 'Echoes', which they also played that night, yet more melodic than anything the Floyd had produced before. It helped that I found a seat at the front of the balcony in an area that had been roped off for the Floyd's lighting crew to do their thing with spotlights. I looked down on the band with nothing to obstruct my view, and during the show someone passed me the kind of cigarette that isn't generally available at street-corner tobacconists, but even without this helpful attitude adjuster I just knew that the music I was hearing was going to be massively popular, though I couldn't have guessed quite how much. On the second night I watched from the side of the auditorium, quite close to the stage, where staff hung around during shows, and it sounded great even without a spliff to enhance my perception.

"Burning flashlights, wind-blown sparkle dust. The pre-recorded voice of Malcolm Muggeridge and a trip to the dark side of the moon all added up the most successful night's business London's Rainbow Theatre has enjoyed since its opening last November," I wrote. "Pink Floyd fans packed the theatre to such an extent that manager John Morris could happily have retained the group for another seven nights."

*

In March I was in New York again, to see Badfinger at Carnegie Hall. Unlike the first time I flew across the Atlantic, I was on my own and there was no one to meet me at JFK. I hailed a cab to my midtown hotel where a message from the group's manager awaited me. The odd thing about this trip was that I was in the city for only 48 hours before I flew home, which is pretty absurd when you consider that flying to America in those days was very expensive, at least compared to today, and comparatively rare.

Badfinger must have liked me. I did my first story on them early in 1971, heading up to north London to their communal house in Golders Green, a large detached mock Tudor place on a winding hill. It was sparsely furnished but there was plenty of evidence that its occupants were musicians, guitars and leads littering the floor and mugs of tea resting on amps. Their girlfriends were in residence too, as was their manager Bill Collins, a big bloke with prematurely white long hair who seemed to me to be a bit too old to be their manager, a bit too set in his ways, rather like a slightly eccentric Latin master.

I didn't know much about them when I went to that house, only that they'd had a hit single with 'Come And Get It' in 1970 and another, 'No Matter What', was doing well when I interviewed them. That first hit was written and produced by Paul McCartney and they were on Apple Records so, perhaps inevitably, I began by asking them about The Beatles connection. This turned out to be a bad move. They were heartily sick of this line of questioning as they made clear to me during the interview.

About a year later I interviewed Joey Molland at the offices of the group's newly appointed PR company in central London, and less than a month after that I was sitting waiting for them to appear at Carnegie Hall, the most upmarket concert theatre in New York, with plush seating that more often accommodated the backsides of classical music lovers. Badfinger were more popular in the US than they were at home, which explains why they wanted me there. The place was full and the audience enthusiastic. They topped the bill over Al Kooper, who was making his name as a record producer after stints with The Blues Project and Blood, Sweat & Tears. I loved Badfinger's songs, exemplary power pop, yet the similarity to The Beatles was unavoidable.

After the show I was taken out for dinner with the group, driving through Central Park in a stretch limo with them and their US manager Stan Polley who, in the fullness of time, would help himself to funds that were rightfully theirs, leaving them penniless. Polley was adamant that I accompany them, seemingly concerned that if I didn't, I might go elsewhere after the show and find something else other than Badfinger to write about. In the event, I did just that, and the next day called my friend Pete Rudge who was helping out Lindisfarne on their American dates. They were supporting The Kinks at Carnegie Hall the following night, so I stayed on for another day to see this show too.

Back at my hotel I encountered a Scotsman I knew only as Jock whom I'd met in La Chasse and who in a few years' time would make a name for himself in the footnotes of the UK punk scene. He was in the lobby and on his arm was a girl whose charms he was evidently promoting. "She's yours for $20," he said. I declined. He then explained that he'd lost his room key – I suspect he didn't actually have a room – and begged me to allow him to stay in my room which, as it happened, had two double beds. In the end I let him and he brought the girl along too. By this time her rate had dropped to $10 but I still wasn't interested. Had I been, I thought provision of the adjoining bed ought to have been payment enough. Either way, I fell asleep to the sound of their congress.

*

In the spring of 1972, the editorial staff of *Melody Maker* were invited to a party at the Wig & Pen Club on London's Aldwych to celebrate the news that the paper had become the best-selling music weekly in the world, its circulation now topping 200,000 copies a week. After a short speech congratulating us on the fine work we were doing, editor Ray announced that *Melody Maker* would henceforth send one of its staff writers to live in New York and report back on the world of American rock. Also, there would be an American edition, printed in Queens, which would be edited by the New York-based writer, trimmed down to 40 pages from the UK edition which by then had anything up to 64 pages a week.

The coveted position of US Editor would not be permanent and, as the paper's News Editor, I wasn't in line for the role, at least not yet. Instead, it was decided that Roy Hollingworth would be the first London-based *MM* reporter to be given the job, staying in New York for six months from the end of May, whereupon he would be replaced by another member of the staff. Roy duly flew off and settled into a fancy apartment in Sutton Place, a chic neighbourhood overlooking the East River in midtown Manhattan.

To say that Roy distinguished himself in the role would be an understatement. Within weeks we were publishing stories and interviews of all that was happening in the world of American rock music, and first-hand accounts of US tours by UK artists. Now that we had a presence in the country, UK acts could no longer exaggerate their popularity in America as they had invariably done in the past. The only downside, at least from Roy's point of view, was the troublesome American edition which was soon abandoned, the victim of IPC's failure to pay graft to the right people in the world of American magazine circulation. IPC – *MM*'s owners – had a New York office that was run by a transplanted Englishman who bristled at paying bribes to shady characters to ensure that the US edition of *MM* hit the newsstands in New York and elsewhere, and as a result most of them ended up on a garbage tip somewhere out near JFK Airport. The few that did hit streets were never displayed prominently on newsstands but hidden away where they couldn't be seen.

The IPC office was on East 42nd Street in the Chrysler Building with its magnificent art-deco spire and they had set aside a room where Roy could work, not that he used it very much. There were no faxes and e-mails in those days, so each week he would type up his interviews, show reviews and a New York news column, together with any photographs he'd managed to obtain, and parcel it all up for a courier to airlift to London. Anything urgent could be sent via a ticker-tape machine operated by a girl in the office. Roy received a weekly $150 living allowance, and all his bills – rent, electricity, phone – were paid for by IPC. Meanwhile, his salary was banked in London and since he wasn't there to spend it, it simply mounted up.

After six months Roy returned to the UK in triumph to be replaced by Michael Watts. Roy was never the same again. New York did something to him and the damage was permanent. In NY he'd stepped out with a beautiful mixed-race girl called Iris Brown, a secretary at *Rolling Stone* magazine. Back in the UK they pined desperately for one another so Iris followed him across the Atlantic. When she had to return to the US, he left *MM* and followed her, settling into her family home in the Bronx and doing his best to establish himself as a singer-songwriter.

Michael Watts' six-month stint was extended to eight months and, to ring the changes, the final two were spent in Los Angeles. In the summer of 1973, however, Richard Williams left *MM* to join the A&R staff at Island Records and Michael was recalled from LA to become our new assistant editor. I would be next but all that was in the future.

8

"Will you cancel the debt if Richard runs into the sea naked?"
Virgin Records employee, Cannes, January 1972

As *MM*'s News Editor, ever hungry for news I spoke regularly with managers
of bands and their PRs, and those who ran the labels for which they recorded.
I found myself rubbing shoulders with most of the big managers of the day:
Robert Stigwood, Peter Grant, Kit Lambert, Tony Stratton Smith, Chas
Chandler, Billy Gaff, John Coletta, Pat Meehan, Steve O'Rourke and more,
though I somehow missed Don Arden, probably for the best. I took Arthur
Howes, the concert promoter, for lunch in a restaurant of his own choosing,
a Chinese in Brewer Street, and while waiting for him in his offices in Golden
Square admired posters on the walls of his reception area, almost all of which
were for Beatles tours in 1963 and 1964. He was a bit old school and I got on
much better with two other concert promoters, Harvey Goldsmith and Peter
Bowyer, who were closer to my age.

Richard Branson became richer than all of these wheelers and dealers put
together and I met him in circumstances he'd probably rather forget. Branson
was a regular advertiser in *Melody Maker*. His Virgin Records began as a mail-
order operation, selling LPs for a few pennies cheaper than shops, and he took
out full page ads in *MM* most weeks. Soon he would fall foul of Customs &
Excise for failing to pay tax on records imported from the Continent, but when
this was cleared up he launched two record shops, one in Oxford Street and
another in Notting Hill. Both Virgin shops encouraged lounging around listening
to albums, with incense burning, bean bags on the floor and shop assistants
with long hair who addressed customers as "man". To ask for a record by Val
Doonican was to invite ridicule.

But Richard Branson had further expansion on his mind and in 1972
attended the Midem Festival in Cannes on the French Riviera, the annual trade
fair for the music industry where behind-the-scenes wheeling and dealing is
transacted, much of it related to the mysterious business of music publishing and
sales of territorial rights on this or that record, song or publishing catalogue.

I too was at Midem that year, reporting on all this even though it was just
that bit outside *MM*'s normal sphere of interest. There were "gala" concerts in
the evenings but it was all a bit showbizzy. This was the year when the clueless

French boss of Midem, Bernard Chevry, wrote to Peter Grant informing him that "Led Zeppelin and his musicians" had been "selected" to appear at the festival. Mr Grant was not amused. He took out a full-page ad in *Music Week*, the industry trade paper, in which the letter was reprinted in full with "Mr Zeppelin Regrets" in bold capitals across the top, causing Monsieur Chevry maximum embarrassment during the week of the event. At least Peter didn't respond in his usual manner when someone displeased him: "Fuck off, ya cunt!" I'll bet he was tempted, though.

I stayed at a small hotel in the backstreets near Cannes railway station, away from the fashionable Croisette that runs along the sea front, and on the first morning shared a breakfast table with an amiable British chap with long blonde hair, a beard, blue jeans and rumpled sweater who was well-spoken and introduced himself as Richard Branson, the Virgin man. He looked like a bit of a hippie, the sort of bloke I could befriend, and told me he was thinking of starting his own record label.

After breakfast my new friend asked me to do him a favour. He explained that he didn't have a pass to enter the Midem Festival hall but that he had a vintage Rolls-Royce, borrowed from his father, in which he'd driven down through France. Would I, he inquired, pretend to be his chauffeur, drive him to the hall and open the car door for him. That way, he reasoned, the doormen would assume he was someone important and allow him entry without even asking for a pass. I agreed to do this favour on one condition: that the following day he would do the same for me, drive me to the hall, and open the door as if I was someone important. He agreed.

Off we went, me driving the elegant Roller with him on the back seat. I negotiated the narrow side streets of Cannes successfully and arrived at the hall, leapt out and opened the door for my "boss". I watched in amusement as the doormen, noting the car, saluted my new friend and ushered him through the festival doors without asking for a pass. I then drove the Roller back to the hotel and left its keys at reception as we'd agreed.

There was no sign of him next morning at breakfast, nor the following morning. It seemed to me that he'd left the hotel and forgotten about me, and his side of our bargain. Then, two days later, I saw him again, on the beach with some cronies, other hippie types, perhaps four or five men and girls, having what appeared to be a picnic lunch. He saw me staring at them all and beckoned me over.

"Thanks for the other day," he said, smiling.

"You promised to do the same for me," I replied.

"I know. I'm sorry. I left that hotel."

"What did he promise you?" asked one of his friends who was eavesdropping the conversation. I explained. "You welched on the deal," he said loudly so that the whole party heard. "You must pay a forfeit."

One of the girls jumped up. "Will you cancel the debt if Richard runs into the sea naked?" she asked.

"Absolutely," I said, laughing.

Without argument, Richard Branson promptly tugged off his jeans, pants and shirt and ran naked into the Mediterranean.

The next time I saw him was two years later, on a London-bound overnight jumbo transatlantic flight. Like me, he was in economy and pleased to note that whole central rows of seats were empty at the rear of the plane. Before we crashed out for the night, he told me that one day he wanted to own his airline. "Don't we all," I replied.

*

In March it fell to me to report with a heavy heart on *MM*'s front page that the Rainbow Theatre, the rock gig I'd tried so hard to promote, was closing. Just as I was at The Who's show when the theatre opened the previous November so I was at the closing show with Humble Pie. "Make the most of it 'cos there ain't gonna be a Rainbow after tonight," yelled Steve Marriott as his band took the stage.

Discussing the Rainbow's closure, John Morris explained that to run the theatre cost £3,500 (about £40,000 in today's money) a week, plus whatever fee the acts charged. "We needed three sell-out concerts a week to break even and four to make any money to pay off rising debts," he told me. "There are not enough groups or artists available with that kind of drawing power 52 weeks of the year. With Pink Floyd, Faces or The Who you are cool, but that can't happen every weekend." John declined to say how much the Rainbow was in debt. "It's heavy. It shocked the living daylights out of me but we don't owe any money to groups."

Among the Rainbow's biggest blows were the cancelled concerts after Frank Zappa was shoved off the stage. Ironically, the same issue of *MM* that reported the Rainbow's closure carried a report about Zappa's assailant being sentenced to 12 months in jail.

It's a shame the Rainbow wasn't able to host a week of shows by T. Rex whose Wembley Empire Pool concert I reported on a week later. "Marc Bolan swept 9,000 hysterical girls into a world of glittery eyes, corkscrew hair and satin trousers," I wrote. Noting that Ringo was filming the event from a roped off area at the front, I compared the scenes to Beatlemania and suggested there might have been an element of déjà vu for the Beatle-turned-cinematographer. "T Rex ripped through their hit singles but at times they were barely audible above the crescendo of screams at his every movement. Even his acoustic set received little reverence from girls who rushed to the front of the arena, only to be forced back time and time again by hard-pressed ushers."

I still wasn't impressed by T. Rex as a live band. As previously noted, Marc Bolan and his bongo-playing sidekick Mickey Finn had recruited a rhythm section with undue haste but the quartet hadn't played together long enough to knit like an experienced group. This didn't really matter when they were drowned out by screams, of course, but it did matter outside of the UK, as Marc would soon discover. At the end, after an encore of 'Summertime Blues' that couldn't hold a candle to The Who, girly underwear littered the stage. "The ultimate expression of delight," I suggested.

*

Somewhere along the line Keith Moon had given me his home phone number, the only rock star of renown ever to do so, and it was by calling him at his home and arranging to drive down to Surrey on a Tuesday afternoon in April that I interviewed him at great length. His home, Tara House, a peculiarly-shaped modern dwelling, consisting of five pyramids and too much glass, was on the outskirts of Chertsey, down a private lane behind a pub called the Golden Grove. The previous July it had been the venue for a launch party for *Who's Next*.

It was set in extensive grounds and there were several expensive cars in the drive, all belonging to Keith, who couldn't drive. There were two Rolls-Royces, one the lilac Silver Cloud III, the other a white two-door Corniche with an open roof; a white Mercedes coupé; a red Ferrari Dino 426 that bit the dust on a nearby double-carriageway; a silver AC Cobra that had once belonged to Led Zeppelin drummer John Bonham; and his "fun" vehicles, a milk-float, an old American "Al Capone-style" car with running boards at the sides, a hot rod and a hovercraft, as well as "ordinary" cars for other members of the household.

"Cars were simply toys for Keith," I was told by Dougal, Moon's long-suffering PA and chauffeur. "Most people see cars as transport, as a means of getting from A to B but for Keith they were things to play with, usually late at night when he was in the mood for a fast drive. He didn't even have a driving licence."

At the time of my visit the household consisted of Keith and his wife Kim, a former model, their daughter Mandy, Kim's mother Joan and her son Dermott who, strangely, was about the same age as Mandy, his niece. All were dismissed as Keith and I settled down to talk in his playroom/bar. He took this interview quite seriously, for him at least. He was sober and, I think, anxious for once to come across as sincere, more than simply Moon The Loon of legend. One thing I remember most vividly was the awe in which he evidently held Pete Townshend. "Pete's a genius," he said more than once, clearly aware that his own good fortune rested squarely on the rather skinny shoulders of The Who's guitarist and principal composer. For some reason this was edited out of the piece that *MM* published.

"They were a bit frightening and I was scared of them," he told me when I asked about his first impressions of The Who, or The Detours as they were then called. "I asked the manager of the club to introduce me to them. I was standing there and I had a few drinks, so I thought I'd play. I crept 'round the side and asked Dave the drummer if I could do a couple of numbers. He said yes… so I got on the drums and I must have been outrageous. I had dyed ginger hair, ginger cord suit. I was horrible. I looked a right state. I did a couple of numbers and broke the bass drum pedal, being rather heavy handed.

"They asked me over for a drink but they didn't say much. They didn't ask me to join the group but they said they were having a rehearsal at some West Indian club. Nobody said I had joined the group but I went along. This chap from Philips Records, Chris Parmenter, turns up with another drummer because they had been offered a record deal by Philips and they badly wanted the other drummer out.

"He set up his kit and I set mine up and nobody was saying anything. The rest of the band just didn't care. They were tuning up in one corner. Then they asked me to play on the first number, but the man from Philips wanted to play. I can't remember if he played or not, but the group said they didn't want him. So, I just stayed with them. Nobody actually said I was in the group. I was just there and I've been there ever since."

That's a small extract from a very long interview that occupied two whole pages of *MM*. Keith Moon would become notorious for rewriting history, for making up stories that were so funny they would invariably be published whether or not they were true, and thus become legendary "Moon The Loon" stories, and it may be that some of what he told me that day was a product of his imagination, but I like to think that most of it was true, that Keith respected me

– and *Melody Maker* – sufficiently not to embellish the truth too much. I was never quite sure, though, not until long after he'd died and much more of the truth came out in *Dear Boy*, Tony Fletcher's brilliant biography of Keith, and other Who books.

Still, this was one of the most enjoyable interviews I ever did for *MM*, and one of the reasons I like it is because it was arranged privately and took place in Keith's home, with no PRs involved, no time limits, and no motive on the part of the interviewee to promote "product", which is the only reason why big name acts consent to be interviewed today.[3]

If Keith was relatively discreet during this interview, the same cannot be said about Ritchie Blackmore, Deep Purple's guitarist, who dissed his group's LP *Fireball* and hinted to me during May that he wanted to launch a new group with Purple's drummer Ian Paice and a bassist/singer he'd recorded with but refused to name. In the fullness of time this would be revealed as Phil Lynott of Thin Lizzy, but the group Ritchie envisaged never came about. Nevertheless, it would explain why in the not-too-distant future Ian Gillan and Roger Glover would be replaced in Purple by bassist/singer Glenn Hughes, with David Coverdale coming in too.

Ritchie and I became quite friendly as I got to know Purple. He was a great admirer of Paul Rodgers of Free, and told me he'd love to form a group with him too. He admired a black fringed suede jacket I'd worn to a Purple concert and wanted one like it, so I steered him in the direction of the shop on Carnaby Street where I'd bought it. One night, he and I went for dinner in a Japanese restaurant on Swallow Street with our girlfriends, which was unusual as this wasn't for an interview, purely social. I'd made the booking and asked for one of the restaurant's small private rooms in which we sat on the floor, ate from a low table and were served by a Japanese hostess who knelt down to pass the food around. In this situation Ritchie was the polar opposite of the extrovert guitarist fans saw.

The next time I saw that particular girlfriend of Ritchie's was at a concert at the Rainbow when it reopened under new management early in 1973. We were standing next to one another at the side of the stage when, during Ian Paice's drum solo, Ritchie beckoned her to join him behind his wall of six Marshall speaker cabinets. I only caught a glimpse of what they were up to but no one within the Purple camp seemed remotely surprised.

*

---

3 *The whole interview was republished by* Drumming *magazine in 1989.*

At the end of May, Slade triumphed at the Great Western Festival, an event partly financed by the actor Stanley Baker who'd revealed his involvement at a press reception in his impressive Thames-side penthouse, the same apartment where disgraced Tory MP Jeffrey Archer would one day host champagne and steak and kidney pie parties for Thatcher and her friends. The crowd in the field at Bardney, near Lincoln, was initially suspicious of Slade's pop leanings – "They were terrified of that audience," tour manager Graham "Swin" Swinnerton would later tell me – and there were jeers when they took the stage. But they hadn't reckoned on Slade's years of experience and within ten minutes they had that crowd in the palm of their hand.

At the end of their set, Noddy Holder was inspired to bring Stanley Baker on stage and urge the crowd to intone the Zulu chant from Baker's best-known film. Such was their impact that Slade made the front page of *MM* the following week.

Slade weren't headlining. The Beach Boys closed the show that night but before they took the stage, and performed delightfully, we were entertained by the team from *Monty Python's Flying Circus*, then allying themselves with the rock world by signing with Charisma and befriending rock's A-list. Their first LP, however, was released by BBC Records who in their wisdom sent one to *MM* for review, and it landed on my desk: "Of all recent comic programmes to arrive on the magic box, *Monty Python's Flying Circus* seems to be the one that most people talk about afterwards," I wrote. "It's become a cult, as a glance at the *MM* club adverts will show. On Tuesdays, groups switch off at ten for half an hour for the patrons to soak up another batch of absolute lunacy from John Cleese and friends. It's all here on the record... dead parrots, albatrosses on sticks, flying sheep, Mr Hitler, dog kennels that mean mattresses and many more of the surreal sketches that result in the director tearing up his script and saying things are getting too silly.... It IS something completely different, hilariously funny and an invaluable souvenir of one of the funniest shows ever broadcast under the BBC banner."

When I reached America, I would have a strange encounter with John Cleese but let's not get ahead of ourselves.

*

In June I was among a large group of long-suffering UK music writers and DJs invited to Toronto and Montreal for the Maple Music junket, an event sponsored by the Canadian government to promote Canadian rock music. For five weary, jet-lagged days our party was shepherded around with unrelenting efficiency like captive prisoners. Early each morning we were roused from our beds and taken hither and thither, to recording studios, to offices, to lunches, to meetings, to press conferences and, finally, to concerts with ten or more acts on bills that lasted up to seven hours, only for the same thing to occur the next day, and again the next, with a six-hour train ride from Montreal to Toronto thrown in too, until we were all so exhausted that all we wanted to do was sleep, but no, off we were marched on further compulsory activities until, on the penultimate day, I staged a protest and instead of visiting yet another boring studio – and when you've seen one, you've seen them all – I absented myself, hired a limo and took two girls from the party off to the Niagara Falls for an afternoon of leisurely sightseeing.

We had a lovely time but when we returned there was all hell to pay. The hosts were angry. We'd abused their hospitality. I pointed out that we'd had no free time for days on end, and that another visit to an airless recording studio was pointless, especially to journalists from a city that boasted Abbey Road and Olympic. The Brits were on my side, and threatened to boycott the evening's concert. Hasty negotiations followed and the next day's daytime plans were cancelled. The organisers gave everyone the day off and even provided a coach to visit the Niagara Falls, which I suspected was a gesture deliberately aimed at slighting me, the trouble-maker, since in doing so they offered a free trip for something for which I had already paid.

But Canada avenged itself on us miserable ingrates. At the airport on the final day, as we boarded our chartered plane, we were handed huge quantities of unexpected, loose carry-on luggage, boxes of records, press folders, books, bottles, t-shirts and miscellaneous gifts bearing the Maple Leaf emblem, which we struggled to carry, along with our duty-free allowance of fags and booze, and our coats and hats and scarves. After we'd somehow crammed all this stuff into the overhead lockers and beneath our seats and taken off into the Canadian night, lo and behold, the plane hit a terrifying electric storm and descended a thousand or more feet in a matter of seconds, causing the overhead lockers to open and all this stuff to come crashing down on our heads, spilling our drinks, landing in our food. We were plunged into pitch darkness as the plane was tossed around helplessly in the unforgiving sky for what seemed like hours but was probably only ten minutes. Many of us vomited from a combination of terror and the lurch of the plane, and I for one was never more frightened in my life... indeed, that was the very worst plane trip I've ever experienced.

I was sat next to David Jacobs, the DJ who had been the host of *Juke Box Jury*. He was as calm as the proverbial cucumber, as urbane and suave as he was on *JBJ*, and I recall his reassuring manner as vividly as the turbulence.

9

"Chantez a bit if you know les mots."
Paul McCartney, Chateau Vallon, France, July 1972

The heady lifestyle afforded by *Melody Maker* didn't stop me from making trips
to Yorkshire to see my dad whenever I could. I went up at Christmas, of course,
and during bank holiday weekends when there weren't shows to attend or rock
stars to interview. I still called in at my local pub in Skipton but thought twice
about mentioning what I did in London to my old friends there. I'd met two
Beatles, two Rolling Stones and Led Zeppelin, many others and to a certain
extent befriended Elton, The Who, Deep Purple and Slade but if I banged on
about them, I'd soon find myself on the end of a sharp Yorkshire taunt.

In the summer of 1972, my girlfriend Deirdre and I joined four couples
from Skipton, among them my sister and her boyfriend, and my friend Chris
Whincup who'd seen Yes rehearse with me in 1968, and his first wife, for a week
in Salcombe in Devon. Deirdre and I stayed in a different hotel from the others
who were in a B&B that I didn't fancy, but it was a good thing because our hotel
was licensed and I could bring in as many guests to the bar as I wanted, and they
could stay late too. At the end of the week, I was told by the hotel manager that
the bar takings that week were an all-time record.

'I Can See Clearly Now' by Johnny Nash was at the top of the charts and
it was played constantly in the bar while my friends and I caroused late into
the night. Reggae music had grown on me slowly. Years ago, I enjoyed dancing
to '007 (Shanty Town)' by Desmond Dekker, a track featured in the movie *The
Harder They Come* and I'd been given the soundtrack LP by Island PR David
Sandison. Bob Marley had yet to come to London or release his first LP on
Island but Trojan Records in London, allied to Charisma, were releasing reggae
albums and I liked them too. Paul Simon had helped legitimise the genre with his
first solo LP, released in January, which contained 'Mother And Child Reunion',
recorded in Jamaica with members of Toots & The Maytals.

"Do you like reggae, Chris?" The question was posed by Linda McCartney.
We were backstage at the Theatre Antique, Chateau Vallon, in the south
of France where husband Paul and his new group Wings had just played the
opening show on their 1972 *Wings Over Europe* tour, the first pre-planned tour by
any Beatle since the group stopped touring in 1966. Fortunately for me, Paul's

tour manager was my pal John Morris, late of the Rainbow, who made sure I got a backstage pass. He told me there were no specific plans for Wings to play in the UK. "Paul wants to play small halls and most of the capacities here are less than 3,000," he said. "He isn't interested in playing the monstrous places which he probably could fill."

The concerts, which featured no support act and no encore, were divided into two sets, but no Beatles songs were performed. The only nod to Paul's past was 'Long Tall Sally' which he'd been playing since his old band rocked Liverpool's Cavern.

I wrote a whole page on the show. "On stage Paul has changed little from the Beatles days. His hair is cropped short but he still stands with his knees bent, his backside constantly shaking, his face forced against the mic as if he is licking an ice cream cone. He shakes his hips but girls don't scream any more. His voice, whether screaming or singing, is everything it always has been and his very presence commands respect, even in France. There's no doubt he's thoroughly enjoying himself."

I noted that Henry McCulloch was given the space to stretch out on a blues jam the band called 'Henry's Blues' and soloed well in 'Maybe I'm Amazed', the best number in the set, and that Denny Laine stepped forward to sing 'Say You Don't Mind'. I was less complimentary about Mrs McCartney. "Linda vamps at the keyboard and chips in with vocals here and there but unfortunately her voice lacks both depth and power," I wrote. "This was brought home demonstratively during her main number, a new reggae song called 'Seaside Woman' which bore a marked resemblance to 'Ob-La-Di, Ob-La-Da'."

After the show I asked Paul why no British dates were scheduled. "We will play there sometime or other, but not right now," he told me. "The audiences are very critical in Britain and we're a new band just starting out, no matter what we've been through before. We have to get worked in before doing any big shows in Britain or America." His mood changed when I asked: "Have you seen your former Beatle mates recently?"

"No, I've got no particular reason to, and I don't really want to," he replied, a tad shortly. "They're into their things and I'm into mine."

Paul was mobbed backstage, so I ambled off and encountered Linda sitting on a travel case, which was when she asked me whether I shared her fondness for reggae. I told her that *The Harder They Come* LP had been on my turntable since I was given a copy two or three weeks ago, and she got a pen out of her handbag and wrote down the title on a piece of paper.

It was a Sunday night and I knew that *MM* would want to publish a story about Paul's gig in the following week's paper. This meant I had to write it up in my hotel room, scribbling in a notebook, and arrange for an early alarm call so I could dictate it over the phone to Marilyne first thing in the morning.

From the south of France, I flew to Belgium, to Brussels where I rented a car and drove to Knokke, there to cover the annual song festival, a sort of junior Eurovision event to which *MM* was invited, along with all the other music papers. Relics from an earlier age, these affairs – I'd attended something similar in Luxembourg the previous year – attracted song writers at the opposite end of the spectrum to the acts that were *MM*'s staple. They were a wealthy, boozy bunch who parked their Roll-Royce Silver Shadows ostentatiously outside the hotel where I stayed, and the vibe within and without the festival was as if Elvis, let alone The Beatles, had never happened. I was obliged to wear evening dress, but got by with a black velvet suit I'd bought for dressy occasions, and a borrowed dickey-bow.

Watching an endless parade of singers, many of them from the schlager school of German oompah music, I thought I was time travelling backwards, suggesting in my coverage that the music performed differed little from 1962, or 1952 for that matter. "It's showbizzy-glamour-schmaltz all rolled into one big sweep of violin strings, penguin suits and glittery dresses. It is broadcast throughout Europe to a potential audience of 200 million who are brainwashed into thinking that the chosen artists are the big stars of the day. There were 32 performers, including five from America. I'll stick my neck out and suggest that Rod Stewart has sold more records in the past 12 months than the whole lot put together."

Britain was represented by balladeer Malcolm Roberts, chanteuse Penny Lane and a pop group called Union Express whose song was a variation on 'Ring A Ring A Roses'. "After a decade in which Britain has produced the ultimate in pop music, from The Beatles to countless others that command world respect, we are represented by a pop group covering a nursery rhyme. What the hell is it all about?"

We won, too. But 1972 was the final year for the Knokke Song Festival. Perhaps they read my report.

*

I never had much to do with Fleetwood Mac professionally, though at the end of July I was sent by *Melody Maker* to interview the pre-Buckingham/Nicks group at their country house, Benifold, near Borden in Hampshire, an 11-bedroom Victorian mansion owned by Mick Fleetwood. Having just released their *Bare Trees* LP, the group seemed to me to be in the pleasant position of not having to work too hard and were unworried about their diminishing profile in the UK.

The house had been turned into a rehearsal space. Big amps, wires, mics and drums battled for space in the dining room, the largest room in a house isolated from neighbours so no one could hear the racket they made. Settling down amidst all this gear, Christine McVie sipped from a mug of tea and told me she'd had her fill of slogging around Britain. "In England it means travelling by road and coming home each night in the early hours," she said. "But in America you are staying in hotels and it doesn't feel like such a tiring drag over there."

With Bob Welch and Danny Kirwan elsewhere during my visit, I spent a pleasant afternoon with Mick Fleetwood, John McVie and Christine in the rehearsal space they'd created for themselves in this elegant but untidy country house. They all believed their future lay in America, though, of course, they weren't to know then how inconceivably correct they were in this regard.

To my mind Christine McVie was the secret weapon that catapulted Fleetwood Mac to mega stardom later in the decade. She was disarmingly modest in a quiet, decent, English way, with a sweet but slightly husky alto voice entirely lacking in ostentation. She didn't need to over emote because the songs she would write in the years to come spoke for themselves: 'Say You Love Me', 'Over My Head', 'Warm Ways', 'You Make Loving Fun', 'Don't Stop', 'Over And Over', 'Think About Me', 'Wish You Were Here', 'Hold Me', 'Little Lies', 'Everywhere' and, of course, 'Songbird', her delicate, understated masterpiece. Her songs, always effortlessly melodic, were outnumbered by those composed by the other members of Fleetwood Mac, but in terms of quality, song for song, her yield was superior to them all.

Thereafter chance delivered me elsewhere whenever Fleetwood Mac played concerts near where I lived and I never reviewed a show of theirs for *MM*. The renaissance brought about by the arrival of Stevie Nicks and Lindsay Buckingham occurred just as my time on *MM* was drawing to a close, and I'd left the paper by the time they played Madison Square Garden in June of 1977. I was working for a music biz company in New York that summer, however, and copped free tickets so I did manage to see the Fleetwood Mac supergroup just the once. Cresting a wave, they were outrageously accomplished and brought the house down. I also copped an invite to an after-show party and recall seeing the five of them sat together in a swanky restaurant. Dressed and looking just like they do on the cover of *Rumours*, they were surrounded by well-wishers, unrecognisable from the group I met in Hampshire five years previously. With flashbulbs going off all round them, they positively glowed.

*

In September I saw The Who again, this time in Rome. They were playing concerts in Europe on a tour that saw them attract 400,000 to a concert in Paris, their biggest ever audience. Aside from that show, it was a low-key outing, with several days off between cities and all bar Keith flew home to the UK between shows. Keith and his driver Dougal drove around Europe from show to show, looking for trouble I suppose.

I caught up with them on the last date of the tour, and spent an amusing hour at a press conference before the show. An interpreter was necessary and I have no idea what was said in Italian, only that Pete's answers – he always did most of the talking – seemed much shorter than the questions. The show was great but the Italian audience was very subdued which troubled the group and caused Pete to smash a guitar at the end, a gesture that was becoming increasingly infrequent as the seventies drew on.

I watched the show from behind the band, on John's side, and noticed that police were patrolling inside the Palasport arena. Later, the promoter told me that fans were scared of police coming down hard on them should they show too much enthusiasm or, heaven forbid, leave their seats, and this explained the muted response.

After the show Keith, Dougal and myself took a taxi around Rome looking for female company in a club or bar, but found nothing, and wound up back at the hotel a bit disappointed. The following day there was a mix-up with the plane tickets. They'd flown me out first class, very nice of them, but the first-class section was overbooked for the return, and I was relegated to coach. Pete thought this was very funny. "*Melody Maker* writers are second-class citizens," he announced quite loudly at the airport, much to the amusement of John and Roger.

Back in London I was at the opening night of a Tom Jones season at the London Palladium but the voice from the valleys was hampered by 'flu, croaking and spluttering, and his performance was brought to a premature end when he signalled for the curtains to be drawn. "His great voice was almost breaking under the strain and he might have damaged it had he carried on," I wrote in my review. "It was an unfortunate anti-climax to what ought to be have been the

Palladium's most exciting night this year."

Jones was accompanied by "Big" Jim Sullivan, the UK's premier session
guitarist alongside "Little" Jimmy Page in the sixties, and he had tutored Ritchie
Blackmore when the Deep Purple ace was a teenager. "Sullivan stepped down
from his rostrum to play delicate Spanish guitar during a couple of numbers
and ought to have received a bigger acknowledgement from Jones," I wrote. "An
instrumentalist of Sullivan's calibre deserves a solo spot in any act."

*

In October I was in Dublin, visiting the Guinness brewery with Lindisfarne
and watching them headline over Genesis and Rab Noakes in a boxing ring
where they performed almost all the songs from their new LP, *Dingly Dell*, to an
audience that came alive only when they heard familiar favourites. It was a brave
move, perhaps too brave, and though the group seemed a bit under-rehearsed I
ended my *MM* report on an optimistic note. "After six gigs it'll doubtless run like
clockwork," I wrote hopefully. I was wrong and not long afterwards Lindisfarne
split in two.

In the same month I interviewed Chas Chandler, then on a roll thanks to
his managerial clients Slade, at his substantial home in Lindfield, near Gatwick
Airport, spending the night there due to his generosity with the scotch. He told
me he hadn't picked up a bass guitar since he left The Animals and wouldn't
dare play one in front of Jim Lea, Slade's bassist, lest Jim laugh at his efforts.

It was a Sunday night, which meant I had to get up early and face the
commuter traffic into London so as to be at my desk for another *MM* news day
and, in the evening, catch a flight to Frankfurt to see the American band Three
Dog Night. While there I interviewed Danny Hutton, one of the group's three
singers, a friendly chap whom I happened to bump into the following week at
the wedding of their booking agent. After the reception Danny, myself and
others ended up at the Speakeasy from where he called his hotel to check for
messages. One, evidently, was from Harry Nilsson, who'd arrived in London that
very afternoon and was at that moment in situ at his Mayfair flat – the same flat
where Mama Cass and, later, Keith Moon died – and wanting for company.

It was very late by this time but I smelled fun and games and accepted
Hutton's invitation to accompany him, along with a couple of girls to whom
we'd become attached along the way. Once there Danny introduced me to Harry
who wasn't best pleased that he'd brought a writer along. "I'm not really here,"
he told me. I understood. Nevertheless, we availed ourselves of his hospitality,

drank hard liquor, flirted with the girls, talked drug-fuelled nonsense and listened to Harry play an upright piano and, with Danny, sing all manner of songs, standards, Beatles, Randy Newman, all sorts, into the early hours until dawn broke. It was fantastic, probably all the more so in view of the state I was in.

It was about 8am when I left, head spinning, by taxi, to where I lived in Bayswater. Sleep was out of the question so I took a long bath, had something to eat and, somehow, made it into *Melody Maker*'s offices by noon, ready to attend the weekly Wednesday conference which that week was chaired by assistant editor Richard Williams. I felt truly awful and didn't contribute much in the way of ideas for next week's paper but I shrank visibly into my chair when Richard said: "I've heard a rumour that Harry Nilsson is in town. Does anyone know anything?" Everyone shook their heads, including me, though it was an effort since it throbbed so bad.

It wasn't until 20 years later that I could bring myself to tell Richard the truth.

*

Before the month was out I saw Pink Floyd again, this time at Wembley's Empire Pool, and commented that it might not be a bad idea if they dropped their muted persona for once and encored with 'See Emily Play'. Far more thrilling was spending 48 hours in Switzerland with Led Zeppelin.

It was Led Zep's habit in those days to play a couple of small gigs before embarking on a big American tour, and they invited an *MM* writer along to see them at the Montreux Pavilion. Chris Welch was closer to Led Zep than anyone else on the paper and had written about them extensively in the past but Ray Coleman decided to send me instead. It was the first of my memorable encounters with the group, but none were as relaxed and enjoyable as this.

I flew out on a Saturday morning and in the afternoon sat in the Pavilion stalls, virtually alone apart from staff and roadies, watching a Led Zep soundcheck during which they played only early Elvis songs, loads of them, and it was fabulous; Jimmy doing note-for-note Scotty Moore, Bonzo tapping away on his rims and snare like DJ Fontana, John Paul on an electric stand-up bass and Robert mimicking The King. They took enormous pleasure in playing songs that had inspired them in their teens, a decade and a half before Led Zeppelin came into being. It shone out from the smiles on their faces, the fun they were having, and I wished Elvis was there to watch.

When they'd finished, I asked them if they'd play a set like that at my wedding – not that I was planning on getting married – and manager Peter

Grant laughed and said, "It'll fuckin' cost yer!" Very good natured it all was, and in the dressing room Jimmy demonstrated to me how to use a new state-of-the-art stroboscopic electronic tuner he'd just acquired. Then he picked up his Martin acoustic guitar, the dressing room went quiet and for a few minutes he played some lovely improvised finger style.

"Led the good times roll!" I wrote in *MM*. "Zep knocked spots off their many rivals with the ease of true professionals. They've been in the game too long to let fashions worry them. Zeppelin are a tremendous live force. They've lost none of the energy that characterises a band who need to work to gain recognition, but the energy has matured into a confidence that allows them to spring off into spontaneous directions during their shows.

"A nod, a wink, a drum roll or a wave of a fretboard and Zeppelin can turn a number back on its heels into songs totally unexpected. Who would imagine, for example, that 'Whole Lotta Love' could end up as 'Heartbreak Hotel'? It can and it does when Zeppelin fly… They've proved themselves with complicated, sophisticated numbers and here the fun starts. 'Whole Lotta Love' moves through a brief history of rock and roll, with Robert Plant taking his audience through the inspiration of Zeppelin and amateurs alike."

On the Saturday evening, after the show, we went out for dinner; all of Zep and their friend, the local promoter Claude Nobs, sat at a long table in a fine restaurant, and because some of their wives were present everyone was on their best behaviour, even boisterous tour manager Richard Cole. The food was magnificent and Peter Grant ordered the largest steak on the menu, a huge prime fillet, a plate of vegetables on the side and several bottles of expensive red wine for us all to drink. He polished it off and waited until the waiter returned to remove his and everyone else's plates.

"Can I get you anything more, sir?" he enquired of Peter, expecting him to order a dessert.

Peter thought for a moment. "Yes, I'll have the same again," he replied.

He polished that off too.

I interviewed Robert Plant in his room at the Montreux Palace Hotel the following day and in my subsequent story wrote: "Countries seem to put up no barriers to Zeppelin, who can consider themselves the unheralded ambassadors of British heavy rock. Unheralded because few reports of the group's foreign activities seem to reach home, and ambassadors because few bands will clock up as many miles in a year as Led Zeppelin. To this end, England has been ignored this year by the group and their popularity has undoubtedly waned."

Unfortunately, I succeeded in offending them – not difficult as they could be incredibly touchy – by suggesting that their popularity had "waned". They took exception to this and in the following week's *Melody Maker* paid for an ad listing the scheduled 24-date UK tour with the words "SOLD OUT" prominently displayed, adding the comment: "and their popularity has undoubtedly waned, Chris Charlesworth, *Melody Maker*, Last Week." Even Robert Plant had a go at me while introducing 'Stairway To Heaven' in Glasgow on December 4. "There was a guy who ah, worked for the *Melody Maker*, Chris Charlesworth, and he said our popularity has obviously waned... Thank you very much."

Drawing attention to my comment was typical of Led Zeppelin, however, and reflected their surprisingly thin-skinned attitude towards anything that might be construed as negative press coverage. Unlike in America, the UK music press had always been supportive, especially *Melody Maker*. Chris Welch was among the earliest writers to sing their praises. Nevertheless, an element of suspicion seemed to cloud their dealings with us and as a consequence their relationship with the press was never as comfortable as, say, The Who whose media-friendliness was one of their many virtues. Outwardly Led Zeppelin appeared to be the least insecure act on the planet, but for all their extraordinary success they maintained unresolved grievances that occasionally bubbled to the surface in unseemly public displays of media bashing that were both unnecessarily petty and, indeed, beneath them. I think that somehow, deep down inside, they and their manager Peter Grant always felt they were owed more respect than they received, but a dignified silence would surely have been more in keeping with their stature.

By this time, of course, Led Zeppelin had become the most popular band in the world among committed rock fans, though by no means the most famous in the world at large. Grant's game-plan deliberately shunned such media friendly activities as interviews with the mainstream press, appearing on television or even releasing singles. Coverage of the band was therefore limited to the music papers and occasional live broadcasts on BBC Radio 1. He believed that word of mouth would spread the news about Led Zeppelin amongst the rock fraternity, and that as word of their prowess in concert spread, so the momentum would build. He was right.

The downside to this strategy was that they were largely ignored by the popular press and that unlike such sixties rock heroes as The Beatles and Rolling Stones, Led Zeppelin would never become "household names", not that they ever really wanted to. Their music and reputation were known only to a cult of loyal, relatively young fans; in effect a secret society, albeit a very large one. And, as they well knew, almost all of them read *Melody Maker*.

They can't have been that upset with me over the "waning" business because I saw them twice again on the sold-out UK tour in December, at the Manchester Hardrock and at Alexandra Palace in London, and they made me welcome backstage. I was a bit critical of the Ally Pally show because the sound in that cavernous enclosure was pretty awful – but that obviously wasn't Zep's fault – and I also recall that midway through the Manchester gig I went to use the dressing room loo and caught newly appointed Zep publicist BP Fallon *in flagrante delicto* with not one but two young ladies.

*

In November, believe it or not, I came face to face with Michael Jackson. He was in London with the Jackson 5 to perform four concerts in the UK, and at a press lunch for the J5 at the Talk Of The Town off Leicester Square (which became The Hippodrome and is now a casino), I happened to be sitting opposite John Peel, with whom I was on nodding terms in those days. Before the J5 performed we were served roast chicken, delivered to us on plates by waiters. Peel, a zealous vegetarian, sniffed at his and frowned. "Waiter," he said in his inimitable Liverpool drawl, "kindly remove this dead animal."

During the J5's performance there was an absolutely magic moment when Michael, who turned 14 in August, did a spin midway through the song 'I'll Be There' just at the point where he screams, "Girl, just look over your shoulder", which is precisely what he did. I gasped, and so did JP, and in that instant we caught each other's glances, silently acknowledging our shared awareness that we had witnessed a moment of true pop wonder, and knowing without need to comment that we had felt exactly the same rush of excitement.

The following day I, along with several other writers, went to meet the J5 at their hotel, the Churchill in Portman Square, now a Hyatt Regency. The square was chock full of fans, almost all of whom hissed at me as I showed my invitation and was allowed through the police lines that held them back.

MJ and his brothers were at tables in a reception room and we were shuffled amongst them. When it came for my turn to sit at Michael's table, I stared into the eyes of the boy who would one day become pop's biggest star and marry Elvis' daughter. He told me he "loved being here in London", he "loved his fans", he "loved being in the J5"; indeed, he loved just about everything and everyone and had clearly been pre-programmed what to say to the press to the point of extreme blandness, but then again what else could I expect? He seemed much younger to me than his 14 years, still a little boy, small for his age and a rather shy and timid one at that.

Reviewing the J5 concert at Wembley Empire Pool in the following week's *MM* I wrote: "Michael Jackson is poised to become the biggest coloured show business sensation the world has ever known. Put his name in neon lights, splash him across the front page, write it in the sky, tell everyone you know… Michael will be a brighter star than anything the Milky Way can serve up. Michel is a ball of soul that bounces uncontrollably around a stage. His little body shakes, dances and moves with the perfection of a talent so natural it's unreal. He stands head and shoulders above his Jackson 5 brothers despite his diminutive stature. He's a star."

I got that right, didn't I? But at what cost?

10

"You laughing at me, boy? I'll whip you any day, boy."
Jerry Lee Lewis, Advision Studios, London, January 1973

In November I visited the US again, flying first class over the Atlantic for the first and only time in my life, my companion John Coletta, Deep Purple's dapper manager, with whom I was becoming increasingly friendly. John was in advertising before he was persuaded to invest in DP, and he told me he considered managing a rock group "an interesting marketing opportunity". I always thought he was a bit out of his depth, especially when it came to controlling Ritchie Blackmore, mention of whom invariably caused John to roll his eyes, but he had a partner, Tony Edwards, who took care of admin while John went on the road with the band. By now Deep Purple was the biggest-selling act on Warner Bros but the label was more attuned to singer songwriters like Neil Young, James Taylor and Randy Newman or rootsy groovers like Little Feat, Bonnie Raitt and Ry Cooder, and had acquired DP in a fire sale when their previous label went bust. Hard rockers like Deep Purple were an altogether disturbing commodity for them.

Travelling first class in those days was the ultimate in luxury. The cabin at the front of the plane was on two levels, connected by a spiral staircase that led to a small bar and dining area above the regular seating – more like arm chairs – where you could stretch your legs and grab an hour or two's sleep if you were so inclined. We flew to New York, spent the night in the Essex House Hotel and the next day flew on to Des Moines, Iowa, to catch up with the group.

This was Deep Purple's sixth and longest US tour of the year. Supported by the pre-Buckingham/Nicks Fleetwood Mac, they concentrated on the West Coast, southern and Midwestern States but I was soon to discover that all was not well within the band. Singer Ian Gillan, whose impending departure was still a closely guarded secret, travelled independently, often staying in separate hotels with his girlfriend Zoe Dean. He had developed a fear of flying and, whenever possible, travelled by road in a black Fleetwood Cadillac. Another reason why he stayed in separate accommodation was that the others weren't happy that he had chosen to bring along his partner, and were concerned that she might observe post-concert debauchery and report back to WAGs back home.

The rest of the band flew from city to city and Ritchie was persistently late at airport check-ins. The tour stretched into December and I joined the entourage for shows in Des Moines and Indianapolis where they were drawing enormous crowds. When I interviewed Jon Lord in his hotel room, he spoke about the need for change and their weariness at the constant touring, so much so that he had difficulty remembering which city he was in. No one was specific about the immediate future, which led me to believe they were hiding something from me. Indications seemed to be that the group would disperse for a six-month period the following year and reassemble having had the opportunity to work on individual projects. Ian Gillan's defection was not mentioned.

As candid as ever, Ritchie confided to me that apart from brief discussions before the evening's set he hadn't spoken to Gillan on the entire tour. Ritchie didn't elaborate, probably because although he knew Ian was leaving, he was under instructions not to tell the press, but when I subsequently asked Ian if it was true he hadn't talked to Ritchie, he confirmed it was.

While the fans at the Veterans Memorial Hall in Des Moines welcomed Deep Purple with open arms, elsewhere the capital of Iowa seemed particularly inhospitable towards them. It was bitterly cold in December, the telephone backstage had a lock on its dial designed to prevent its use and in the hotel bar those members of the DP entourage enjoying a late night drink after the show were rudely interrupted by a couple of abrasive local cops who insisted that the bar close immediately and that unconsumed drinks remain untouched. Clearly disapproving of our hair, clothes and demeanour, the cops threatened to arrest us all if we demurred.

Perhaps this explains why, on a plane flight from Des Moines, Ritchie indulged in a prank that ranks among his best ever – or worst, depending on your point of view. We were sat together and when the plane reached cruising speed he produced from his hand luggage a fearsomely offensive pornographic magazine with obese women, some dressed as nuns, doing extraordinary things with animals, astride pigs, beneath dogs. Realising that the magazine was of the same dimensions as the in-flight magazine published by Braniff Airways, Ritchie systematically substituted pages from one to the other, carefully replacing the staples before tucking the reconstituted flight brochure into the pocket provided. "Shame we won't be here when the next person picks that up," he said when the mischief was complete.

I left Deep Purple to their own devices and returned to the UK via New York where I had arranged to meet my *MM* pal Michael Watts who earlier in the month had taken over from Roy Hollingworth as our US correspondent.

Michael took me to PJ Clarke's, a long-established bar and restaurant on the East Side, where we ate their famous burgers and drank a lot of beer, so much so that I almost missed my flight back to London that night. Running very late and far from sober, I hailed a yellow cab on Third Avenue to take me to JFK. I really thought I was too late to check in but I hadn't reckoned with how airport staff treat first-class passengers. "That's not a problem sir," said the lady at the Pan Am check-in desk as I produced my ticket and apologised for my tardiness. "Please step this way." Never again would I be escorted through customs and onto a plane. I collapsed in a large comfy seat and promptly fell asleep. Two hours later, I awoke with a start and began to scribble about Deep Purple in a notebook, and when I landed at Heathrow I went directly to the office and typed it up.

As an aside here it is worth mentioning that to have been flown first-class across the Atlantic at the expense of those with a financial interest in the career of Deep Purple might seem to the untrained eye as if I'd been bribed to write positively about them. This was what was known in the trade as a "facility trip" and it wouldn't have come about had it not become clear to everyone involved that I liked the band. Nevertheless, it could be construed as an indirect bribe since travel and hospitality doled out in such largesse might make it churlish on the part of the writer not to acknowledge gratitude in the form of favourable coverage. It's a dilemma *MM*'s staff faced time and again.

However, this sort of thing was widespread in the music business during the period I worked for *MM*. I'll stick my neck out here and state that almost all flights undertaken to see acts overseas by writers from the UK weekly press – not just *MM* – were paid for by someone else, usually their record label. Indeed, of the hundreds of flights I took during my seven years of *MM*, many between 1973 and 1977 when I was working from the US, I paid for only two, both private holidays.

It never occurred to any of us to question this, nor to become curious as to who might have paid for it all in the long term. I suspect now that it was the acts who footed the bill for entertaining us writers, probably not directly but in the form of debits from their royalties or add-ons to whatever debt in the form of an advance they had already accrued with their label.

Indirect bribery like this didn't necessarily take the form of expensive air travel and accommodation. Publicists buying a round in the pub or lunch in a restaurant might feel the gesture warranted a favour in kind, and the only favour they'd be interested in would be mention of their client in the paper. "Lunch?

Certainly, and here's a copy of my client's new album to review. I recommend the Chablis with the lobster." The bill for both, in the form of expenses, would arrive at the office of the group's manager who, after paying it, would add it to whatever expenses were owed them by their client, or their record label.

Either way, it's a pound to a penny that the musicians paid in the end.

*

In the third week of December, as 1972 was drawing to a close, I spent an afternoon with John Entwistle at his semi-detached house in Ealing. By this time, I knew John reasonably well and he and his wife Alison welcomed me into their home. Aside from the fact that the house was packed with curios, it was the kind of home you might expect a moderately successful businessman to live in with his family, comfortable but not ostentatious, perfect for the character in The Kinks' song 'A Well Respected Man'.

I remember two things in particular from the visit. John had just bought a table lamp with those swishy frond-like tentacles that lit up at the ends and I'd never seen one before. Nowadays they're a bit kitsch but I was fascinated by it. Even more impressive was the first video machine I'd ever seen, a grey box the size of a micro-wave oven with lots of knobs and cassettes the size of cigar boxes. John demonstrated it for me, and then took me upstairs to admire his guitar collection. Outside of a music shop, I'd never seen so many guitars in one place.

"Boris the spider sits in a glass case behind John Entwistle's private studio control panel, and the ten little friends that inspired the opening track on *Whistle Rymes* flank him on either side," I wrote. "The spider in the case didn't actually inspire the early Who favourite: it was bought later, along with all the rest of the bric-a-brac that makes John's house part museum, part instrument gallery, part studio and part home. Entwistle's castle really is impressive. If the £14,000 custom-built Cadillac resting outside in the drive (it's too long for the garage) doesn't hold your attention, then the suits of armour, gun collections, swords or goldfish will.

"And if you're still not satisfied there's no fewer than 32 guitars of different makes, shapes, sizes and uses waiting to be plucked. There are a couple of rare Gretschs that Chet Atkins must have been reluctant to part with. There is an acoustic bass with an outsize body to make the notes hum and there are guitars that are simply there because John was given them by eager manufacturers, anxious to use the Entwistle seal of satisfaction in their advertising copy.

"There are Gibson basses with Fender necks and Fender basses with Gibson pick-ups, and all manner of combinations of bodies, fretboards and electronics. There are as many brass instruments as there are guitars, and the studio offers facilities for every home record maker. The electronic drum beater provides constant rhythms to play to, and a couple of muses (musical computers) provide a steady supply of notes in ever-repeating patterns.

"There's a grand piano and a couple of Keith Moon's cast-off drum kits. And there's a Moog synthesiser proper that's guaranteed to keep anyone with the slightest interest in music occupied for hours."

In the fullness of time John would amass over 200 guitars and probably owned a larger collection of bass guitars than any musician in the world.

After John's death on 2002, about 90 of his bass guitars, among them several he had played onstage with The Who, were sold at Sotheby's Auction Room in South Kensington, along with a similar number of guitars and many brass instruments. Watching the auctioneer's hammer come down alongside me were grieving fans eager to bid for a little piece of John Entwistle. In the last decade of his life, they had seen him performing not only with The Who but also with bands of his own, and these loyal fans deeply appreciated not just John's immense skills as a musician but the touching allegiance he had always shown towards them. Within the Who fan community it was well known that after both his own and Who shows, John would remain behind to socialise, happy to answer questions about his equipment, his playing style and The Who, and sign autographs for one and all. I cannot think of any other rock star of his stature who was more gracious to fans, the lifeblood of the music industry after all, than John, nor fans who appreciated this princely attitude so much.

The last time I spoke to John was backstage at Wembley Arena after a Who show on November 15, 2000. The hospitality area was crowded with men and women far younger than me or the group and there was no sign of Pete or Roger but, as ever, John was in the midst of the throng. Grey-haired and looking older than his 56 years, he was slightly tipsy, and when he saw me, he offered a warm smile of recognition.

"I don't know a soul here apart from you," I said to him.

"Neither do I," he replied, laughing.

*

With the exception of Don Everly, I had somehow eluded the first wave of rock 'n' rollers during my time on *MM*, but one of them – the scariest of the lot – was in London in January and I must have pulled the shortest straw. Jerry Lee

Lewis was recording an LP to be titled *The London Sessions* at Advision Studios in Bloomsbury, where a host of British musicians had been recruited in much the same way as B.B. King and Howlin' Wolf collected British names to add a touch of glamour to their respective *London Sessions* albums. During the week no lesser personnel than Alvin Lee, Klaus Voormann, Rory Gallagher, Kenney Jones, Delaney Bramlett, Peter Frampton, Ric Grech, Tony Ashton and most of Heads, Hands & Feet showed up at various times to accompany Jerry Lee.

Two uniformed security guards stood impassively by the doorway to the studio, and every visitor was checked against a list of names at reception before entering Jerry's presence. Even then admittance wasn't guaranteed. It rather depended on whether Jerry liked the look of your face or not.

The band was playing 'Proud Mary' with Jerry's son, Jerry Lee Lewis Jr, on vocals when I arrived. Jerry was on piano, Albert Lee and Delaney Bramlett on guitars, Chas Hodges on bass and Kenney Jones on drums, with three girl singers. After two rehearsals and two takes they were done. About 24 numbers had been recorded in this way. Vocals, guitars, piano, everything was put down all at once. Recording one instrument at a time just wasn't Jerry Lee's style.

The control room was more than crowded. Apart from the musicians there were Jerry's "men". He called them "gophers" because they'd go for things for him — like sandwiches and beers. His manager, Judd Phillips, the son of legendary Sam of Sun Records, was also on hand, as was Jerry's woman, a Southern Belle, who was constantly at his side.

When a playback stopped there was stony silence. The kind of respect that Jerry commanded was not only musical. He could cut anyone up with words too, so few dared to disagree with his opinion. "Ah, ah like it," he drawled. Discussion followed on the next song. 'Satisfaction' was mooted. "Ah'd like to do a song of Mick's," Jerry said. "But Mick did that one so good, me singing it would be sticking a greasy noodle up some critter's ass." It was a cue to laugh. Often Jerry's comments, though difficult to catch through the Southern drawl, were incredibly funny.

When he sat in a chair that belonged to a technician, the thoughtless technician asked Jerry to move.

"You move me, boy." Silence. "I'll give you five-hundred to a thousand you won't move me, boy." You could hear a pin drop in the room, and no-one's sure whether Jerry was really as mean as he made out or it was all a big joke. His piercing eyes cut through the opposition. "I'll whip you any day, boy. Any day." But then he laughed and broke the tension. It was a joke, but one that brought home how proud Jerry Lee was of his Southern upbringing. Southern Comfort, cotton, short hair, the Good Book and the country music. I wondered how he made out with Chuck Berry and Little Richard.

Later Jerry was holding court again in the control room while others rehearsed a number around the piano in the studio. "They're rehearsing a song I don't wanna play," he drawled. In company with everyone else, I laughed and shook my head. "What's you shaking your head and laughing for, boy?" It was aimed at me. "You laughing at me, boy? Don't you believe me? I'll whip you any day, boy." Silence. My face turned red. Everyone got this treatment from Jerry. Unpredictable, tension-filled moments when the words just don't arrive in time.

But it passed, and Jerry smiled and laughed and I told him I was laughing at the musicians in the studio who were rehearsing a number they're weren't going to play and he agreed that it was funny, so we laughed together. It seemed we were friends but I was glad to get out of there.

*

The tenth anniversary of The Beatles topping the *MM* charts for the first time, with 'Please Please Me', occurred in March and I was called on to somehow summarise their 1963 achievements in a double page spread. I relished this kind of opportunity, did a bit of research and came up with: "At the end of the year seven separate Beatles records occupied places in the charts – two singles at one and two, EPs at 13, 17 and 25, and their first two albums at one and two in the LP charts. During the year a Beatles record had been at number one for 19 weeks. For much of the year Beatle records had been at number two or three, or songs penned by The Beatles but recorded by other groups had occupied the top spot. A social revolution coincided with the arrival of The Beatles but even if their presence was not directly responsible for the social changes, The Beatles provided the soundtrack for all that occurred. In the parade of the young, The Beatles were the band we marched with."

Now, 60 years later, it is sometimes forgotten how all-encompassing was The Beatles' domination of pop music during the early years of their career. Setting aside for a moment the chart statistics I quoted in that 1973 feature, and the chaos they caused outside theatres wherever and whenever they performed, and at airports or anywhere else they happened to be, including, in Australia, public spaces where hundreds of thousands of fans gathered to watch them wave from balconies, setting aside all that, there is the music – a dozen peerless LPs, countless singles – that continues to enlighten, inspire and entertain.

Over the past 50 years many acts, usually boy bands, have been lazily tagged as being "bigger than The Beatles" but only for two or three years, at which point they cease to be "bigger than The Beatles" until the arrival of another one. However, no one ever says that this or that band is bigger than the last act that was said to be "bigger than The Beatles". No act is ever described as being bigger than, say, The Bay City Rollers, or Take That, or One Direction, or BTS, or whichever boy band, or girl band – for a while, ludicrously, The Spice Girls were "bigger than The Beatles", as I recall – is currently doing pretty well. Being "bigger than The Beatles" is a meaningless comparison drawn by those seeking a standard with which to measure popularity, and the only standard ever worth applying is The Beatles.

Meanwhile, statistically, dozens of acts can legitimately claim to be "bigger than The Beatles". In the years since The Beatles were active as a group, everyone from Michael Jackson to Taylor Swift has released albums that have sold many more than any single album by The Beatles. Similarly, attendance figures at Beatles' concerts have been overwhelmingly surpassed by pretty much every act that's risen to arena or stadium status in the past 50 years, not least their sixties rivals, The Rolling Stones. On internet lists of highest grossing tours, The Beatles don't even get a look in.

Nevertheless, as a measure of popularity, it's The Beatles – and only The Beatles – who are used as a yardstick, which merely serves to solidify their impregnable status. The more acts who claim to be "bigger The Beatles", the bigger The Beatles become.

*

It was pure coincidence that my musings on The Beatles occurred in the same issue of *MM* as my report on the arrival in the UK of The Osmonds, the sibling act from Utah, whose manager Ed Leffler was the proud owner of a watch inscribed by Brian Epstein, thanking him for services to The Beatles on one of their US tours. He showed me the watch at the offices of Polydor Records in Stratford Place, off Oxford Street, where his charges had gathered for a press conference and where their presence close to London's principal shopping street had become known to fans, hundreds of whom had gathered on the street below.

"There were no scheduled public appearances but when you're Donny Osmond, every step out of doors is a public appearance," I reported. "A royal wave, a smile to flash a perfect row of whiter than white teeth and the shrieks ricochet off the buildings in Stratford Place. Office workers in adjacent buildings stop work to gaze out of windows, police are drafted into the area, taxi-drivers flee after dropping their fares and shoppers, unaffected by puppy lust, jostle each other to see what all the fuss is about. The fuss, dear shoppers, is because Donny Osmond, Lord High Priest of Weeny-Bopper Land, and jewel of the Osmond family, is waving out of the window of Polydor's fourth floor offices."

I reported on the press conference and the following month found myself in the company of one of The Osmonds' chief rivals, David Cassidy – another was the far superior Jackson 5 – who was on a tour of Europe. Less squeaky clean than The Osmonds but still surrounded by heavy security, doubtless for his own protection, it was difficult not to conclude that Cassidy was a pawn in the game, easily manipulated, poorly managed and deeply insecure. His management were determined to keep everyone, including the press, at arm's length, but somehow the wall of security had been breached by a man called Anthony Fawcett who had at one time worked as a PA to John Lennon and Yoko Ono. In the course of this employment Fawcett had acquired a black velvet jacket, Edwardian style with a high collar and many buttons, that once belonged to Lennon and had evidently gifted it to Cassidy, a gesture that secured Cassidy's fierce loyalty, at least temporarily.

This development did not sit well with Cassidy's management but they were impotent to prevent their charge from retaining Fawcett as a close advisor, purely on the strength of the Lennon association and the jacket, which Cassidy wore everywhere apart from on stage. Everyone connected with the tour, including the press, was on a private plane, a big one, and a class divide arose between the star and his staff and everyone else, though to a certain extent Fawcett acted as an intermediary, a state of affairs that displeased his managers. Indeed, when the plane touched down at Luton Airport, a helicopter was on standby to take Cassidy and his immediate entourage to somewhere closer to the centre of London. There was a bit of a scramble for seats among those who felt they were entitled to them and at least one member of his management team was greatly put out when their seat was taken by Fawcett.

All of this offered a rich source of tittle-tattle for the posse of journalists following the tour when we gathered in hotel bars after the shows to exchange notes or, back in the UK, sat at the back of the coach that brought us, the second-class citizens, back to the city. Journalists love a bit of gossip, especially those employed by the popular daily press, and the stress-level we observed in those connected with the tour, not least Cassidy himself, was a goldmine for speculation and cynical humour.

I saw three Cassidy shows, two on the Continent in Germany and Holland, before returning to the UK and attending another at Wembley's Empire Pool. With no interview of substance to fall back on, back at *Melody Maker* I wrote about the circus surrounding Cassidy and the concerts themselves which, although musically lacklustre, were Grade A scream fests in which no one, not the band, audience or Cassidy himself, could hear a note of music anyway. Cassidy had a habit of turning his back to the audience, bending over and wiggling his bottom at them, which was a cue for screeching that rivalled the din at any pop concert I'd ever attended. His band were also travelling with us and seemed as bemused by it all as we were, professionals doing a job and getting paid well for performing music that was far from taxing.

I sensed Cassidy's frustration, that he wanted something a bit more profound than all this, but he was trapped in the syndrome that afflicted so many of his peers in the sphere of entertainment to which he had been unwillingly assigned. *The Partridge Family*, the US TV show in which he starred, was aimed at children, young girls especially, and his winsome looks, fluffy hair and easy smile were perfect for a teen idol. His management knew this full well – and also that the jump to serious musicianship was perilous and might see their client in limbo: alienating fans of his popular oeuvre while failing to attract older ones because of it. It's a dilemma they all face when the screaming stops.

I came away feeling a bit sorry for him. I don't think he even had a girlfriend with whom to confide when the lights were out, which was deeply ironic considering that a good proportion of the female population of the western world between the ages of 15 and 25 would have jumped into bed with him in the blink of an eye. Like everyone else, he seemed very stressed and this manifested itself in an outbreak of spots that required make-up to disguise. It seemed to me that only John Lennon's velvet jacket brought him some comfort; a token of where his head was at and where he really wanted to be.

A year later, in May of 1974, a teenage girl fan would be killed in the crush at the front of the stage during a Cassidy concert at White City Stadium in west London. This sad incident presaged Cassidy's gradual withdrawal from such concerts, and from the circus that surrounded him.

*

Not many fans screamed at Elton John – he wasn't the right shape – but since I first saw him at that festival near Halifax in 1970 he'd become just about the biggest pop act on the planet. He'd also moved into a mansion on the Wentworth

Estate at Virginia Water where *MM* photographer Barrie Wentzell and myself spent a pleasant Saturday afternoon towards the end of March. It was the day of the Grand National steeplechase and Elton had placed a bet on a horse that failed to show. He didn't seem to care but then, why should he? In the drive were a Rolls-Royce Phantom, a Bentley and a Ferrari.

"The lyrics to 'Your Song', the song that launched EJ, are a parody," I wrote. "Elton has a lot of money and a big house which he's built with the help of Bernie Taupin, a Steinway grand piano and a lot of hard work."

I talked to Elton at length while Barrie took photographs and Elton's mum Sheila brought us cups of tea in the games room, and afterwards I challenged him to table tennis. He wasn't bad and seemed surprised that I, too, could play a bit, a legacy of playing for Skipton B-team in the local league back when I was 17. He was very competitive, though, and won narrowly, which I put down to my being out of practice.

That same issue of *MM* contained my concert review of Roxy Music. Viewed at first with some suspicion by traditionalists, the Roxy project began as a hybrid that updated old influences while forging ahead into unexplored areas of music, style and ideas that shifted the same axis David Bowie was tilting, albeit without quite the same extravagant allure. Roxy were sharp operators who attracted the interest of Richard Williams, then also the presenter of BBC2's *The Old Grey Whistle Test*, by sending him a demo tape before they had a record deal. Liking what he heard, Richard took an interest in their career that boosted their fortunes but the truth is we were all captivated by their flair and ingenuity. At Richard's prompting, we stuck them on the front page before they'd earned the distinction, and not just because they were incredibly photogenic.

There was something slightly camp about Roxy Music and this prompted me to write a tongue-in-cheek review of their Rainbow Theatre concert. "Gee, you guys from Roxy sure do have style. Mmmmmmm, yummy yummy. What I couldn't do to that Bryan Ferry if he dropped around my place sometime. He's so... er... and the way he... er... well you know what I mean... So fabulous. I saw them last night at the Rainbow, dear, and I'm speechless. Talk, about pleasure... wow never mind about blowing that sexy little bitch's mind, you blew mine too. Golly gee... let me tell you all about it."

I was fast losing the Yorkshire in me.

11

"You can get a roast chicken dinner for a quid."
Graham "Swin" Swinnerton, Slade tour manager, London, 1972

During 1972 and 1973, as Slade became the UK's top pop band, I spent more and more time with them, interviewing them all, though mostly Noddy, and travelling all over, often with manager Chas Chandler for company. He was as down to earth as they were, albeit a lot worldlier, and he liked to tell tales about his past in The Animals and managing Jimi Hendrix, never sugar coating his stories. He cut through bullshit like a knife through hot butter and liked to get stoned a lot. He was an old school manager, hands on in every way, in awe of Slade's skills as a live band and as dedicated to their cause as Peter Grant was to Led Zeppelin or Brian Epstein had been towards his Beatles.

Over time I came to realise that Slade looked on their calling differently than most of their contemporaries in the rock trade. For a start, they were as hard-headed as Chas, with thick Black Country accents that made it seem as if everything they said was a question. They were very funny, forever cracking jokes among themselves, and like Chas they enjoyed a drink and a spliff or three. They were also very frugal. Not for them the delights of London's honeypot clubs like the Speakeasy and Revolution or fancy hotels, expensive restaurants and big black limousines. Even as the hits piled up, they continued to live with their parents near Wolverhampton and their chief roadie, Swin, drove them from gig to gig in a red Vauxhall Velox PB saloon before depositing them back home with mums and dads in the early hours. They recorded at Olympic in Barnes, a studio of choice for many top acts where Chas had worked with Hendrix, but he drilled into them that before a session started, they had to know the song back to front. There was no wasting time in the studio, which could be costly. When they had to spend a night in London, to do a gig, record at Olympic or tape *Top Of The Pops*, they stayed at The Edward Hotel on Spring Street near Paddington Station which was close to where I now lived. "It's only £4 a night," Swin told me "And you can get a roast chicken dinner there for a quid."

I spent a few pleasant evenings with them in the bar in the Edward Hotel basement where no one ever hassled them and one night they came around to my flat, all four of them. One of my flatmates' girlfriends was a fan and we were in the kitchen having a beer when she walked in. She couldn't believe her eyes.

"We were an enigma," Jim Lea would tell me. "No-one knew what to make of us because we hadn't changed at all. I still used to meet my girlfriend Louise [to whom he remains married] during her lunch break and take her for coffee. Our lives didn't change except that we were busier."

If any of them was an enigma it was Jim. While Noddy, Dave Hill and Don Powell were born extroverts, hell bent on enjoying their fame, Jim seemed perpetually worried, pondering the significance of the group's success with a knotted brow, and less inclined towards the outlandish attire that became de rigueur for Slade as the hits rolled off the production line. In contrast, Noddy was brash and outspoken, seen by all as Slade's natural leader and he played up to the image, at least on stage and on TV. With success came dazzling, over-the-top outfits, red check pants and yellow tops, and he grew out his side whiskers, crowning the Dickensian look with a top hat festooned with mirrors in which he kept saucy fan mail from girls. Entering into a spirit of competition, Dave – "H" to the others – went even further, generally wrapping himself in silver foil, adding glittery make-up and, of course, his famous Superyob space-age guitar. On occasion Dave would change in the dressing room toilet to avoid jokes from the rest of the band. Moments before Slade appeared on *Top Of The Pops* promoting 'Cum On Feel The Noize', he emerged in his spectacular metal nun costume. Faced with Jim's open-mouthed amazement, he retorted: "You write 'em. I'll sell 'em."

Slade toured diligently long before the charts beckoned, honing their skills and drawing crowds on their reputation as a lively, fun-to-watch showband. Jim told me that backstage at their first *Top Of The Pops* appearance in 1971, he looked at the other acts on the show and scoffed. "When we saw the competition, I knew we'd make it," he said. "I looked around and laughed. We could slaughter that lot." Like Chas, Jim always talked it like he walked it.

Once within Slade's orbit, I clung on for a topsy-turvy ride that lasted about five years. I don't think any music writer wrote more about them than myself. I observed their extraordinary chart success, watched them grow as performers and saw them on stage many times in the UK, Continental Europe and America. I became their "official" biographer in 1983, and contributed sleeve notes galore for both vinyl and CD albums, all the way up to 2005. The earliest were for their 1972 *Slayed* LP.

"It was Samantha who first introduced me to Slade," I wrote, trying to be witty about the club where I first saw them perform. Chas paid me £20 in cash for the *Slayed* sleeve notes, and in them I invented some fictitious Slade fans, all of them couples, including "Chris & Janet". The truth is I wanted to impress a friend of my sister called Janet Hill at the time and this was a coded message that I thought might boost my chances with her. It was partially successful too.

At the beginning of 1973, on January 7, Slade appeared at the London Palladium, a gig somehow connected with celebrating the UK's entry into the EEC. Chas asked me to introduce them on stage. "Here they are…," I began into a microphone. I was booed on and booed off because all the crowd wanted was Slade and I can't blame them. I watched the show with Chas from the side and watched the balcony sway as fans jumped and stamped their feet. I honestly thought it might collapse at one point, and drew Chas' attention to the potential danger, not that he'd have been able to do anything about it. "Fook me, Chris, mon," he said in his endearing Geordie accent, gazing up at the fans in the circle. "Whatever you do, don't say nooothin'. They might stop the fookin' show, mon, and if they did there'll be a fookin' riot."

In April of '73 Slade left Gatwick Airport for their second US tour and, in an attempt to drum up publicity, their newly appointed PR Les Perrin, assuming that scores of fans would be there to wave them on their way, invited reporters to watch the fun. Alas, there were none to speak of. Still, I was photographed on the runway alongside them and a couple of Air Caledonian stewardesses with the plane in the background. As time would tell, America was a bridge too far for Slade and the rather forlorn Gatwick episode seems now to be an omen for what lay ahead.

Back in the UK there was no stopping them however, and in July they played the biggest show of their career, at Earls Court. Slade were only the third band to play at London's huge exhibition centre, after David Bowie and Pink Floyd, and Chas was all too well aware that the Bowie show had been a disaster. His PA system was inadequate, the acoustics were terrible and the band performed at floor level, all of which led to serious crowd disturbances, with blame centred on Bowie's management for skimping on costs. Chas was having none of that for Slade. They performed on a huge stage with massive amplification and even had CCTV in operation beaming close-ups of the band on to a huge screen behind the drums, the first time I'd ever seen this at a rock show.

As at the Palladium, I watched from the side of the stage with Chas alongside me and midway through the show, as we gazed out at 20,000 Slade fans having the time of their lives, he was yelling into my ear, just like he did way back at Samantha's and at the Palladium: "All yee've got to do in a foookin' place like theese is to build a big fookin' stage and light it properly, mon. And get a decent fookin' PA. It's as fookin' simple as that, mon."

I was feeling a bit smug in the office the morning after that Sunday night show. Not many of my *MM* colleagues shared my enthusiasm for Slade, preferring instead Marc Bolan's slightly more cerebral T. Rex, but Slade had outpaced them statistically chart-wise and professionally gig-wise. "It's Monday morning and my ears are still ringing," I wrote that day. "Last night, I was among the 20,000 fans that packed London's Earls Court to prove beyond doubt that Slade are Britain's most popular pop/rock group. For them and me, it was an emotional occasion. You see, three years ago I knew this was going to happen to Slade sooner or later. Three years ago, I gazed into my crystal ball and predicted in these very columns that within a year or so, Slade would become household names. Needless to say, I was scoffed at.

"So, despite the singing and ringing and the dumbness and the numbness, I am a happy man this Monday morning. So, I should imagine, are the boys themselves – not forgetting manager Chas Chandler – all of them now waking up in their Swiss Cottage hotel that the Sunday papers reported had been under siege at the weekend.

"Under siege indeed! I can recall the first time I watched Noddy, Dave, Jim and Don perform. It was at Samantha's Club, off London's Regent Street, when barely 20 people turned out to see them. And they were mostly foreign tourists visiting the club to drink and chat up members of the opposite sex. Not much sieging went on that night outside the Edward Hotel in Paddington where they stayed in those days."

The fickle hand of fate dealt Slade a cruel blow for within days of the Earls Court concert Don Powell was seriously injured in a motor accident in which his girlfriend was killed. Thereafter, things would never be quite the same for them. The only outstanding show on Slade's date sheet was at the Isle of Man for which Frank Lea, Jim's brother, played drums. I was there, too, soaking up the emotion, though what I remember most about that night is that staying in the same hotel on the IoM as the band and myself was Julie Webb, my former girlfriend, who wrote for *NME*. Slade, of course, were well aware of our past relationship and found the strained atmosphere between us highly amusing. Noddy in particular seemed intent on reuniting us, even if only for one night.

"Go on Chris," he kept saying in the bar after Julie had retired for the night. "Get up there, knock on 'er door and give 'er one."

*

Slade's triumph at Earls Court was one of many notable concerts I saw during the first half of 1973. I watched Paul McCartney and Wings again, this time at the New Oxford Theatre, bussed there with several other music writers, and was pleasantly surprised at the improvement since the show in France the previous year. He closed his show with 'Long Tall Sally', the only nod to his Beatle past and still, to my mind, the best rocker they ever recorded, including those they wrote themselves.

I was at the Pink Floyd show at Earls Court that preceded Slade and stressed in my review how much better Floyd had coped with the arena than Bowie. "I hope every manager, agent, promoter and musician in the land was at Earls Court on Friday," I wrote. "I hope especially that those responsible for the David Bowie concert were there, and even more especially I hope that those who are due to present rock concerts in this vast arena later this year were there too. For on Friday evening – and on Saturday too – Pink Floyd demonstrated in no uncertain way exactly how to present a show in front of such a massive audience. They were faultless in every department, and at the end of the show 18,000 fans left Earls Court shaking their heads in bewilderment."

In June I was at the Royal Albert Hall to see one of two wonderful Paul Simon concerts at the great dome by Hyde Park. "They clapped for five solid minutes when Paul Simon, humble and tiny as ever, emerged from the tunnel, guitar in hand and on to the stage," I wrote in a lengthy, page-long review. "They clapped for much longer when he left. And Paul, as humble and tiny as when he began, just smiled and looked faintly embarrassed. He did four encores and only the house lights could put a stop to the adulation bestowed upon him by these adoring fans."

I was very impressed by the skill and professionalism of Paul and his musicians but felt it my duty to convey the news that, prior to his arrival in the UK, he had packed two newly tailored white suits that he intended to wear on stage at the RAH. After checking into his hotel, he sent them to a dry-cleaners to be pressed. Alas, the pressers shrank the suits, leaving Paul with nothing to wear. By all accounts he was furious, though this didn't impact on his performance. "Dressed all in black, he kept his audience spellbound for over two hours. When he laughed, they laughed and when he got down to the serious business of playing music, you could have heard the proverbial dropping of pins."

Simon was accompanied on stage for certain songs by Urubamba, a group of South American musicians, and for others by the Jesse Dixon group, a quartet of gospel singers, who helped him out on 'Bridge Over Troubled Water'. "This built up to an ear-shattering climax with the three girls chanting the lyrics behind Simon and Jesse Dixon trading lines until all their voices came together to bring the song to a close."

The concert ended with Simon alone on stage singing 'America', much requested by the audience. "Time and time again Simon reappeared to bow, smile and look shyly embarrassed at the pandemonium he had created. We knew it was all over when he walked up to the mic, waved and said, 'It's good to be home'."

That same issue of *MM* contained a lengthy interview I did with Cat Stevens who was perceived as among Paul Simon's main rivals, one of many who didn't stay the course. Nevertheless, I was positive about Stevens' LP *Foreigner* in the same *MM* that carried my Paul Simon review, even if I did suggest there was little on it to compare with 'How Can I Tell You' or 'If I Laugh' from *Teaser And The Firecat*. I still feel the same way.

*

While Michael Watts was in New York reviewing Elvis Presley at Madison Square Garden, a source of great envy to me as I would never see Elvis in person, I was at Wembley Empire Pool alongside Chris Welch being bored to tears by Jethro Tull who unwisely delivered the entirety of their new LP, *A Passion Play*, to an indifferent audience. Even the girl from the press office of Chrysalis, Tull's record label, was bored, as she and I went off to a quiet corner for a snog halfway through while my colleague Chris observed – and wrote – about how the audience amused themselves by tearing pages from the concert programme and folding them into paper planes that were thrown over everyone's heads. "One particularly fine hurl – I think it was from row 28 – earned a round of hearty applause as a dart shaped like Concorde travelled in a neat parabola before executing a perfect landing in the central aisle," he wrote, adding, perhaps more seriously, "It began to occur to me that this was very poor music indeed."

Such was the opprobrium heaped upon Jethro Tull that the group promptly announced their "retirement", blamed by their manager Terry Ellis on the abuse they received at the hands of critics. This was front page news but it later transpired that the story was a hoax, cooked up by Ellis and our editor Ray Coleman, who didn't say a word of it to his staff. Even Tull boss Ian Anderson was ignorant of what went on and was as surprised as anyone to read in *MM* that he and his group had "retired". "The whole scam was ridiculous," he commented later.

One star who did retire around this time, however, was Ziggy Stardust, David Bowie's alter ego, and I was at the Hammersmith Odeon on July 3 to see Ziggy's last concert, not that I or anyone else much beyond Bowie's tight inner circle knew it at the time. Michael Watts, who in early 1972 had done the famous "I'm gay" interview with David, and Roy Hollingworth had become *MM*'s Bowie-men but I'd somehow wangled tickets for this show, and went with Barrie, our photographer, who as soon as the show started leapt out of his seat to the front to take pictures.

It was an emotional night. The stage manager alerted everyone that something odd was going to happen when he announced, "… for the last time… David Bowie" but it wasn't until after the last number, Chuck Berry's 'Round And Round', for which Bowie was joined on stage by Jeff Beck, that the penny dropped. "Not only is it the last show on the tour, but it's the last show we'll ever do. Thank you."

After the show there was a lavish knees-up at The Café Royal in Regent Street where a host of celebrities danced the night away. Barrie and I tried to get in but couldn't get past the beefy doormen.

*

In August Ray called me into his office to tell me that Michael Watts was returning from America to become our new assistant editor, taking over from Richard Williams who was leaving to join Island Records. That left a vacancy as *MM*'s man in the US that was mine if I wanted it. I didn't hesitate. Indeed, I was as happy as a pig in shit. Michael had spent the last few weeks in Los Angeles so to my delight I would head out there at the end of the month instead of New York.

Before I left, I interviewed my pal Pete Rudge, now in charge of the circus surrounding The Rolling Stones who were about to tour Europe. "At every date the promoter is expected to provide 50 security men, five limousines, a doctor, ten dozen roses, two bottles each of whisky, bourbon and tequila, three bottles of iced white wine, one bottle each of brandy, vodka and coffee liqueur, a gallon of apple juice and orange juice and assorted mixes. Fresh fruit, cold meat, good cheeses and Alka Seltzer are also required," he told me, adding with a sly grin that the Royal Family had been in touch inquiring whether he might be available to organise their next tour of the Commonwealth.

I also interviewed former Animals singer Eric Burdon, session keyboards superman Nicky Hopkins and George Wadenius, guitarist with Blood, Sweat &

Tears, in town to promote their new LP, before heading up to Yorkshire to tell my dad and sister I wouldn't be seeing them for a while, not until the following spring as it turned out.

Then I sold my car and packed my bags. California here I come.

12

"Some of those girls are only 12."
Girl at Rodney Bingenheimer's English Disco, Los Angeles, 1973

I flew from Heathrow to Los Angeles LAX on Sunday, August 26, 1973, 12
hours in a TWA 747, my ninth flight across the Atlantic but my first visit
to California which was stiflingly hot and there was a two-hour delay in
immigration. I was met on the other side of customs by Jenny Halsall, a friendly
English girl who'd worked for EMI in London but was now at Elektra Asylum
Records in LA. Jenny drove me to the Chateau Marmont, my temporary berth,
to drop off my single case and thence to the Hollywood Bowl, a revered outdoor
concert venue, to see America, the acoustic trio, supported by Jackson Browne.
Backstage I encountered David Crosby smoking a joint and a beautiful blonde
called Victoria who offered to drive me home. On the way we passed a street-
scene being filmed for a movie and she waited while I got out of her car to take
a look. Then she drove me to the Chateau but declined my invitation to join
me for the night, probably for the best as I had neither showered nor slept in 36
hours.

I spent my first month in Los Angeles in the same suite of rooms my
predecessor Michael Watts had vacated at the Chateau, a mock Gothic castle
set back from Sunset Boulevard opposite Schwabs, the bright pink drugstore-
cum-diner where underdressed starlets hung out in the hope of attracting film
producers. Built in 1929, the Chateau wasn't like any hotel I'd stayed in before.
There was no bar or dining room, no public areas to speak of, and the rooms
were spacious apartments in the main building, or bungalows in the grounds,
though there was a communal swimming pool and basement garage. I briefly
befriended a man who imported vintage cars from the UK and parked them
there, a line of old Rollers, and one day he took me for a ride in one.

Unlike today, the Chateau Marmont in 1973 was too shabby to be described
as luxurious. Nevertheless, many famous Hollywood names had occupied its
rooms over the years and a whiff of scandal lingered in its dusty corridors. The
dressing room alongside the bedroom had floor to ceiling mirrors and when I
retired for the night in the enormous bed, I couldn't help but wonder how many
adulterous assignations between the rich and famous had occurred in the room,

maybe even the bed, where I now slept.

Michael had left me a list of contacts and so on my first morning in LA I called up several PRs at record labels, introduced myself and hoped for the best. Sure enough, within days LPs started arriving, though I had nothing on which to play them, along with concert tickets, invitations to parties and solicitations to interview musicians. The man from Atlantic Records sent me a back-catalogue order form and invited me to tick off every album I wanted, and Motown's PR asked me to dinner at his house where he showed me his exercise bikes and extensive collection of pornographic magazines.

Michael had befriended a freelance music writer called Peter Philbin who became my friend too, and he helped me open a bank account at Wells Fargo, chosen because I liked the name and their cheques featured Western scenes. I deposited about $400 of IPC's money and Peter took me shopping for groceries and on a tour of Hollywood, Beverly Hills and Santa Monica. He explained that driving was mandatory in LA as there was next to no public transport and no one walked anywhere, so I leased from Avis a red Ford Pinto, a sporty little two-door, and parked it alongside the elderly Rollers beneath the Chateau.

I didn't need to take driving lessons or even to have a California driving licence, but I got one anyway as it was required for ID purposes. I was told that if I were stopped by police without ID I ran the risk of being arrested for vagrancy, but it was useful in bars should the need arise to prove I was over 21, the legal drinking age. When I took my test, the examiner noted that I seemed far older than most of those being tested and asked me how long I'd been driving. "About nine years," I replied, pointing out to him that my UK licence enabled me to carry on driving even if he failed me. He took the hint, told me to drive round the block and announced I had passed.

Unlike London, Los Angeles was baked by an ever-present sun that turned everyone but me golden brown. Pale and interesting was more my style, so I tended to avoid the Chateau's swimming pool. On my first and only visit I encountered Lorraine, wife of Dave Mason, late of Traffic, a thin, statuesque model who was sunbathing in a bikini. She asked me whether I had anything to drink and five minutes later, still in her bikini, was lounging seductively on the carpet in my suite sipping iced vodka and orange. Unsure of the etiquette in these situations, I was on the verge of propositioning her when she got up and left, only to reappear a couple of hours later and, because Dave was detained elsewhere, ask me to escort her to a small gathering that same night in a bungalow at the Beverly Hills Hotel. Happy to go along with this, it was there that I met Lisa Robinson, the well-connected New York music writer, and John Cale, the largely unsung Welsh hero of the Velvet Underground, both of whom became useful contacts in the years to come. In the apartment he shared with Lorraine, I did an interview with her husband a couple of weeks later.

The Chateau suited me just fine as it was within a few minutes' drive from everywhere I needed to go: the Whisky A Go Go, the Roxy, the Rainbow Bar & Grill, the Troubadour, various record company offices, the Hyatt House where all the rock stars stayed, and Rodney Bingenheimer's English Disco where, in return for three copies of that week's *MM* which Rodney left on the bar – probably the first to be delivered anywhere in LA – I could drink for free and meet jailbait. Rodney's was a favourite haunt of Led Zeppelin whenever they passed through LA, a trashy, decadent dive on Sunset patronised by the less discriminating strain of rock star, mostly English, and a glittery crowd of skinny boys with bare chests and groupie girls in hot pants and halter tops who were too young to need bras. One night I took one of these girls back to the Chateau, seduction in mind, but backed off when, to my surprise, she mentioned she was only 15.

"You look much older," I said.

"I know," she replied. "Some of those girls are only 12."

I drove her straight back to Rodney's English Disco.

*

In complete contrast to the clientele of Rodney's, my first interview in LA was with The Carpenters, the soft-rock brother and sister duo who were selling records by the truckload. Driven to their home in Downey, a conservative suburb south of LA, by Doreen Louer, A&M's PR chief, I was astonished that Richard and Karen, aged 27 and 24 respectively, still lived with their parents on an upper-middle-class estate where their large detached house had been turned into a showcase for their many awards, all prominently displayed on shelves and in glass cabinets. At the back of the house was their own recording studio where we sat down and talked while Ma Carpenter delivered tea and biscuits.

Sweet as they were, Richard and Karen seemed strangely naïve about the rock world, set apart from it in many ways yet rubbing shoulders in the charts with the likes of Led Zeppelin and the Stones. I suppose that in a roundabout way they were the American equivalent of Abba, creators of expertly produced pop music that catered for a large but undemonstrative constituency discomfited by the vigorous sedition of long-haired musicians in tight jeans with wailing guitars. Led

Zeppelin's drummer John Bonham was furious when Karen, as slim and graceful as Bonzo was corpulent and lumbering, was voted the world's best drummer in *Playboy*'s musicians' poll the following year.

After the interview Doreen introduced me to tacos and fajitas at a Mexican restaurant in downtown LA, and we remained friends for the duration of my American adventure.

*

Within three weeks of my arrival in Los Angeles Gram Parsons was found dead in a motel room in the Joshua Tree National Park, down in the southeast corner of California, a local rock story given great prominence because Parsons' friend and road manager Phil Kaufman, acting on instructions from the deceased, made off with his body and cremated it nearby. It was the talk of the town in rock circles and I duly reported these events for *MM*'s readers back home.

Keenly aware of how much the Eagles were indebted to Parsons, I thought it best not to mention this when I interviewed Glenn Frey and Don Henley two weeks later in a sprawling ranch-style house atop one of the hills between West Hollywood and the Sherman Oaks valley. We talked in a spacious living room strewn with guitars while a succession of gorgeous blonde girls in tight jeans and loose t-shirts wandered in and out delivering cups of coffee. I got the impression the senior Eagles were accustomed to being waited upon by beautiful handmaidens under edict to cater to their every whim.

This was before the Eagles became multi-platinum brand leaders of the laid-back LA country rock sound born chiefly in the barroom of Doug Weston's Troubadour Club on Santa Monica Boulevard and soon to come largely under the control of Asylum Records boss David Geffen. It was a movement I was duty bound to cover for *MM* and to this end I also interviewed Jackson Browne, who, along with Frey, wrote the Eagles' first hit 'Take It Easy', and also Linda Ronstadt, both alumni of Weston's club.

Weston was a canny businessman who habitually coerced musicians into signing contracts with options that guaranteed they would play three or more seasons at his club for the same or only marginally increased fees. This ensured that should they become enormously successful in the meantime he would have the right to re-book them cheaply or, even better, promote their shows in a much larger venue. If they baulked at this he would point to the early contract and threaten legal proceedings unless substantial payment in lieu of the appearances was forthcoming.

I met Linda Ronstadt in her bijou house in the hills beneath the Hollywood sign and chatted with her while Emmylou Harris, her houseguest in mourning for Parsons, worked on a crochet in the corner of her living room. Pete Frame, the editor of *Zig Zag* and later to become renowned for his Rock Family Trees, sat in on the interview. We circled one another warily. *MM* was a big circulation weekly, the rock paper equivalent of a major label, while *Zig Zag*, the monthly magazine that Pete had founded with his great friend John Tobler, was like a cool indie label. Nevertheless, Pete and I remained good friends from that day onwards and a decade later, as editor at Omnibus Press, I published several books of those Rock Family Trees.

That same week I saw Linda perform at the Roxy Club where she dressed for the stage in a blue Boy Scouts uniform complete with skimpy shorts, a yellow kerchief and activity badges sewn on to her shirt, and very fetching she looked too. She had told me about an English pub in Santa Monica called The Brigadoon but I was too shy to invite her to go there for a drink with me. Perhaps I should have done, as I subsequently discovered that her boyfriend at the time, the songwriter JD Souther, another contributor to Eagles recordings, was two-timing her with Joni Mitchell, a former beau of Jackson Browne; very incestuous this lot in those days.

My arrival in LA coincided with the opening of the Roxy, a 500-seater joint on Sunset next to the Rainbow Bar & Grill, owned and operated by a consortium of A-list rock and roll businessmen that included Geffen, Ode Records' boss Lou Adler, record producer Peter Asher, Whisky A Go Go proprietor Elmer Valentine, and Elliot Roberts, who managed Crosby, Stills, Nash & Young and Joni. I was there to watch Neil Young play on the opening night, rubbing shoulders with the great and the good of the LA rock biz establishment, slightly wary of the company I was keeping and trying desperately not to appear gauche amidst them all.

Neil Young was preceded on stage by Cheech & Chong, the stoned comedians, and Graham Nash, who'd been recruited at the last minute to take the place of Nils Lofgren who had laryngitis. Nevertheless, Nils was well enough to take his place in Young's back-up band and play guitar during an hour-long set of new material from Young's forthcoming *Tonight's The Night* album, a highlight of his long career. I evidently agreed. "The new songs reflect a change from the lost soul that Young has moulded for himself," I wrote in *MM*. "On all but one he was attacking a Fender Telecaster instead of an acoustic jumbo and the music slotted more into rock than folk category. Of the new songs, the one

I preferred was called 'Open Up Those Tired Eyes', a track apparently written as a warning to dopers in which Neil offers advice apparently from personal experience."

Upstairs at the Roxy was the private On-The-Rox Club where, for the first time ever, I played a computerised slot-machine, a ping-pong game that involved knocking a blip back and forth between two illuminated bars. Customers queued up to put their quarters in the slot. Its popularity augured well for this sort of thing, I thought, never realising that the day would come when computer games would outsell records and the uses to which a computer could be put would one day deal an almost fatal blow to the record industry of which I was now a part.

*

My second visit to the Hollywood Bowl was to see Elton in his glorious pomp. In LA that September Elton was hot. A giant billboard advertising *Goodbye Yellow Brick Road*, his new album, looked down on Sunset Strip. He threw a lavish birthday party for his manager John Reid at the Beverly Hills Hotel to which I was invited and some wag, maybe Elton, gave him a bronze sculpture of an erect cock and balls that delighted Elton's mum, Sheila, who inspected it closely and declared it fit for purpose. That same week I watched him spin the discs as 'EJ The DJ' at a local radio station and a day later he appeared in the open air at the Bowl. Introduced by porn star Linda Lovelace, he was preceded on stage by an array of famous guests, all four Beatles, Charlie Chaplin, Batman & Robin, Groucho Marx, Elvis, the Queen, the Pope and Frankenstein, all lookalikes of course. "And here he is," screamed Linda, "the co-star of my next movie… Elton John."

"Last to make this spectacular entry was Elton and group," I wrote for *MM*. "As he walked towards the front of the stage the lookalikes gathered themselves around five grand pianos, lifting the lids to reveal the letters E-L-T-O and N, and simultaneously released 400 white doves over the heads of the stunned audience. Elton, dressed in a white and silver jump suit with feathers and hat to match, grinned over his white glasses and settled down to open his music with 'Elderberry Wine'. It was the most spectacular entry on to a stage I and probably everyone else at the Bowl had ever seen."

The party afterwards, at the Roxy Club, was a 'must-have' invitation and my date was Victoria, the blonde who drove me home on my first night in LA, but she abandoned me for a man who arrived in a vintage Rolls-Royce, probably acquired from my friend at the Chateau.

*

I was still living at the Chateau when I interviewed the singer and songwriter Tim Buckley whose *Starsailor* album I liked a lot. He was a rather intense young man, handsome but distracted, almost Byronic, and his death from a heroin overdose two years later took me completely by surprise. "Buckley is no spaced-out American hippie, nor pretentious underground figure," I wrote in *MM*. "He's a serious young man with thoughts on all manner of subjects apart from music; he's educated and articulate more in the fashion of a forward-thinking college professor than a contemporary musician."

Ray Manzarek of The Doors, who'd just released a solo album called *The Golden Scarab*, was my next interviewee; pleasant enough but a bit pompous, very aware of his own, or at least The Doors', importance, I thought. My appointment with him was arranged by the group's aide-de-camp Danny Sugerman, who remained a friend for two decades and went on to marry Fawn Hall, the former secretary to Lt Colonel Oliver North, the soldier notorious for his role in the Iran-Contra affair in the eighties. Danny lived in a house on a hill behind the Hyatt House where he welcomed all manner of rock 'n' roll strays, some of them castoffs from the female clientele at Rodney's, and I slept there once or twice, not necessarily alone.

Danny introduced me to a glamorous publicist named Diane Gardiner who, I was reliably informed, was the LA girlfriend – simultaneously – of Ahmet Ertegun, the boss of Atlantic Records, and Chuck Berry, both of whom she would entertain whenever they were in town. Diane invited me to a birthday party she hosted at her house for Chuck, the only time I ever met this touchy genius of rock 'n' roll's first flowering, and though I'd like to have cornered him for an interview, this wasn't the right moment. Diane had given Chuck, or Charles as he preferred to be known, a Polaroid Land Camera as a present and the great man was much taken with this gift, so much so that he took photographs of everyone at the party, me included. Also present that October night was Diane's best friend Pamela Courson, Jim Morrison's lover, who was with him in Paris the night he died; a sad, beautiful creature who in six months would herself succumb to a heroin overdose. "She was the most dangerous girl I ever met," Diane would later write in the preface to *Break On Through*, a book on Morrison by James Riordan and Jerry Prochnicky.

These encounters were not the kind of thing I could convey to the readers of *Melody Maker* and now – looking back – it astounds me that within the space of a few weeks I'd penetrated LA's rock world so easily. My rooms at the

Chateau had a corner tower that overlooked Sunset Strip and here, on a circular dining table, was where I worked, stuffing A4 sheets into my Olivetti portable, transcribing the words of my interviewees as I watched the traffic below. Each week I mailed a package to London and inside were stories about, and pictures of, Dave Mason, Elton, Linda, Jackson, Glenn & Don, Ray and Tim, guitar heroes Duane Eddy (twang) and Chet Atkins (country), and also actor/singer Richard Harris, who signed a copy of his poetry book *I, In The Membership Of My Days* for me, and show reviews of Neil at the Roxy, the Allman Brothers at the Forum, Van Morrison at LA Town Hall and, at the Hollywood Palladium, Mott The Hoople and Sly & The Family Stone.

Mott were ideally suited to the tacky glitz of the Palladium which was only a stone's throw from Rodney's decadent dive, and after the show some of them ended up swigging beer in my suite at the Chateau. Their lead singer Ian Hunter, with whom I would have a memorable falling out two years later in New York, was not among them but their tour manager, Stan Tippins, whom Hunter had long ago superseded as the group's lead singer, brought along a free-spirited, immodest girl that he intended to marry, or so he said. No sooner had Mott left LA to continue their US tour, however, than she was out on the town again, behaving nothing like a betrothed fiancée, as I had occasion to experience for myself. Waking up at her house one morning I was advised by her to hide in the closet as an "ex-husband" was on the way over, and he was twice my size. I did as she suggested. To my relief he didn't cross her threshold.

The Sly Stone concert at the Palladium lived up to the star's reputation as the most capricious of performers. He made but a token appearance, leaving the stage after just over a half hour and three songs, apparently satisfied that the customers had had their seven dollars' worth of entertainment.

"There was a dissatisfied yelling coming from the stage and the drummer re-appeared, commencing the same solo a second time," I wrote in *MM*. "Two minutes and Sly reappeared with band to give us two more choruses of 'I Want To Take You Higher', and wave to one and all in the manner usually associated with performers who have been on stage for a couple of hours or more. Then he disappeared and so did everyone else. The house lights went up and everyone went home surprisingly peaceably after what had occurred. For what there was of it, the music was tight and entertaining. But other aspects of this show left me with a bitter taste in my mouth. Seven dollars is almost three pounds sterling for half an hour's music – the worst deal I've ever come across."

I would encounter Sly Stone twice more during my American adventure, on one of these occasions attempting – and largely failing – to interview him.

*

I was back at the Hollywood Bowl on September 21 to review Procol Harum, who performed with an orchestra, and I took along Bruce Johnson of The Beach Boys whom I had befriended through his girlfriend Connie DeNave, an A1 Hollywood scenester and Elton's PR. After the show Bruce and I met up with Connie at an after-show party at the nearby Universal City hotel where Bruce spotted a grand piano in the lobby. He sat down to play and sang 'Disney Girls', his fragile song of lost innocence that appeared on The Beach Boys' *Surf's Up* LP.

Somehow the news that a Beach Boy was playing the hotel's piano spread through the lobby and a crowd began to form, among them a large group of Engelbert Humperdinck fans en route to see their hero in Las Vegas.

"Do you know Engelbert?" one of them asked when Bruce had finished.

"Of course," he replied. "He's gay you know."

The fans looked shocked to the core.

"Is Engelbert really gay?" I asked when we were out of earshot.

"Of course not. I just wanted to see the expressions on their faces."

Bruce had promised to introduce me to Brian Wilson and a week or two later he and Connie picked me up in his silver Porsche and took me for a Sunday brunch of avocado omelettes at an open-air restaurant in the Hollywood Hills. Afterwards we stopped outside Brian's house at 10452 Bellagio Road, Bel Air. On the bell push on the gate was a sign that read 'Speak Normally', but when Bruce rang it no one answered so I didn't get to meet Brian after all.

Bruce did introduce me to Dean Torrence though, one half of surf duo Jan & Dean, one-time rivals of The Beach Boys. As blond as the California sun, Dean had long since given up music and was now a graphic designer specialising in LP sleeves but I turned this encounter into an *MM* story that related the tragic tale of how in 1963 he and the other half, Jan Berry, recorded 'Dead Man's Curve', a celebration of pop devil-may-care about an unofficial auto race in Hollywood. The song ends in a mighty pile-up and it sold almost a million copies – but in all the ironies of rock 'n' roll there are few to match Jan's story. Three years later he drove his Stingray into the back of a truck in Beverly Hills, severely injuring himself. That was the end of Jan & Dean.

13

"I'm working for John now. Would you like to meet him?"
Tony King, PA to John Lennon, Los Angeles, November, 1973

I had a month to find somewhere cheaper to live than the Chateau Marmont so it was lucky that among the many music business folk I encountered was PR and rock 'n' roll archivist Michael Ochs, the brother of singer and activist Phil. When I mentioned to Michael that I needed a new home in LA he suggested Phil's place at 8812 Rangeley Avenue, just across Santa Monica Boulevard at the bottom of Doheney, a convenient walk from the Troubadour and Dan Tana's, the Italian restaurant next door where music biz types hung out. It was in Dan Tana's that I was introduced one night to Andy Williams who was so short that when he stood up to shake hands, I thought he was still sitting down. Michael explained to me that Phil was in southern Africa, seeking out revolutionaries with whom to write and sing, and was unlikely to return for at least three months.

Rangeley Avenue was a quiet, tree-lined, one-way street, and Phil's apartment was on the first floor of a building divided into four flats. It suited me to a tee and I moved in a few days later and found myself living in Phil's world, soaking up his character through his possessions. He had an extensive record collection that was falling out of a dozen cardboard boxes beneath the dining table, and I played them on his record player while I sat in his chair and ate from his plates. It was a wide-ranging collection and all jumbled up: Elvis might be alongside Mozart, The Beatles alongside Miles Davis, Dylan next to Sinatra.

I was familiar with Phil's best-known song, 'There But For Fortune', from the Joan Baez version, but the rest of his work was a mystery to me until I played his own records. I found the album that featured Phil on the cover wearing the gold lamé suit modelled on the one worn in 1957 by Elvis and chuckled at the title, *Gunfight At Carnegie Hall*. I didn't realise until then that Phil, essentially a protest singer, had performed a set of early rock 'n' roll covers at New York's Carnegie Hall and been barracked for his trouble.

Pictures of Phil were everywhere and I decided he had a kindly face. Evidently untroubled by any sartorial leanings, he looked a bit shabby, even on his LP sleeves, so the gold outfit must have come as a shock to his fans, like Robert Plant in a business suit or Mick Jagger with a crew cut. Through reading his many books and listening to his records I came to understand that he was a deeply-committed left-wing activist, probably more so than any of his contemporaries who emerged from Greenwich Village alongside Bob Dylan ten years earlier. Although he had a sense of humour, he was a serious radical, a brave position to take in the USA. In an earlier era, he'd have been blacklisted like those in the movie industry who felt the wrath of right-wing demagogue Senator Joe McCarthy. The closest contemporary musician to whom I can compare Phil is Billy Bragg.

One of Phil's books that caught my eye was *The Sexual History Of The World War* by Magnus Hirschfeld, with mouth-watering chapters on 'Eroticism of Nurses', 'War Eunuchs', 'Sensuality in the Trenches', 'Army Brothels', 'Behind the Lines Lust' and 'Debauchery Back Home'. In reality it was a rather dry academic study.[4]

In the closet was the Elvis-style gold lamé suit Phil had worn at Carnegie Hall and one morning I tried it on but it was far too big for me. Naturally, he owned a copy of *Elvis* by Jerry Hopkins, the first serious biography of Presley. Reading it in that flat inspired me to contact RCA, Elvis' record label, optimistically requesting an interview. I was asked to apply in writing to Col Tom Parker, Elvis' manager, c/o RCA Records, and though I was assured by RCA's press flunky that the letter was forwarded, Parker didn't even have the courtesy to reply. I guess it was filed away among 1,000 other similar requests.

The nearest I got to Elvis was relaxing in his dressing room at the Hilton Hotel in Las Vegas where I was taken to see and interview Glen Campbell, a friendly star in the country idiom whose skill as a guitarist was less well known than the heart-breaking vignettes by Jimmy Webb that he turned into massive hits. I actually saw two shows in Vegas, Tony Orlando & Dawn at the Riviera, where I stayed, and Campbell at the Hilton.

Dawn's set lasted just 25 minutes and cost a reported $50,000 to stage. "Dancing girls, old time music and heavy reliance on 'Tie A Yellow Ribbon' made up an act which was slick in the best showbiz fashion," I reported. "It was typical nightclub stuff, entertaining in a jolly sort of way but not the kind of act I'd pay to watch. The steaks in the showroom, incidentally, cost $18.50 a time," I added. That's $128 today.

Across the street at the Hilton Glen Campbell was a different kettle of fish. "He's an all-round entertainer in the strict sense of the word," I reported, "not only singing but playing guitar (expertly), impersonating Elvis (not so expertly)

4 *It can still be bought on Amazon.*

and playing the bagpipes (competently but not spectacularly). The highlight for me was the 'Duelling Banjos' sequence, closely followed by the *Lone Ranger* theme, played at breakneck tempo, accompanied by a film of the masked cowboy himself, astride Silver, galloping across the Nevada plains."

Glen used the same dressing room as Elvis and what I remember most about it was a custom-built TV with two screens back-to-back, so that those sitting on one side of the dressing room could watch a different show than those on the other side. Not everyone shared Elvis' taste in TV shows, I concluded.

If Los Angeles was a giant step for a Yorkshire-born son of the Dales, then Las Vegas was another world together, a Mecca to the fast buck where the hotels are in reality massive residential casinos, skyscraping monuments to unfettered greed where the activity hums around the green baize tables rather than around the lobby, dining rooms or bars.

Reporting from Vegas in the guise of a travel writer, I informed *MM*'s readers that "casinos take up almost the entire area of the ground floor, making it impossible for the visitor not to miss them on their way to various parts of the hotel. To walk from the lift to the lobby, from the lobby to the bar, from the bar to the dining room, or from the dining room to the show room always involves a trip past the lines of tables where hopeful punters risk their greenbacks on the spin of the wheel, the drop of the cards, or the shake of the dice. There are no clocks in any of these rooms and neither are there any windows, the absence of daylight designed to discourage gamblers from heeding the passage of time. Night and day thus merge into one long, never-ending passage of time."

I'm glad I went but I never went back.

*

The only other trip I made from LA that required a plane flight was to San Francisco where I and several other music writers gathered for lunch in the Dipti Nivas Vegetarian Restaurant and Natural Food Store at 216 Church Street in the Mission district, an unassuming area of the city where road works were ploughing up the streets to make way for BART, the Bay Area Rapid Transport system. The restaurant was owned and run by Devadip Santana, formerly Carlos until his guru Sri Chinmoy counselled a change of name, and serving at the tables was his wife Urmila, formerly Debbie, who flitted about with a cloth among the cheese, tomato and avocado dips.

I was sipping my carrot juice and reluctantly observing the no smoking rule when Devadip arrived, all smiles and healthy of countenance, spiritually beaming, delighted that his divine enterprise was doing good business today. A master of sustain on the electric guitar, he now wore his hair very short, his clipped moustache the only clue to his former identity as leader of the band named after himself that wowed Woodstock with Latin rhythms fused with American rock. His clothes, too, were conservative: a navy-blue blazer, unfaded denim pants, a t-shirt with an Indian design and a badge with the face of his guru. He was remarkably thin and greeted everyone with clasped hands, bowing meekly in the manner of an elderly clergyman greeting his flock leaving church after matins.

Carlos/Devadip talked to me with a Latin-American accent and was primarily interested in discussing how his meeting with, and acceptance by, Guru Sri had changed his life. "My main purpose in music," he told me, "is to inspire people to learn about the Supreme. I am not interested in whom they pray to, how they do it or why they go to see, as long as they realise they all have a supreme, a father of the Universe, to recognise. Intellect and wisdom are two different things and what I am trying to do is inspire people to get up in the morning and have a direction to live for. They can do it through Jesus, Buddha or Krishna or whatever. It doesn't matter as long as they do it."

Duly inspired by Devadip's sermon I spent a pleasant hour as a first-time tourist in San Francisco, gazing out across the bay to Alcatraz Island and wandering around Ghirardelli Square. The air was crisper than LA, and the day was bright and clear. In Fisherman's Wharf I was entranced by the human juke box – a sentry box a bit like a garishly painted upright coffin, inside of which was a man who played requests on a trumpet – which was doing good business, and I opted for 'When The Saints Go Marching In', a popular choice. I knocked on the front, placed a dollar in the hand that emerged from hole at waist height, made my selection and backed off as a trumpet appeared through another hole higher up. The crowd that gathered burst into spontaneous applause when it was over, by which time I'd wandered off to admire a VW Beetle painted in psychedelic colours whose bodywork was covered entirely in sea shells. I had an appointment to keep.

Back in London a few months earlier two *Melody Maker*-reading, Grateful Dead-loving free-spirits from San Francisco had turned up at the office with the express intention of befriending the writers whose stories they'd read and whose by-lines they'd memorised. This didn't happen often, and when it did it was usually schoolgirls who were after pictures of Marc Bolan or Donny Osmond.

These American ladies, however, were certainly not schoolgirls. They wore suede dresses, lots of jade jewellery and moccasins, and they garlanded their waist-length black hair with beads and dried flowers. Both had seductive Latin complexions and smelt of patchouli oil, and they seemed very exotic indeed to us pale-skinned Englishmen. Those of us who were unattached sensed an opportunity. We took the girls for a drink in the Red Lion behind the Fleet Street offices, where they turned a few heads, and then on to the Speakeasy where they had difficulty keeping up with the pace of our British drinking habits. As I recall, they spent the next few nights of their stay at photographer Barrie Wentzell's flat opposite the Nellie Dean in Soho, where Roy Hollingworth occupied the spare room. I was more than slightly envious.

The two girls left a week later but they kept in touch with us and one of them discovered through reading *MM* that I was now living in LA. She contacted the London office, inquired of my whereabouts and sent me a postcard with her phone number. I responded and we met up that afternoon in San Francisco, and over coffee in Ghirardelli Square I invited her to spend a few days with me in LA. She readily agreed and the following weekend flew down to stay in Phil's flat. Apart from a liking for sex, and plenty of it, however, we had absolutely nothing in common which isn't surprising really, so after three days she packed her bags and went back to San Francisco. I never saw her again. It didn't help that I never much liked the Grateful Dead.

No sooner had she fled than I was introduced to Caroline, an English rose from Kent who had somehow infiltrated the Rainbow Bar & Grill on the arm of a photographer I'd met called Richard Creamer. She explained to me that she'd travelled by Greyhound bus across America with her English boyfriend but that he had abandoned her in Los Angeles and hitchhiked down to Mexico. Without much money and at a loss what to do, she had found a job in Santa Monica as an au pair looking after two young children of a prosperous family. I sensed she was displeased with the errant boyfriend and asked her out, thus embarking on a relationship that lasted about six weeks.

On our first date I took Caroline to Calabasas, a 25-mile drive from Santa Monica, where the Sundance Saloon, a Western-style bar, hosted music nights. It was a fun thing to do, imagining ourselves transplanted to the wild west of John Wayne movies, but our night out took a turn for the unexpected when we decided to play pool. While we were at the table another costumer placed a quarter on the edge, thus signifying his wish to play the winner. I won and faced him. As it happened, I'd played a bit of snooker back in the UK so pool, with its smaller table and bigger pockets, was quite easy for me. I won again, and again, and again, eventually retiring undefeated. Meanwhile, Caroline was sat at the bar accepting drinks from several admirers and when we left it was clear to me that she'd overdone it. Slurring her words and walking haphazardly, she was in no state to return to the house where she was employed. She threw up on the drive back to LA and when we got back to my apartment, I helped her up the stairs, laid her down on my bed, took off her shoes and jacket, threw a rug over her and went off to sleep on the couch.

Caroline woke up quite early the following morning with a roaring hangover and while she showered, I cleaned off her clothes as best I could before driving her to Santa Monica. These courtly attentions on my part endeared me to her and sealed her loyalty, at least for the time being, and that night she returned to Phil's apartment and cooked me a roast chicken dinner, after which she was reacquainted with the bed, this time with me alongside her.

Because she was English, easy to talk to and as pretty as a picture, Caroline was the first girl I'd met in LA to whom I was minded to remain faithful, but I'd already realised that the role of *Melody Maker*'s man in America simply wasn't conducive to steady relationships. Casual was the name of the game in this job, and I was probably fortunate that many American girls felt the same way, especially those in some way connected to the music industry.

*

I stayed in Phil's flat for two more months and wrote more about the musicians of LA on Phil Ochs' portable typewriter, sitting in the room he used as an office opposite a page from a newspaper, cut out and Sellotaped to the wall, that advertised the best "round the world" in Hollywood. I never found out what "round the world" was but the illustration on the advert suggested it involved a female tongue and would probably have made Queen Victoria blush.

I also wrote about English acts passing through: The Who on their problematic *Quadrophenia* tour, Rod Stewart and the Faces at the height of their powers but soon to be laid waste as Rod's ambition destroyed their unity, and my pals Slade, desperate to get a foothold in America but somehow fated to wind up as also-rans, at least until many years later when MTV could showcase them in their true colours. My biggest catch, though, was John Lennon, on the run from Yoko, who was shacking up with Yoko's lovely Chinese assistant May Pang at a Bel Air mansion owned by Ode Records boss Lou Adler. By chance, I was introduced to John for the first time in mid-October. He was carousing in the private club above the Rainbow Bar & Grill with May and Tony King, a smooth-talking gay PA to rock stars, now in John's employ, whom I already knew because he also worked for Elton.

"Is Elton here?" I asked him at the bar.

"I'm working for John now," he replied. "Would you like to meet him?"

"Doesn't everybody?" I replied.

Tony led me over to where John and May were sitting. He was wearing dark blue jeans and a faded blue denim shirt and he seemed much smaller than I'd imagined him to be, thinner too, with small round glasses perched on his narrow, pointed nose. Although it covered his ears, his hair wasn't particularly long, quite smartly cut in fact. Tony introduced us and John seemed pleased to meet a writer from *Melody Maker*, especially one lately arrived from London. His voice, that light Scouse accent, was unmistakably Lennon and I was entranced. He began quizzing me about life in London, what was happening on the London rock scene, what Paul was up to, what the weather was like, what the government was doing, how much a pint of milk cost and even how the royal family were getting on. I got the impression that he seemed to be very isolated; or rather he had chosen to isolate himself. It was almost as if he was homesick, though he would later deny that. He was just curious about what was going on back home.

John was very friendly and I did my best to answer his questions. Because I'd interviewed Paul in the past 18 months and twice seen his group Wings, I was able to debrief him on these matters. Chatting to John Lennon like this, casually and without prior notice, seemed a bit like a hallucination to me, especially as I was conveying to him news about the bloke who played a violin-shaped bass with whom he wrote most of the Beatles' unforgettable music.

After a few drinks I plucked up the courage to request a formal interview with John. He told me to ring Tony King in the morning and, over the phone the following day, I arranged another meeting with John for the following Monday, October 22. It took place by the pool at the Lou Adler-owned Bel Air mansion where John was staying with May, whom I would come to know better as the years went by. The house was a single-storey spread set well apart from the neighbours, and as I walked through the rooms to meet John on the patio, I noticed a dark red Gibson Melody Maker guitar leaning against a sofa. It seemed like a good omen for what turned out to be one of the best interviews I ever did for *MM*.

The only problem was the noise from low-flying aircraft on their way to LA Airport. John and I talked for 90 minutes by the side of Lou Adler's pool, sipping cokes and smoking English cigarettes. It was a wide-ranging conversation:

his new album *Mind Games*, his love for America, the state of his marriage to Yoko, his immigration problems, his thoughts about recent Beatles greatest hits packages, his lack of live appearances, his views on the current music scene and, of course, his relationship with the other ex-Beatles.

My last question, inevitably, was whether or not The Beatles might get back together again. "There's always a chance," John replied. "As far as I can gather from talking to them all, nobody would mind doing some work together again. There's no law that says we're not going to do something together, and no law that says we are. If we did do something I'm sure it wouldn't be permanent. We'd do it just for that moment. I think we're closer now than we have been for a long time. I call the split the divorce period and none of us ever thought there'd be a divorce like that. That's just the way things turned out. We know each other well enough to talk about it."

And then he leaned over and switched off my tape machine.

The informal manner in which I arranged this interview with John Lennon set the tone for all my subsequent dealings with him, two further interviews in New York, a couple of chats on the phone and the odd social meeting, of which much more later.

Three Beatles down and one to go.

14

"Will you swim after him if he gets into difficulty?"
Corel Starr, Iggy Pop's girlfriend, Los Angeles, October 1973

I soon got to know my way around The City Of The Angels, driving here and there and even taking my chances on the absurdly complex freeway system that cuts across this sprawling conurbation. It was important to know which freeways went north, south, east and west and to move into the correct lane long before the off ramp you needed. I missed a few before I got the hang of it. I was also getting used to the idea of validating parking slips in shops or offices and having someone park your car for you when you rolled up at clubs or restaurants, and one night as Caroline and I left the Troubadour, a man in an open-topped car mistook me for the parking attendant.

"Where shall I park?" he asked me.

"Over there. It's one buck," I replied.

He handed me a dollar bill just as the real parking attendant emerged from behind another car. Caroline and I lost no time getting into my car and as we headed for the exit too quickly for comfort the driver and attendant were both shaking their fists at me. I gave her the dollar bill and told her never to spend it as it would bring bad luck, and she promised not to, giggling all the way home.

She wasn't with me on my only other car-related incident involving, of all people, Iggy Pop whom I watched performing with his group The Stooges at the Whisky one night in November. Mildly shocked by a show that degenerated into a free-for-all between Iggy and the audience, I wandered out into the night at the close and accidentally drove the wrong car home.

While to innocently drive the wrong car home might seem more than preposterous to most ears, the Whisky was one of those places, quite common in LA, where when you arrived at the front door a car hop gave you a ticket and drove your car to a private car park within easy reach. When I left that night the car hop wasn't around so I walked to the car park at the rear of the club and got into what I thought was my car – same make, same model, same colour, same rental company – found the ignition key beneath the seat and drove it home.

The following day I was due to interview Iggy and on my way to his hotel in what I thought was my red Ford Pinto I noticed my map of LA was missing, as was a carton of Marlboros I'd left in the glove compartment, and on the back seat was a pair of blue jeans that weren't mine. When I got to Iggy's hotel, I found a hotel room key in the jeans pocket and I asked him if I could use the phone in his room. No problem, he said. I called the hotel, the Hyatt House, got put through to the room on the key fob and asked the guy who answered if he'd lost his jeans. "Yeah… and I lost my fucking car too!" It was only then that I realised what I'd done.

So, with Iggy and his girlfriend Corel in the back, I drove to the Hyatt House and we swapped cars. Turned out he was a roadie for some band or other and he'd driven off in my car, albeit after I'd driven off in his. They were, of course, identical. Iggy just accepted this strange business as if it were commonplace.

Iggy suggested that we go to a beach to do our interview, a great idea as, naturally, it was a lovely sunny day. Corel was incredibly beautiful with hair down past her ass, spray on faded jeans and a loose white shirt. I drove the two of them to a seaside suburb south of LA, and when we got to the beach Iggy stripped down to his underwear and swam out to sea, his tough, wiry frame floating over the waves, dyed blond head bobbing among the ripples, his strong arms and fluid crawl easily coping with the choppy Pacific. Soon his head was nothing more than a tiny dot in the grey-blue ocean. Corel began to look concerned. She gazed out to sea, shielding her eyes from the sun's glare with her hand, letting her waist-length hair catch the breeze to form a billowing mane. I thought she looked like a mermaid.

"He's crazy. He always has been," she said. "He's always after a challenge of some kind. It doesn't matter what it is, and today he's challenging the sea. Will you swim after him if he gets into difficulty? Please!"

Fortunately for me Corel had underestimated Iggy's swimming skills and ten minutes later he was back with us, towelling off. He'd brought a couple of golf clubs and some old balls with him and, while we chatted, he stopped every now and then to hit the balls into the ocean. He had a pro golfer's swing, and he whacked these golf balls way out into the water, looking well pleased with himself. I was amazed that Iggy, the wild man of rock, could swing a club as well as he did, especially as golf is a bit of a pedestrian sport, but he told me about his dad and how he was a sports freak and how he'd been brought up on healthy exercise.

"You know if I had never been into music, I'd have liked to be a professional golfer," he told me. "Some years ago, I was pretty good at golf, playing off around a four handicap, but I haven't played for two years now. One of my roadies took my clubs to a pawn shop because I owed him money. I think I'd have been good at anything I tried. Maybe I could even have been the president."

His mermaid, sunbathing alongside us, nodded in agreement.

*

I saw the Faces at the Hollywood Palladium, and while the group was in town interviewed Ian McLagan and Kenney Jones at the Century Plaza Hotel where they were staying. The schism between the group and their singer Rod Stewart had yet to explode into hostility but Mercury Records, to whom Rod was signed as a solo artist, didn't help matters by throwing a party for him – not the group, which was signed to Warner Bros – at the posh Greek Café. The rest of the Faces were present but didn't seem pleased that the spotlight was on Rod.

Because Caroline was required to stay home with her young charges that night, I took along the lovely Victoria, more as arm candy than in hope of third time lucky, and when Rod walked in wearing an all-white outfit, his tinted blond rooster-cut shimmering beneath fairy lights, it was like he was luminescent, a sparkling jewel amidst a throng of devoted sycophants.

Victoria simply melted when I introduced her to Rod, not one of my better moves. Her eyes were like saucers and from the salivating smile on her face I thought for a moment she was going to grab hold of him and not let go. She had long blonde hair and was wearing a very short dress, just the kind of thing Rod liked, and when he smiled back at her I thought she'd melt. I'm convinced that she would have followed him anywhere that night, done absolutely anything for him, if only he'd asked. I lost her in the crowd and never asked her out again.

In the first week of November, I interviewed Peter Wolf, the singer with the J Geils Band, in his suite at the Continental Hyatt House. Wolf's girlfriend, the actress Faye Dunaway, sat in on the interview and, when it was over, she asked me about England, about the royals, about our customs and why our policemen didn't carry guns. She was quite tiny, birdlike almost, and very beautiful, and she spoke to me in a word-perfect English accent. Maybe she was practising for a part.

That night the JGB played at Long Beach Arena, supported by my friends Slade who were largely ignored by a partisan crowd. After having watched the vastly experienced Slade blow away everything in their path in the UK, it was galling to see them being snubbed in LA. I'd have thought that the Geils' crowd, obviously fans of the raucous R&B their band played, would have enjoyed Slade if only they'd given them the time of day. I could understand an antipathy towards Slade if they'd been on a bill with, say, the Eagles, but J Geils and Slade were a decent match. Perhaps Noddy's garish outfit put them off, or maybe it was his OTT stagemanship which, in hindsight, wasn't a million miles away from four New York chancers who hit the jackpot by painting their faces to resemble cartoon-book villains, or even a Telecaster-wielding ball of energy soon to emerge from an apprenticeship on the New Jersey shore and become the future of rock and roll. It can't have been Noddy's voice, which was a match for anyone anywhere.

I watched their show from the side of the stage and remained there for the JGB's set, during which Faye, in a pale blue silky dress, turned up, made eye contact and stood next to me until it was over. It's always too loud to make conversation at the side of stages so we didn't talk much but I gathered from her that she'd be at the after-show party, as would I. "See you there," she said as she dashed off just before the final number was over. An experienced celebrity, she knew precisely when to leave.

The party was aboard the Queen Mary liner, now permanently docked nearby after renovation as a posh hotel, and when I made my way into the room where it was being held, I noticed that Faye was sitting on her own. Peter Wolf had evidently not yet arrived or had left her alone to have his picture taken, and she beckoned to me to join her. We chatted for a few minutes then, to my surprise, she suggested we take a stroll along the deck together. As we did so we fell into an improvised dialogue, imagining ourselves as English aristocrats crossing the Atlantic by liner at the turn of the century, perhaps even on the *Titanic*. It was another of those lovely warm LA evenings and as we ambled along together we warmed to our roles, linking arms flirtatiously beneath the stars. The conversation, inspired on my part by Jeeves & Wooster, went something like this:

"Tell me Lord Charles, how was the conversation at the Captain's table tonight?"

"It was very agreeable, Lady Faye. The Countess of Avignon joined us and was most amusing. I see you dined with the Duke of Marlborough this evening. How are the Duke and Duchess? I often shoot at his estate in the Highlands, you know."

"The Duke is very well but the Duchess has a touch of mal de mer."

"Oh, how tiresome. I do hope she's well enough for the deck quoits tournament tomorrow. She's a spiffing player you know."

"Spiffing?"

I had her there but it was a hoot. I was thoroughly enjoying this, and I think she was too. We came to a step-ladder that took us to a higher level and I followed Faye's pert little bottom up to an observation deck where we continued our adlibbing. The truth is we were flirting with each other, all very tongue-in-cheek of course. The thought of taking Faye Dunaway into my arms was simply too outrageous to contemplate for me. Then we heard Peter Wolf shouting from below. He'd evidently been alerted to the scandalous reality that his famous girlfriend was out on the deck with another man, and he sounded peeved, probably thinking something was going on between us. As if.

Faye smiled at me and squeezed my hand. "Thank you, my English friend," she whispered, pecking me on the cheek, "but I have to go."

She excused herself and went back down to soothe her irate boyfriend. Musing on this fairy-tale encounter I lingered a while, smoking a cigarette, looking up at the stars and staring out over the moonlit blue Pacific, and when I finally made it back to the party both had left.

Faye Dunaway married Peter Wolf the following year but they were divorced in 1979. I never met either of them again.

*

On November 16, I drove down to Anaheim with Caroline for a Beach Boys concert at the 8,000-seater Convention Center. This was a really big deal for me, not just because it would be a fun weekend for myself and Caroline, but because I'd loved The Beach Boys for years, and she was a fan too. I'd seen them in London a couple of times, at the Albert Hall and Crystal Palace Bowl, but now I was going to see them in their own backyard, in Orange County in Southern California, which was like seeing The Beatles in Liverpool or The Who in Shepherd's Bush.

I dressed the part, white jeans, tight t-shirt, trainers; Caroline too, and she was blond with an hour-glass figure which helped, though neither of us were sufficiently tanned to be the real deal. In the car park were woodies with surf boards on roof racks, so the locals took it as seriously as we did.

It was a fabulous concert, just a great big fun-filled rock 'n' roll party, with the group swept along by an arena-sized sell-out crowd that danced in the aisles and sang along to every song they played, hit after hit after hit. No doubt out of respect for its mellower tempo and gorgeous harmonies, the only time they quietened down was when the group performed 'Surfer Girl', superbly too.

If there was a clear favourite among all the hits they played, the odds were on the unofficial state anthem. Indeed, there's nothing closer to Beach Boys heaven than hearing *real* California girls, like thousands of California girls, singing along to the glorious tribute that Brian Wilson wrote for them: countdown… "I couldn't wait to get back in the state", ignition… "back to the cutest girls in the world", lift-off… "I wish they all could be…", and the whole sodding place simply exploded into song. Magic. Caroline thought so too.

We stayed at the nearby Disneyland Hotel that night and on the TV in our room watched David Bowie's *1980 Floor Show*, filmed at the Marquee in London and featuring Marianne Faithfull as a nun in a backless dress *sans culottes*. We spent most of the next day at Disneyland, going on all the rides. We might even have gone on Pirates Of The Caribbean twice.

I wasn't to know it but this romantic weekend, this ultimate five-star Golden State of California experience I'd gladly given Caroline, was the culmination to our time as lovers. That night, after we'd driven back to LA, she asked me to park on the street where she lived and turn off the car's ignition. Then, hesitating slightly to deflect the impact, she told me her errant boyfriend, the bloke who'd left her in the lurch and hitchhiked down to Mexico, was returning and she had decided to forgive him. He was, after all, her childhood sweetheart from Kent, the only other bloke with whom she'd ever stepped out. I guess she had known about this all weekend but hadn't had the heart to tell me earlier. So, as nicely as she could in light of the fabulous few weeks we'd enjoyed together, Caroline dumped me.

C'est la vie.

*

On November 22, six days after my trip to Disneyland, I was at the LA Forum for the first of two shows by The Who, but the word was out that this tour, on which they played virtually every song from *Quadrophenia*, their new album, wasn't going as well as they'd hoped. Two nights previously, on the opening date at the Cow Palace in San Francisco, Keith had collapsed towards the end of the concert whereupon, at Pete's behest, a member of the audience had climbed on stage, settled himself behind the drums and played along for three more numbers.

I hadn't seen The Who for over a year, my longest gap between Who shows since joining *MM* in 1970. I was desperately looking forward to seeing them again, the only sad note being that I wouldn't be able to bring Caroline along to the Forum to witness the wonder of The Who in full flight alongside me.

Tour boss Pete Rudge gave me a yellow laminate with the nuclear radiation symbol on the front, for some reason the *Quadrophenia* tour all-access pass, and all seemed well in the dressing room, but when The Who arrived on stage, I knew something wasn't quite right. The show lacked the reckless spontaneity of previous performances I'd seen, the reason being that most of the songs from *Quadrophenia* required them to play along to tapes of pre-recorded synthesisers. This restricted their free-flowing style, so the hell-for-leather momentum that surged through The Who at their best was missing somewhere. The problem was exacerbated when Roger and Pete paused the set to explain the story of *Quadrophenia* – Mod-related and therefore difficult for Americans to grasp – between songs, and this simply interrupted the flow of the concert. At the far side of the stage John looked pissed off, as if he wished they'd just shut up and get on with it, but Keith was his usual cheery self, clearly unfazed by what had happened in San Francisco.

Still, when they were done with *Quadrophenia* they were as good as ever, which was probably frustrating for Pete if not the other three. The crowd still adored them, as I made clear in my *MM* review. "19,500 fans had stomped and cheered for over 15 minutes in the Forum, refusing to leave even though the house lights had been raised and probably well aware that The Who rarely did encores," I wrote. "But tonight their enthusiasm was rewarded with just that. The group came back and did an encore – actually 'Baby Don't You Do It' – only the second time I've seen this happen in watching The Who around 20 times... they blasted through the song, climaxing with Townshend unstrapping his Gibson Les Paul and, gripping the fretboard as if it were an axe, bringing it down on to the stage with a resounding crash time and time again until it cracked around the twelfth fret."

The following night I went to the second Forum show, which was an improvement on the first, and beforehand visited Keith in his suite at the Century City hotel. In the bathroom there was a gaping hole in the wash basin where the plughole ought to have been.

"What happened here?" I asked after using his loo and hesitating before turning on the tap to wash my hands.

"I had an accident," said Keith. "Use the bath."

*

In the first week of December Ray Coleman rang to tell me to relocate to New York asap, just like that. The reality was that in both time and distance

Los Angeles was simply too far away from London for the practicalities of doing this job. In the days before faxes, let alone e-mails, communication from the west coast of America was difficult, the post took too long to deliver my work, the eight-hour time difference was problematic for phone conversations. I didn't have much, just one suitcase for clothes, a portable typewriter and a stack of LPs that I had no choice but to give away. Still, LA had two more surprises for me.

Because I'd been using Phil Ochs' typewriter to write my *MM* stories, I'd loaned my inferior Olivetti portable to Caroline who could touch type and liked to use it for writing letters home. In the rather delicate circumstances that surrounded the end of our fling, I'd more or less forgotten about it. I knew that by now her boyfriend would have returned from Mexico and might even be staying with her in Santa Monica, so she – let alone he – probably wouldn't welcome my dropping round. Nevertheless, I needed to get my damn typewriter back. I called her house, got her on the phone and explained my dilemma. She agreed I could stop by so she could hand it over.

I made that difficult call on the day before I was due to leave LA. In the early evening I had just emerged from the shower and was preparing to head out to collect the typewriter when I heard the front door being opened with a key. With only a towel wrapped around my waist, I walked down the corridor towards the living room where I was confronted by none other than Phil Ochs, in person. I recognised him instantly. He didn't look well. He was overweight, unkempt and sweating. He carried two plastic bags full of cans of beer and he sat down and opened one. I don't think it was the first he'd had that night.

"Michael told me you would be here," he said. "I just came by to use the phone."

"That's fine," I said. "Pleased to meet you Phil."

"Are you going out?" he asked.

"Yes. I need to finish getting dressed."

"OK. Sorry to barge in."

"It's your flat. But I'm leaving tomorrow."

"I know. Michael told me."

He looked around his living room and saw that nothing much had changed. Then he went over to the stereo and put on an album of classical music, very loud, *fortissimo*. Then he switched on the TV news and cranked up the volume so that it could be heard above the music. Then he picked up a telephone and made a call, yelling into the phone. The din was far, far louder than anything

142

I had made in the previous three months. Phil drained his beer, threw the can on the floor and opened another. The music and TV blared on and when I was dressed and back in the living room, I sussed that he was ringing round trying to find a bed for the night. He virtually ignored me. After about five calls he found one, and promptly left as suddenly as he had arrived.

"I gotta rush," he shouted, gathering up the bags of beer cans. "See you around."

He slammed the door behind him and I turned off the stereo and TV and sat down. The silence was deafening. I'd wanted to tell him about how I'd enjoyed living in his flat, about how I'd appreciated listening to his records, about how I'd taken advantage of his library, maybe even discuss his book *The Sexual History Of The World War*. I wanted to tell him that I was genuinely grateful for having had the opportunity to live among his possessions and that it had been an enlightening experience for me. But he was gone.

Half an hour later I drove to Santa Monica, to the house where Caroline worked as an au pair, to collect my typewriter from her. I rang the bell and she came to the door with it but instead of simply handing it over she stepped outside into the night and walked down the path. I followed her until we were a short distance away from the house, out of earshot. It was an awkward moment, the first time we'd seen one another since the return drive from Disneyland.

"Thanks for letting me borrow this," she said, handing over the typewriter.

"It was a pleasure," I replied. "And so was everything else."

I looked up and in the doorway a few yards behind her was the silhouette of a young man I didn't recognise but assumed was her boyfriend. He was staring down at us, unsmiling. I didn't know how much he knew about what had passed between Caroline and I while he was in Mexico.

"Yes, I know," she was saying, almost whispering. "And thank you for everything else too. It was… it was lovely. You were so lovely to me. I felt like a princess. I won't forget it."

She touched my cheek, a last act of affection, and I squeezed her hand. Then we turned our backs on one another, both of us assuming that this really was the end and we wouldn't see each other again, ever. A few minutes later I was driving back to Hollywood. I didn't feel like going out on the town on my own, so on my last night in LA I ate alone at Ben Franks on Sunset, then went back to Phil's apartment, watched TV and had an early night.

The next day I packed my case, closed my Wells Fargo bank account by withdrawing all my dollars, dropped off the Ford Pinto at LAX and flew to New

York, checking into the Gorham Hotel at 136 West 55th Street. From now on, and for the next three years, I would be *MM*'s US correspondent based in the Big Apple, like Roy Hollingworth and Michael Watts before me.

15

"Well, he has a temper on him and he usually carries a gun."
Capricorn Records employee, January 1974

New York's Gorham Hotel – now renamed The Blakely – was a dump. Tucked
around the back of Carnegie Hall on West 55th Street, it was much used
by English musicians unable to afford the more expensive Drake or Essex
House, let alone the St Regis, Waldorf Astoria or Plaza. I hated it and had to
find somewhere else to live. Peter Philbin, my friend from LA, now worked
for Columbia Records in New York, and he came to my rescue, finding me a
one-bedroom apartment above a deli on Lexington Avenue between 55th and
56th Streets. It belonged to a friend of his, a girl who'd gone to live with her
boyfriend, quite hurriedly it seemed as she'd left all her possessions behind:
books, records, furniture, kitchen stuff and a closet full of her clothes too.

She didn't have many records but among them was her copy
of *Revolver* which I scrutinised closely. It seemed to be lacking three tracks, and
I couldn't figure out why. This was my first indication that American Beatles
albums were different from the UK ones, something I'd never realised until now.

Meanwhile, life became even more hectic on the rock front in New York
than it was in LA. My first assignment was a quick trip to Chicago where,
with *MM* photographer Barrie Wentzell for company, I caught up with Emerson,
Lake & Palmer, reviewing a show at the International Amphitheatre on
December 3. I think Barrie had been asked by ELP's management to take some
live shots of them for promotional use and he'd checked into the Gorham on the
floor below me, which meant I had a drinking partner in New York, for a few
days anyway. Roy Carr, the *NME* writer, had come over to do a story on ELP
too.

ELP were not really to my taste and I was a bit surprised that their brand
of bombastic pseudo-classical rock found such an enthusiastic audience in a
Chicago shed. Although they closed their shows with a vigorous stab at 'Nut
Rocker', the much-loved variation on Tchaikovsky's 'Nutcracker', ELP's music
was in sharp contrast to the perennially popular US-style non-stop boogie. They
were big on special effects and showmanship, not least Keith Emerson abusing
his Hammond organ with knives, and I figured this was what probably won over
US audiences.

After the show Barrie and I copped a ride back to the hotel in the same stretch limo as Keith. I'd first met him when he was in The Nice, when he and his Danish wife Elinor used to drink in La Chasse on Wardour Street. He was a friendly, down-to-earth fellow, quietly spoken and quite different off stage to the knife-throwing extrovert his audiences thought they knew. We were chatting away about mutual friends in the back of the limo when the driver turned around and informed us we were being followed. Then he drove like a madman, skipping lights, making quick unsignalled turns and alternately slowing down and accelerating really fast. Keith, Barrie and I grabbed on to straps, hanging on for dear life. "We've lost him," he announced after about five minutes.

This was the first of many visits I would make to Chicago and O'Hare Airport, the world's busiest. Each and every time I passed through, I was accosted by ingratiatingly subservient young women in smock tops, ankle-length skirts and sandals with flowers in their long straight hair, promoting religious cults, all smiles and platitudes but chillingly persistent. "Thank you but I'm not interested," I would say politely, mindful of what happened to Jeremy Spencer of Fleetwood Mac. Then they'd follow me and try again. After a while I realised the only way to get rid of them was to be offensive. "Fancy a fuck?" usually did the trick. Worked with Moonies too.

My next assignment from New York occurred just over a week later, watching Alice Cooper in action in Madison, Wisconsin, and Ann Arbor, Michigan, flying from La Guardia with his shrewdly clever manager Shep Gordon. There was snow everywhere and it was unbelievably cold. The exquisitely fragrant actress Cybill Shepherd was also accompanying Alice, covering the tour for some up-market woman's magazine. We interviewed Alice together in his hotel suite, and for a moment I thought Cybill and Alice were an item but they weren't. Of course, I found it difficult to purge the image of her stripping naked on the diving board in the famous swimming pool scene from *The Last Picture Show*. Most unsettling it was.

At this time Alice Cooper was the name of the group, not just their lead singer who subsequently took the name for himself and replaced the band with hired hands. But the writing was on the wall, as during the concerts there was a hidden guitarist called Mick Mashbir playing the tricky parts in the wings where the audience couldn't see him. No-one tried to hide this from me. It was regarded as perfectly normal but I remember thinking how outrageous it would be if, say, The Who or Led Zeppelin had a guitarist in the wings covering for Townshend or Page – unheard of! And the Cooper band was aspiring to the same level.

My connection with the Cooper crowd was eased by a solid friendship with Ashley Pandel, his publicist who worked for the Cooper set-up, Alive Enterprises, run by Shep. Ashley would soon go on to form his own PR company in New York, the Image Group, with Alice, Lou Reed, Todd Rundgren, the New York Dolls and a few more as clients. My ex-*MM* colleague Roy Hollingworth, who moved to New York, went to work for him as a copywriter and on Friday nights a gang of us – Ashley and his girlfriend Nancy, Roy and his girlfriend Iris, Mandi Newall, who also worked for Ash, and myself – would head up First Avenue to an Australian bar called Waltzing Matilda and play darts. That December we were joined by Barrie, Roy Carr and Lorraine Alterman, the music writer who covered New York for *MM* before us Brits arrived, and Mandi took a few pictures of us all in the bar. They're only contact sheets so a bit small but every time I look at them, I'm reminded of this period of my life, how nights like this, out with friends, made up for being 3,000 miles away from home.

It was during my first year in New York that Alice's tall blond drummer Neal Smith married another statuesque blonde, a model by the name of Babette, followed by a reception on board a boat that circled Manhattan, to which I was invited. Because police intervention could come only from another boat that could be seen approaching, parties held off shore like this offered opportunities for extreme debauchery, and this was no exception; gallons of booze, shitloads of drugs, casino-style gambling and private cabins for intimate liaisons – you name it. It was well after dawn when the boat docked and its dishevelled, bleary-eyed passengers disembarked. It was on that boat that I first set eyes on Lisa Stolley, a beautiful, pixie-like model with twinkling eyes whose boyfriend worked on Alice's road crew. I would have an unrequited crush on Lisa for years.

It being close to that time of the year, back in New York I wrote up my Alice Cooper story as a spoof whodunnit in the style of a Sherlock Holmes Christmas story, in which I became the great detective on the hunt for Alice and his gang, solving the mystery of the distinction between the identities of Alice and Vince Furnier, his real name.

Christmas was fast approaching, my first away from home, and I didn't fancy spending it alone. More out of hope than expectation, I called Caroline in LA, inviting her to join me in New York for the holiday, offering to pay for her flight. To my astonishment and delight she accepted. She was due to return to the UK soon anyway and, providentially from my point of view, her boyfriend had preceded her. In a mature and, for me, uncharacteristic understanding that rarely happens in the real world, we agreed that our attachment was strong enough to withstand the switch from romantic to platonic, from lovers to friends.

After a chaste night in bed together on Lexington Avenue, on Christmas Day morning of 1973, Caroline and I bundled up against the crisp New York winter and took in the splendour of Central Park from the back seat of a horse-drawn carriage. Later in the day we had Christmas dinner with my friend Pete Rudge, his wife Frankie and their two kids. Knowing how much he loved sport I bought him a grid football outfit, complete with ball, helmet and the shoulder padding that US footballers use. I can still remember the look of delight on his face as he ran off to his bedroom to try it on.

After a second chaste night, I took Caroline to La Guardia in a cab and saw her off as she flew back to LA. I would see her again only once, in London some years later.

*

I was now on my own in New York and had to fend for myself. Americans don't celebrate Boxing Day so, as I did in LA, I called up all the record and PR companies to inform them of my presence here and, sure enough, the promo LPs started to arrive again, along with tickets for gigs and invitations to interview all and sundry. This time I at least had a record player on which to play LPs, albeit one belonging to her who's flat I now occupied.

Like Roy Hollingworth and Michael Watts before me I presented myself at the offices of IPC, *Melody Maker*'s parent company, several flights up in the Chrysler Building at 205 East 42nd Street which, with its stunning Art Deco spire, is still the most elegant of all New York's many skyscrapers. Here I became acquainted with the man who ran IPC America, a plump old squadron leader type of chap, complete with bushy moustache, who suggested I find myself somewhere to live in Yonkers, wherever that may have been. I had other ideas. I wanted to live in Manhattan, where the action was, and decided to ignore his housing advice. He introduced me to a pleasant Italian girl called Gina who would occasionally retype my stories on a ticker tape machine, this being the fastest way to relay text from New York to London. Gina would also call me with occasional ticker tape messages or cables from London.

"Mr Coleman wants you to interview someone called Lou Reed."

"OK. Thanks Gina."

"Who is he?" she would ask. "Is he famous?"

Once established, each Thursday afternoon for the next three years I would leave my package of typed pages and photographs at these offices, from where a courier picked them up for delivery on Friday mornings to *MM*'s office in London. I would also collect my weekly living allowance cheque for $150 and on the way home deposit it at a nearby branch of Hanover Trust, the bank where I opened a new account. The rent on my flat, the phone bills, gas and electric were all paid for by my squadron leader.

New York in January was very cold but, as in LA, I was warmly welcomed into the rock fraternity. I was invited to dinner at the home of Lisa and Richard Robinson who had the biggest private record collection I'd ever seen, and they showed me all their American Beatles LPs, thus satisfying my curiosity on that score. I was astonished by one that featured The Beatles on one side and The Four Seasons on the other. Lisa published her own magazine, *Rock Scene*, and wrote a New York column for *New Musical Express*, while Richard was the record producer largely responsible for Lou Reed's re-emergence after the Velvets called it a day. Their friend Lenny Kaye, another writer, joined us there and he invited me to check out Bleecker Bob's Golden Oldies record store where he worked part time, which I did a day or two later.

I was also invited to a party at the midtown apartment that *Newsday* rock critic and *Rolling Stone* columnist Dave Marsh shared with his partner Barbara Carr, who worked in the press office at Atlantic and who before long would go into partnership with writer Jon Landau in the management of Bruce Springsteen. They had a hell of a lot of records too. Dave and I bonded over our deep love of The Who and at his place I met fellow rock critics Bob Christgau of the *Village Voice*, John Rockwell of the *New York Times*, and Paul Nelson who wrote for *Rolling Stone* and, while working for Mercury Records, signed the New York Dolls, which cost him his job at the label.

I was already moving in the right circles but at the same time noting how earnestly all these writers viewed their calling, invariably seeking a deeper meaning in the rock music they wrote about, a bit like Pete Townshend I suppose, which is why they all loved The Who but looked askance at Led Zeppelin who for all their skills lacked intellectual depth, at least as far as they were concerned. I think some of them looked askance at me too, a fairly happy-go-lucky Brit whose domestic circumstances were cushioned by the big selling music paper for which I worked – perhaps a source of envy – but it seemed to me that my *MM* brothers and I had far more fun writing about rock music than they did and, in any case, I always subscribed to the notion that rock 'n' roll's basic function was to entertain first and educate second.

Meanwhile, Peter Philbin's position as press officer at CRI – Columbia Records International – had special responsibility for looking after visiting foreign press. Since I was the only foreign music press guy on a semi-permanent visit to the city, that meant he was mainly looking after me. Very opportune, I thought, as every single Columbia LP release, from rock and pop to country, jazz, classical and more, including even *How To Speak Spanish*, came winging my way.

*

In January I went to St Louis see my pals Slade playing the sold-out Ambassador Theater, capacity 3,000. This was a bit of an anomaly for them. Because a local DJ took a liking to them and played their records regularly on his radio station, Slade were massively popular in St Louis, of all places, and later in the year they would sell out the 10,000-seater Kiel Auditorium, again with me on hand as a prejudiced observer. We stayed at Stouffer's Riverfront Hotel, a tall circular tower with a revolving restaurant on the top floor, next to the Gateway Arch, then the world's tallest arch and at over 600 foot the tallest man-made monument in the western hemisphere.

The concert was a riot of fun, just like Slade shows in the UK. This was the first time I'd seen Slade headline in the US and I was surprised Noddy didn't tone down his exuberant patter for American audiences, who were traditionally less inclined towards getting their boots off, getting down and getting with it. Afterwards the usual gaggle of fans, mostly female, found their way back to Slade's hotel, and in the bar I befriended a blonde heiress called Debbie who told me she was a model, and from the look of her I wasn't about to argue. We spent the night together and a couple of weeks later she came to stay with me in New York where I took her out to dinner with Peter Gabriel and his manager Gail Colson. Gabriel, who had a keen eye for the female form, seemed quite taken with her. Debbie and I hooked up on my subsequent visits to St Louis and in the spring, immediately after a quick visit back to the UK, we took a week's holiday together in New Orleans.

As it happened, it wasn't long before I was back in St Louis. In February, I stayed in the same Riverfront Hotel with Black Sabbath whose manager Pat Meehan, the man of many cars, was gobsmacked when I walked into the bar with Debbie on my arm a mere 30 minutes after having checked in. Only rock stars were supposed to have a glamorous girl in every city. The next day I flew to Chicago with Sabbath in a small plane, a 12-seater I think, my first ever flight in this type of aircraft, and saw them perform in the same shed where ELP had played.

Black Sabbath's brand of what soon become universally known as heavy metal was not really to my taste but, as with ELP, there was no denying the enthusiasm of their fans who loved Tony Iommi's doomy solos, Ozzy Osbourne's peace-sign posturing and the relentless, machine-like drive of their rhythm section. Backstage in their dressing room I was surprised to see the cheap luggage in which they transported their unwashed and rather grubby stage clothing, a sharp contrast to the five-star valeting practices employed by acts like Elton, Led Zeppelin and The Who. Pete Townshend always took the stage in newly dry-cleaned and sparkling white clothes, Jimmy Page's embroidered stage suits were lovingly maintained and Elton's many outfits were shuttled from place to place in state-of-the-art portable wardrobes. Ozzy's fringed tops looked soiled and shabby to me, however. They're not being cared for properly this lot, I thought to myself, and in ways that went far beyond the care of their laundry.

*

Travelling on Amtrak for the first time, catching a train from Penn Station beneath Madison Square Garden, I enjoyed watching the real America flashing past me, the energy of the American heartlands, the towns and the factories, the buildings and the billboards on tall towers, the wide roads that sometimes ran alongside the railroad track, the places that rock writers don't normally see. When you're in the rock 'n' roll trade and fly everywhere, as I did, you don't see the Jonestown companies that Springsteen would one day sing about, but you get a sense of them from a train.

I didn't write about these impressions in *Melody Maker*, of course. Bruce had yet to find the river, and I thought it unlikely that our readers would be interested in my thoughts on the American landscape. I was on my way to Philadelphia, a journey of about 250 miles, to see the Electric Light Orchestra, and in keeping with their name opted to review them for *Melody Maker* in the style of a classical music critic. "We are gathered together, ladies and gentlemen," I began solemnly, "for a recital by that promising young group of British musicians who call themselves the Electric Light Orchestra. Please take your seats quietly and refrain from rustling your programmes. Tonight's recital will include works by Bach, Beethoven and Chopin as well as pieces written and scored by the Orchestra themselves."

I was probably among the first writers to draw attention to similarities between their sound and that of The Beatles in their mid-to-late period psychedelic phase, the *Magical Mystery Tour* era, but I was amused – and pleased

– to note that their repertoire included a couple of singles that I'd bought when I was a teenager and learned to play on my first guitar. Just like The Cougars and Nero & The Gladiators, ELO rocked up versions of *Swan Lake* (Tchaikovsky) and 'In The Hall Of The Mountain King' (Grieg).

"We're happier working in the States than anywhere else," Jeff Lynne told me after the show. "We've been here for six weeks and have had favourable reactions everywhere we've played."

I wished him luck and caught the train back to New York where my next assignment, a bit of a shift in cultural perception, was reviewing Liza Minelli at the Winter Gardens. "Having never seen her perform before, I enjoyed it a lot," I wrote. "Could it be that it made a welcome change from rock and roll for a few hours for me, or could it be that I found her rather cute, like a loveable puppy? She's short, very dark and pert; full of fun, very natural and almost a little overawed at herself. When the audience claps, she claps too: a sure sign she's subconsciously thrilled at having pleased her audience – and herself."

Whatever enjoyment I felt was tempered by the cost of the seats; not that this kind of thing ever impacted personally on a reviewer like me but I sometimes felt the need to put myself in the position of the paying punter. "Despite an outstanding ovation, she didn't sing an encore," I wrote. "The show commenced shortly after eight and finished before ten. With almost half an hour's interval, that made it rather short by my standards. My seat would have cost me $12.50 and whether it was value for money is certainly debateable."

*

Also that January I flew down to Macon in Georgia, my first trip south of the Mason-Dixon line. This was arranged by Capricorn Records whose owner Phil Walden had managed Otis Redding, so he was worth an interview in himself, and in the three days I was there I also interviewed the Marshall Tucker Band, Wet Willie, Allman Brothers Band keyboard player Chuck Leavell, nowadays the Stones' first choice keyboard player, and Gregg Allman himself.

The highlight of the trip was spending an afternoon at Gregg's ranch-style house where he played his guitar and sang for me, talked about his late brother Duane and discussed musicians he loved, among them Steve Winwood, Van Morrison and, perhaps surprisingly, Cat Stevens. I wrote almost 4,000 words about Gregg, one of my longest interviews ever. "Gregg Allman picked up an old Gibson acoustic guitar and allowed his nimble fingers to slide over the six new strings," I wrote. "He tuned it and cursed and tuned it again. It was a 1920 model that had once belonged to his brother. Soon he picked notes as crisp and clear as the Georgia countryside surrounding his small estate. He played 'Come And Go Blues' from *Brothers And Sisters*, the Allman Brothers Band's album. Then he tuned it a little more and his picking became familiar again. He played and sang Paul McCartney's 'Blackbird' perfectly. 'That McCartney... shee-it!' he said.

"He swopped guitars, choosing a 1942 blond Martin. More tuning and into the chords for 'Long Black Veil', the tear-jerking traditional song about a man hung for a killing he didn't do, loath to attest his alibi lest it shame his lover, his best friend's wife. A brief pause, another tuning adjustment and Gregg played 'Will The Circle Be Unbroken', the song the Brothers sang at Duane Allman's funeral two years ago.

"It was like sharing a moment of reflection," I continued, "a very private moment I had no right to. I wondered what exactly he was thinking, but I never really found out, even after speaking with him for over an hour. I don't think anyone in the world knows what's going on inside Gregg Allman's head. He gives out his music and keeps the rest to himself."

Gregg's long blond hair habitually got in the way of the guitar's fretboard. He spoke in a deep Southern drawl that was at times difficult for me to understand, but he was hospitable to a tee. "Help yourself to the cocaine," he said at one point, indicating a bowl full to the brim with white power on the coffee table. Never having seen so much cocaine in my life, I thought it was sugar. Throughout the interview we sipped Dom Perignon champagne which he referred to as "a little white wine from Fraaiyanse". His fridge, a walk-in affair, was jam-packed with it.

When the interview was over we shook hands and as I was leaving he stood in the doorway of his luxury bungalow, one arm around Janice, the second of his seven wives, the other waving goodbye. "Mind y'all come back soon now," he said in the way that Southerners always do.

In the evenings in Macon – pronounced Maykin as I discovered – I was entertained by the staff from Capricorn's press office, among them a Southern Belle I tried to impress by giving her a coveted Alice Cooper medallion given to me by Shep Gordon. She accepted the gift graciously and we were billing and cooing in the darkest corner of a bar when she suddenly went cold on me.

"What's wrong?" I asked.

"Wayyell, Chris," she said, stretching her vowels like Elly May in the *Beverly Hillbillies*, "Butch Trucks from the Brothers Bayyaaaand has just walked in."

"Well?"

"I think he fayyaancies me."

"I don't blame him."

"The thing is Chris, he won't take kaiiindly to me being with you."

"So?"

"Well, he has a temper on him and he usually carries a gun."

I withdrew.

*

Back in New York I scoured the pages of the *Village Voice* looking for somewhere better to live than the poky little flat on Lexington Avenue. I needed a place where I could work as well as live and my budget, controlled by IPC's office in Manhattan, was $400 a month. Two serviced flats I saw were unsuitable because they were far too small, but I hit third time lucky when I found apartment 3D at 51 East 78th Street. It was well-nigh perfect, a dining area on a raised level as you entered, then a step down into a large living area, with a chunky table I could use for a desk, a big bedroom off to the left, a separate – and, as it happened, chronically underused – kitchen with a massive fridge. It was fitted out with deep pile red shag carpets, comfortable for sleeping on if I didn't make it to the bedroom but I soon learned that the best feature was actually the bathroom. Like the room itself, the tub was tiny but the water from the shower was scalding hot, so much so that if you left it on for five minutes it became a sauna, especially if you closed the window, placed a towel at the base of the door and stood on the loo seat where the extra height had a Turkish bath effect that sweated off hangovers.

The neighbourhood was tidy. The building was between Madison and Park Avenues and directly opposite was Finch College, an up-market private girls' school whose alumni included Tricia Nixon and Grace Slick. Less than a block away on Madison I found a shop that stocked day-old British newspapers, a Baskin & Robbins that sold the best ice cream I'd ever tasted and a Greek coffee shop where I ate scrambled eggs and home fries most mornings for breakfast, washed down with freshly squeezed orange juice and coffee. There was a Jewish deli on the corner where one day an elderly waitress queried my age – I was 26 – when I ordered a beer, and a small supermarket next door. Central Park and the Metropolitan Museum of Art were a couple of blocks away, and close by was a small lake where old men sailed lovingly tended model boats. Nearby was a statue of Alice in Wonderland and a short walk brought me to Bethesda Fountain where Latinos sold loose joints.

IPC were remarkably efficient at paying my eye-wateringly high phone bills. In LA I'd run up enormous bills calling the UK and when I ordered a couple of phones for the apartment, two brand-new white push-button jobs were delivered and hooked up within a couple of hours. Ma Bell recognised a good customer when she saw one. Answering machines not yet having been invented, I contracted an answering service so that my phone was answered on the third ring by someone somewhere who took down messages and relayed them back to me when I called with my personal code. Since I was out a lot, the girls who answered my phone were the nearest thing I ever had to a PA in New York, and although I spoke to them all the time, I never met any of them, ever.

In hindsight I ought to have rented an apartment downtown, perhaps in Greenwich Village, but I soon got the hang of the subway system which took me downtown and back again remarkably quickly on the local and express trains, a system unlike the London Underground but far more efficient, for only 25 cents a trip. Although the subway was dirty and incredibly noisy and the carriages were covered in graffiti, it was a taste of New York's underbelly that contrasted sharply with my rather bourgeois rock 'n' roll lifestyle. But I didn't mind. Whenever I took the subway downtown, I dressed the part, scruffy, looking like I only had a few cents in my pocket. And since when I got to where I was going, it didn't matter what I looked like and everything for me was usually free, that's pretty much all I ever needed anyway.

16

*"Why would I want to see Bob Dylan? I know what he looks like
and he's too short to see anyway?"*
Lou Reed, New York City, March 1974

Newly installed in the apartment on East 78th Street, the first thing I did was
buy a stereo on which to play the LPs that kept arriving. I was still typing on the
Olivetti portable I'd brought back from LA, the one that Caroline had borrowed,
and it worked just fine on the farmhouse-style wooden table. I always made
a carbon copy so that if my work got lost en route to London I could send a
duplicate. The copies piled up on a spike. What would I have given for today's
emails?

No sooner had I finished writing about Gregg Allman and the trip to
Macon than I was back in the Bible Belt, invited to Nashville to attend Columbia
Records' annual sales convention. I flew down with Mike O'Mahoney, the
company's PR whom I knew because he used to work for CBS – as Columbia
was known in the UK – in London.

We stayed at Roger Miller's 'King Of The Road' Motor Inn, named after
his 1965 hit song, and it was crammed with country music cowboys. It had a
weird system of room service whereby a dozen or more large tubes extended
from the basement right up to the top floor, running through the rooms, on
which orders were delivered. You placed your order and 15 minutes later it
appeared on this cockeyed dumb-waiter system. I later learned that it fell down
when guests realised they could help themselves to food and drink on its way to
floors above them and no one could figure out who'd put the snatch on it.

Mike was blessed with the traditional Irish gift of eloquence and that
evening I found myself dining with Goddard Lieberson, the President of
Columbia, and other executives, in a private dining room. At the other end
of the table was David Essex, newly signed to the label, who spoke with an
exaggerated Cockney accent that I thought was wildly affected and made him
sound like a prize prat. Offered the opportunity to interview Essex, I declined. I
hadn't come to America to write about second division British pop singers.

A far better prospect reared its head the next day when, much to my
surprise, Mike somehow wangled it that we could borrow the Columbia

executive jet for a few hours, an even fancier plane than the one I flew in two weeks before from Chicago to St Louis with Black Sabbath. So here I was, with just Mike for company, in the nearest thing to a spaceship I'd ever flown in. Up we went, heading east over the Blue Ridge Mountains to the nearby state of Virginia to see two shows by an act for whom the label had very high hopes, another in the endless parade of New Dylans. The pilot dropped us off in Richmond and headed straight back to Nashville. Only the top brass could tell him to wait.

The Mosque in Richmond, and the Chrysler Theater in Norfolk, where we went the next day, were small old-fashioned venues and both are still operating today, though The Mosque is now called The Landmark. I don't think either was sold out on January 25 and 26, 1974.

"He stands there looking like a cross between Elvis Presley and a reject from Sha Na Na with faint Dylanesque overtones," I wrote in *MM* after seeing the shows. "A battered Fender Telecaster hangs low enough for him to qualify for a place in The Ventures. His hair is short and curly and there's a wispy beard that never seems to grow any longer. On his nose rests a pair of square shades which stay in place all the time during his shows, which make him look more like Dylan of 1965 than Dylan of 1974. He wears jeans and a red vest and maybe a denim jacket, all of which make him look a bit like James Dean too, only smaller, skinnier and more vulnerable.

"And he clicks his fingers now and then like Presley's supposed to do and like Tom Jones does. He shakes his Fender back and forth and twists his hips around, looking as if he means business. He conducts the band with his fretboard, sometimes grinning and sometimes looking perplexed, like he's not quite sure what's happening next. And then he'll surprise you by discarding the guitar and playing a tender love song at the piano. He dismisses the group, who return later with a change of instruments and takes up a stance at the front with the regular bassist playing a tuba and the keyboard man strapped behind an accordion. The tuba makes a strange deep noise that reminds me of a colliery silver band from South Yorkshire.

"After all that seriousness he'll start rocking again, the big black cat on the saxophone coming on as a bass vocalist for an old rock and roll number. If you're lucky he'll finish his set with a rendering of 'Twist And Shout' complete with the ascending build up between verses that sounds just like John Lennon was standing beside him, crouched over a Rickenbacker and yelling his loudest to drown out the screams."

It was, of course, Bruce Springsteen and his E Street Band, whom I was seeing for the first, but certainly not the last, time. Bruce had already attracted the attention of *Melody Maker*, my colleague Michael Watts having written about him extensively. I took pleasure in relieving him of the baton.

Mike and I stayed in the same hotel as the band and I chatted with Bruce in the coffee shop on the morning after the show. He was eating a burger and fries washed down with Coca-Cola, and wasn't very talkative, shy almost, maybe a bit tongue-tied. He was thin in those days, quite unlike the muscular hunk he is today, with that wispy beard, and intense, like he had a lot on his mind. He wasn't up for a real interview so I didn't press him, just told him how much I'd enjoyed the show the night before, and he was grateful for the compliment. He was humble, courteous, like I imagine the young Elvis would have been in his Sun Records days, like Elton had been on that rainswept moor near Halifax.

Norfolk, Virginia had a particular resonance for me. During the Second World War my dad served as a gunner on troop and supply ships criss-crossing the Atlantic between British ports and the American naval base here. Dad had told me that, off duty one summer's afternoon in 1940, he took a bus to the beach, and an elderly coloured lady carrying several parcels of shopping got onto his bus and remained standing. A good-hearted Yorkshireman brought up to be respectful to ladies, Dad offered her his seat. The lady explained that because of the colour of her skin she was not permitted to sit in his seat, only at the back of the bus where all the seats were occupied. Dad, utterly ignorant of local custom, was appalled, so he made a point of standing for the remainder of his journey even though the seat on which he had been sitting remained vacant, and when the lady got off the bus, he helped her with her packages. "May I help you madam," he said to the astonished woman. "Thank you, kind sir," she replied, so Dad recalled. "I will remember this for a long time."

When Dad reached the beach, he wrote a postcard home to Betty, his wife, whom he had married – in uniform – earlier that same year. So it was that on my visit to Norfolk to see Bruce Springsteen for the first time, I did exactly the same thing. I did some exploring and from a distance saw the naval base, then I bought a postcard and went to the beach where I wrote on it something like, "Dear Dad, following in your footsteps 35 years later," and mailed it off to the old home in Yorkshire that same day.

The two Bruce Springsteen concerts blur together a bit so many years later and I can't actually remember which one it was – and it might have been both – that Bruce and his band played 'Pretty Flamingo', Manfred Mann's great

1966 chart topper, but what I remember as clear as day was Bruce's long, witty and gloriously uplifting monologue that prefaced it. As it was my introduction to Bruce live, his monologues were quite new to me, surprising, captivating and unique.

The 'Pretty Flamingo' story began with Bruce telling us how he once lived on a street in Jersey down which a beautiful girl would walk every day after work at five o'clock, so he and his buddies from the block would gather there at a quarter to five every day just to watch her stroll by. While the band ticked over in the background, idling like a car in neutral, Bruce conjured up in a few pithy sentences the image of a shapely heartbreaker that he and his buddies, by inference some of the band, were too self-conscious to approach. They were desperate to know her name but too shy to ask, even some crazy guy in Bruce's gang who often did really brave stuff because he was far too crazy to care about the consequences.

And so it went on, with the girl walking by for weeks, maybe months, and Bruce and his buddies still watching her every day, and no-one knew what she was called. By this time, we in the audience were all hopelessly in love with her too, just as Bruce and his pals obviously had been, and they'd coined a nickname for her. "And then… like I moved away," said Bruce, disappointment clouding his face. "We never found out what her name was. We used to call her something. What was it that we called her Clarence? Can you remember? What did we call her Steve? I remember. Should I tell 'em?"

Then, louder, repeated, his right arm raised. "Should I tell 'em?"

"Yeah," called Steve and Clarence in unison. "Tell 'em Bruce."

"Should I tell 'em?" He was screaming now.

"Yeah!"

Bruce brought his arm down. A chord.

"On our block all of the guys called her Flamingo."

Guitars and drums exploded. Perfect. Just fucking perfect. The incredible tension of the build-up was finally released and like a great tidal wave crashing through the theatre Bruce and his band launched deliriously into this terrific song. The crowd went nuts. But he wasn't finished with us. Two, maybe three, minutes in, just after the first verse, after Flamingo had brightened up the neighbourhood like she just could, he brought the band down again, let them tick over again, and he had us captive again.

"What can I do Clarence?" he asked, even more passionate than before. "I gotta find that girl. I'm gonna hire a detective, someone good, like Charlie Chan."

He was laughing now, full of fun, and we were holding on to his every word. "And when I get her I know what I'm gonna tell her. I know what I'm gonna tell her. I'm gonna tell her I'm in a band. *I'm in a band!*"

And off they went again, careering downhill like men possessed.

"*Some sweet day, I'll make her mine, Pretty Flamingo.*"

That night I saw the rock star we all of us wanted to be in our dreams.

*

Looking back on it now, that month, January 1974, was one of the most musically eventful of my life: based in New York and visiting Chicago, St Louis, Philadelphia, Macon and Nashville, with the trip to Virginia to see Bruce an added bonus. And it wasn't over yet for, on January 30, the icing on the cake was seeing Bob Dylan for the first time. What's more, I was sat in the front row at Madison Square Garden, Dylan a few feet away.

My friend Mike from Columbia, the same Mike who'd introduced me to Bruce, excelled himself again, somehow managing to get hold of four front row centre tickets, the best seats in the house, for this opening show of a three-night run with The Band. He distributed them to four of us individually before we arrived.

As it happened I arrived first, just as the lights were dimming and the crowd was roaring in anticipation, and it took me some time to push through to the front, the security all assuming – until they saw my ticket – that I was a frenzied fan intent on getting as close to the stage as possible. When I reached the front row there were four empty seats and so, cheekily, I draped myself across all of them, lounging as if on a sofa. Those around me must have wondered who the hell I was, someone who could obtain four front row centre seats for himself, just so he could stretch out lethargically as he might in his living room, right there in front of Bob Dylan.

Talking of whom, the man himself had launched into his opening song, 'Most Likely You Go Your Way (And I'll Go Mine)' by the time I took my seat(s), and he peered down quizzically at me, no doubt also wondering just who the hell was this bloke who seemingly had four seats to himself, right slap bang in the middle of the front row. I think I put him off his stride for a moment or two, and he was well into the second song of the night, 'Lay Lady Lay', by the time the other three ticket holders arrived and order was restored.

That night Dylan played many of the songs I wanted to hear and he was effortlessly supported by The Band, then at the peak of their game. Their fluent

(clockwise from top left) CC's mum & dad, Jim & Betty Charlesworth, on their wedding day, Bingley Parish Church, April 6, 1940; Jim & Betty at Malsis Hall, 1959: 'Malsis was where I first heard Little Richard singing 'Tuttu Frutti'.; with his treasured Futurama III guitar, rehearsing with John Holmfield & their group The Pandas, in his bedroom at Skipton, 1964; on the beach at Filey with Mum, Dad & sister Anne, summer 1957

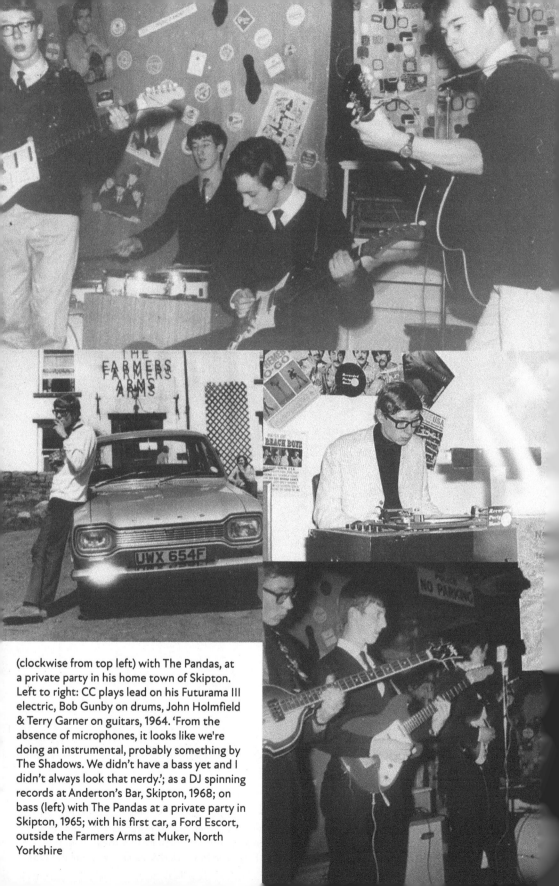

(clockwise from top left) with The Pandas, at a private party in his home town of Skipton. Left to right: CC plays lead on his Futurama III electric, Bob Gunby on drums, John Holmfield & Terry Garner on guitars, 1964. 'From the absence of microphones, it looks like we're doing an instrumental, probably something by The Shadows. We didn't have a bass yet and I didn't always look that nerdy.'; as a DJ spinning records at Anderton's Bar, Skipton, 1968; on bass (left) with The Pandas at a private party in Skipton, 1965; with his first car, a Ford Escort, outside the Farmers Arms at Muker, North Yorkshire

PRIORITY PASS
Melody Maker
RAZ...

VALID FOR ALL AREAS

ROCK AT THE OVAL
Concert in Aid of the Famine
in Bangla Desh – Sept. 18, 1971

pass

Rainbow

name Chris Charlesworth

72   signature

WHO
U S
TOUR 71
BACKSTAGE
PASS

(clockwise from top) MM staff group shot, taken on the flat roof outside the Fleet Street office in London, 1971: back row, left to right - Laurie Henshaw, folk writer Andrew Means, office manager Roy Birchall, Michael Watts, Chris 'Any Questions' Hayes, features editor Chris Welch, assistant sub Neil Roberts & front row, left to right – CC, Roy Hollingworth, Jeff Starrs (Barrie Wentzell); CC's Rainbow Theatre pass - access all areas at all times; backstage pass given to CC at the start of The Who's US tour, October 1971; backstage pass for the Oval Concert, headlined by The Who, September 18, 1971

ASHLEYS
CHARTER MEMBER
CHRIS CHARLESWORTH #001
59 FIFTH AVENUE AL5·8744

(clockwise) walking into the party thrown by Paul McCartney at the Empire in Leicester Square, behind Tony Blackburn & his girlfriend actress Tessa Wyatt, November 8, 1971; with Elton John & Ashley Pandel (centre) at Ashley's Bar & Restaurant in New York shortly after it opened in June 1975 (Bob Gruen); Charter Member No 1 – CC's membership card for Ashley's; the *MM* office in 1972: back row, left to right – assistant editor Richard Williams, editor Ray Coleman and chief sub Alan Lewis (seated) & front row, left to right – Michael Watts, CC, Features Editor Chris Welch and Mark Plummer (Barrie Wentzell)

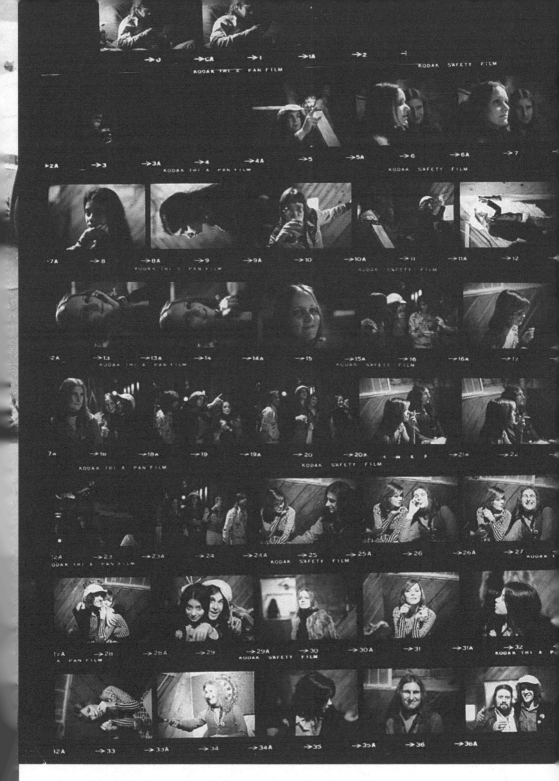

(opposite, above) with Slade at Gatwick Airport on April 17, 1973, before they embarked on their second US tour (unknown) & (opposite, below) with Ian McLagan & Kenney Jones of the Faces in LA, October 1973 (Richard Creamer); (this page) CC and friends, including *MM* photographer Barrie Wentzell, Ashley Pandell, Roy Carr, Roy Hollingworth, Iris Brown, Nancy Bianchi & Loraine Altermann at Waltzing Matilda, New York, December 1973 (Mandi Newall)

(above) with Bruce Springsteen & Mike O'Mahoney from Columbia Records, backstage at the Chrysler Theater, Norfolk, Va, January 26, 1974 (unknown); (opposite) with his date, Debbie Harry, at the New York party following The Who's four-night run at Madison Square Garden, June 19, 1974 (Bob Gruen)

(clockwise from top left) with David Bowie & Ava Cherry at an after-show party at New York's Shun Lee restaurant following Todd Rundgren's concert at Carnegie Hall, April 19, 1974 (Bob Gruen); with Alice Cooper at an Upper East Side bar, New York, summer 1974 (Bob Gruen); with Keith Moon & Who sound engineer Bob Pridden, backstage at Madison Square Garden, New York, June 1974 (Bob Gruen); Section A, row 1, seat 8 – CC's ticket stub for Bob Dylan at Madison Square Garden, New York, January 31, 1974

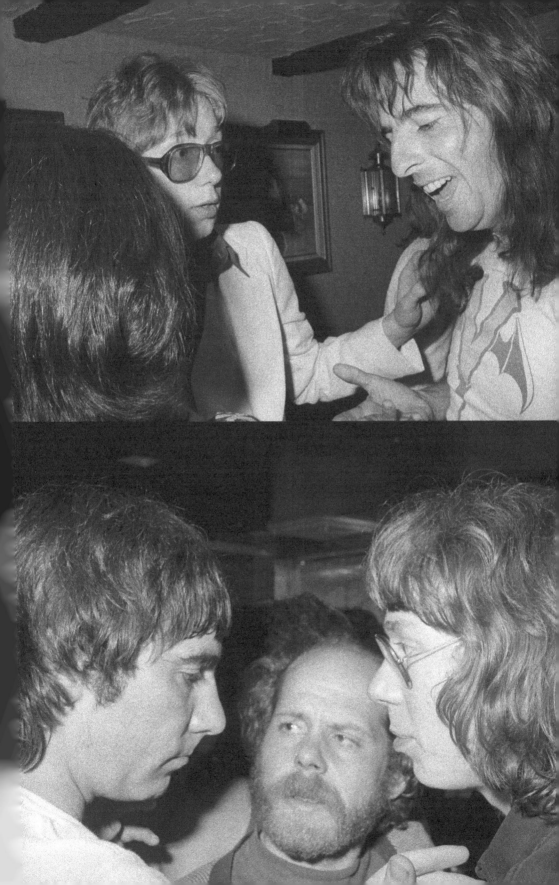

(this page) with Pete Townshend at the reception following the New York premier of the *Tommy* movie, March 18, 1975 (Bob Gruen); (opposite) with John Lennon & Yoko Ono at the 17th annual Grammy Awards at the Uris Theatre, New York, where John was presenting an award, March 1, 1975 (Bob Gruen); CC's postcard from John after Lennon declined his request for an interview in 1975

Chris,

comment
→ stern reply!
→ invisible

love
John L
ono

C. Charlesworth

51 East 78th St.

apt 3D.

NEW YORK

N.Y. 10021

JOHN HINDE
ORIGINAL

PROCLAIM LIBERTY THROUGHOUT ALL THE LAND
USA 13c

SMALL
200 Y
BUILDING

NEW N.Y.
28 JAN
7

DANCERS make the scene at most festivals and
functions. To the accompaniment of Chinese
gongs and cymbals, this colourful lion shows its
the Haw Par Villa where Chinese mythology and
are artistically featured in mortar and stone.

de Limited, Cabinteely, Co. Dublin, Republic of Ireland.

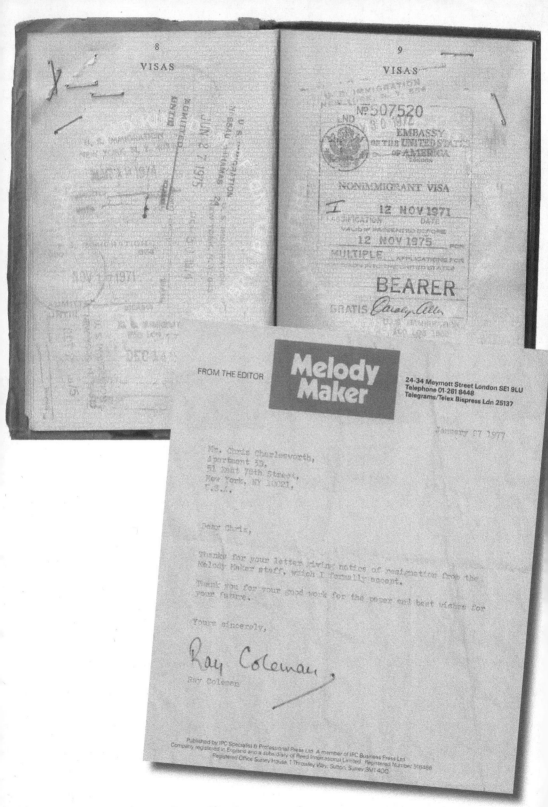

(above) CC's passport showing the number of times he entered the US; (below) Ray Coleman's letter accepting his resignation

musicianship, the result of hundreds of hours of ensemble playing during ten years together, made for a terrific contrast with Dylan's more casual, impromptu style, each supplying the other with exactly what was needed to serve up a perfect feast.

There was an acoustic set within the main set, featuring Dylan alone, during which a roadie nipped down to ask one of our party to stop taking photographs as it was putting him off his stride. When he put his camera away, Dylan looked down and nodded, acknowledging the gesture. My only complaint was that he failed to sing 'Mr Tambourine Man', a favourite of mine, but he did play 'Like A Rolling Stone', another favourite, which closed the show. For a final encore he sang 'Blowin' In The Wind', by which time the house lights were on and the audience jammed up at the front all around me. Truly a great night.

I reviewed the show for *MM*, dated February 9. "They cheered and clapped and waved for 15 minutes even though the house lights were up and 'Greensleeves' was playing through the PA system and Bob Dylan had already played a couple of encores," I wrote. "[Promoter and tour manager] Bill Graham, at the rear of the stage, looked perplexed and wondered when in hell the 20,000 Madison Square Garden crowd was ever going to leave. Then Bob returned on his own and looked slightly sheepish. He'd discarded his black suit and was wearing a blue ice hockey jersey with a white maple leaf on the front. The cheering reached greater heights as he walked towards the microphone and looked as if he was going to say something. Then he changed his mind and walked across the stage, smiling and holding his arms aloft like a prize fighter who'd just knocked out the champ. Then he went back to the mic. 'Thank you. See you next year,' he said. Then everyone knew it was all over."

I would get closer to Bob on one more occasion, backstage at a Rolling Stones show at the Garden in 1975, but I would never get to interview him. And it was two and a half years before I next saw him, on stage, on the *Rolling Thunder Revue* up in New England, but that's another story.

*

February was only marginally less busy for me than January. I never kept a diary but back issues of *MM* reveal that I interviewed John McLaughlin, Blue Öyster Cult, Black Oak Arkansas, had a sneak preview of a new album by Maggie Bell, and reviewed The New York Dolls, supported by Elliott Murphy, at the Academy of Music on East 14th Street, and Stephen Stills at Carnegie Hall.

I would come to know the Academy well, seeing upwards of 30 shows there in the coming years, and I was soon on nodding terms with Howard Stein, New York's leading rock promoter, who put on most of the shows there, and a few elsewhere too. The number two promoter was Ron Delsener who in time would topple Stein.

In fact, the Academy was a rather tacky old theatre, once an opera house, that in 1976 would change its name to the Palladium. Either way it reminded me a bit of the Rainbow in London, except that at the rear of the stalls was a big standing area, its floor littered with cigarette butts, paper cups and trash. The Academy always stank of grass, and loose joints could be bought for $1 a pop from dealers who operated outside, tending to the needs of those queueing to get in. Having become acquainted with Paul Simon, I bumped into him there one night wearing a parka with its fur hood up, just like on his first solo LP, and when a look of recognition crossed my face, he put his fingers to his lips. He was incognito.

This was the second time I'd seen the Dolls – the first was at the Whisky in LA – and in my review I remarked on an improvement in their show. Roy Hollingworth before me had introduced *MM*'s readers to the Dolls in a series of flattering reviews, and I would see them perhaps half a dozen more times over the next couple of years, a period that – alas – saw their fortunes slipping and sliding. At the Academy, however, they were still on a pedestal, their set preceded by a short film that had been made by Bob Gruen, New York's busiest rock photographer whom I would soon come to know well.

Nevertheless, I felt duty bound to point out the similarity between the Dolls and The Rolling Stones. "There isn't a shred of originality about their entire performance," I wrote. "[It is] based so obviously on The Rolling Stones that one tends to think that maybe it's some kind of Mike Yarwood of rock and roll out there on the stage. The early half of their set was surprisingly tight. They've obviously been rehearsing recently and taken an instant course on how to play guitars. The latter half, however, descended into a deafening musical abyss, all stemming from David Johansen's vocal work which gradually lost its pitch amidst his enthusiasm. By the end he was yelling his head off. But the Dolls are the Dolls and in New York before their own audience it doesn't really matter how well – or how badly – they play."

I was far more complimentary about Stephen Stills at the Carnegie, New York's premier classical music venue that made the Academy look like a pigsty. I noted that he played six different guitars, opening with 'Love The One You're With' and moved through an electric set, then acoustic, before winding up on electric again, and offered songs from all the phases of his career. I was particularly impressed when he dismissed his band and played solo. "Though his voice sounded a little croaky, his guitar style – so deceptively simple but hugely fluent – was a joy to hear. He gave us 'Change Partners', 'Crossroads', 'You Can't Catch Me', McCartney's 'Blackbird' and '4 + 20', a huge favourite of mine.

"It's not until you see Stills performing on his own," I continued, "that you realise how talented he really is. He's casual in the extreme, lighting cigarettes during numbers, tapping his foot to keep the time signature, and he creates an aura of respectful silence from his audience. Unquestionably one of the best guitar players rock has produced, he's equally at home on either the acoustic or electric instrument. The mood was marred only by the inevitable yelling for requests between songs but Stills gritted his teeth and played only what he wanted to play.

In New York Stills stayed at the Carlyle, a classy hotel on Madison Avenue only two blocks from my apartment, and I was introduced to him there the following day. I liked him a lot, and he took to calling me "English", a nickname that stuck on those occasions when I bumped into him over the next year or three.

*

"Why would I want to see Bob Dylan? I know what he looks like and he's too short to see anyway?"

I thought it was a reasonable question, Bob being the talk of the town after his Madison Square Garden shows. Lou Reed thought otherwise. I had been warned that he could be contrary. Observing instructions Gina had conveyed to me from Mr Coleman, I set up an interview with Mr Reed that took place in late February. Although I knew all about the rise and fall of the Velvets and had made the acquaintance of John Cale – not something I mentioned by the way, perhaps wisely – I wasn't really prepared for the taciturn ill will with which Lou approached the interview.

Lou faced me from the far end of a long table on the 37th floor of a Park Avenue office block facing north that commanded an expansive view of Central Park with Harlem way out in the distance. It was a cold day with snow on the ground, as it often is at this time of the year in New York, and Lou was as cold as the weather. He sat in a swivel chair and looked uncomfortable. I had been told that he sometimes brought a friend along to interviews to smooth out the atmosphere and encourage conversation but when we met no such friend was available and he seemed a little lost for words, and rather than say something he didn't want to say, he simply didn't say anything at all. As the years rolled by he became more and more aloof towards journalists sent to interview him and, the difficult Dylan question aside, I think I got off quite lightly in the end.

"His appearance has changed yet again," I wrote. "Today, and for at least the next few weeks, he has very short hair, almost a crew-cut, dyed black, and without any growth at all descending below the height of his ears. Last week he had an Iron Cross dyed into the back, but it's gone today. He looks, in fact, rather like a convict or a soldier. He is very thin. His blue denim jacket tends to drop off his shoulders and his jeans would be tight on others if not on him. He talks very quietly. Also very little."

On his appearance, Reed said he altered it continually through boredom. "I found I couldn't really solve the boredom by changing my appearance but at least I could stop some of the hassle. I don't have to comb my hair now because there isn't enough of it."

We talked about his current band, a recent live album and where his career was headed. I mentioned David Bowie. "He's very clever," Lou admitted. "We found we had a lot of things in common."

I suggested his career took an uplift as a result of his flirtation with Bowie. "David learned how to be hip," he replied with a glint in his eye. He wasn't about to admit that Bowie's patronage had in any way contributed to his career upswing. "Associating with me brought his name out to a lot more people, too. He's very good in the studio. In a manner of speaking, he produced an album for me."

He was disparaging about other artists, mentioning that when he played London's Rainbow on his last UK tour he kept thinking about how Frank Zappa was pushed into the orchestra pit. When I told him I saw the incident, he thought for a moment. "I hate Frank Zappa," he said. "It made me so happy to think about that."

For no apparent reason, Lou next launched into a scathing critique of Jefferson Airplane, expressing the view that they represented the worst in everything, both musically and ideally. "I hate everything about them, the way they dress, the way they look, the way they play, the cute name. I despise every San Francisco group except Moby Grape and they broke up."

It was then that I asked him whether he'd been to see Bob Dylan on his recent tour. "Are you kidding?" he replied, evidently shocked that I had the insolence to ask such a question. "Why would I want to see Bob Dylan. I know what Bob Dylan looks like and he's too short to see anyway. I saw the back of his head once. I didn't want to go to see him, especially if he is giving his money to Israel. If he gave some to Israel and some to the Arabs it would be different."

We moved on to the New York Dolls, the sort of group I imagined he *would* like. "You know, I tried so hard to like the Dolls but I couldn't. I like the titles of their songs. It's such a shame. They're just another glitter trash band." Then, inexplicably, he launched into a tribute to Fats Domino. "I'm still mad that Fats never made it properly. He could have been a blues artist in the tradition of Bessie Smith."

And with that last comment, Reed offered a limp handshake and disappeared into the afternoon.

In time my relationship with Lou, at least when I wasn't interviewing him, became less frosty and a couple of years down the line he gave me three television sets, but that's another story.

*

In March Yes came to town, bringing with them Harvey Goldsmith, the London rock promoter whom I knew well. I was invited to a get-together at their hotel, the Warwick, where Harvey collared me and asked which new American acts he should bring to London this year. "Bruce Springsteen," I replied without hesitation.

Later in the year, in July, Harvey would return to New York and I would take him to see Bruce at the Bottom Line, courtesy of my friend Peter Philbin, my man at Columbia International. It would be another year before Bruce made his celebrated London debut at the Hammersmith Odeon, a show promoted by Harvey. I wasn't there, of course, but I played a small part in bringing Bruce to the UK for the first time.

There was something awfully *Melody Maker*-ish about Yes, the result of Chris Welch's almost unqualified support for the group, and this close relationship led to their two shows at the Garden being co-promoted by the paper, an unusual state of affairs which in the more enlightened 21st century might look like a conflict of interest for its editorial staff. At 50 years remove I'm hard pressed to recall the details of our promotion but I suspect some money changed hands for *MM*'s logo to appear on the tickets and posters advertising the shows.

The get-together in Yes' hotel suite was notable for two incidents. *MM* celebrated their American success with a front-page story stating that the gross takings from the two Madison Square Garden shows would exceed

165

$200,000. Their bass player Chris Squire was less than happy that *MM* had chosen to "reveal" Yes' earnings and he berated me over the story. I responded by pointing out that anyone with a calculator could work out what they were grossing each night, simply by multiplying the average ticket price by the number of seats, but Squire seemed to think that we had exposed some dark secret. He didn't like the idea of fans knowing how much money they made but there really wasn't any secret about it, and I thought it a bit rich coming from him as he always seemed to me to be the most money-conscious member of the band. The others didn't care about the story at all, and neither did Brian Lane, their manager. Rick Wakeman certainly didn't care and he joined in the argument on my side.

The other incident caused the party to end in disarray. Harvey Goldsmith was thrown fully clothed into a bath tub, a jape instigated by Rick. Harvey was all dressed up, ready to go to the Garden when suddenly Rick and some of the others in the room picked him up and chucked him in. He was furious, really angry, soaked to the skin and obliged to change his clothes. Personally – after the row I'd just had with him – I'd have preferred to see Chris Squire dumped in the bath.

I went to both shows and in a lengthy report that included an interview with Rick concluded that Monday's show – the first – was far better than the one two nights later. Chris Squire offered an explanation: "We lost our rhythm through having a day off between shows. When we play night after night it comes natural but we had a day away shopping in New York and I think that affected us."

The concerts showcased the group's *Tales From Topographic Oceans* album, right down to the way in which the stage depicted a fairy-tale landscape, but it had been roundly criticised as the epitome of their self-indulgent tendencies, and Rick seemed aware of this when we talked in his hotel. "A band of our standing reaches a dangerous position when it can put out records that will sell no matter how good they are," he told me. "We have realised we did make some mistakes but I think these problems have been ironed out now."

In my report I suggested Yes fans didn't come to their shows to dance but to take notes.

17

"There's this singer, a blonde girl, looks just like Marilyn Monroe."
Bob Gruen, New York rock 'n' roll photographer, April 1974

By the end of March, I had been in America for over six months, working pretty much all the time without a break. There is a school of thought that might consider my work as a form of leisure insofar as interviewing rock stars and watching them perform isn't the most taxing of occupations and, indeed, for someone as partial to his rock and pop as I, much of it was a pleasure. I will always consider myself tremendously lucky to have been on the staff of *Melody Maker*, let alone in the role of US editor, and as a result never gave in to the temptation to become lazy. That would have been all too easy when you operate on your own initiative, as I did in New York.

When I applied for my American visa at the US Embassy in London's Grosvenor Square, I was given an 'I' classification, stamped "Multiple", which meant I could enter the US as many times as I wanted, at least until my passport expired, and at immigration a slip of paper was stapled onto the page saying how long I could stay on each visit, usually six months. It was the same as would have been issued to all foreign media whose publications paid for their expenses on American soil, like the BBC's White House correspondent or New York correspondents for the UK's national dailies.

I was introduced to a few of these journalists at record company receptions but like most Fleet Street types in those days they were interested only in rock performers they defined as "celebrities", like Beatles and Stones, and primarily with what might be termed scandals, usually involving drugs or abandoned wives. It was almost a decade since I'd been told been told that Fleet Street was the pinnacle of this profession, the writing game, but now, older and a tiny bit wiser, I knew this was no longer the case. The longer I worked for *MM* the more I thought I'd made the right decision to opt for music. The question of what I might do after *MM* had yet to occur to me.

The only other British music writer who lived permanently in New York was Ian Dove, a pop critic for the *New York Times* and for music trade magazines like *Billboard* and *Cash Box*. Ian was a jazz nut but he knew the New York music world as well as anyone I knew and although he was one of nature's born cynics I enjoyed his company and appreciated his advice. Another face I saw everywhere was Fred Kirby who wrote about rock and pop for *Variety*, the entertainments business trade paper that covered movies primarily but made room for music too. Fred, white-haired and well fed, was a jolly old soul, a generation or two above me, and though his style of writing was strictly geared towards the dollars and cents end of the business he recognised a promising band when he saw one.

By now I had made myself thoroughly at home in the flat on 78th Street. It was effectively *MM*'s office in New York for up in Apartment 3D I tirelessly bashed out many thousands of words – interviews, reviews, news columns – every week on that small Olivetti portable. In one corner of the living room was a growing pile of *Melody Makers*; in another a stack of albums, hundreds of them; and stuck to the wall opposite my desk was a big blue quilt on which I pinned buttons and badges, backstage passes, invitations, concert tickets (rarely less than three shows a week) and bits of paper with phone numbers and scribbled notes reminding me of appointments. If I'd been out of town for a day or two the telephone answering service relayed messages galore when I returned.

The rate at which LPs now arrived soon eclipsed anything I could ever have dreamed about as a pop mad teenager back in Yorkshire. As well as the teach-yourself-a-foreign-language LPs, Columbia's five-star mailing list entitled me to box sets of works by Beethoven and Mozart, dull as dishwater country records from Nashville, military bands and Greek balalaika music, you name it, in addition to all the rock and pop from every other label, big and small. Also, I got duplicates of LPs by A-list acts, one from the record company, another from the act's PR and sometimes even one from the management company if I happened to know someone who worked there. Soon the postman complained so I had to get myself a PO box at the nearest post office and visit once a week to pick them all up, then bring home all these LPs in a cab as they were too heavy to carry. The packaging alone filled my waste bin for a week. Back at *MM*'s office in London, of course, all these LPs would have been shared out amongst the staff for review but in New York there was no one else to share them with so I got the lot – and I didn't even have to review them. Another writer put me in touch with a shop in Brooklyn and once every two months a girl arrived at my apartment, looked through what I didn't want and gave me a wad of $20 bills from a stash she kept in her cowboy boot. I spent the money she gave me on clothes or grass.

Over a late breakfast in the Greek coffee shop, I read whatever day-old English newspaper I could find at the newsagents on the other side of Madison. Then it was back to the flat to write or make phone calls. No day was ever the same, weekdays blurring into weekends as rock 'n' roll never stops. My deadline was always Thursday afternoon, 3pm, when I delivered my weekly parcel to London to IPC's office on 42nd Street, a packet of 20 or more sheets of A4 paper and usually some photos, often taken by Bob Gruen, my photographer of choice in New York.

The weekly parcel also contained my New York news column, always the last thing I wrote on Thursday mornings, compiled from press releases, anything I could crib from the *Village Voice* or other NY culture mags and my own wanderings around the city's music spots. A good example of this was bumping into David Bowie at an after-show party following Todd Rundgren's concert at the Carnegie Hall on February 19. I managed a quick word with David, and my report of this sighting was typical of the items in my weekly New York news column. "Looking casual in blue denims David drank champagne with his companion Ava Cherry and fled when the flashbulbs began to irritate," I wrote. Bob Gruen was on hand to photograph me sat at a table chatting with him.

In April I took a two-week break and flew back to London. I asked Steven Gaines, who wrote for *Circus*, a monthly music magazine, to take over for the duration, writing a news column and sending reviews of shows back to London for me. He proved a good choice and for the next couple of years deputised for me as required. Steven was gay, the first real gay friend I had, and lived on West 11th Street with a plaque on his front door that read: "The Greta Garbo Home for Wayward Boys and Girls." It was the venue for lots of parties, one of which – the following year – introduced me to the ecstatic charms of Donna Summer and 'Love To Love You Baby'.

I found somewhere to stay in London for a few days, turned up at the *MM* office like the Prodigal Son, then went up to Yorkshire to see my dad and sister. Ten days later I flew back to the US and on to New Orleans for a few more days' holiday, picking up my girlfriend Debbie in St Louis along the way. We stayed in the French Quarter, drank mint juleps and listened to jazz and R&B in bars and clubs along Bourbon Street. I dropped my $2 into a hat at Preservation Hall to listen to black jazzmen as old as time itself playing 'When The Saints Go Marching In'. My best memory of that short break was surprising Debbie by speaking French to a maître d' in a Creole restaurant.

Then it was back to New York, 78th Street and my little Olivetti.

*

New Yorkers will tell you that the season they call the fall and we call autumn is the best time to be in the city but I preferred spring. The colours of the trees in Central Park as they shed their leaves and turn gold were a beauty to behold, but Manhattan winters were mighty cold so it was a big relief when the winds that whipped around those blocks eased off and what the weathermen called the wind chill factor was no longer an issue, especially for the likes of someone who'd been mollycoddled by our temperate British climate.

One Monday morning not long after I'd returned from New Orleans I walked the length of Fifth Avenue, from 78th Street all the way down to Washington Square, a distance of about three miles. I'd lived here since the beginning of the previous December and it was high time I tasted Manhattan on a sunny day. I wanted to look at the people, the shops and cafes, to watch the yellow cabs whizzing by, to gaze up at the Empire State Building as I passed 34th Street and the Flat Iron Building where Broadway disrupted the grid pattern at 23rd Street. I wanted to get a fix on the city I now called home, the skyscrapers, the lattice-like layout of one-way streets, bisected by Fifth Avenue, that alternated east to west or west to east, apart from the big wide ones every ten blocks or so. I didn't do traditional sight-seeing during my time there. I was less interested in seeing the established tourist sights than getting to know my way around this concrete world and, of course, experiencing its rock 'n' roll.

When I reached Washington Square old men were playing chess on stone tables with chequered boards etched on to their surfaces and young men were playing Martins, their velvet-lined cases open in front of them to collect change. A crowd had gathered around one busker. "Far from the twisted reach of crazy sorrow... let me forget about today until tomorrow." I smiled at the thought of Bob carrying his guitar across this square in maybe 1964 or '65, writing the songs for *Bringing It All Back Home* and this one in particular, or earlier when he lived on West 4th Street with the lovely Suze Rotolo, with whom he was photographed, hunched up against the cold, for the cover of the *Freewheelin'* LP.

The grid pattern loses its symmetry below Washington Square and the maze of streets beyond, known collectively as Greenwich Village, have names instead of numbers. I would come to know Bleecker, the most famous, well. Further south was Soho – which stands for South of Houston (Street) – and then Little Italy, Chinatown and, finally, the Wall Street financial district, not really my cup of tea. But they'd have to wait until another day as after three hours walking I was hungry. I bought a sandwich – probably ham and cheese on rye – in a deli and ate it while I listened to the busker. I gave him fifty cents, then took the subway back to 77th Street, walked back to 51 East 78th Street and settled down to write up a review of Rick Nelson & the Stone Canyon Band, whom I'd seen two nights ago at the Bottom Line.

Back in Skipton I owned two of his singles on the ever dependable black and silver London American label; 'My Babe', which we played in Sandra & The Montanas, and 'Poor Little Fool'. He was Ricky Nelson then, and from the age of eight he'd appeared in a prime-time US family-friendly TV sitcom called *The Adventures Of Ozzie & Harriet*. A career as a teen idol followed, his records enhanced by the guitar playing of James Burton, whose nifty little bent-note solos impressed teenagers Geoffrey Arnold Beck and James Patrick Page, among others. I'd been given to understand that Rick was now a mature performer, leaning towards country. Indeed, his song 'Garden Party' was geared towards giving the impression that he'd shaken off his earlier image and entered into the seventies in a spirit of renewal. Unfortunately, that didn't seem the case to me.

"Nelson is as much steeped in nostalgia as the rest of them," I wrote. "His set at the Bottom Line Club was about two-thirds drawn from his old repertoire with very little added to the basic arrangements. Nostalgically, it was mildly entertaining, but musically it was flat… all his songs sounded pretty much the same. They all seemed to be in same key, sang at the same pitch and at a similar tempo. They were all a little countrified thanks to the steel guitar wizard in the band, but Nelson's own sorties on the guitar hardly qualified him for the virtuoso league.

"He still looks good, though, in his Nudie western shirt with rhinestone collar, but it was all too easy going for me; sort of supermarket pop brought up to date. The material included some out and out rockers like 'My Babe' which was a hit for him long, long ago; some of the traditional Nelson melodies like 'Hello Mary Lou', 'Travellin' Man' and 'Lonesome Town'; and some new material which, of course, included by far his most impressive recent offering 'Garden Party'.

"The audience lapped up the older material but remained totally indifferent to the newer stuff, which probably frustrates Nelson when he tried to introduce something new along the way. One member of the audience insisted on yelling for 'Poor Little Fool' between every other number, but it transpired that the Stone Canyon Band (bass, lead, drums and slide) didn't know it."

The Bottom Line, which held about 400, hadn't been open long when I arrived in New York, and I would see many shows there, at least one a month, among them Bruce Springsteen and Little Feat, and most times I had a tab from the record company whose acts were playing. This meant I was entitled to free drinks. I asked the waitress for whatever I wanted and gave her my tab so she could add it on, and at the end of the night handed it in at the bar. I can't remember if there was a limit – there probably was – but the bill was then sent to the record company.

All of which meant that I never needed to have much money on me when I set out for evenings like this. The Bottom Line was on West 4th Street, not far from the Bowery and Lower East Side, an area I'd been advised to avoid at night, so I always made a point of dressing like someone who wasn't worth mugging, which more or less meant I fitted in quite easily with the clientele at the Bottom Line. After a show there, I could catch the subway back uptown, switching from local to express for 72nd Street, and be home in less than half an hour, all for a quarter. The trains ran all night too, unlike London's Underground.

*

My *Melody Maker* credentials had made it remarkably easy to infiltrate New York's rock 'n' roll scene. The paper was selling 200,000 copies a week back in the UK and labels were well aware that coverage in *MM* would help their acts sell records there. I soon became a familiar face among the rock 'n' roll cognoscenti. I saw the same men and women at clubs like the Bottom Line and Bitter End or backstage at gigs or at record company parties, and I was soon on Christian name terms with all the city's music writers, PRs, record company folk and a few managers and concert promoters. It was a bit of a closed world but, boy, did we enjoy ourselves.

As far as I was aware, there were three principal rock photographers operating in New York in those days: Bob Gruen, who was everywhere that mattered, Leee (note the three e's) Black Childers, who was outrageously gay and favoured the glam world, and Chuck Pulin, who worked for *Sounds*. Leee's pictures had already appeared in *MM* when Roy Hollingworth was our man in NY but my instincts told me Bob was the man to approach as my photographer of choice to accompany me to interviews and shows where I needed a picture to illustrate my story. We cut a deal that suited both of us. Any picture he took where access was enabled by me belonged to *Melody Maker* for one month. Thereafter it was his to sell to all and sundry in perpetuity. We saw a lot of rock together and became good friends. Still are.

Bob operated out of a cramped apartment on the Lower West Side and could be counted on to fill me in on whatever was happening in the New York rock world. Every time I called Bob he'd say, "What's happening, man?" and sometimes he'd call me and open up the conversation with the same question. Of course, Bob always knew what was happening more than anyone else I knew in New York, whether it was on the streets or in the clubs. It was instinct with him, and I liked the fact that he was just as enthused about taking pictures of some unsigned punk band as he was taking pictures of The Rolling Stones, Led Zeppelin or John Lennon, with whom he developed a close relationship. Bob was an energetic, wiry little fellow with afro-styled hair. He drove a beat-up old VW Beetle, always wore a black leather jacket, t-shirt and jeans and more often than not had a tiny spliff clamped between his lips. For all his energy, he was as laid-back as anyone I'd ever met, unflappable, Mr Cool. Still is.

Bob introduced me to New York's underground. It was a matter of routine for me to write about acts, famous or otherwise, that were contracted to record labels but it was quite another thing to venture out on my own initiative to see an act that wasn't signed and wasn't expecting any interest from a paper like *MM*. I'd heard a bit about rowdy young bands playing in a rough downtown bar on the Bowery called CBGBs and in a joint not far away called Club 82, and I wanted to check out this scene for myself. I was a bit unsure about it so I called Bob for advice. He suggested I join him a couple of nights later in Club 82 where a band he liked called The Stilettos was playing. "There's this singer, a blonde girl, looks just like Marilyn Monroe," he said on the phone. "Check her out man, you won't believe it."

Club 82 was an old-style drag club with mirrors everywhere, famous in its day for its risqué floor shows but now fallen on hard times, and the girls who worked it, all of them of a certain age with short cropped hair and dressed in dark men's suits with buttoned-up shirts and ties, figured that a bit of rock 'n' roll might keep the creditors at bay. For a while it became a sort of sister club to CBGBs, of which more later, but it was never as well-known. Still, it was fun, with more of a party atmosphere than CBGBs. On the night Bob suggested I paid my $3 on the door – no freebies for *MM* writers here – and went inside, bought a beer and found him by the stage, camera at the ready.

The Stilettos turned out to be supporting Wayne/Jayne County, with whom I was already familiar because I'd seen him/her at Max's Kansas City, a hangout for artists, among them the Andy Warhol crowd, and musicians in Union Square. They were a trio, backed by guitar, bass and drums, who took their cue from the girl groups of the pre-Beatles sixties. There was a black girl, a redhead and a blonde who stood in the middle and appeared to be the leader, and Bob was right. She wore a clingy, low-cut, full-length, satin ball gown in all gold with a halter top that flattered her figure, and she was a dead-ringer for Marilyn, with platinum hair, a cute smile and strawberry lips. Their set was under-rehearsed and short – everybody's was down there – and afterwards Bob introduced me to her.

Her name, of course, was Debbie Harry. Up close she was incredibly beautiful, but she was also cool, committed, sassy. I tried not to let her appearance interfere with my interviewing technique as we talked about this and that while Bob took pictures of her. She told me she wanted to be a full-time singer but she had a daytime job in a New Jersey beauty parlour. She hoped someday to get into the music business full time. I told her I'd stay in touch and she gave me the phone number of where she worked. Bob took some more pictures, and I went away and, in a week or two, mentioned her and The Stilettos in a generic piece I wrote about several unsigned New York bands that were operating downtown.

"Never had I seen the 82 more crowded than about three weeks back than when Wayne County topped the bill over The Stilettos," I wrote. "Wayne came out in full drag which was pretty stunning, but the music was overly loud and uninspired for my taste. He went down a bomb though."

The piece mentioned ten other acts, but I found room for Debbie. "The Stilettos, who opened up, had more potential but less rehearsal. Fronted by a cuddly platinum blonde called Debbi (sic), they're a girl vocal trio with a male guitar/bass/drums back-up band. The three chicks take turns to sing solo while the other two chant away behind, and some of the songs were well worth putting on vinyl. Ninety-five per cent were original, but the style was taken from the late fifties-era of vocal groups."

There is good reason to believe that the 75 words quoted in that paragraph – out of a total of about 1,500 in the whole piece – were the first ever mention of Debbie Harry in a British paper, music or otherwise. Similarly, *MM* was the first magazine to print a photograph of her. Bob had given me a few of his pictures of The Stilettos that I sent over to London and, somewhat inevitably in the light of her appearance, the subs desk at *MM* opted to use one to illustrate the feature. A week or two later, that issue of *MM* landed on my doorstep so I called her up at the beauty parlour where she worked and told her that her picture was in *Melody Maker*. She was very excited about this. It was evidently the first time she'd ever had her picture in a magazine, or so she told me, and she seemed desperate to get her hands on a copy.

A night or two later, Debbie drove up to my apartment on East 78th Street in an old green banger with bench seats. I gave her two copies of the paper and took her out to dinner at a Japanese restaurant on the West Side. Over sushi, tempura and sake she told me that The Stilettos were breaking up and she was forming a new band with her boyfriend, Chris Stein, their guitarist, its name as yet undecided. I took note of this and mentioned her plans in my next *MM* New York news column, no doubt the first mention of the fledgling Blondie anywhere.

It was around midnight when Debbie drove back through Central Park to drop me off on the East Side. Before getting out of her car I pulled her towards me across the bench seat, kissed her on the lips and invited her inside. But I was too late – she'd already met that other Chris.

18

"People who take their clothes off are into rhythm and we're into that."
Donald Fagen, New York City, April 1974

The best thing about being *Melody Maker*'s man in New York was that the job was all my own, so tickets to concerts weren't shared around as they were in London. Those I reviewed were nothing if not eclectic. A glance at back issues of *MM* reveals that in April, May and June of 1974, I saw, amongst others, Rick Nelson, Steely Dan, Greg Allman, Grand Funk Railroad, Todd Rundgren, Roger McGuinn, Charlie Rich, Harry Chapin, Roxy Music, Sly Stone, The Who and David Bowie.

I was particularly looking forward to seeing Steely Dan. When their first LP, *Can't Buy A Thrill*, was released in late 1972 a copy arrived in *MM*'s offices and, curious, Richard Williams put it on the office record player. It wasn't long before those of us there that day stopped what we were doing to listen. "This is great, who the fuck is it?" someone asked as we gathered around the low-fi deck that IPC Business Press had so generously bestowed upon the massive cash cow that *MM* had lately become. For the next few months *CBAT* was on and off that deck more than any other LP.

On the same day as Steely Dan's April concert at Avery Fisher Hall, I interviewed Walter Becker and Donald Fagen at their record company's offices, which was not quite as challenging as I had been led to believe, by which I mean they were friendlier than I expected. Perhaps this was because I was among the first British journalists to interview them. Also, bearing in mind their intellectual approach, I had taken the time to read up about them and play their music a lot. Come to think of it, I still do.

By this time, Steely Dan had released three LPs. The most recent, *Pretzel Logic*, a firm favourite of mine, was their first to reach the US LP Top 10, and Becker and Fagen had now emerged as co-leaders of the group, composing all the material and laying down the law as far as strategy was concerned. But there was trouble afoot. These two were increasingly reluctant to tour and appeared to be demoting the rest of the group. They had yet to become a studio duo backed up by skilled session musicians but it was on the cards, and Becker and Fagen hinted at it while we spoke.

"Fagen is a tall, thin man with a slight hunch, probably caused through leaning over a piano for much of his life," I wrote after a brief summary of their career thus far. "He's a serious musician who isn't afraid to voice his opinions on current rock giants, for whom he has little respect. Becker is pretty much the same, except that he's short and tubby. Both would sooner spend an evening in a jazz club that at any rock concert you'd care to name."

The main reason why the terminally interview-phobic Dan men had agreed to speak to *MM* was because they'd be playing concerts in the UK the following month. Fagen was looking forward to it. "I have a feeling that European audiences will be more appreciative of our music. American audiences are fantastic but I don't know what they appreciate."

"You can't tell what they're into at all," said Becker. "From the stage, you see people at the front and they're obviously into volume, a self-abuse trip. As for the rest of the audience we don't know. We hope it's the music."

"People who take their clothes off are into rhythm and we're into that," said Fagen enigmatically.

When I turned the conversation towards which groups they did and didn't like it was clear they were hard to please. Indeed, they disliked almost every rock group on the planet, especially those from the world of glam. Their most hated group of all appeared to be my friends Slade, with whom they had shared a bill. "How they ever managed to get enough money together to come here and tour is a miracle," said Becker.

I got to the Avery Fisher Hall – a bit like London's Festival Hall – early, determined not to miss anything. In the event it started late due to "technical" problems that marred Steely Dan's set throughout, a failing monitor system to blame, along with whining feedback. It was so bad that they stopped one number shortly after it started and began again.

Having mentioned all this at the start of my review, I continued as follows: "It would, I feel, be unfair to judge them on this display. It doesn't happen often but it has a nasty habit of happening in New York. Fagen is the focal point of the outfit. His grand piano is placed squarely in the centre of the stage and he frequently abandons his stool to conduct the rest of the band with his hands, turning his back on the audience as he does so.

"The accent is very much on percussion with two kits and a conga player. Perhaps it was that sound system, but frequently the percussion drowned out the rest of the band. The twin guitars flow in unison for much of the set, and at times they sounded very influenced by Santana. At their best they were magnificent, but this high was only reached occasionally. Problems or not, it was obvious that Steely Dan have set themselves a high standard and, as they told me earlier, were not content to sit back and play their rock and roll like everyone else.

"Most of their numbers are fairly short, and the material was mainly from their new album *Pretzel Logic*. They finished with 'Reelin' In The Years', their first major US hit, and a sympathetic audience brought them back for an encore. The band looked grateful, but it was obvious they were far from happy with the evening."

The next time I saw Steely Dan was at Hammersmith in the year 2000. There were no sound problems that night.

*

Rock shows at Carnegie Hall were a bit of a rarity during my stint as *Melody Maker*'s man in New York. I can recall seeing The Chieftains there and being slightly alarmed at Irish independence sympathisers outside collecting openly on behalf of the IRA. "Spare some change for the old country," they exhorted. I kept my mouth shut. But there was an element of prestige involved in playing the Carnegie and Gregg Allman pulled out all the stops at his show there in late March. Alongside him on stage were 29 other musicians, with a backdrop and scenery designed to suggest that he'd brought 'Maykin, Jawjar' – as he called his home town – to the Big Apple.

The show was produced by Shep Gordon, Alice Cooper's manager, who never did things by halves and brought a touch of grandeur to the proceedings. My only complaint was that the effort necessary in presenting Gregg in this way caused the show to start almost an hour late. Although the now legendary group took their name from Gregg's surname, he was not the front man when I last saw The Allman Brothers, at the LA Forum the previous year. Guitarist Richard 'Dickey' Betts was the star of that show while Gregg hid behind a Hammond to stage left, shyly taking an occasional bow and content to be out of the limelight.

For the solo concert, all this was changed. The Hammond stood in the centre of the stage, decked out with flowers and lit candles. The show was clearly aimed at pushing Gregg forward, thus working against his natural shyness, and as a result he looked uncomfortable amid the splendour of the smart-suited orchestral back-up.

In effect we were seeing half of The Allman Brothers Band. There was Chuck Leavell in a straw hat playing a grand piano at stage left, and Jai Johnny

Johanssen alternating between bongos and a regular kit. The rhythm section was Cowboy, a quartet of session players from the Capricorn Studio in Macon, and the rest were strings, brass and backing singers with comedian Martin Mull bringing the complement up to 30 by acting as MC.

The evening opened with an orchestral piece played by Leavell at the piano. As strings and brass came on strong, the rhythm section joined in and Allman made his entry to the delight of the crowd and chagrin of the stern Carnegie Hall staff who were kept busy returning fans to their seats throughout the entire show. "Dressed in denims and looking his usual dishevelled self, Allman appeared somewhat out of place," I wrote. "His long blond hair covered his features and even though the spotlight shone firmly down on him, he still managed to hide away behind his instrument for most of the time. He sways on the stool so much one imagines that any moment he's likely to slip off on to the floor. It never actually happens though."

Predictably, the set comprised material from his 1973 solo album, aptly titled *Laid Back*, and Gregg's contributions to the Allman Brothers' song catalogue. "With such a huge band, the music sounded not unlike Joe Cocker's Mad Dogs & Englishmen band," I continued. "It was all very well-rehearsed, but Allman's voice was frequently drowned out by the force of everything else. He doesn't have the strongest of voices, but when it does shine through, he sings with a loping, casual Southern accent, slurring words together, sounding rather like a mean gunslinger.

"During the entire show, he picked up the guitar only once – to sing 'Midnight Rider'. This was a shame. He's as good a guitar picker as you'll find anywhere, and I'd have preferred to hear him on either the acoustic or electric instrument instead of endlessly pumping away on the organ. He's a competent, if not brilliant, organist but he was given few opportunities to solo and when he did it was nothing too spectacular."

Oddly, the second half of the show featured Cowboy on their own, with Allman returning for the finale, the massed congregation offering 'Turn On Your Lovelight'. For an encore Gregg played a new, unaccompanied piece at the piano before one and all joined in again for 'Will The Circle Be Unbroken'.

*

A day or two later I interviewed Todd Rundgren at the offices of Bearsville, his record label, on East 55th Street, and for reasons best known to himself he brought along his main squeeze, the model Bebe Buell. Perhaps it was to show her off. Ms Buell, of course, was strikingly beautiful and in the fullness of time her name would be linked with Mick Jagger, Jimmy Page, David Bowie, Elvis Costello and Steve Tyler, with whom she had a daughter, the actor Liv Tyler.

Although Rundgren dressed outlandishly onstage and gave the impression that he was an extrovert, in reality he was a sober, clear-headed, clean-living chap who adopted a methodical attitude towards his calling as a musician and record producer. Indeed, he had worked it out so that his successful career in the studio making records for others financed his critically acclaimed but less remunerative career as an artist in his own right.

"I discovered that I didn't like most of the people involved in the so-called music business, so the fewer people I had to meet the better," he told me matter-of-factly. "I figured a producer didn't need to meet too many people. I like people better nowadays but it's still not right, so I continue to disinvolve myself as much as possible from the business aspect."

Most recently Rundgren had been brought in to produce Grand Funk Railroad, and he certainly added some much-needed sparkle to this immensely popular but rather dull hard rock group. The resulting album, *We're An American Band*, compared favourably with all their former efforts and as an added bonus there was a number one single from the title track – something Grand Funk had never had before – and also a modicum of critical acclaim, also new to GF.

"I would say now that Grand Funk are better musicians than the world believe," said Todd. "It is possible to make a band sound worse than they are in the studio which may have happened with Grand Funk. That's very easy to do, much easier than it is to make a band sound good."

We talked a bit about his own band and he was modest enough to admit that though he considered his live performances far more important than his albums, he loses money going out on the road. "I rack up tour debts though and that's where the money that I make from producing goes. Everything evens itself out in the end."

I would experience Grand Funk Railroad for myself a few days later, at Madison Square Garden, and was dumbfounded by the volume at which they played.

"Ringing ears are a symptom of excessive listening to loud rock and roll," I wrote in *MM*, opening myself up to a charge of stating the bleeding obvious. "When the ears tingle after a gig, you know the band in question has pushed out plenty of juice. When they're still ringing the following day, then that band must have employed a brave sound engineer to control the volume setting. When the ringing's still there as you head for bed the following evening, it's something else entirely. I've experienced those ringing ears the following morning, but only once have I known it to last the entire day and into the night.

"That was last Tuesday. On Monday evening I experienced a two-hour concert by Grand Funk, who, regardless of what the *Guinness Book Of Records* says about Deep Purple, go down in my book as the loudest band I've ever heard and, hopefully, the loudest band I'm ever likely to hear."

I was sat near the front, a mistake though I wasn't to know this beforehand. In any case, review tickets were almost always decent seats, a description that, in this case, was certainly moot. Still, after all the atrocious reviews I'd read, they were better than I expected, though much of their attraction lay in the effects they laid on: their state-of-the-art lighting rig, the movies shown on a screen behind them and, of course, that terrifying volume.

"Their reception at New York's Madison Square Garden on Monday evening was nothing short of unreal," I wrote. "From the opening note, 20,000 fans stood on their chairs and cheered wildly until it was over. The ovation surpassed anything I've seen in the States, including Dylan at the same venue, and the enthusiasm knocked current scream-idols flat.

"One young lady, for example, rushed at guitarist Mark Farner from her pitch at the front of the stage. She was roughly hauled aside by a member of the road crew and left to find her own way back to her rightful place at the front of the crowd. Somehow or other she managed to claw her way through the throng to the front again. Not satisfied with her earlier attempt, she dashed the stage yet again to clutch at Farner. Again, the same girl was bundled off. At the end of the show she was back up front again, having somehow pushed and shoved her way back to pole position beneath the sprightly lead guitarist."

Oddly, towards the end of the show the band deserted the stage while a short film about themselves was shown. Designed to depict the members of the group in their natural environment, one was seen riding a horse, another a motor cycle, another in a fast car and the fourth water skiing. Back at my flat later that evening, unable to sleep due to the ringing in my ears, I imagined how it would look if The Who adopted something similar during their concerts: Pete worshipping at the feet of his guru Meher Baba, Roger ploughing his fields, John chasing spiders and Keith hurling a heavy object through a window. Nah – it'd never work.

The following morning, my ears still painfully aware of the previous night's experience, I breakfasted with the group at their Manhattan hotel, the St Regis. They were all thoroughly likeable guys, though none were particularly talkative, least of all Farner, the leader on stage if not off. Though he's a bona-fide rock superstar, his conversation was on ration. Drummer Don Brewer was more talkative, while keyboard player Craig Frost, the newcomer, sat back to let him do the talking. Bassist Mel Schacher was still in bed, suffering from 'flu.

We talked about the group's early days as Terry Knight & The Pack, losing Knight – who had exerted a disproportionate influence on them – and how Todd Rundgren had brought about a resurgence in their fortunes.

Someone took my picture lighting a cigarette after breakfasting with Farner, who can be seen in a mirror behind me. I'm wearing a replica St Louis Blues ice-hockey shirt that I bought on one of my visits there. Warm, loose and practical, albeit deeply unfashionable, I went through about half a dozen ice-hockey shirts during my spell in America.

19

"I write on the toilet 'cos no one bothers me there."
Sly Stone, New York City, June 1974

You'd be hard pressed to find any music writer who didn't admire The Byrds and I had long hankered to chat with Roger McGuinn, the flock's mainman. My friend Peter Philbin at Columbia International obliged by driving me out to Roslyn in Long Island to finally meet him in early May. Afterwards we took in his show at My Father's Place, a cool little club nearby where entry was just two dollars and beer less than 50 cents a glass, cheap by New York standards.

"It's a far cry from The Byrds' flights across America in their heyday when they could expect to fill massive basketball arenas," I wrote in *MM*. "McGuinn isn't even carrying his own PA system, preferring to rely on that provided by the club rather than pay expensive air freight charges for his own gear. He's just got a couple of guitars, a banjo, a Pignose amp and some electronic gadgetry that makes one guitar sound like three."

Dressed all in denim, his long, straggly hair parted in the centre, Roger turned out to be a quiet, thoughtful and dignified fellow, friendly enough and happy to discuss the demise of the group he had led since 1964, the year before they recorded their magnificent electrified version of Dylan's 'Mr Tambourine Man'. Now the architect of that remarkable record was sat opposite me on a double bed in an unremarkable Holiday Inn hotel room, telling me all about the group's demise and defending his decision to perform Byrds classics as a solo performer. "I feel just as qualified to sing The Byrds' songs as anyone else," he said. "I was one of the writers on 'Eight Miles High' and I feel the same about the Dylan songs. I changed the timing on them and it was my idea for The Byrds to do their versions of them in the first place."

McGuinn had finally disbanded the group, of which he was the sole original member, the previous year, because the five original Byrds – McGuinn, David Crosby, Chris Hillman, Gene Clark and Michael Clarke – had got back together to make the album for Elektra/Asylum, and he didn't want two sets of Byrds on the market, the originals and the most recent variation. "It would have been ludicrous to have two Byrds with two albums out at the same time, so I thought it would be best to have the original group and nothing else. There was talk of the original band going out but it wasn't warranted by the number of album sales on that record. It didn't sell well at all. I was unhappy about that but in retrospect I can see why the general public didn't like it.

"It was a bit of an anti-climax, and the last version of The Byrds was the same. Some combinations of musician that made up The Byrds were OK and some weren't. The last band wasn't to my liking. Clarence [White] and I fired each other as a joke, but nobody had the right to fire me as I was the leader and I'd fired everybody else by that time anyway."

Although Roger told me that his solo act was a cross between new material and old songs associated with The Byrds, in actual fact his show that night was 90 per cent Byrds material, with only three new songs. First he played acoustic guitar, then banjo for one number, and then turned to the electric Rickenbacker 12-string, his trademark in earlier days. With the aid of his electronic gadgets, he produced a whining, droning guitar sound that managed to cover up for the sparse instrumentation.

"It was, however, rather a patchy performance," I wrote. "The material made up for this – everyone likes hearing those old Byrds hits – and one and all, myself included, had a whale of an evening. Surprisingly, he attempted a solo version of 'Eight Miles High', perhaps most electric of Byrds songs. And there were a host of others – 'Tambourine Man', 'Turn, Turn, Turn', 'Easy Rider', 'Wasn't Born To Follow', 'Fifth Dimension', 'Chestnut Mare', 'My Back Pages', 'So You Wanna Be A Rock and Roll Star' and 'Mr. Spaceman'.

"McGuinn was seated for the performance and offered deadpan introductions. The polite claps turned to cheers and he wound up doing around four encores; it was the atmosphere that the grand old Byrd created, rather than the musical output, that made the evening such a success.

"Inevitably it was the old songs that the crowd were rooting for, and they got what they wanted," I wrote. "At the end he seemed genuinely moved by the ovation which was surely intended as an appreciation of his career as much as for the evening's performance."

*

Earlier in the year, back in the UK, the ruggedly-handsome country singer Charlie Rich had enjoyed hits with 'The Most Beautiful Girl' and 'Behind Closed Doors' and this prompted Ray to request I interview him. Like McGuinn, he was on Columbia and their ever-obliging press department informed me he was playing at Disney World in Florida. Did I fancy a trip a trip to the Sunshine State and a couple of nights in the hotel on the resort complex? Of course I did.

My companion this time was Mike O'Mahoney, the same CBS PR who'd introduced me to Bruce Springsteen earlier in the year, and when we arrived at the Century Hotel he asked for a suite which was duly served up: two huge bedrooms with en-suite bathrooms linked by a vast lounge, dining, bar and kitchen area, the sort of hotel room that could accommodate a family of six for a year. It was, in fact, the best accommodation in the entire hotel and Charlie was not best pleased when he dropped by for our interview. Evidently, he had a slightly smaller suite on the floor below.

"At 41, he's a distinguished-looking man," I wrote. "His silver hair – natural, by the way – and his large physique reminded me of that great cowboy Hopalong Cassidy. He has a lived-in look, a face that's seen much in the last 20 years, and retained it all. He looks tough, but is really a gentle giant. His appeal lies as a father figure but teenage girls actually screamed at him during his performance."

Charlie was happy to run through his career for the benefit of *MM*'s readers, recall a few anecdotes of working at Sun Records which, like Elvis, he left for RCA. Then came Epic, part of Columbia, and success after well over a decade's worth of effort. During that time, of course, he had changed his style a lot, beginning as a rock 'n' roller but gradually moving over to country simply because he preferred it.

Three hours after our chat, a 5,000-strong audience was gathered around Cinderella's castle in the heart of Disney World awaiting Charlie's arrival on stage. There were two ways to enter Disney World. One was through the main gate and the other, more exclusive, method was to make your way around the back, walk through a series of tunnels beneath the complex and rise up in an elevator to your chosen area. We chose the latter, which afforded me an insight into the mechanics of the resort. Beneath the Magic Kingdom was a vast complex of air ducts, machines generating power, replacement pieces, a giant strong room where the cash was kept and, oddly, costumed staff taking their meal breaks. I resisted the temptation to chat up Snow White.

As there was no backstage area, no dressing rooms or similar facilities, Disney security people formed a tunnel for our party from Cinderella's Castle to the stage. When the show started, it was surrounded by fans pressed tight against the front. A host of amateur photographers had their Instamatics ready.

Charlie used a four-piece backing band – two guitars, bass and drums – augmented by four brass and three black girl singers called The Treasures, and played a grand piano at the front of the stage. They struck up the opening notes of 'The Most Beautiful Girl', a few fans shrieked but most clapped, and a local country station DJ introduced "The Silver Fox, Mr Charlie Rich", who surprised no one by getting straight into the music, following their cue on 'Most Beautiful Girl'. A good percentage of the crowd sang along.

Charlie wore shades and a sensible hot weather safari-type outfit with a gold chain and medallion dangling from his neck. With his silver hair blowing in the slight breeze, he had the air of an aging film star, as if Cary Grant had turned to singing in his twilight years. He looked very classy, the kind of celebrity who's seen vaulting between Rolls-Royces with stunning blondes on either arm. Still, he's a rocker at heart and 'Lonely Weekends' was essayed as a forceful rock number. He hit the piano keys like Jerry Lee as arms reached out from the front to touch him. At the close he shook a few and drank from a cup of water that more eager arms reached out to grab.

The show lasted about 45 minutes and was very tightly arranged. At one point Charlie left the stage to allow guitarist David Mayfield, a young blond riff rider, to lead the band in some out and out rock. Then The Treasures got a chance to sing a song on their own. Charlie returned with 'A Very Special Love Song', then warmed up through his "evolution medley" – a segued selection from his past – to 'Behind Closed Doors'. This led to more squealing from the girls in front. At the end he left abruptly, declining to encore.

When he'd gone two girls got into a fight over the beaker from which he was drinking.

*

Later in May I was in the company of Bryan Ferry of Roxy Music, then pretty much an unknown quantity in America. In the UK Roxy had been fast-tracked to success on the strength of their inventive records, positive press coverage and the way they dressed but none of this cut much ice in a country the size of the USA where the accepted wisdom was that success came only to an act that toured extensively. As a result, Bryan, on a promotional tour of the US, was exhausted.

"Not much lounging for the lounge lizard this week," I wrote in *MM*. "All go. Up at dawn to another city. Another round of interviews. Another airplane. Another late night. Another early call. Six days on end. Somehow his black hair maintains its usual crisp quiff even if his eyes blink a lot and need a good rub to prevent the lids from clamping together. A cup of tea. An untidy suite. A television with picture and no sound. An album set containing 72 of Frank Sinatra's greatest hits, a prized possession indeed.

"In the past five days he's flown from London to New York, spent a day in Cleveland, a day in Detroit and a day in Chicago, and also visited Philadelphia and Boston. Each day was crammed with press and radio interviews, and each evening was spent discovering the delights of America."

"The first American tour was a terrible bring down really,' Bryan admitted to me. "It was the only time we've ever been... er, not appreciated. It was sandwiched between two English tours which were rave tours and to come here and be totally unknown was obviously a bit of a downer. People I spoke to on that tour who had the first album never even knew we were due to play in the town on that day. What we should have done was to play in small halls rather than support big bands in the big arenas."

Like other acts that targeted a more sophisticated audience than American-style boogie-all-night-long rock fans, Roxy found themselves more appreciated in the big cities on the coasts than in the great hinterland in between. A party was thrown for Bryan in a loft in downtown New York where trendy taste-makers from among the Andy Warhol crowd gathered to inspect this rock star who looked and dressed more like a fifties crooner than Robert Plant or Roger Daltrey.

This was the first time I'd ever been inside a New York loft. Unlike what we in the UK call the space beneath gable roofs of houses, in New York lofts are apartments originally designed as workshops, most often found downtown where small industries like textiles and bespoke furniture once flourished. As a result, they are vast open spaces, without interior walls, like XXL studios I suppose. Bryan was the centre of attention at the party, and enjoying it, but I managed to corner him for another chat, sitting on beanbags as I recall, not the most elegant lounging position for this most elegant of loungers.

"We were very fortunate to be successful from the first record onwards in England, maybe because of the mechanics of the English system," he continued. "There isn't a huge rock press over here, and in England we were always written about from the very beginning so people were aware of us before even the first album came out. Here people are more influenced by FM radio and they're more unadventurous in their outlook. There seems to be a dreadful musical snobbery between AM and FM radio and Roxy doesn't seem to fall into either of these accepted categories. We're too weird for AM, and considered too flash and too image conscious for some of the FM stations.

"Americans aren't so preoccupied with style as the English are, but it could be changing. When I was in Detroit, I got a phone call from Canada during a radio interview and this kid said that he cut out photographs of me and took them along to his hairdressers so that he could imitate my hairstyle. I was very flattered."

The promotional visit previewed Roxy's June 2 concert at the Academy of Music, following which the artist Larry Rivers threw an after-show party in his East Village loft studio that was attended by David Bowie. On his arm was Amanda Lear, the cover model from Roxy's *For Your Pleasure* LP. "Roxy's image has attracted a clique following of film stars, artists and general Warhol-type personalities and they turned up in droves for the after-show party," I reported in my weekly *MM* NY news column.

*

Two days later I found myself face to face with Sly Stone who proved even more difficult to interview than Lou Reed. The encounter took place in a small apartment on New York's Westside that adjoined his manager's offices. I was told he didn't like hotels. I suspect it was more a case of hotels not liking him but thought it best not to air this opinion. By his side during the interview was his fiancée, Kathy Silva, whom he would marry on stage at Madison Square Garden on June 5, the first American wedding to which I was invited, though probably not a typical Stateside tying of the knot.

They made a handsome couple. Sly had dressed for our interview as he would for a concert; a gleaming all-white leather outfit with tassels and rhinestones, topped off with his huge afro. Silver sunglasses hid his eyes. Kathy was wearing a matching ensemble except for a petite mini-skirt that exposed plenty of shapely leg. This may have inspired what occurred midway through our chat when she and Sly decamped to the adjoining bedroom to do what comes naturally to men and women in bedrooms, quite noisily too. In the meantime, I was left in the company of his publicist, a long-suffering girl who tried to make small talk in the temporary absence of her client. It was excruciatingly embarrassing, albeit quite funny in hindsight.

The interview got off to a bad start. "He extended a hand but looked elsewhere," I reported. "Who could tell where his eyes focused beneath those silver shades? He gripped and I felt a pain through the middle finger on my right hand. He grinned and disappeared. About half an hour later I found out what had caused the pain. On his two little fingers were a couple of matching rings. Spelled out in diamonds were the words 'Sly' (right hand) and 'Stone' (left).

"Meeting Sly is like coming face to face with an ugly cop. He isn't social. He isn't friendly. He resents intrusions on his privacy. He doesn't like to talk. He's a star and he acts like a star ought. Moody, mean and magnificent."

What actually happened was that when Sly arrived, preceded by a white personal assistant, he breezed into the adjoining office, disappearing almost immediately, allowing me just a glimpse of him. After ten minutes he re-appeared, taking us through to the apartment which was tiny by rock-star standards. I offered him a copy of *Melody Maker*, pointing out that it contained an article on him, a retrospective in our Rock Giants series, which prompted him to retire to his toilet to read it. He was gone for another ten minutes.

While waiting, we were joined by Kathy. Then Sly re-emerged to the sound of plumbing and sat on a couch, still reading the *MM*. Thereafter the interview spluttered on with Sly answering my questions, largely in monosyllables, and Kathy chipping in here and there to offer support. Their decision to retire to the bedroom after about ten minutes seemed motivated on his part by a need to prove his macho credentials in the face of a white man with a British accent with whom he decided he had little in common.

"Do you get bored always playing very familiar material like 'Dance To The Music' and 'I Want To Take You Higher'?" I asked when he returned. "No," he replied. "They like it and they keep on liking it and you gotta keep telling people you like it, too. I love every period of my career."

I asked about who played on his records and he told me he played every instrument, implying that it was disrespectful of me to suggest otherwise. "I just overdub everything," he said.

"Where do you write?" I asked. "I write on the toilet 'cos no one bothers me there. I enjoy myself best on the toilet and I wouldn't invite you there."

This last remark brought the interview to an inevitable conclusion. Sly's assistant showed me to the door while the man himself curled up on the sofa with his fiancée. "You know something," said the PR girl. "He really opened up this afternoon. Usually, he just grunts at writers. He's done a few interviews this week and he said more this afternoon than he's said all week."

On June 5, I was at the Garden to report on Sly's marriage to Kathy. "The ever-unpredictable Sly Stone married the mother of his nine-month-old son in front of 20,000 fans at Madison Square Garden on Wednesday evening," I wrote in *MM*. "Following a set by Eddie Kendricks, Sly's mother came on to the stage to call for quiet. Then she introduced Sly's 12-year-old niece who sang a gospel hymn like someone twice her age before the stage filled with friends and relations all dressed in gold costumes.

"A dozen girls holding palm leaves high in the air formed a backdrop as Sly himself loped out last, dressed all in gold with a gold cape. The preacher – brought in specially from San Francisco – called for hush and the service began. Appeals for the audience to keep silent because of the solemnity of the occasion were largely ignored, but the words of the marriage service were clearly audible through the PA system. When the words 'Do you, Sly Sylvester Stewart, take this woman' were uttered, a huge cheer went up. The service closed with the traditional 'Let no man put asunder' line which prompted the crowd to go crazy.

"Then everyone trooped off. The whole affair was over in less than 15 minutes. There was another delay before the band came back on, followed by Sly who ripped into a long set, at least by his standards.

"The new Family Stone included a violinist and there were several new songs in his repertoire as well as old favourites," I informed *MM*'s readers. "'Dance To The Music' opened and closed the set. Musically, Sly was as good as ever, alternating between organ, guitar and harp. He seemed to rise to the occasion and actually addressed the audience between numbers instead of merely jumping from one number to the next to hurry the proceedings over as quickly as possible."

Two years later Sly and Kathy separated. "He beat me, held me captive and wanted me to be in ménages à trois," Kathy later told *People* magazine.

20

"I don't want The Who to end up on stage playing because they have to but playing because they want to."
Pete Townshend, New York City, June 1974

I never felt closer to The Who than I did in New York during the second week of June, and this includes the period, between 1993 and 2000, when I worked on and off for them on a box set and back catalogue reissues. I tried to maintain my neutrality with them but I admired them so much, both as a group and as individuals, that becoming close to them was somehow important to me and, of course, it helped me get the hot Who scoops for *Melody Maker*.

I'd formed certain opinions about them by now. Pete was an idealist, Roger was practical, John was professional and Keith was simply unquantifiable. Pete and Keith were reckless, Roger and John cautious. Pete wanted progress, the others were content with the way things were. They were bound together musically but not socially. Management was an issue, and they were not as rich as the world imagined them to be, a legacy of the penance they paid to original producer Shel Talmy. To survive they needed to work, performing live as often as possible, perfecting the show and pocketing the fees they could command. This had the additional benefit of making them the greatest live band in the world.

On June 10 they opened an unprecedented four-concert run at Madison Square Garden, shows that sold out on the strength of one radio announcement, all 80,000 seats. No other act had played the Garden four times in one week before and to say I was anticipating these shows eagerly would be an understatement. I was at every one, either in a good seat or at the side of the stage, and in their dressing room.

It therefore pained me to report that The Who weren't at their best in New York this time around. Equipment glitches were partly to blame but an exacerbating factor was a fan down at the front on the opening night who yelled "Jump Pete, jump" to Townshend, which shocked him enormously. For the first time, he said later, he felt he was parodying himself, even resembling a circus act. Furthermore, he found he needed to force his uniquely athletic stage style, which had previously come naturally to him and was so much a part of the excitement of The Who's stage shows. In the short term this contributed to an unsatisfactory run of concerts, at least by the absurdly high standards The Who had set in the past. In the long term, what he experienced at the Garden had a profound effect on his attitude towards the group. Most fans loved them regardless, of course, and their blind faith depressed Pete still further.

From where I was sat on the first night I couldn't see the fans up front but I could tell something wasn't right. I put it down to sound problems, and the fact that they hadn't played for a while. The Who were like elite athletes who needed regular training to obtain optimum results. When they took on a lengthy tour the first few shows might have been slightly under par but when they hit their stride, Olympic fitness as it were, they were supreme, untouchable. When they played the odd show here and there, as they did in 1974, they suffered through being out of condition – and sometimes it showed.

This was the first time they'd played the Garden so the acoustics were new to them. I thought they'd iron out the problems after the first night but they didn't, not really. It was only later that I realised the real problem ran far deeper, and I suspect that the band used the dodgy sound as an excuse when they, or at least Pete, knew the problems lay deeper too. They hadn't recorded any new material since the previous year's *Quadrophenia*, so the set they played was a run-through of their past, a kind of greatest hits selection. The only real surprise was that for the first time since the *Tommy* era they re-introduced 'Tattoo' into the set which the fans (and I) loved but which somehow contributed to a slightly unsettling feeling of nostalgia that had hit me earlier when I saw High Numbers t-shirts on sale outside the Garden. Pete always wanted to progress but the others were content with the way things were, and this was also part of the problem. It was a problem that would never go away, not while Keith was alive anyway.

"A huge roar greeted the arrival of The Who and the first half hour of Monday's show was quite electric," I wrote in *MM*. "But from then on it slid into a murky mess of badly mixed sound, flared tempers and general untogetherness. Things went wrong from 'Behind Blue Eyes' onwards. Daltrey had difficulty pitching the 'See Me, Feel Me' lines and at one stage he kicked over a monitor speaker in a fit of rage. Townshend could be seen shouting at the sound men and the taped synthesiser backing tracks were too loud. Towards the end the sound did improve but by this time it was too late to count. Townshend even apologised but it didn't seem to matter. They still got a standing ovation, but it was a hollow victory for the band."

My friend Pete Rudge, who handled The Who's US affairs, had given me passes for all four nights and backstage I overheard a terrible row after this opening concert. The Who were screaming at each other behind a locked dressing room door. Their co-manager Kit Lambert, who wasn't often seen at Who concerts by 1974, had turned up unexpectedly, drunk as a lord, and was demanding to mix the on-stage PA the following night, a ludicrous suggestion that exacerbated an already fraught situation. Long serving soundman Bobby Pridden ran out of the dressing room shouting that he was through with The Who, and I took him aside into another room and spent about ten minutes beseeching him not to quit, and of course he didn't. Poor loyal Bob, the real fifth member of The Who. He caught it in the neck so many times but he loved them far too much to ever quit.

Eventually things calmed down and Rudge asked me to do everyone a favour by quietly steering Kit away from the scene which I somehow managed to do, perhaps because Kit, who was openly gay, was eyeing me up. On our way back uptown to the Navarro Hotel I asked his limousine driver to stop so I could buy a pack of cigarettes and Kit, bless him, rushed into a liquor store and returned with two cartons of Marlboro – 20 packets! – for which I was grateful, albeit still unwilling to join him for drinks in the hotel bar.

The concerts improved as the week went by but The Who never really fired on all four cylinders that week. Tuesday was much better than Monday, though, and after this show I took Pete, John and Keith downtown to Club 82 where Television were playing. Pete had mentioned to me that he wanted to see some young New York bands, and I thought Television's spiky, unsettling minimalism might be his cup of tea. He liked them but John, ever the traditionalist, hated them. We lost Keith in the crowd.

Wednesday was a night off and during the afternoon I interviewed Pete at his hotel. He seemed in a bad way, stressed out through working on the *Tommy* film soundtrack, drinking too much brandy and torn between the wishes of the fans, the band and what he wanted to do himself. I think he felt a great responsibility to everyone: the other three, the fans, the film producers and, of course, his young family. Everybody wanted a piece of him, even me interviewing him for *MM*, but he needed a break from everything. It was telling that when I knocked on his hotel room door he took a long time to answer. I might even have woken him up, and I'm pretty sure he was dreadfully hung over.

"We were acting," Pete told me as we discussed whatever it was that afflicted the group on the opening night. "We've been able to act and look as if everything's OK for a while now but we can't keep it up if the sound doesn't get better. It didn't and we couldn't act for the whole show."

He seemed grimly aware of the expectations of his audience. "These fans feel that they own The Who. They were there in the front row at the Murray the K Shows [in 1967] and now that The Who have reached this stage they feel that as they've been so loyal they have a prior claim to what numbers we're going to play and things like that. New York to us is like what the Goldhawk Club is like to us in England.

"Most of these kids, the ones I've met, seem to have a similar attitude to life. The ones you saw freaking out at the front are the fanatics and they all seem to be deeply intellectual people who are very worried about life. They find The Who to be a kind of gut release which is what I get from The Who, too. They're people from the dead suburbia of New York who need a release from everyday life.

"The trouble with all of us in this group is that we have such incredibly defined traditional ways of playing that we tend to be bogged down by them in some senses, but I like to go out and do a solo on single notes instead of the usual routine. Without becoming alarmist about it I guess that I don't get as much out of performing on the stage as I used to. I don't have the same lust for gut feedback that I used to and more and more I want to get feedback from pure music.

"I think The Who are going to have to allow themselves time to breathe without allowing their sense of identity to dissipate. I don't want The Who to end up on stage playing because they have to but playing because they want to. If it turns out they don't want to play together, then I don't think they should, but at the moment we don't play that often and when we do it's because we want to. I can't wait to get back on stage tonight."

During their stay in New York, Pete stayed in a different hotel – The Sherry Netherland – to the rest of the band who took suites at the Navarro on Central Park South, their regular New York berth. It was the first time that the whole group hadn't stayed together in the same hotel, which I thought was telling, but Pete stayed in touch with developments at the Navarro by using a rudimentary cordless mobile phone, probably one of the earliest of its type, that had been assembled by the group's sound crew.

At Thursday's show 'My Generation' morphed into Van Morrison's 'Gloria', a rather disjointed stab at The Kinks' 'You Really Got Me', sung by John, and ended with 'Big Boss Man', a Jimmy Reed blues staple from their early days. It seemed to me they were loosening up, finding a semblance of form at last, but try as they might the shows somehow never reached the peaks of the touring that followed the release of *Who's Next*, or the closing shows on the *Quadrophenia* tour for that matter.

After that show Keith, his assistant Dougal and I visited John Lennon in his suite at the luxurious Pierre Hotel, where he was living with May Pang. The Pierre, on Fifth Avenue at the south east corner of Central Park, was as swanky as they get and Keith, Dougal and myself rode there in a limousine from the Garden, then headed up in the elevator. John seemed pleased to see Keith. They'd been pals back in London in the sixties and had been hanging out together in LA earlier in the year. In truth, Keith was a Beatles groupie, eternally in awe of them, and also a good pal of Ringo whose son Zak – who drums with the 21st Century Who – was the recipient of at least one Moon cast-off drum kit.

Keith, being Keith, suggested to John that we all have a drink, assuming, wrongly as it turned out, that John would have a huge bar stocked with booze. In the event, all he had was one bottle of shockingly expensive red wine, a fine vintage red, given to him by his former manager Allen Klein. John said he thought the bottle cost $1,000 but was a bit spooked by this because Klein was suing him and might therefore have good reason to poison him. He suggested that someone in our company should taste the wine before everyone else took a drink.

Looking around he said, "Well Keith, you can't taste it because you're the drummer with The Who so you can't die, and you need your assistant Dougal. I'm John Lennon, a famous Beatle, and I can't die either. May Pang is my companion at the moment and I don't want her to die, therefore the only one of us left to taste the wine is you Chris... so here you are."

The bottle was duly opened, John poured some wine into a glass and I sampled it as the others all stared at me. There was a moment's silence while they waited to see whether I would keel over on the spot, and I was half tempted to clutch my throat and make a gargling sound – but to this day, that was the finest glass of wine I've ever tasted in my entire life, so rich, so full-bodied, bursting with flavour. "It's absolutely fantastic," I said. It was duly shared out, but once the wine had gone Keith was eager to move on, so we left.

As we were waiting for the elevator Keith needed to take a pee but was reluctant to return to John's suite and disturb him. So he peed down the Pierre Hotel laundry shaft instead.

On Friday, the final night of The Who's week of shows at the Garden, Pete smashed three of his Gibson Les Pauls and Keith joined in, chucking his drum kit everywhere and smashing the fourth and only remaining guitar. I was told that Bob Pridden had taken delivery of around a dozen Les Pauls from Manny's, the music shop on West 48th Street, and would return the unused ones at the end of the week.

I took along my new friend Debbie Harry, and we sat together on John's side, a few rows up from the stage. No doubt keenly aware how Chris Stein had saved up for his guitars, she was appalled by the destruction. Backstage in the dressing room after the show Roger tried to put the make on her – "Fuckin' 'ell Chris, that bird looks just like fuckin' Marilyn Monroe" – as did Keith, equally unsubtly. She didn't respond to either of their advances, I'm happy to report, which didn't please Roger whose success rate in this department was always very high.

Debbie spent the rest of the evening with me, taking in an after-show party at a roller-dome where we danced a lot and Bob Gruen, ever on my trail, took more photographs, including several of us together. It was a lavish affair where 1,500 guests, among them Elton and assorted Beach Boys, were entertained by Ronnie Spector & The Ronettes.

The Who wouldn't perform together again for 14 months.

21

"Chris, do you know Pattie?"
Robert Stigwood, Pittsburgh, July 1974

Shortly before *Diamond Dogs* was released in late May I was summoned to Mainman's New York HQ to hear it. Tony Defries, David Bowie's manager, firmly believed that to be a star you must look and behave like one, even if you are not, and since by now David certainly was a star, the circus surrounding him was bordering on the absurd, on a par with Elvis. To this end I was restricted to a single hearing of *Diamond Dogs*, not allowed to record it – I was temporarily relieved of my cassette recorder – just take notes, and generally treated like some sort of sub-species by the unpleasant people there, one of whom lingered as I listened, observing me as a warder might a high-risk prisoner.

In these circumstances reviewing a record isn't easy, and I wasn't even given a lyric sheet, so to come up with 900 words, as I managed to do, was quite an achievement. "Bowie's new album really is excellent," I wrote, not my most insightful review, when I returned to the flat and read back my scribbled notes. "It's a departure from his previous records in that the Spiders are no longer with him, and it's also a departure in that the whole production of the songs is far more lavish than anything he's previously attempted. For most of the tracks, he's adopted a 'wall of sound' technique, borrowed not a little from Phil Spector, but the richness of it all enhances his voice no end. He's also moved further into rock and roll – there's hardly a slow song on the album – and played all the chunky guitar licks himself, according to the sleeve credits."

Because of the almost paranoid secrecy surrounding David and his activities, I wasn't to know that this record would form the basis of a new stage show I would watch in Canada on June 16. Invited to the O'Keefe Centre in Toronto to review this third show of his *Diamond Dogs Revue* tour, along with a party of other music writers, I was convinced that David had re-invented the concept of rock theatre.

It could be argued that Alice Cooper started it all but, compared to what David did on this tour, Alice was a Punch and Judy show. It being a Sunday night I had to write up my longish review very quickly, in longhand on hotel notepaper, then wait until about four in the morning to call London (10am UK time) and dictate 1,600 words over the phone to Marilyne. We'd progressed from carrier pigeons but e-mails were as remote as Major Tom. It filled page three of that week's *MM*.

"A few thousand lucky Canadians witnessed a completely new concept in rock theatre when David Bowie opened his North American tour in Toronto on Sunday," I wrote. "It now seems likely that Bowie was speaking the truth when he announced his retirement from rock on the stage at the Hammersmith Odeon last year. For the act that David presents on this tour has as much to do with rock and roll as Bob Dylan has with the gloss of Las Vegas.

"The one-and-a-half-hour, 20-song show is a completely rehearsed and choreographed routine where every step and nuance has been perfected down to the last detail. There isn't one iota of spontaneity about the whole show. It is straight off a musical stage – a piece of theatre, complete with extravagant mechanical sets, dancers and a band that stands reservedly to stage right and never even receives so much as a cursory acknowledgement, like an orchestra in a theatre pit.

"The show belongs on Broadway or Shaftesbury Avenue rather than on the road. The whole concept takes a complete turnaround from what a rock audience anticipates, but at Toronto on Sunday it left them stunned. Perhaps the crowd at the O'Keefe Centre literally couldn't believe their eyes... not once did Bowie address the audience, or even allude to their presence other than an odd grin... He was dressed in a light grey suit with blue and white polka dot, collarless shirt, and red braces. He retained the same outfit for the entire performance, apart from removing his jacket. He appeared without any noticeable make-up and gone was the spiky hair style of last year and the year before. In its place was a neat parting; it left little doubt about the masculinity of the performer.

"Fittingly there was no encore and the applauding audience was greeted with the announcement ten minutes after the show stopped that Bowie had already left the theatre. The Colonel Parker touch is forever there."

This show never came to the UK. I would see it again at Madison Square Garden in July but the theatrics didn't really work in an arena and it wasn't long before the expensive props were put away for good. In the meantime, Bowie's band – led by session bassist Herbie Flowers – had threatened to go on strike after a show in Philadelphia was recorded and they received no additional remuneration. It was released as *David Live*.

Without the props, the tour continued on the West Coast, merging the *Diamond Dogs* songs with David's increasing interest in soul music, after which he retired to Los Angeles to lick his wounds, anaesthetising them with cocaine. The following year he released his blue-eyed soul LP *Young Americans*, its funked-up US No. 1 hit single 'Fame' a collaboration with John Lennon that savaged his relationship with manager Defries.

*

Among other acts that I interviewed during the first half of 1974 were Dr Hook, Rick Derringer, Loggins & Messina, Buffy St Marie, Harry Chapin and Gary Puckett, whose 'Young Girl', a 1968 hit with his band The Union Gap, had mysteriously re-entered the UK charts in June. Editor Ray was always asking me to chase up oddities like this and, as it happened, Gary was in the Philippines shooting a movie so I spoke to him on the phone since no one offered to fly me there.

I went to see Dr Hook at a club in New Jersey, driven there in a limousine courtesy of Columbia Records. I chatted with Ray Sawyer who wore an eye patch, the result of a car crash, and Dennis Lacorriere, their singer, in a cramped dressing room and watched a lively show afterwards. They were a light-hearted lot that reminded me a bit of Lindisfarne but what I remember most about my night out with Dr Hook was that someone with a gun took a shot at the limousine as we were leaving. The driver sped off down the road and after a couple of minutes got out to inspect the damage. Sure enough, there was a scratch where the bullet ricocheted off the bodywork at the rear. I have no idea why this happened. Perhaps our rifleman simply didn't like limousines.

I liked Harry Chapin a lot. He reminded me of a schoolteacher but his heart was in the right place and that was where his songs came from. After a career in which philanthropy played a key role, in 1981 he was tragically killed in a motor accident, aged just 39.

My mid-summer highlights, however, were seeing Eric Clapton at Three River Stadium in Pittsburgh, PA, on July 5, and Crosby, Stills, Nash & Young, at Denver in Colorado two weeks later. On the same bill as Clapton were The Band, friends of his from Big Pink days who'd steered him away from the excesses of Cream, but their music, Americana at its very best, was lost on the massive crowd eager to see their guitar hero. I was looking forward to seeing him too as I'd been sent an advance copy of *461 Ocean Boulevard* which I liked a lot. What I remember most about this trip, however, was meeting Pattie Harrison, George's wife, who arrived at the side of the stage midway through Eric's set.

With their affair yet to become public knowledge I was ignorant of the whole business until I saw her being ushered in by Robert Stigwood, Clapton's manager. I recognised her, of course, but couldn't for the life of me figure out why she was here. Before long, however, the affectionate glances between her and the chap in the middle with the Fender Strat around his neck led me to the obvious conclusion.

"Chris, do you know Pattie?" asked Stigwood as the two of them assumed a position close to where I was standing.

"Er, no," I stammered. "Pleasure to meet you."

As we shook hands I could see where the attraction lay. Pattie Harrison was indeed lovely; slim of figure in tight-waisted bell-bottom jeans and a pale blue silky top, angelic of features with soft blonde hair that tumbled down around her shoulders, the slight gap in the top row of her teeth giving her a childlike innocence that was enormously becoming. Keith Moon had declared his admiration for her to me at his house in Chertsey when I interviewed him there three years past, but Keith, though a model of indiscretion in most respects, was far too deferential towards The Beatles to proposition one of their wives, as Pattie then was and, for that matter, still was, at least on paper. Eric was evidently more determined – or more infatuated.

In hindsight, I have reason to believe that Pattie's arrival was engineered by Stigwood in the hope that she might curb Eric's consumption of alcohol. In the event he was wrong, for July 5 happened to be the 31st birthday of Robbie Robertson, the leading figure in The Band. To be honest, though, Eric didn't need an excuse to hit the whisky bottle in those days, being pretty much pissed as a newt most of the time. Before the show he was staggering around backstage trying to discover the whereabouts of The Band, then elsewhere in the vastness of Three Rivers Stadium. Each time he asked someone they'd reply something along the lines of "right here, Eric."

"Not my band, THE Band," he'd say, exasperated. "It's Robbie's birthday today and... there's gonna be some bovver tonight."

Remarkably, Eric's inebriated state made not one iota of difference to the vigour of his performance. Perhaps facing 42,000 fans – the biggest crowd ever at Three Rivers – had a sobering effect, but when he walked on stage, acoustic in hand, followed by his group and preceded by Legs Larry Smith, the English country joker, late of the Bonzos, acting as compere, he seemed completely in control.

Legs Larry had been hired to play down the superstar angle that Eric wanted to shake off, as had Yvonne Elliman, an easy-on-the-eye Hawaiian singer whose main contribution to the set came early on, during the acoustic songs. Eric, wearing a floppy hat and shabby dungarees, opened the show with 'Smile', the old standard written, oddly enough, by Charlie Chaplin that came as something as a surprise at first but seemed more and more apt after continued hearings. It sent out a message of good vibes from the start – "Smile, when your heart is achin'" – and quietened down an audience eager for high-powered rock. 'Smile' moved into 'Let It Grow', another easy-going acoustic song with Eric and Elliman singing harmoniously together, then 'Can't Find My Way Home', Steve Winwood's Blind Faith song. Slotted hurriedly between them at Pittsburgh was a spontaneous 'Happy Birthday' for Robertson who was now standing at the opposite side of the stage to where I was. Its significance was lost on the crowd.

With the acoustic exchanged for a Stratocaster we were into the main course. During 'Blues Power', the first electric number, Eric was hit hard on the side of the face by a well-aimed missile that turned out to be a New Testament, wrapped in a small chain with a message from the local Jesus freaks. Not knowing what had hit him, he fumed for a bar or two, picked up the tempo again and bellowed his disapproval down the microphone. Then Pattie arrived, soothing the situation as the set progressed, Eric for the most part delivering songs from the forthcoming *461 Ocean Boulevard*, with 'Motherless Children' and 'Mainline Florida' offering ample opportunities for everyone to stretch out.

The closing song of the set proper was Chuck Berry's 'Little Queenie', enlivened by a re-appearance of Legs Larry who smashed a plastic ukulele à la Townshend, hurling the debris into the crowd. As encores, after much cheering, there followed 'Tell The Truth' and a lengthy, turbo-charged 'Crossroads' that generated the most inspired soloing of the night.

For those who seldom experience it, there is something positively awe-inspiring about standing on a stage a few feet from a rock superstar playing to an audience in excess of 40,000; the vast sea of faces stretching out into the distance, the waves of adulation they release, the deafening on-stage volume of the music, the whole experience amplified for me this night by the freshly realised knowledge that the superstar's mistress, the wife of a Beatle no less, was standing right next to me. Surreal is a much-overused expression, but it certainly applied here. She was smiling towards the man with the guitar, and every so often, as 'Crossroads' surged like a tsunami, he would glance across as he played and smile back at her.

Back at the hotel Eric found The Band, or they found him, and even Pattie was unable to curb the carousing that went on well into the night. Robertson, a man of fairly sober habits next to his team mates, retired early but Rick Danko and Richard Manuel kept the party going in Danko's room until dawn broke, by which time Pattie had dragged Eric back to their suite. I recall seeing him reeling down a corridor, the slight figure of his paramour steadying him as they lurched along. As it happened, that night I befriended Danko who two years later would try to put the make on my sister after a Band concert in New York – but that's another story.

*

Almost three weeks after the Eric Clapton concert, on July 25, I was at the side of another big stage before another huge crowd, this time Crosby, Stills, Nash & Young at Mile High Stadium in Denver. Unstable and prone to outbreaks of verbal squabbling between themselves, CSN&Y nevertheless set aside their differences to undertake a big tour of the US in the summer of 1974, proving to one and all that they were unquestionably the most popular American band of the era. As with Eric, I watched from the side of the stage, gazing out over a vast crowd though this time it was two wired up Americans, one cool Canadian and one delighted Englishman a few feet away from me.

Flown in from New York courtesy of Atlantic Records, I stayed in the same hotel as the group and in the afternoon interviewed Graham Nash. Stephen Stills had been quoted as saying that the first time CS&N went out on the road was for art, the second time for the girls and this, the third, for the dollars, but Graham took exception to this. "We're doing it for the music, man, because all of us know that none of us can make as good music together as we can apart," he told me. Unlike Crosby and Stills, Nash was thin and wiry, and he spoke so passionately that I couldn't help but believe him. Stills wandered into the room at one point, and was very friendly. Nash introduced us. "This is Chris, from *Melody Maker* in London."

"Hi English," said Stills, recognising me from our earlier meeting in New York.

Later in the afternoon I found myself in the elevator with Neil Young, a pure coincidence, but was too overawed to speak. He was thin and wiry like Graham, and travelling separately from CS&N in a motor home with his wife and dogs. "Each night he packs up his guitar, wife, baby son and dog and hits the road," Crosby told me after the show.

It was a warm night and watching the show from the stage was another unforgettable rock experience. At 9 pm, three-quarters of an hour after The Beach Boys, CSN&Y appeared to a standing ovation, and for the next three hours they joyously celebrated their reunion alongside Tim Drummond on bass, Russ Kunkel on drums and Joe Lala on congas. The ovation washing over them, the four principals moved to the front, Stills to the left and Young to the right, with Crosby and Nash in the centre bobbing between mics and occasionally sharing. They opened with Stills' 'Love The One You're With'.

The show was divided into two halves with a 15-minute break. The first, the longest, opened with an electric set and switched to acoustic, with the second half all electric, and different combinations of CSN&Y took songs in turn. Those numbers where all four played and sang together were undoubtedly the highlights.

Crosby's 'Wooden Ships', with Young at the grand piano, followed 'Love The One', then Nash went over to the keyboard for 'Immigration Man', Stills taking the guitar solo. A new Neil Young song, 'Traces', followed with Young playing a huge Gretsch White Falcon and trading guitar breaks with Stills. Crosby stepped up next for 'Almost Cut My Hair', screaming out the vocals above the combined backing. For this song, Nash moved over to the organ, but again it was Stills' guitar that carried the weight. Young's turn came next with 'Cowgirl In The Sand' and the first electric set ended with all four joining together for 'Pre-Road Downs'.

Five minutes later about a dozen acoustic guitars were set up around two stools and four mikes. Firstly, Young appeared alone to sing 'Only Love Can Break Your Heart' and 'Old Man', then Crosby followed with a new song called 'For Free', and Nash followed with two songs at the piano, 'Simple Man' and 'Prison Song'. For the latter he was joined by the whole band and they stayed in place for Young's 'Sugar Mountain' which inspired a mass sing-along, appropriate as we were in the foothills of the Rockies.

Stills offered 'Change Partners', sung by the whole band, and 'Questions' which he played alone. I'd have preferred '4 + 20'. The acoustic set closed with 'Suite: Judy Blue Eyes', all four tearing into this mythical song and, although some of the harmonies were occasionally a little off-pitch, they handled a long and difficult piece with the kind of assurance that comes only from those who'd created it.

The second half opened with Crosby's 'Long Time Coming', followed by Young on 'Don't Be Denied' and Stills with a new song called 'First Things First' on which he played congas. Crosby offered 'Déjà Vu' before Young played two more new songs, 'Revolution Blues' and 'Pushed It Over The End', on which both he and Stills soloed at length. The concert ended with 'Ohio', a great crowd favourite, another sing-along, but they returned for one encore, a lengthy 'Carry On' that proved equally popular.

The cheers were deafening but after a quick wave they left the stage fast, Neil heading for his camper truck and the others to black limousines. On the way past me Stephen stopped for a second. "Hey, English," he shouted. "What da ya think?" I couldn't think what to say so I just gave him a thumbs-up.

I lingered for a while as the crowd was leaving, taking in what I'd seen. As with Clapton, I'd found myself it a position to watch a gigantic crowd from the performer's standpoint, seeing them react to songs, the waves of delight, the ovations, the sheer pleasure of experiencing all this on a warm night in Colorado amidst the Rocky Mountains. What a fucking great job I had.

I watched the crowd disperse then knelt down next to a monitor and scribbled away in a notepad, anxious not to forget the songs they'd played and whatever thoughts I had while still fresh. After a while I put my notepad away and spotted a blonde girl in jeans and a yellow top on her own, down at the front, gazing up at the crew clearing the stage. I shouted to her, asking if she'd enjoyed the show. "It was great," she yelled back. "What are you doing later?" I asked. She shrugged. "Come to the party at the hotel," I shouted and lobbed my hotel room keys down to her. She caught them and laughed so I hoped for the best.

There was a party in the hotel, in a reception room high up on the top floor. Stephen kept calling me "English" and David didn't stint on the wine. I'd taken my pocket tape recorder along. "Where's Neil?" I asked David. "He's two miles out of town by now and so high on the show that nothing can touch him," he replied. "He's out there so happy. He came and did what he had to do for three hours and knows he did it well. Nothing can make a man happier than that."

David and Graham seemed the most enthused by the show, Graham especially. In fact, he seemed as high as a kite, rushing here and there and refusing to stop talking to anyone who'd listen. "It was a dramatic want to play music together again. A real need, man," he replied when I asked point blank what motivated them to reunite. "I think we realised about a year ago that we had a really fucking hot band if we wanted and we could really make this hot music. We missed each other, y'know. We missed that bounce off. When there's four of yer up there and there's Stephen at one side and Neil at the other and me and David in the middle. Just watching them converse with each other. That's it, y'know. That's it. Like tonight, when we did 'Sugar Mountain', we stopped playing and heard 60,000 people sing back at us. Do you know what a rush that is?"

Of course, I knew. I was about 20 feet away from him for the whole show.

I stayed at the party for a couple of hours hoping my friend with the room key would show up but she didn't. It was the only disappointment of another fabulously memorable night.

22

"It's Mr Grant to you, ya fuckin' cunt."
Peter Grant, New York City, August 1974

In the summer months I was a regular visitor to the Wollman ice skating rink in New York's Central Park, not to skate as ice froze only in winter, but to see rock shows at the Schaefer Music Festival, a series of open-air concerts held there in June, July and August. The arena held about 6,000 and entry was cheap, $1.50 and $2.50 closer to the stage. In August, the hottest month in the city, two shows stood out for similar reasons: Anne Murray and Foghat.

Anne Murray's management made the terrible mistake of having Bruce Springsteen as her opening act. Not only were they musically incompatible but so were their fans, many of whom either left when Ms Murray came on or chanted "we want Bruce" during her set. "If Bruce is unclean but emotional Anne is clean but unemotional. Bruce could harm but Anne is harmless," I wrote, noting that her audience included many gay women. "Although poles apart Bruce Springsteen and Anne Murray mean a great deal to a great many," I added.

Foghat were similarly overshadowed by their support act, in this case Bad Company whose eponymous debut LP, released in May, went to number one in the US *Billboard* charts, while the single they picked from it, 'Can't Get Enough', went Top Five. Managed by Led Zeppelin supremo Peter Grant, Bad Co were formed from the remnants of Free – singer Paul Rodgers and drummer Simon Kirke – along with guitarist Mick Ralphs from Mott The Hoople and bass player Boz Burrell from King Crimson. As if this wasn't sufficient to guarantee instant success, in the US they were on Led Zep's own Swan Song record label with all the promotional clout of Atlantic Records behind it.

In fact, Bad Co's debut LP was number one the week they supported Foghat at the Schaefer show and when Jimmy Page joined them on stage for an encore, it was icing on the rink. The audience went berserk; a tough act to follow and many in the crowd began to leave after Jimmy skipped off. I saw Foghat looking mighty pissed off backstage, and accepted Peter Grant's invitation to head back to the Essex House hotel for a drink with him, Jimmy and Bad Co.

There were two limos backstage for Page, Grant and Bad Co, and I was offered a ride in the one with Jimmy and Peter. Alas, as he climbed into the back seat the driver slammed the door shut, catching Peter's foot in it. Unwise.

Peter exploded. "What the fuck do ya' think ya' fuckin' doing, ya' fuckin' cunt!" Displeasing Led Zeppelin's fearsome manager was no laughing matter and the luckless driver compounded his sin by calling Peter by his Christian name when he apologised. "Who the fuck told ya' you could call me Peter? It's Mr Grant to you, ya' fuckin' cunt!"

You could have cut the atmosphere with a knife. All the way back to the Essex House he continued to yell at the driver, 15 minutes or more of relentless abuse. "You'll never drive another fuckin' car again, ya' fuckin' useless cunt!" Jimmy looked on impassively. We sat there in embarrassed silence, not daring to speak while Peter shouted and ranted. I thought it unwise to remark that, professional as they were, in my opinion Bad Company lacked the sprightliness of Free and that Mick Ralphs wasn't as imaginative a guitarist as the doomed Paul Kossoff.

*

At the other end of rock's class divide, I maintained my interest in promoting unsigned acts by writing a feature about those who performed at CBGBs, which really was an unholy dump – the loos ought to have been condemned – and the undulating fortunes of one of them, Teenage Lust, a band that had an unexpected, albeit brief, brush with the big time when their trio of girl singers found themselves backing John Lennon alongside Elephant's Memory at Madison Square Garden in 1972. "When we get rich," said comely Laurie Malone, who like her fellow Lustettes dressed for the stage in black underwear, "we're gonna open up a lounge where we play all the time. It'll be called the Lust Lounge and we'll make it."

Alas, they didn't but they had fun trying.

A week later I was back at the other end of the divide, mixing with both Rod Stewart and Ron Wood. Still notionally Faces, both were in New York together but roaming separately, Rod touting his forthcoming *Smiler* LP and Ron his first solo outing, *I've Got My Own Album To Do*, and in a seemingly pointless spirit of competition, both record companies – Mercury for Rod and Warner Bros for Ron – hosted lunches in posh restaurants for their artists on the same day, thus creating a dilemma for me since I was invited to both. Lunch with Rod or lunch with Ron? I opted for Ron, largely because I had an interview scheduled with Rod the next day and needed to write something about Ron too.

Honest Ron was a great luncheon companion, hilariously indiscreet about the rivalry between him and his Faces pal with a similar haircut. Probably due to the competing luncheon elsewhere in town, there weren't many of us around the table and since he was a natural comedian he kept us all entertained with his banter, a bit of cheek, a bit risqué, a bit "cor-blimey guv". The idea was to promote his solo LP but I don't recall him mentioning it at all. Mick Taylor had yet to leave the Stones so the issue of his replacement wasn't on the table, but like pretty much everyone else observing the trajectory of the Faces, I wasn't surprised by the vagueness with which Ron spoke around the subject of their future. "Don't ask me?" he said. Which rather begged the question, well who do I ask? Rod didn't seem to know either, or was unwilling to dwell on the subject. Ron was more affable, a good deal friendlier than Rod, and I turned what he had to say into a few paragraphs in my weekly New York news column. Rod, on the other hand, required something more substantial.

I'd met Rod Stewart several times already. He'd paid his dues the proper way, rising up from the clubs where I saw him that time with Steampacket, but he was a bit of a cocky bugger, a sort of cross between a cockney Jack the Lad (which he wasn't, of course) and a canny Scotsman (which he was, sort of) whose wallet required a jemmy to prise it open. I'd been a big supporter of the Faces, writing glowing reviews of shows in both the UK and US, and he seemed well disposed towards us on *MM*, not least because he won our Top Male Singer poll award in 1972 and came to the presentation. He liked to win awards. He liked to be the centre of attention. He liked applause. I suppose he had every right to be a cocky bugger.

He had a house at Windsor in the early seventies and occasionally dropped into the Fox & Hounds, the pub in Englefield Green where I once lived and still had friends. I used to go back there from time to time to see them and one night I was there when Rod turned up. He wasn't expecting to see me and looked at me warily. Unlike in pre-arranged situations, or backstage or even in clubs frequented by musicians, unexpected encounters between music writers and rock stars like this, in out of the way places, can be slightly awkward, as was this. I watched him playing to the crowd as regulars bought him drinks. He invariably asked for a large brandy, but he never bought a round himself which caused a bit of muttering among the locals. I suppose he was used to lackeys buying him drinks and had difficulty adjusting to a different environment. That night when he left the pub he found he'd left the lights of his yellow Lamborghini on and the battery was flat, so he went back into the pub and asked for a push. No one volunteered and there were a few smirks but I felt a sort of filial duty to someone from what was now my world and went outside to take a look. Of course, there was no way in hell that one person could push a Lamborghini, especially a yellow one, so he had to get a cab back home and, presumably, return the following day with a mechanic, all of which would have cost him considerably more than a round of drinks.

I think there was a touch of hubris about the way in which his relationship with the press deteriorated. He didn't like criticism. Promoting his fifth solo LP *Smiler* in New York in 1974, he was on the defensive, perhaps sensing that the tide was turning and the unanimous acclaim he'd enjoyed during that glorious run of solo LPs, beginning in 1969 with *An Old Raincoat Won't Ever Let You Down* up to 1972's *Never A Dull Moment*, might be drawing to a close. Perhaps in his heart of hearts he knew that *Smiler* wasn't in the same league.

In the past he'd been chatty, friendly, but now he was behaving as if he expected the interview to turn into a confrontation. "Well, what do you want to know?" he asked when I switched on my tape recorder. "Come on Chris, ask me questions." It was as if he'd decided to attack before I could, assuming that was my intention. He was unnecessarily abrupt, almost aggressive, though he knew full well I'd been a supporter but he didn't trust us writers any longer. Still, I managed to scratch together a 1,500-word piece for the following week's *MM*, dated August 31. It was headlined "I Dream Of A Solo Concert", a quote from the interview. "There's gotta be a chance of it happening with all the people that appear on my albums," he said, his eyes glistening at the thought. "I've asked them and they all say I ought to do it someday. Mmmm, lovely acoustic guitar behind me. I'll get around to it. It's just a question of time."

He was right there.

*

In September I reported on a Beatles fan convention at the Commodore Hotel. The brainchild of 24-year-old Beatle fan Mark Lapidos, I believe it was the first event of its kind to be held anywhere, a precursor to countless fan conventions for all manner of acts today. Mark had run the idea past John Lennon and got a thumbs up, so much so that as competition prizes both John and Paul donated guitars, George a tabla and Ringo some drum sticks. False rumours suggested that John, heavily disguised, actually attended but he didn't. Instead, he sent along May Pang to pick up any Beatles memorabilia on sale that she thought John might like, and when she spotted me she asked my advice about what to buy for him. John had already told me he was keen on collecting Beatles bootlegs but since I didn't know what he already had, I wasn't sure what to recommend to May. But I reasoned that John wouldn't mind having more than one copy of a bootleg, and since money was no object she invested in several that I thought he might like.

I also saw some original pictures of The Beatles in Hamburg, taken in 1960 by their friend Jurgen Volmer, including one where John was stood in a doorway wearing a leather jacket with his hair in a rocker's quiff. I drew May's attention to this, and we chatted with Volmer who was selling his pictures. May bought a print of it and the next time I saw that picture of John in the Hamburg doorway it was on the cover of his 1975 LP *Rock 'N' Roll*.

Talking of the Commodore Hotel, I interviewed Lowell George who met his Dixie Chicken beneath a streetlamp in one of many great tracks recorded by his band Little Feat. They played at the Bottom Line in September, packing the club out for two shows and in the audience was Bob Dylan, keeping a low profile, albeit surrounded by friends who prevented anyone from approaching him. Truth is, I loved Little Feat, still do, and Lowell was one of the humblest musicians I ever encountered, this despite the reverence in which he was held by his peers. "Mostly we play music with what I would call a stream of consciousness," he told me in the Warner Bros offices the day after the show. "We want to explore all sorts of areas together. I love country and western music so we play country songs with a twist in them."

This was the first of three interviews I would do with Lowell over the next two years but other interviews I did that September were with George McCrae, KC & The Sunshine Band, Don Covay and Loudon Wainwright III, a droll character unimpressed by the trappings of fame. When I asked Loudon what he liked to do in his spare time he replied, "Watch TV and smoke cigarettes." I saw him for the first time in London in 1971, supporting The Everly Brothers at the Royal Albert Hall, where Teddy Boys booed him off. When I mentioned this he said, "Yes, I remember that too. Everybody remembers me as that guy who walked off stage. It was just a question of the wrong venue for me really but I think I've made it up in England since." He was a very funny fellow, given to quite strange utterances, and he told me that the song about a dead skunk was based on a real incident. "It really did stink."

I also found myself in Hammond, Indiana, reporting on how Hawkwind's equipment had been impounded by Internal Revenue Service agents, allegedly for not paying taxes owed to the US government. "The agents were waiting for the group when they came off stage," Hawkwind's manager Doug Smith told me. "They literally took the guitars off their back as they went to the dressing room."

The equipment, he told me, was locked in a room at the venue in Hammond with stickers saying "Property of The US Government" on it. "It's worth between $25,000 and $30,000 which is a great deal more than the tax they claim we owe them." A show in Toledo, Ohio, was cancelled. "The way Hawkwind work is on a day-to-day basis, paying their way as we go along, so we can't afford to miss shows because of things like this."

I'd been invited along to report on the tour but found myself unable to do so. Instead, I opted to defend Hawkwind against the Blue Meanies from the IRS. "It was a particularly odious act by the authorities to impound their instruments and thus prevent them from making their livelihood," I wrote. "Would they confiscate a carpenter's hammer or a painter's brush in similar circumstances?"

*

Unlike today, biographies of rock stars were something of a rarity in 1974, which was why I chose to lead my New York news column with an item about *Me Alice*, a biography of Alice Cooper written by my friend Steven Gaines, the music writer I'd appointed as my deputy when I was out of town. As part of his research Gaines played a few rounds of golf with Alice. Not to be outdone, so did I, along with Alice's PR and sidekick Ashley Pandel, now a close friend. The three of us spent a Saturday afternoon on Pelham Bay, an 18-hole course in the North Bronx, and it was soon clear that Alice – like Iggy Pop – could swing a club like a pro. One chip from the fairway actually found the hole, much to his delight.

Chatting as we played, it seemed to me that Alice wanted to clean up his image. In real life he was very different from the monster he portrayed on stage, though it was this side of his personality that created a problem the last time he passed through immigration at Heathrow Airport. "Am I still on the 'unwanted' list at customs in England?" he asked me on the third tee. I told him I hadn't a clue, so he recounted the incident to me. "I showed my passport at customs at Heathrow and the next thing I knew I was taken aside and kept for an hour while inquiries were made about me."

"Sorry about that," I said, as if I, being English, was somehow responsible.

"It seems that trouble with Leo Abse [a Welsh MP who tried to get Cooper banned from the UK] had caused my name to get amongst a list of undesirables. In the end they let me in but that MP caused plenty of trouble. I'm thinking of dedicating my next LP to him and his daughters who brought the matter up in the first place.

"I mean, I've never been busted or had any drug convictions. I'm not a revolutionary who preaches communism and yet I'm placed on the undesirable list all the same. I even did a commercial here in the States recently telling kids to keep away from drugs. I said, 'If I catch you taking drugs I'll come around and bite your puppy's head off' which got me into even more trouble. Can't seem to do anything right these days."

One thing Alice did right was play golf. He completed his round in 82 shots, only 12 over par, while Ashley and myself, hacking away in and out of the rough, were somewhere in three figures, a failure we flippantly put down to the conditions, wet and windy. Back in the clubhouse, Alice signed his autograph for the golf professional who'd somehow learned the identity of the long-haired player in white.

"I'm off to the Bahamas next week for a few day's holiday," said Alice as he wiped down his immaculate set of clubs. "All that sunshine and all that golf… can't wait."

*

My first spell as *Melody Maker*'s man in America was drawing to a close. Just before I left I reviewed clean-living John Denver at Madison Square Garden – "The first time I've attended a Garden show and not smelled the sweet aroma of marijuana as I took my seat," I reported – and Joe Cocker at the Academy of Music, a man whose dedication to the art of not living cleanly was beginning to tell.

"It is with a heavy heart that I take up my typewriter to inform you that Joe Cocker is a shadow of his former self," I wrote. "The once great voice that thrilled thousands has succumbed to the punishment Joe has enjoyed during his lay-offs. No longer does it have the power and range but, more importantly, no longer does it have the soul that cried out for pity so well in years gone by. That cry of pity comes today from the head rather than the heart. While not going as far to say Joe's all washed up, I can say without hesitation that Cocker is but a shadow of the best white soul singer he once was. On stage he was Joe Cocker acting out the Joe Cocker act, or trying to anyway. He came over, in fact, as a stumbling drunk. The audience cheered former glories rather than the night's performance."

Relieved of my posting as *Melody Maker*'s man in New York during the last two months of 1974, I missed John Lennon's last ever appearance on stage, with Elton at Madison Square Garden on November 28, always a source of disappointment to me. Michael Watts briefly resumed the role of American Editor so that I might re-acquaint myself with what was happening in the UK, so I packed my one suitcase, left the key to the apartment with a neighbour and took a cab to JFK.

I knew I'd be back, sooner than expected too.

23

"Sometimes I get people tramping through my garden and asking for my autograph because they've heard I'm in a pop group. They probably think we're like Gary Glitter."
Rick Wright, Glasgow, November 1974

Ray Coleman was at a bit of a loss to know what to do with me when I arrived back in London. Before I left for the US I'd been the paper's News Editor but this role was now filled, with distinction, by Rob Partridge. In the event, because I'd spent so much time travelling he decided I'd become *MM*'s Roving Reporter, a new position, and to this end I went to Belfast to report on rock, or lack of it, in the capital of Northern Ireland, to Manchester and Glasgow to report on the state of commercial radio in those cities, and to Clearwell Castle in Gloucestershire where Bad Company were rehearsing for a forthcoming tour. I was even coerced into writing a two-part feature on airports, flying and how to avoid getting busted in customs. Pure filler really.

I also reviewed concerts outside of London, the most memorable of which were Pink Floyd in Edinburgh on Bonfire Night, The Bay City Rollers on tour for three wildly chaotic shows in Cardiff, Hanley and Edinburgh, and John Entwistle, who took his own band on the road in December.

Of all the globally elite British groups of the seventies, none kept a lower profile than Pink Floyd. They didn't employ a PR, relying on their record company to send out review tickets to music magazines, interviews were conducted with great reluctance and if EMI insisted on throwing a party to launch an album, as they did with *Dark Side Of The Moon* at the London Planetarium, then the Floyd famously sent along cardboard cut-outs of themselves, partly as a sort of a droll joke but mainly because they simply couldn't be bothered to attend. They once boasted that after a gig at New York's Madison Square Garden they actually mingled with the crowds who were leaving and weren't recognised, and there was even a press ad that featured the backs of their heads.

The members of Pink Floyd maintained a sort of aloof, couldn't-care-less attitude, as if courting the press and giving interviews was somehow beneath them. This may have stemmed from the affluent upbringing of Nick Mason and Rick Wright, well-heeled folk being traditionally ambivalent towards the media, but it was also a symptom of the anonymity they sought: none of the increasingly successful albums that followed *Ummagumma* in 1969 featured photographs of them on their sleeves and on stage the four musicians eschewed spotlights, obscuring themselves beneath a giant circular screen on which were projected light shows and eye-catching film footage, or giant mobiles that drew attention away from the boys in the band.

With press contact minimal I opted to ambush Pink Floyd in Edinburgh. I simply found out the hotel where they were staying by ringing around and booked myself in. I gained admittance to their concert at the Usher Hall by buying a ticket from a tout, which was most unusual since virtually every other act on the planet laid out the red carpet for *MM* staff in those days. "As in previous Floyd tours there was no supporting act and the concert was in two halves," I reported. "For the first hour the group played three new pieces and for the second *The Dark Side Of The Moon* in its entirety. They also came back to play 'Echoes' as an encore, after considerable persuasion and football-style chants of 'We Shall Not Be Moved' from the audience."

Afterwards, hanging around in the lobby, I was looked upon with deep suspicion by Floyd's entourage. Fortunately, the promoter was Harvey Goldsmith and through him I somehow managed to ingratiate myself into the large Floyd party and eat a sumptuous post-gig supper with them around a huge table in a private room. At first, I sat alongside their manager Steve O'Rourke who seemed an agreeable chap if you were prepared to talk about fast cars but before the food arrived, I was asked to move by Storm Thorgerson from the Hipgnosis design team. "There's something important I need to discuss with Steve," he told me. Over dinner I detected an atmosphere of civilised maturity; none of the japes, womanising and loutish behaviour brought on by a surfeit of alcohol or drugs that were the hallmark of post-concert parties thrown by so many other groups. Pink Floyd, I realised, were adults, and they behaved like them too.

I was determined to get an interview and collared Steve O'Rourke before everyone retired for the night. He said he'd do his best. None of them really wanted to be interviewed by me but the following day I found myself face to face over a tape recorder with keyboard player Rick Wright, who'd evidently drawn the shortest straw. I would have preferred to interview Roger Waters but he was unwilling as he wanted to play golf, there being many fine courses close to Edinburgh. I was astonished that Waters, whose lyrical preoccupations were space-flight, insanity and death, was a keen golfer.

Unlike almost all of their contemporaries Pink Floyd in those days performed new songs on stage before they had actually been recorded, a fairly brave move since bootleggers might record shows and release material before it came out through official channels. At the Usher Hall the previous night they'd performed 'Shine On You Crazy Diamond' which wouldn't be made available until *Wish You Here* was released a year later and two other new pieces, 'Raving And Drooling' and 'Gotta Be Crazy', both of which eventually surfaced on *Animals* no less than three years later, in 1977, retitled 'Sheep' and 'Dogs' respectively.

"I can't think of any other bands that work this way," said Wright over a cup of tea in the hotel lobby. "Usually bands record songs and then play them but we feel that if you do a few tours with a number, then that number improves immensely. We will probably record them after the tour."

Wright turned out to be a friendly, loquacious interviewee, to some degree dispelling the aura of non-communication that surrounded the group. It seemed to me that once you'd penetrated the shell, it was plain sailing, and we talked at some length about the extraordinary success of *Dark Side* which seemed to have taken the group by surprise. "It's changed me in many ways because it's brought in a lot of money and one feels very secure when you can sell an album for two years. We knew it had a lot more melody than previous Floyd albums and there was a concept that ran all through it. The music was easier to absorb and having girls singing away added a commercial touch that none of our other records had."

We talked about the visuals that enhance their shows, how he and David Gilmour were keener on touring than Waters and Nick Mason, how each member of the Floyd had plans for solo albums and wanted to spend six months of each year on this and six months with the group. In hindsight this seems like wishful thinking but at the time, before Waters' domination threatened their future, it made good sense.

I couldn't resist raising the issue of their anonymity. "We are not trying to sell ourselves, just the music," Wright ventured after a moment's pause. "Right from the start we adopted this policy. We have never had a publicity agent and we've never found it necessary to employ one. We don't go to all the 'in' parties and we don't go to all the 'in' clubs. People don't recognise us on the streets and even if they did it wouldn't be a problem. It's changed since I moved out of London to Cambridge where people don't know anything about the Floyd.

"Sometimes I get people tramping through my garden and asking for my autograph because they've heard I'm in a pop group but they don't know what the Floyd do. They probably think we're like Gary Glitter."

Wright further admitted that he, and by extension his colleagues too, maintained a discreet distance from the contemporary music scene. "I ignore the way pop is going," he said. "I have completely lost touch with the singles charts. I don't listen to what is being played on the radio. I don't watch *Top Of The Pops* and I don't watch *The Old Grey Whistle Test*. I don't even know how the rock business is going, expect that I think the bubble will burst fairly soon."

Wright was astute enough to predict a long career for the group. "It could last forever," he said. "We still have much to do together. We probably do things much better with each other than we could with anyone else. We're not underground anymore, despite what people say. At the UFO it was underground but you can't be underground when you sell out every concert hall and your album goes to number one. No, the Pink Floyd can't claim to be underground anymore."

The conversation over, Wright excused himself, and I caught a train back to London happy in the knowledge that I'd secured a small scoop for *MM* and found a way to penetrate this most impenetrable of groups. Unfortunately, whatever bridges I thought I might have built between Pink Floyd and the press were swiftly demolished. Punk rock was still at least two years away, but in some quarters the tide was already turning. Reviewing Pink Floyd's performance at Wembley Empire Pool less than a fortnight later, *NME*'s star writer Nick Kent laid into the band without mercy, describing their performance as "a pallid excuse for creating music". Even more controversially, he opened his review with a complaint about the state of David Gilmour's hair, describing it as "seemingly anchored down by a surfeit of scalp grease and tapering off below the shoulders with a spectacular festooning of split ends". It was to prove too much. A furious Gilmour demanded an audience with *NME* to address the review.

Pink Floyd's wall – not for the first time or last time – was back up again.

*

That same month I found myself in Cardiff, Hanley and Edinburgh – their home town – observing The Bay City Rollers in action amid scenes of mayhem not seen since Beatlemania gripped the nation in 1963. But while The Beatles would go on to far greater things, their music spiraling into unimaginable sophistication and becoming multimillionaires in the process, the Rollers would tumble into tragedy, squabbling amongst themselves while the millions they earned slipped through their fingers and into the hands of those appointed to advise them.

The term "boy band" nowadays refers to an act assembled through auditions by businessmen with an eye on the financial return. The Rollers did not begin their career like this but along the way their manager Tam Paton hired and fired boys according to what he perceived as their appeal to pubescent girls, which made them the first such act of note in the UK, though in the US they were beaten by The Monkees. But while The Monkees achieved a degree of artistic recognition, the Rollers were deemed too lightweight for serious appraisal. Nevertheless, some of their singles, notably 'Keep On Dancing', were as good as anything else in the pop charts, even if – like The Monkees – they neither wrote them nor played on them.

"In the same week that Muhammad Ali regained his heavyweight boxing title, the featherweight crown of pop, too, has changed hands," I wrote in *MM*. "The fickle crown of pop now rests firmly on the well-coiffured heads of The Bay City Rollers."

I talked to them in their dressing room but they didn't have much to say though singer Les McKeown, the most animated, made a joke or two about Gay Liberation which seemed odd to me. It never occurred to me at the time that manager Paton was a predatory sex abuser who did his best to coerce various Rollers into sex acts, all the while barring them from having girlfriends. He even instructed me in no uncertain terms not to invite any girls back to the hotel, fearing that if I did so it might somehow tarnish the group's unsullied reputation. Usually when I'd been on the road with groups this was positively encouraged and loads of girls were invited back, the more the merrier, and invariably a few stayed for breakfast.

Later in life Paton became openly gay and was charged with gross indecency for which he served a prison sentence.

"They don't have girlfriends and live a claustrophobic life in a tiny circle that includes only themselves and Tam, the manager," I wrote. "On the road they always stay at a town at least ten miles away from a theatre they're playing (so the fans won't get near them) and share rooms, fish and chips and hair dryers. It's all too easy to be very cynical about a group like The Bay City Rollers whose appeal lies essentially in their looks and mannerisms rather than the music they produce. But however unfavourably they compare with the rock giants of the seventies, The Bay City Rollers are a phenomenon that cannot be ignored.

"The music the group performs is barely audible, partly because of their woefully inadequate PA system but mainly because 2,000 schoolgirls can create a horrendous din if the mood takes them. Their set lasts about 60 minutes and is happily amateurish compared with other groups whose appeal lies within the Rollers' age group. Musically they're as competent as the average cabaret band, and as most of their material comprises standards like 'CC Rider', 'Great Balls Of Fire', '(Let's Have A) Party' and 'Be My Baby' it would be easy to confuse them.

"Critical assessment, however, is virtually impossible under the extraordinary circumstances of a Rollers' performance, but they do sing in tune, play their own instruments and occasionally Eric Faulkner bounces through with a fairly nifty guitar passage. All the concerts I saw were repeats of the previous evening in every aspect."

At Hanley I rode with the group in the unmarked white van they used for quick getaways. Its side door was opened as it pulled up so close to the backstage door that not even the slimmest girl could squeeze between van side and wall. "Inside the cold, dark van are five colourful blankets for the five Rollers to cocoon themselves as they lie on the floor of the van to avoid being torn to pieces should their presence be detected," I continued. "Usually they're in the van seconds after leaving the stage, and away down the road before even the most determined girl can make it to the stage door. It's a punishing routine, especially in winter, rushing while piping hot and covered in sweat then forced to bear the cold van for ten minutes until the panic is over."

In Edinburgh the Rollers' show was brought to halt midway, and as I watched the chaos from the side of the stage I couldn't help but think that someone somewhere would one day be seriously injured in the mayhem. "Using every ounce of effort, hundreds of girls packed themselves at the front of the all-too-low stage in the Odeon Theatre," I wrote. "Even the 35 firemen hired for the night (at £5 a man) couldn't stem the tide and the more inexperienced became unnecessarily violent as the push gained momentum. Girls were being trodden underfoot in the melee and the front row of seats became dislodged from the floor and smashed as more and more surged into the crowd. There were at least a dozen cases of fainting, and twice girls pretended to be overcome in order to be lifted up on stage. On both occasions they immediately came to life within inches of Eric Faulkner."

After the show I joined a couple of the firemen for a pint in a pub across the road. "Better this lot than that Bryan Berry or whatever he's called," one of them said to me. "Ferry said we ruined his show by being there at the front. I'd like to have seen him get on without us. That'd 'av bin' fun."

The other fireman said he preferred Pink Floyd to Ferry or the Rollers.

"Outside the theatre," I continued, "are two anxious fathers and one anxious mother. All three have flown up from London searching for their daughters who have run away to see the Rollers. All of them are reunited after the show and no doubt a few harsh words will be exchanged between parent and offspring on the night express down to London.

"Outside Tam Paton, in a white suit, is still talking to anyone who'll listen to him. I bid him goodnight and tell him I'm leaving in the morning. He tells me to keep in touch with him. 'Ye nivir know,' he says, 'one day they might be as big as The Beatles and then I'll giy'er a beeg exclusive.'"

Two years later I was with the Rollers in America.

*

John Entwistle's Ox sold only 300 tickets for their show at Newcastle's City Hall and John seemed surprised that he'd sold that many. This was the one and only time during the career of the original Who that any of its members undertook a full tour away from the band and it was an expensive whim for their bass player. When I inquired how much it had cost to take his four-piece band, plus two backing singers, out for eight dates in the UK and a further sixteen in the US in the New Year he replied: "Oh, I dunno, about twenty-five grand. I mean, what's money for? You can't take it with you so you might as well spend it."

At the show in Newcastle the volume was deafening, far louder than The Who. "Next gig, I'm gonna leave some of them speakers behind," said Bobby Pridden, pressed into service by John. "Bleedin' daft. There's enough gear for a gig in Hyde Park and be 'eard in 'Ounslow."

Nevertheless, there was more than a hint of The Who in the sound that John's band made on stage because his style of playing and the sound he got from his equipment was unique. It brought home to me, and probably other Who fans who were there, how much John contributed to The Who's sound.

*

Still at a loss what to do with me in London, Ray pressed me into service when *MM* received an invitation from Warner Bros Records to visit Los Angeles and two other US cities during the third week of December. I was to interview six of their acts that were shortly to visit the UK. I flew to LA where I picked up a rental car and drove to the Beverly Wilshire Hotel. As soon as I arrived, I called MCA Records and managed to obtain a number for Keith Moon whom I knew was living there, and later, sleepless of course, drove out to join him and friends at the Palamino, watching Rick Nelson. The next day I had lunch with Joe Smith, the boss of Warners Records at his Bel Air mansion and in the afternoon met up again with Lowell George who led Little Feat.

It was always a pleasure to spend time with Lowell. We talked about guitars, his past, his influences and his hopes for his band, and as we chatted, I was again struck by his humility and that he seemed to have absolutely no idea of the respect in which he and Little Feat were held in the UK. Dressed in loose overalls that accentuated his rather portly figure and with his shoulder length hair and none too tidy beard, he eschewed all pretensions of rockstardom. He was completely and utterly free of ego, quietly spoken and humble, without doubt one of the most warm and endearing rock musicians I would ever meet.

The next day I flew up to San Francisco to interview Larry Graham, leader of Graham Central Station, who told me he played bass on Sly Stone's records, which Sly had disputed to me earlier in the year. Larry laughed out loud when I told him that Sly claimed to have played bass on Family Stone records. After spending the following morning with horn blowers Tower of Power, it was back to LA to interview Ronnie Montrose and a group called Bonnaroo, then off to see The Doobie Brothers in Kalamazoo where I also visited the Gibson guitar factory. I was pretty much exhausted by this time – but the truth was I didn't know the half of it.

I was shown around the Gibson factory by an obliging PR man I'd called an hour earlier after finding the number in the phone book by my bedside. During an absorbing hour I saw the whole process, how a plank of wood was turned into a Les Paul, a Flying V or a J45. There were mechanical saws that cut the wood to patterns, varnishing rooms and hot air drying cupboards, benches where beading was attached and an electronics department where pick-ups were assembled and mounted. At the end of the production line were half a dozen booths in which guitarists played every single guitar for about 15 minutes each to check they were OK to leave the factory. Those that weren't went into a reject room, even if all that was wrong was a scratch or slight discolouration. Most of them would end up in the furnace I was told, but the PR wouldn't let me take away a condemned guitar as a souvenir. No chance, he said.

I was given a little book about the history of the Gibson company and its distinguished-looking founder, Orville H Gibson (1856-1918) which I still have. Like Orville, the book looks really ancient, but it's very charming and is probably a collector's item by now.

From Kalamazoo it was but a short hop to Detroit and a connection back to London but the next 24 hours brought the most wearisome flying experience imaginable. When I tried to check in at Detroit the nice girl at the British Airways desk told me the travel agents had made a mistake and no London flight was leaving that particular evening. This meant a delay while they sorted something out, which they did, and because another BA girl's boyfriend just happened to be the pilot on a Delta flight to Chicago I could squeeze onto that plane and get a connection to London from there. Carrying my luggage, I was marched across the tarmac to this plane, searched at the top of the steps, and directed to a first-class seat. Off we went into the December sky, with me settling back with what turned out to be the first of an endless supply of free drinks.

O'Hare Airport was snowed in and we went into a holding pattern that lasted for two hours. More free drinks appeared, and as I sipped my vodka, I watched the hands on my wristwatch slip past the time that my connection to London was due to leave. Christmas was rapidly approaching. Would I spend it at O'Hare? Eventually we landed. O'Hare was a madhouse, overcrowded, chaotic, bags and delayed passengers everywhere, many of them asleep. The runways were snowbound. Planes could take off only in brief windows when a runway was cleared. I established that my connection to London had not yet taken off and somehow managed to check-in, hours late, and be given a boarding pass and, yes, vouchers for free drinks at the bar nearest the departure gate. I took advantage of them until the bar ran out of booze then wearily joined my fellow passengers waiting to take off for London.

Eventually, somewhere around 3am, we boarded, took our seats and waited until a runway was cleared. Once in the sky, perhaps an hour later, we were offered – yes – free drinks "to compensate for our inconvenience". Then came the bombshell. The plane would not fly direct to London but call in at New York JFK first in order to refuel. Evidently the snow on the runway had prevented refuelling at Chicago.

Many passengers, animated through drink, protested but to no avail. About two hours later we touched down at JFK and stayed on the ground for at least three hours. The fact that several other passengers boarded at this time suggested the airline may have had an extra incentive to land at JFK and this was noted by some of the more indignant passengers. Then, sleepless but fortified by more free drink, we took off, crossed the Atlantic and, at around seven in the evening, more than 12 hours late, landed at Heathrow. It was the night before Christmas Eve and I was exhausted, jet-lagged, hung over and sleep deprived.

My friend Chris Whincup met me at Heathrow with the news that he was throwing a party at his house in Englefield Green to which I was invited. I went but passed out on a bed long before midnight. The next day I was reliably informed that later in the evening an amorous couple had joined me in the bed, undressed, did what couples do in that situation, put their clothes back on and left. I slept through the entire encounter.

Next day, Christmas Eve, I drove a rented car to Skipton where I spent Christmas with my dad and sister, mostly asleep. On the day after Boxing Day I drove back down to London, wrote up all my interviews from the US trip and, on December 29, flew back to New York to resume my duties as *Melody Maker's* US editor.

The Manhattan skyline looked majestic as my plane descended into JFK.

24

"I don't wanna see one fuckin' word of this finding its fuckin'
way into your fuckin' magazines."
Richard Cole, Led Zeppelin tour manager,
somewhere over Colorado, January 1975

Back in New York, my first big assignment of 1975 was covering Led Zeppelin's
tenth US tour which opened in Minnesota and moved on to Chicago where I
checked into their hotel, The Ambassador, watched two shows at the Chicago
Stadium and then found myself on an unscheduled flight to Los Angeles with
three-quarters of the group for company. I also interviewed Robert Plant, who'd
arrived in the freezing Windy City dressed in a lightweight, open-fronted blouse
more suited to a pre-pubescent girl, the kind of thing he liked to wear on stage,
and while there he succumbed to a nasty cold, his health deteriorating steadily
during the run.

After the first show I and most of the LZ party went out to a drag club
because they were unlikely to be hassled in a gay environment but on the
morning after the final show Robert was pronounced too sick to continue the
tour, causing the postponement of a concert in St Louis. Since the following
night was a night off anyway, much to their chagrin Led Zeppelin found
themselves stranded in cold, unwelcoming Chicago for 48 hours.

This was deeply unsettling for everyone. Led Zep were in their pomp, as
high and mighty as it is possible to be in the world of rock; rich, powerful and
unused to setbacks like this. A meeting was called. What to do now? They had
their own plane at the ready, after all, and they were paying for it on a daily
basis whether or not they actually flew anywhere, so there was no need to stay in
Chicago. Page, who got his own way in situations like this, wanted to fly to Los
Angeles, into the arms of a ravishing teenage model. Robert would stay behind
to be nursed and everyone else would go to LA, me included unless I preferred to
return to New York. Sensing fun, I opted to tag along.

There was an odd incident as the Led Zeppelin party left the hotel. A large
group of press photographers and reporters were hanging around in the lobby,
and when Led Zep emerged from the elevator Richard Cole assumed the media
were waiting for them and tried to shoo them away. Turned out he was mistaken.
Lieutenant Hiroo Onoda, a Japanese soldier who'd continued to man his post

in the South Pacific long after World War Two had ended, was staying in the same hotel, evidently in Chicago to promote the book he had written about his experiences and it was his presence that had attracted the media, confusing everyone.

In the scramble for limousines I found myself in one with Bonzo, who was swigging from a bottle of Smirnoff Blue Label vodka. He wasn't a happy man. Eternally homesick on US tours, he'd wanted to use the down time to fly home to his wife and kids in Redditch in the Midlands but time constraints precluded this. He opted to get very drunk instead.

The flight to Los Angeles was not without incident. As the plane headed west Bonzo succumbed to the effects of the vodka and crashed out in the bedroom at the rear of this spacious plane. I settled into a comfy seat towards the front and passed the time of day with Cameron Crowe, the only *Rolling Stone* writer sympathetic to Zeppelin, and Neal Preston, their photographer of choice, also along for the ride, and hope that Page might grant me an interview. He did but it was brief. He spent most of the flight with Peter Grant and Cole in the meeting room, a small area furnished with scatter cushions and beanbags just along the fuselage from the bedroom.

The area where I sat had tables with shiny tops and comfy seats such as are to be found in the first-class compartment of regular commercial flights, and there was an open area in the centre of the plane where two arm chairs were fixed in place by swivel-style fittings, opposite which was a long couch. TV screens showing movies, some pornographic, were suspended from the ceiling. On the next table to me John Paul Jones was engaged in a game of high-stakes backgammon, and in the background hovered two pretty, short-skirted stewardesses, employed by the owners of the Starship to cater to our comforts, distributing canapés and periodically refreshing our drinks from the bar. I was told by one of them that the Starship was licensed to carry 42 passengers, though the plane itself was built for almost three times that, so with less than twelve of us on board today the journey was all the more agreeable.

Peter Grant stopped by.

"Enjoying yourselves lads?" he asked brusquely, the glint in his eye suggesting he had it in his power for this enjoyment to abruptly cease. At 20 stone plus and standing six foot and three inches, he was without question the most intimidating man I would ever meet. The pitch of his voice was strangely light, which somehow added to the calm menace he radiated, even on the phone, as *MM* editor Coleman had cause to find out when he called to protest about a cartoon we published that depicted him as a whale, with Led Zeppelin and ELP on rafts in its belly and £5 notes gushing from its blowhole. And he wasn't just angry about the inference he was soon to manage ELP as well as Zep.

"Yes thanks, Peter," I replied.

"Wanna see the front?"

"OK."

Peter took me into the cockpit where, for the next half hour or so, I sat between and slightly aft of the two pilots, gazing out at the horizon. The panoramic vista afforded by the front window made it seem as if we were floating on a giant bed of shaving foam, and in the distance, many miles away, I could see one or two other jets, quite tiny, in the uninterrupted clear blue sky. The plane was on auto-pilot and the pilots were sipping coffee. I chatted with them and they asked me if I'd like a go, so I moved over to sit behind one of the joysticks and "had a go", pulling the stick ever so slightly towards me so that the plane lifted slightly, then pushing it away so that it dipped. The movement of the plane was visible on a small screen in the centre of the controls, a bit like a satnav. It occurred to me that somewhere over Colorado the fate of Led Zeppelin was in my hands.

When I returned to the main cabin, Peter was sat where I'd been sitting, so I took another seat.

"Enjoy that?" he inquired.

"Yes, I flew the plane for about ten minutes."

Peter laughed, a deep chuckle, and shook his head so the coonskin hat covering his massive cranium wobbled slightly. "That's nothing. Bonzo flew us all the fuckin' way from Los Angeles to fuckin' New York on one tour."

Relieved that Bonzo entertained no such ideas today, I resumed my conversation with Cameron and Neal and before long Richard Cole came over. Aware that I had shared a limousine with Bonzo en route to the airport, he was anxious to know exactly what the errant drummer might have consumed that had rendered him insensible.

"Only vodka, but plenty of it," I told Zeppelin's anxious Mr Fixit.

"No pills? No coke?"

"No, not that I saw. He was just swigging vodka, straight from the bottle."

"Nothing else?"

"No."

Richard seemed satisfied with this explanation and the mood lightened. A meal was served, seafood and fillet steak, and afterwards, as the skies darkened and we flew over the western states, most of the party gathered around the electric organ that was attached to the end of the bar amidships. John Paul took his natural place behind the keyboard and began to play a selection of old English music hall songs, 'Any Old Iron', 'Bye Bye Blackbird' and the like, much to the evident pleasure of Peter who sang along lustily.

I had by this time enjoyed several beers, a few glasses of wine and moved on to spirits, and just as I was beginning to think that life couldn't really be much better, that I was probably in the best place in the world right now, hurtling towards sunny California with the world's biggest rock band in their sumptuous private airliner, Bonzo, forgotten amidst the merriment, emerged from the bedroom dressed only in a loosely-fitting red bathrobe. Unseen until too late, he lurched drunkenly into us and, without even having been introduced, propositioned one of the stewardesses by lifting up her skirt at the rear and forcing her to the ground in a clumsy attempt to mount her from behind. Peter and Richard wrenched Bonzo away from the shocked girl and led him struggling back towards the bedroom. The girl's screaming alerted a pilot who appeared from the cockpit, demanding to know what was happening. He was very angry. The girl was sobbing. Peter re-emerged from the bedroom to assure him that everything was under control. Jimmy led the distressed girl off to soothe her. Calm ensued.

The incident cast a pall of gloom on us all, however, and the remainder of the journey passed virtually in silence, except for when Richard strode down to where Cameron, Neal and myself were seated. He wasn't smiling. "I don't wanna see one fuckin' word of this finding its fuckin' way into your fuckin' magazines. Right."

Right. Fuckin' right.

*

Jimmy Page mentioned to me that he had injured a finger when a carriage door closed on his hand as he was alighting from a train at Victoria Station, leaving him with only three fingers on his left hand with which to play guitar. As a result, 'Dazed And Confused', Jimmy's showcase, was dropped from the set.

This unscheduled trip to California was the closest I ever got to Led Zeppelin and it afforded a unique opportunity to assess their characters. I sensed that Jimmy operated on a different daily timetable to most others on the planet, that he went for several nights without sleep, tempting fate, walking along a precipice to see how far he could go, and what might happen. He certainly had an otherworldly presence about him that contrasted with his fellow Zeps who, by and large, seemed quite unaffected compared to their leader. Robert, when well, was easily approachable, usually genial and generally friendly towards journalists; John Paul was sociable enough albeit reticent in a slightly aloof fashion, a bit like Pink Floyd, as if talking to writers was somehow beneath him, not worth the bother, and, in any case, his low profile suited his reserved nature; and Bonzo, although down-to-earth in the manner of the Midlands brickie he once was, was simply best avoided because his temper was so unpredictable. Peter was a key fifth member of the group, deeply committed to the cause, ready to physically confront anyone who sought to profit at their expense or otherwise break their stride; well versed in the mechanics of the music industry and how money flowed within it, he offered Led Zeppelin a platform on which to operate without the least concern for their physical or financial security.

I didn't see much of Led Zeppelin during the stopover in LA. After a trip to the Rainbow on the night we arrived, they kept their own company, Jimmy no doubt wrapped in the arms of his coltish courtesan, Bonzo recovering from hangovers, John Paul disappearing into the ether as he was wont to do, maybe even getting in a day's session work at the Record Plant. I had a girlfriend of my own to visit in LA in those days so I stayed out of everyone's way. A day later I was back with them on the flight back to the East Coast, to Greensboro, North Carolina, a trip that necessitated rising very early as we flew against time changes. As a result, the journey was uneventful, most of us keeping our own company and dozing fitfully for the entire flight from west coast to east.

The evening's concert was at the Greensboro Coliseum where Robert, now recovered and having taken a commercial flight direct from Chicago, awaited us. The usual convoy of black limousines greeted the Starship on the runway, five in all, a slightly enlarged party now alighting to occupy them, staff from Atlantic Records in New York having flown down to join the fun. However, everyone in the inner circle was tired, the group weren't really up for the show and, to make matters worse, outside the venue a shortage of tickets had caused violence to erupt. About 500 fans had attempted to storm the rear of the building, throwing broken bottles, stones and pieces of scaffolding. Three of the five limousines, those parked outside, came under attack and were damaged.

The show, not one of Zeppelin's best, went on regardless. It being January, the building was cold, which dampened the atmosphere, and the acoustics were awful, the sound a great wash of impenetrable noise. Firecrackers were set off amid the audience and as Zep waded through their songs I had an uneasy feeling that things might turn ugly; that the mood in this hideous great place was not sympathetic to the emotions of those on stage nor to the music they were trying to play. It's difficult to maintain your concentration before a restless crowd like this at the best of times, and tonight was amongst the worst.

For an hour or so I watched the concert alongside Peter Grant from the side of the stage where the din was so great you could hardly hear yourself think. Peter bemoaned the lack of 'Dazed And Confused'. "First time I can ever remember a tour without it," he said sadly.

After about an hour, Peter was summoned to resolve an issue involving the limousine drivers and, out of curiosity, I followed him down the stairs into the area behind the stage. Evidently the drivers of the three limos parked outside, fearing further damage, had removed them and the other two drivers, whose cars were parked inside, wanted to take theirs away too. This, of course, would have left the Led Zeppelin entourage stranded when the concert was over and this realisation prompted whoever was manning the loading doors to decline to open them until Mr Grant gave the OK.

Mr Grant was not going to give the OK. In fact, he was having none of it and a confrontation quickly ensued. "You can't take ya fuckin' cars away. We need 'em," he shouted into the faces of the drivers.

"We're sorry. We have to take them away. They'll get damaged."

"You'll get fuckin' damaged, ya cunts."

"We have no choice."

Peter looked at the drivers with contempt. "Alright, how much do you want for ya fuckin' cars. How much are they fuckin' worth? Forty thousand dollars each? I'll fuckin' buy them from you right now, ya cunts."

Peter carried with him a large briefcase and I was left in no doubt that there was sufficient cash within for him to honour this offer.

The drivers protested. "We can't sell them. They're not ours to sell."

Peter dismissed this response as if swatting a fly, and beckoned to some of Zep's road crew who gathered around. "In that case, I'll fuckin' steal them. I've offered to buy them and if ya can't fuckin' sell them, I'll just fuckin' take 'em."

The drivers protest further. "You can't do that!"

"Don't be fuckin' stupid ya cunts," said Peter derisively, moving towards them so that his massive bulk acted as a buffer, pushing them backwards into the crew who stood their ground. "Of course, I can fuckin' do that. I can do what I fuckin' want, can't I?"

By this time Peter is yelling into their faces, mere inches away. "I've got twenty fuckin' men working for me. There's only two of you, ya cunts. Ya can't fuckin' stop me, ya' fuckin' cunts."

The dispute concluded in Peter's favour, a compromise of sorts was reached while the music blared on. The members of the group and Richard, with Peter at the wheel, would leave the arena in the first of the two limousines; all the rest of us, with a roadie at the wheel, would occupy the second, something of a squeeze as it turned out. The drivers would pick up their limousines at the airport later. Our exit would be speedy.

"We don't fuckin' need you, ya' cunts," said Peter to the dispossessed drivers, bringing the issue to a close. "We'll drive the fuckin' cars ourselves. So fuck off, just fuckin' fuck off."

Peter turned away and resumed his position at the side of the stage for the remainder of the show which ended, as always, with 'Stairway To Heaven'. The four members of Zeppelin left the stage but, instead of heading to the dressing room for a quick cigarette, a toot and swig of booze, Richard immediately appraised them of the transport situation, advising them to wait out of sight of the audience for less than two minutes before returning for the encore, 'Whole Lotta Love'.

As Robert did his best to re-excite everyone with every inch of his love, Richard hustled us hangers-on into the second limo and, as the final notes echoed throughout the arena, Jimmy, Robert, John Paul and Bonzo tore down the steps towards the first limo. Richard handed out their large, red, hooded towelling robes as they jumped into the car with Peter at the wheel, already revving the engine. The applause was reaching a crescendo as our cars sped off. The huge stadium doors opened and the angry mob of fans that didn't make it into the show surged forward into our path. Peter blasted a way through, his horn blaring, and the crowd parted like the Red Sea. Our truncated convoy reached speeds of up to 80 mph in a heavily built-up area as Peter led the way, driving through red lights and on the wrong side of the road through the town of Greensboro. This was far more exciting than the concert.

Then, when we reached the area of the airport where the Starship sat, a funny thing happened. Peter drove round and round, circling the huge aircraft, tyres screeching, faster and faster, burning rubber. When he finally skidded to a stop, the four members of Led Zeppelin tumbled out, hysterical with laughter.

Someone asked him what he was playing at. "The band was placing bets on whether I'd crash it into the fuckin' plane," he shouted, equally hysterical. "Fuckin' useless pile of fuckin' junk!" he continued, kicking the limo hard, denting a door. "Way off tune... my Bentley goes twice as fuckin' fast!"

And so we all stood there laughing into the night, totally exhilarated by it all. Then, happier than we'd been all day, we climbed aboard the plane and flew on up the East Coast to New York, drinks in hand, relieved that this long day was finally over, party time again.

Unforgettable. Led Zeppelin – the only way to fly.

25

"I don't know my phone number. Yoko is always changing it."
John Lennon, New York City, spring 1975

With Led Zeppelin done and dusted for the time being, I interviewed Harry
Nilsson who was staying at the Plaza Hotel and who met me in the lobby loaded
with parcels, presents for his friends and relations back in LA, he explained. We
talked over lunch at the Park Lane Hotel overlooking Central Park and for coffee
were joined first by Harry's Irish girlfriend Una and then by Alice Cooper. The
head waiter insisted we wore jackets which meant Harry had to keep his anorak
on and remove his flat cap, much to his displeasure. He told me he was having
trouble with his record label, RCA, who disapproved of his preferred title for his
new LP, *God's Greatest Hits*. "They're winning," he said, mournfully, sipping on a
double Chivas Regal with ice.

I reminded Harry that we'd met before, at his flat in London, but he didn't
remember. Can't say I was surprised. Harry, of course, was pally with John
Lennon, his hero, and not long after our interview would take John along to a
meeting with the boss of RCA, a negotiating ploy designed to convince the label
to grant him a sizeable advance. "Me and John will be making records together,"
he lied to the RCA bigwig who, salivating at the prospect, happily signed a
cheque for seven-figures.

The following month I bumped into John in the lobby of the Uris Theatre
where he was a presenter at the Grammy Awards, which he attended with Yoko.
Wearing a black beret, white shirt and black jacket with a prominent silver
ELVIS badge on its lapel, John appeared on stage alongside Paul Simon and
Andy Williams, and there was a bit of hilarity about "my partner Paul" before
John awarded the record of the year prize to Olivia Newton John for 'I Honestly
Love You'. Alas, Olivia was detained elsewhere and the award was accepted by
Art Garfunkel.

"Are you guys getting back together again?" quipped John as Art arrived on
stage.

"No, how about you?" replied Art.

I grabbed a quick word with John after the presentation. I wanted to arrange
a talk with him about his immigration problems, which were creating news at
this time. For some years the US government had been trying to expel him, the

hypothetical reason his marijuana possession conviction from 1968. Of course, the real reason was his radical politics, in particular his vocal opposition to the Vietnam War. A hero to the youth of the country, the Nixon administration considered him a potential troublemaker, so the dope bust was simply a ruse to deny him the green card that would enable him to travel freely. In all likelihood the miniscule quantity of cannabis found in the Mayfair flat where John was staying with Yoko had been planted by the infamous Metropolitan Police Sergeant Norman Pilcher, who made a career out of busting rock stars, but rather than argue the case John had pleaded guilty in order to save Yoko from being charged with obstruction and possibly deported.

In March I wrote a story for *MM* entitled "John's No. 1 Dream", and reported that John's negotiations to remain in America would reach a climax within the next three months. I visited the office of John's lawyer, Leon Wildes, who told me that he had "... information that shows that the Government deliberately ignored his application [for a green card], actually locking the relevant document away in a safe. This was because of a memorandum which was circulated by an unknown Government agency to other Government agencies which stated that John and Yoko were to be kept under physical observance at all times because of possible political activities." Leon said that he was currently trying to find the source of this document and if he did it would "break the case wide open and prove that there has been a miscarriage of justice".

Either way, something underhand was going on, hardly untypical of Nixon and his cronies, and it would be another year and three months before John was awarded his green card. Only then would he be able to travel outside of the United States in the certainty that he'd be allowed back in on his return.

Soon after encountering John at the Grammy Awards I bumped into him again at a private party in the apartment of a music industry executive on the Upper East Side. I watched as he autographed an Italian Beatles LP for the host, one that featured the group on a stage, and he wrote a few words in bubbles from the mouths of his old bandmates. Above George he wrote: "Anyone fancy a curry after the show?"; above Ringo: "What song are we playing?"; above Paul: "Come on lads, we need to rehearse more"; and above his own picture he wrote: "I'm leaving to form my own group."

It was at this party that, rather cheekily, I asked him for his phone number. "I don't know it," he replied, unfazed by my request. "Yoko is always changing it." Then, to my amazement, John made me an offer. "If you send me a cable to our flat in the Dakota with your phone number on it, I promise I'll call you back within 24 hours, all assuming I'm in New York."

I reached for my notebook and wrote it down: "John Lennon, 1 West 72nd Street, New York, NY 10023." Thereafter, whenever I wanted to speak to John I sent him a cable: "John, please call: 212 628 9378 Chris C, MM." He kept to his word too, invariably announcing himself as "Johnny Beatle" when I picked up the phone.

Writing that last sentence now, 48 years later, fills me with a peculiar mixture of wonder and sorrow; wonder that John Lennon, among the best-loved rock stars in the world, a musician revered for having been the founder of The Beatles, still the yardstick by which success in popular music is measured, could be so utterly nonchalant about his monumental fame as to agree to this means of communication with a music writer, and sorrow that he is no longer with us, murdered in cold blood by a fan whose mind was deranged by religion. In the 21st Century it is unthinkable for a star of Lennon's magnitude not to be surrounded by layers of insulation that would make such a gesture absurd. Yet John, as famous as it was possible to be, idolised by millions, a hero of the counter-culture yet pursued by the US government, was sufficiently comfortable in his own skin to grant me this favour.

I suppose he must have liked me. I have no idea why.

*

The first interview with John I arranged by this method took place later that same month at the Capitol Records offices on Sixth Avenue, its main purpose to discuss his soon-to-be-released *Rock 'N' Roll* album. Before our chat, a buoyant John talked on the telephone to no less than 35 different disc jockeys simultaneously across America. "I like 'Stand By Me' and 'Be-Bop-A-Lula' is one of my all-time favourites," he said, before going on to discuss the problems he had in making the album. "There's been more trouble with this album than Soft Mick," he stated, using an expression that I'm sure 99 per cent of his listeners had never heard before.

In the modern era what John was doing would be called a podcast, albeit without video links. When it was over, we settled down in another office where he outlined the *Rock 'N' Roll* album's chequered history: "I just finished *Mind Games* when I started the new album and I just wanted to have some fun. It was so soon after *Mind Games* that I didn't have any new material. I wanted to just sing and not be the producer. I thought, 'Who's the one to do it with?' and I thought of

Phil Spector. We went down to the Record Plant and started cutting and, well, it got pretty crazy... it really got wild at times. But we managed to cut seven or eight in the end before it collapsed... which is the only way to put it.

"Next thing Phil had apparently had an auto accident. Only he knows whether he did or didn't, but that's what the story said. That was the end of it then, because he'd got the tapes and I didn't get them back until two days before I went into the studio to cut *Walls And Bridges*. When I did get into them, I found that out of the eight, there were only four or five that were worth using. The sessions had 28 guys playing live and a lot of them out of tune, which is too much, even for rock and roll. So I didn't know whether to forget it or carry on, but I hate leaving stuff in the can. I thought about putting out an EP – remember them? But they don't have them in America, and thought about a maxi-single. In the end I decided to finish it off and produce the rest myself.

"I did ten tracks in three days in October, all the numbers that I hadn't got around to with Phil. I had a lot of fun and mixed it all down in about four or five days. My one problem was whether it sounded weird going from the Spector sound to my sound, from 28 guys down to eight. But they match pretty well I think. So there it was, I suddenly had an album."

I mentioned to John that Paul would profit from the album because he'd acquired Buddy Holly's song catalogue and John had covered 'Peggy Sue'. "What a clever move that was," he replied. "I hope he gives me a good deal. I don't care who gets the money. With Paul it's cool, 'cos we're pals, and even Klein's all right really. I'm not gonna get much money from this album anyway."

John seemed happier with his past than at any time since 1970. "I've lost all that negativity about the past and I'd be happy as Larry to do 'Help!'. I've just changed completely in two years. I'd do 'Hey Jude' and the whole damn show, and I think George will eventually see that. If he doesn't, that's cool. That's the way he wants to be."

John also mentioned that he was now back with Yoko. "I'm happy as Larry," he beamed, "and she is... I hope. We've known each other for nine years. I met her in 1966. We had a sort of breakdown last year, one way or another, but we called each other often even when I was going crazy out on the West Coast, and I probably said a lot of barmy things to her which I'll regret."

*

In the same month I spoke to John, I saw Queen at the Avery Fisher Hall, a fairly prestigious gig for the band who'd made their New York debut the previous year supporting Mott The Hoople. I wasn't impressed: "… tedious, and their on-stage presence (an essential quality if you choose to run the heavy-rock-with-glitter-overtones race) was an almost laughably bizarre mish-mash of every other more successful band of their genre. Freddie Mercury came over as a pompous, arrogant duplication of all those who have gone before; his stage movements seemed forced and stereotyped instead of smooth and flowing with the rhythms his band were creating. Brian May is a competent, but far from spectacular guitar player. His long solo relied entirely on the tape loop of an echo chamber which, I suspected, had the sustain control switched up to the fullest level."

I had a good word only for their drummer, Roger Taylor, who "… came to the rescue with some nifty infills time and time again," but found it necessary to point out that my view of the concert contrasted with that of the majority who went home satisfied. Nevertheless, within a week both the *New York Times* and *Rolling Stone* published similarly unflattering reviews.

In contrast, my fondness for Bruce Springsteen knew no bounds. I saw him again at the Westbury Music Fair, a theatre in Jericho on Long Island. Weirdly, the gig was on a revolving stage in the centre of a room that held about 1,800 people. It wasn't sold out. The venue was run by Italian gangsters, and the backstage area was patrolled by olive-skinned men in dark suits and ties with bulging shoulders, all of whom looked like extras from *The Godfather*. Peter Philbin, the Columbia Records PR guy who'd driven me there, recognised this before I did and advised me not to make eye contact. We went backstage to chat with Bruce after the show but, as ever, he was tight-lipped, pre-occupied with the issues surrounding the release of his next LP, *Born To Run*. I didn't know about the dispute between his manager Mike Appel and future producer and manager Jon Landau, which had yet to break out into the open.

In the review I wrote for *Melody Maker*, I drew attention to his violinist, Suki Lahav, who "not only improves the aesthetic of the set but adds considerably to the crushing atmosphere that Springsteen, street poet, extraordinaire, creates." Sadly, this was Suki's last appearance with the E Street Band.

That same month I watched Entwistle's Ox at the Academy of Music and felt a bit sad for John as there were plenty of empty seats, a far cry from The Who's four-night sold-out run at the Garden the previous year. "The audience gave him a hero's welcome," I reported, "but reserved their biggest cheers for the songs he's contributed to The Who's catalogue over the years. Opening with 'My Wife' and closing with 'Heaven And Hell' was a shrewd move."

Mick Jagger was at the show and also at a party afterwards at the Rainbow

Room, and I sidled up to him to inquire whether or not a replacement had been found for Mick Taylor in the Stones. He kept mum.

Also at the party were four members of the *Monty Python's Flying Circus* team who were in New York to promote an LP about to be released in the US. They had signed with Arista and the label held a reception for them at which label boss Clive Davis made a short speech and played a track about Thomas Hardy writing a new novel while his fans watched him at work. Afterwards the Python men answered questions in an appropriately silly fashion and I, for one, was bemused to learn that their half-hour TV shows would be broadcast on Channel 13 – the educational network.

*

Topping the US charts in February with their catchy instrumental 'Pick Up The Pieces' was the Average White Band, five Scottish musicians and a drummer from Brighton who now lived on the tip of Long Island, the densely populated island that extends for 120 miles or so eastwards from New York City. This called for an interview so I took the train, through Freeport and Patchogue, and as I chugged along on that crisp February morning I discovered that the farther you travel the less populated the island becomes until you reach the easternmost tip where very rich people live, out in the Hamptons, Great Gatsby land. Here I took a taxi from the station and pulled up outside a grand mansion that belonged to Ahmet Ertegun, the boss of Atlantic Records, and inside, a bit gobsmacked at their good fortune, I found them.

"They play rhythm and blues music with such authority that the majority of Americans think they're all black musicians," I informed *MM*'s readers. "They spend their days kicking a fitba' around the grounds of one of Ahmet Ertegun's many mansions, and their nights creating music under the baton of some of the greatest rhythm and blues producers on the Atlantic label."

I discovered that a family of 13 occupied the house: six musicians in the band, a couple of roadies, three WAGS, manager Bruce McCaskill and one small child belonging to tenor player Malcolm "Molly" Duncan. The big house had a big room, probably intended as a ballroom, where the AWB's instruments were set up, and I listened to them rehearse for a while before we sat down to talk. They gathered round to tell me their story, which was not without its share of ill fortune, and a week later *MM* carried my long report about the band and its history, almost 3,000 words.

Realising their fortunes lay in the US, they had decided to settle in the New

York area for at least a year and probably longer, and when they weren't on tour, I would bump into them in and around NY's music clubs over the next 18 months or so. As transplanted Brits, we enjoyed one another's company but their success wasn't to last. It rarely did for white bands that played this type of music, no matter how competently, and soon there was strong competition from several US acts – Earth, Wind & Fire, The Ohio Players and Parliament-Funkadelic among them – whose colour was no doubt in their favour with audiences. Still, I reckon the guys in the AWB will look back on the spring of 1975 as a once in a lifetime experience that none of them ever regret.

*

Flying had by now become a way of life for me, and, in the spring of 1975, I took trips to Miami, Des Moines, Detroit and Los Angeles. In Miami, where I watched and interviewed Billy Joel, I made the silly mistake of accepting an invitation to go sailing with him and a friend in a small boat with no protection from the blazing sun. The following day my skin was red raw and merely putting on clothes was agonising. When I got back to the apartment in New York I spent two days home alone, sitting around naked and covered with soothing lotion since clothing exacerbated my condition. Fortunately, I was able to get dressed again in time for the trip to Des Moines to see and chat with Joe Walsh, who had yet to join the Eagles, though it was Eagle Glenn Frey who chatted with me in LA, as did Minnie Riperton, the connection being their manager, Irving Azoff, a short, stocky man with frizzy hair who would go on to become one of the US record industry's biggest power brokers.

Minnie was lovely, as "fizzy as a soda bottle shaken on a hot summer's day", I wrote. Her five-octave vocal range was extraordinary and my afternoon with her coincided with her biggest hit 'Lovin' You' reaching number one in the *Billboard* charts. She had every reason to be fizzy, and I came away utterly charmed. Sadly, a year later she was diagnosed with breast cancer to which she would succumb in 1979. In the 2000s I met her husband, record producer, Richard Rudolph, who was in the London offices of my employer Music Sales. Recognising my name from the *MM* article, he told me he'd cut it out and kept it to show to their children. "I still have it," he told me. I was immensely touched.

In Detroit I watched my old golfing partner Alice Cooper present a new show based on his album *Welcome To My Nightmare*. By now Alice had dropped his old band and much of the shock-horror theatrics, which is not to say that his show wasn't theatrical, just a bit more tasteful, or perhaps less distasteful. A

feature of the show was a screen made from thin strips of material on which
a film of Alice and four dancers was shown; the strips enabled him and the
dancers to slip in and out, real life characters one moment and movie images the
next. "The new show is not as macabre as previous Cooper outings," I reported,
"and for once Alice has displayed a semblance of good taste in his on-stage
activities. One of Cooper's virtues in the past was the essential tastelessness of
his act: hopefully his audience will have grown with him otherwise much of the
'nightmare' may go over their heads."

I didn't need to fly to New Jersey which required a trip through the Lincoln
Tunnel beneath the Jersey River that flows along the west side of Manhattan.
Cherryhill was a two-hour car journey away, next to nothing in a country the
size of America, and at the Latin Casino I saw Al Green whom I rated as the
equal of Otis and Marvin in the hierarchy of soul singers. I simply loved his
records, still do for that matter, and was astonished at how women reacted to
him. "Whether by good management or good fortune, Al Green has turned into
a black sex symbol on the lines of Tom Jones or even Elvis Presley," I reported.
"The only difference is that Green's worshippers are generally younger. The
passion and frenzy is the same, as are the screams that greet this man from
Memphis with his silky voice and shameless sexuality."

I interviewed Al at length after the show, and found him loquacious and
funny, and he had a habit of laughing very loudly at his own jokes. What was no
joke was the recent incident at his home in Memphis when a girlfriend poured
boiling grits over Green's back while he was taking a bath, then fatally shot
herself. I was a bit cagey about bringing this up but to my relief he spoke quite
freely about what had happened.

"It was a situation where a girl was visiting me and she stayed longer than
she said she would when she arrived," he explained. "It wasn't a situation where
I had 20 women living with me in the house at the same time. There were just
three people living there including myself and I have to say that I adored the
girl in question to the highest degree. It was very tragic and very unfortunate
because she was a sweet, lovely lady. I guess I've got this image because I have
had pictures taken with my shirt off — I wouldn't go any further than that — for
magazines, not necessarily what I'd call sexy magazines. I guess that explains it to
some slight degree, but I don't think I'm the playboy that people have made out."

In 1976 Green, perhaps realising the godlessness of his ways, established
a church in Memphis and became an ordained minister. Mostly he recorded
gospel-only records thereafter.

All the while more interviews piled up: Frankie Valli, Ozark Mountain Daredevils, concert promoter Jerry Weintraub, song publisher Don Kirshner, Bachman Turner Overdrive, guitar maestros Jeff Beck and John McLaughlin, street poet Gil Scott Heron, future Springsteen sideman Nils Lofgren, Journey, BJ Thomas, Freddy Fender, ZZ Top, Ritchie Blackmore and Ian Hunter and Mick Ronson, now joined at the hip in the Hunter-Ronson Band. There was also a big feature on The Beach Boys and Chicago, touring together, which saw me in Chicago, appropriately enough, and concert reviews galore, among them The Kinks, Bruce (again) at the Bottom Line when I took Harvey Goldsmith along with me, and Phil Ochs in Central Park, a wonderful afternoon and evening show staged to mark the end of the war in Vietnam. The songwriter in whose apartment I lived in Los Angeles performed alongside Paul Simon, Richie Havens, Joan Baez, Peter Yarrow, Pete Seeger and Tom Paxton, and I wrote a lengthy review for *MM*'s Caught In The Act page.

"The crowd joined in on the choruses and the years fell away to the period when it was hip to protest against the hostilities in the Far East," I wrote. "With Baez, Phil was hesitant (it was the first time the two – songwriter and hitmaker – had ever duetted on 'There But For Fortune') but they traded lines across Phil's Martin; it wasn't the moment for musical subtlety anyway. Ochs closed with 'The War Is Over', relating how the song was originally written during a demonstration in New York's Washington Square some seven years ago. On that occasion Ochs and various colleagues decided to declare the Vietnam offensive over themselves. Slipping into a lower octave for the verses, Och's throat strained to hit the higher notes without much success. Again, it didn't matter. The feel was what counted.

"Paul Simon was the biggest star of the day, John Lennon having excused himself on the grounds of 'not being in a singing condition at the present time'. Lennon probably declined to attend because of his decision to lie low while the courts decide his future in the US. Publicity surrounding his appearance at this kind of event would do more harm than good. There was a rumour that George Harrison would show, but he never did.

"Simon, never a spontaneous artist, looked his usual nervous self. He opened with a flawless rendering of 'Bridge Over Troubled Water' while photographers literally fought to snap his profile. He received a tremendous ovation but looked hesitantly around him for encouragement from the other artists waiting to appear. Attempting a tune-up, he slid into 'American Tune', a particularly appropriate song but it never got off the ground. While tuning his guitar and singing at the same time, he hastily decided to abandon the song – which was beginning to drag – and liven up the proceedings with the jerky intro to 'Me And Julio Down By The Schoolyard'.

"He completed about half this song before giving up on the guitar, bowing and picking up his young son Harper, and encouraging him to say 'peace' into the microphone. He did just that and was rewarded with a cheer that rivalled his famous daddy. 'I wasn't quite prepared for that,' a flustered Simon told me backstage while being trodden underfoot by yet more cameramen. He made a hasty getaway."

*

It seems to me now that I was subconsciously working as hard as I could, churning out copy relentlessly, week after week on my little Olivetti portable because I had come to love my life in New York and knew that apart from the brief period in the UK at the back end of 1974 I'd been in America for the better part of two years and my time might soon be up; unless, of course, I made myself indispensable through relentless efficiency. I was partially correct.

On May 1 The Rolling Stones famously played from the back of a flatbed truck rolling down Fifth Avenue between 9th and 8th Streets, a surprise press stunt to promote their forthcoming tour of North America. Pete Rudge had advised me to be there but, as ever, the Stones were late arriving at the hotel where a press conference was supposed to be held. I and many others listened to a comedian kill time until someone rushed in and advised us all to step outside where we were astonished to see the Stones bashing out 'Brown Sugar' in a slight drizzle on a truck that turned into Fifth from West 8th and made its way slowly along the Avenue.

"Mick wore faded denims worn Bay City Rollers-style and a Brando leather jacket and tennis shoes," I reported in my NY news column. "The rest of the band, including Ron Wood on guitar and Billy Preston on piano, were more formally attired. Keith Richards appeared to be in charge musically, conducting them through their chops and grinning an absurd grin in the directions of onlookers. At one stage Jagger dropped his microphone and had to sing into Preston's boom mic over his keyboards. It was the only hitch in a stunt that gave the band maximum publicity."

Traffic was halted, a rapidly accumulating mass of fans blocked the way and after tossing out leaflets to astonished passers-by, Mick and his men jumped off the truck into waiting limousines and sped away. I was told later that Charlie had suggested the stunt in emulation of how jazz bands in New Orleans promoted forthcoming shows.

That same week a new bar and restaurant opened up at 59 Fifth Avenue, just over the road from where the Stones played. It was called Ashley's and its nominal proprietor was Ashley Pandel, my pal who'd been Alice Cooper's press agent and later ran his PR outfit The Image Group. Ashley christened me Chuck and told me about his past, how he'd studied catering at college and once managed a hotel in a resort town on the shores of Lake Michigan. He'd come up with the idea of only accepting bookings from single women, so the place soon got a reputation amongst blokes as a great place for finding them. "Bar was packed every night," he laughed. "Guys came from miles around knowing they'd find it full of girls. Takings tripled."

It was this background that inspired Ashley to quit the PR business and open his own bar and restaurant with two partners, his brother Carl and a catering professional called Ed Martin. Ashley hung Art Deco pictures on the walls and on the opening night it was packed to the gills with music business types. Steven Gaines and I sent Ashley a gigantic bouquet of flowers shaped like a horseshoe for the opening, the sort of thing we thought Mafia gang bosses would send to funerals of rivals they'd eliminated, and the bar soon became the place to go and be seen for New York's rock world. I became a charter member, my membership card number 001.

For the next two years Ashley's bar and restaurant became my home from home in New York, a bar like the one in the TV show *Cheers* where everybody knows your name and they're always glad you came. Ashley, a natural mixer, went from table to table, greeting and telling jokes, laughing and smiling, topping up drinks, putting quarters in the juke box, making absolutely sure everyone was having a great time, night after night, week after week. He had a way of ensuring that rock stars who visited were never bothered by fans. Upstairs there was a dance floor and a DJ and it was supposed to be members only but this wasn't strictly adhered to, and there was an office where favoured guests could talk in private, hoover up coke on the mirrors provided and, with the door firmly locked, do what comes naturally to the birds and the bees.

Ashley's soon became party central, and a list of those who visited reads like the inductees at the Rock 'n' Roll Hall of Fame. They flocked to Ashley's like they flocked to Jay 'The Great' Gatsby's house, and there was something about Ashley Pandel that reminded me of Fitzgerald's greatest character as he welcomed Beatles, Stones, Whos, Led Zeps, Pink Floyds, Faces, Elton,

Aerosmiths, NY Dolls, you name them, into his tavern. One of the guys from Kiss often came in, without his make-up of course, and ducked under a table if a photographer was snapping away; the New York Dolls were regulars, their music blaring out from the juke box; Lou Reed too, along with friends of uncertain sexuality; Jonny Podell, the booking agent whose father Jules had famously run the Copacabana for mobster Frank Costello, and Jonny's petite girlfriend Monica; Alice and his clever manager Shep Gordon; the lovely models Lisa Stolley, who played Bee Gees' records on the jukebox, and Babette, wife of Neal Smith, Alice's drummer; Steven Tyler and his managers and girlfriends; Bleecker Bob who ran the best record shop in the Village; a wise man who spoke seven languages and worked at an embassy; and a golf pro called Sam Anziano who ran an indoor golf course and took Ashley and I golfing to a club with five courses on Long Island and, afterwards, to an Italian restaurant run by one of New York's Five Families.

All these and many more came to Ashley's, to drink and have fun, and at the centre of it all, grinning from ear to ear, shining like a diamond, radiating a special kind of magic, was Ashley Pandel, the best pal I had in New York City.

26

"Hooray, hooray, the first of May, outdoor fucking starts today."
Graffiti on the ladies' bathroom wall, O'Henry's pub, New York City,
1975

I had long ago realised that the peculiar nature of my role as *Melody Maker*'s man in New York was unsuited to forming close romantic relationships, and my two predecessors had coped with this dilemma in different ways. Roy Hollingworth, who rarely looked before he leapt, had fallen hook, line and sinker for his Iris and she followed him back to the UK. After quitting *MM*, he had followed her back to America to face an uncertain future. Michael Watts, more discreet than Roy in every way, had an English partner called Tessa who joined him in New York where she found a job as PA to the manager of Miles Davis. When Michael was recalled in 1973 they returned to the UK together.

I had no such attachments. Reluctant to embark on a steady relationship lest Ray Coleman recall me to London without much notice, I defied the edict laid down by that sharp-tongued social worker at St Mary's Hospital in Paddington and opted for promiscuity. Enjoying sex in New York in the seventies did not signify emotional commitment for me and, perhaps unsurprisingly, the music industry and its broader environs attracted plenty of independent-minded young women who felt the same way. Sex for us was a leisure pastime, like reading or board games or sport. This resulted in a number of agreeable but fairly meaningless sexual encounters and a few escapades that were unlikely to have come my way in the more prudish UK, let alone back in North Yorkshire, where many girls still treasured their virginity, to be surrendered only in the honeymoon bed.

In complete contrast, the female position on sex in New York was best expressed by graffiti on the wall of the ladies' bathroom in O'Henry's, a historic bar in Greenwich Village, where I took a date for a drink one night. Returning from the loo, she was giggling stupidly.

"What's up?" I asked.

"The graffiti. Someone's written 'Hooray hooray, the first of May, outdoor fucking starts today' on the wall."

I spent a night with a woman of colour whose enthusiasm took my breath away. On at least two occasions I was despoiled and brusquely discarded by women a bit older than myself which I found slightly humiliating, albeit a fair price to pay for what had occurred. One night I was involved in a foursome with two girls and a bloke who worked for Billy Gaff, the manager of the Faces, in Gaff's splendid apartment in a high rise on the East Side, and on another occasion enjoyed a threesome with two girls, watching them making love to one another before joining in, a stunningly erotic experience. One of the girls worked for Mainman, the company run by David Bowie's manager Tony Defries, and after the exertions on the bed, as we sipped beer and smoked grass, she mentioned that Bowie had at one time pleasured her, as he did many of the girls that worked there.

Two women who shared my bed on an irregular basis had husbands back home and one of them introduced me to the delights of phone sex, calling me every so often to talk dirty. After she seductively locked the door to her office, I attended to the needs of a girl who worked high up in the Black Rock, Columbia Records HQ on West 52nd Street, and when it was over we realised to our amusement that we could have been observed by those on the same level as us in another skyscraper across Sixth Avenue. I allowed a cheating friend in the music business to use my apartment for trysts if I was out of town, the quid quo pro a lavish dinner in a restaurant of my choosing, paid for by his company credit card. Something similar happened with a visiting English friend who needed somewhere to be alone with the wife of a well-known rock star who was away on tour, so I lent him the key for an hour.

It was through these escapades that I began to believe that being English in the USA at this time, before the advent of Freddie Laker's cheap flights across the Atlantic, was looked upon by the more venturesome slice of American womanhood as being a member of an exotic species with whom it was advantageous to mate or, at the very least, a guinea pig on whom they could satisfy their curiosity. While I took full advantage of this, some I encountered, among them an accomplished chess player, certainly tugged at my heartstrings.

So it was that although I lived alone at the apartment on East 78th Street I didn't necessarily sleep alone or always wake up in my own bed. Indeed, in the summer months when New York became unbearably humid, I occasionally woke up on the deep pile carpet in the living room cradling last night's date, our clothes strewn everywhere. My bathroom steam room was a bonus and some mornings I'd invite my date to refresh herself alongside me in my improvised private sauna. Since it worked best if we somehow raised ourselves off the floor, we'd stand on the loo seat clutching one another, our naked bodies drenched in sweat.

On the morning after the opening of Ashley's bar and restaurant, in May of 1975, I awoke in a studio apartment on Manhattan's West Side that was the home of one of the waitresses, name of Gail, who had six kittens that climbed all over us on the bed and a wardrobe full of antique floral print dresses. She was free-spirited and very pretty, slim but curvy in the right places with big blue eyes and curly dark hair that tumbled loosely over her forehead, and she disdained underwear. A bit of a wild child, I was very taken with her and we became an item for a few weeks though I was mindful that having been in New York since the beginning of the year there was a good chance that Ray might order me back to London at any time, which was precisely what happened at the end of June.

Before that I took her for a few days to Paradise Island in the Bahamas, where passengers alighting at the airport were entertained by a reggae band in the customs area. We sat in the sun, ate well and lost a bit of money in a casino. While there, however, Gail told me she was bisexual and much as she enjoyed our time together she preferred sex with her girlfriend. Knowing that I was about to return to the UK for an indefinite period anyway, I swallowed this unforeseen but disheartening development and, holding my emotions in check, took her to see The Rolling Stones at Madison Square Garden on the night we flew back to New York.

My friend Pete Rudge, tour managing the Stones, introduced me briefly to Bob Dylan who was loafing around backstage, the only time I ever met the great man. Swigging greedily from a flagon of white wine, he inquired briefly about the wellbeing of Max Jones, our jazz expert who in 1962 was the first British journalist to take an interest in his career, then turned away to resume his conversation with a girl in a red dress. Neither this nor my premium Stones seats impressed Gail and after the show she went back to her own apartment, her need to be reunited with her kittens evidently greater than a final night with me, and I never saw her again, ever, but someone later told me that once my back was turned, she was seen on the arm of a New York journalist who went on to make a name for himself writing about fashion and American society.

*

After a holiday in Austria where my sister now lived, I was back in London and aghast to discover that, while I was in the US, *Melody Maker*'s offices had relocated from Fleet Street to a prefabricated building on spare land in Meymott Street, south of the river close to Waterloo Station. Many of the magazines from

IPC Business Press, of which *MM* was a part, had been rehoused at IPC's base in Sutton but the management, mindful that *MM*'s staff would have mutinied at this, opted for prefabs that had once seen service as a staff canteen.

I couldn't help but feel we'd been downgraded, that despite the paper's success and the vast sums that continued to roll in from advertising and sales, the directors at IPC had no real respect for *MM*, its staff, its readers or the subject that filled its pages. A few refugees from Fleet Street, and *NME* from their offices in Carnaby Street, were rehoused in nearby Kings Reach Tower, a newly-built tower block, but *MM* was consigned to a bomb site surrounded by barbed wire. I am not alone in believing that the move symbolised the approaching end of *Melody Maker*'s glory years. Those who worked there referred to it as "Colditz".

"Ruffians from *NME* would periodically come and jeer at us through the barbed wire," said Michael Watts. "They all but threw bananas."

The move to Meymott Street was not the only unwelcome change that had occurred in my absence. Gone was Richard Williams, to whom I had looked up as a source of knowledge and good taste; dry-humoured production editor Alan Lewis had been replaced by Michael Oldfield, not the musician but a chap who loved American West Coast music; my mate Roy Hollingworth now lived in the US; and also missing were Mark Plummer and folk writer Andrew Means. In their place were several newcomers, among them the roguish Allan Jones, perhaps the funniest writer *MM* ever employed, who would go on to become the paper's editor and also editor of *Uncut*; Rob Partridge, who had my old role of News Editor and would, like Richard, go on to work for Island Records; and folk writer Colin Irwin, soon to distinguish himself in that field. Chris Welch, always cheerful, was still there, as was Chris Hayes, Mr Lugubrious turning up every Tuesday to inquire whether someone or other played a Gibson or a Fender.

All of this only added to my dissatisfaction. I was truly homesick for America and New York especially. I missed the excitement of the city that, like John Lennon, I looked on as the centre of the world, the open-mindedness of my American friends, the easy availability of cheap grass and the independence that went with the job there. I wasn't to know it but the writer sent to replace me would for reasons unexplained return to the UK within four months and I'd be sent back there. In the meantime, I gritted my teeth, bought a used MGB GT, found somewhere to live in South Kensington and fell into the welcoming arms of Maureen, the estranged wife of another music writer.

My first *MM* assignment was covering Pink Floyd headline at Knebworth. I felt they were becoming stale and needed fresh material to revitalise their act which, as it had done for three years now, relied largely on *Dark Side Of The Moon*, by now one of the best-selling LPs of all time. I figured there were two reasons for this: its state-of-the-art production made it perfect for testing upmarket stereo systems, and its slinkier songs, not least 'The Great Gig In The Sky' with Clare Torry's ecstatic moans, made it good for the bedroom. "The afternoon contained no real excitement," I reported of Knebworth. "There was none of the glorious anticipation of being on hand to witness an event that would go down in the musical annals, alongside more profound events that took place earlier this decade."

Much more exciting was a trip to France the following month to report on the Orange Festival near Avignon. Staged in a spectacular Roman amphitheatre where gladiators once fought with lions, it promised much but delivered less due to several star name no-shows, bands running late and interminable delays between sets. Coupled with the hard stone seats, it's not surprising there were outbreaks of ill-feeling amidst the crowd. Nevertheless, it was memorable in all sorts of ways.

I watched a set by Fairport Convention but whatever enjoyment I felt was tempered by an altercation in the backstage bar I had earlier in the day with their bass player, Dave Pegg. Pegg, not in the first flush of sobriety, had taken exception to an *MM* review of his group's last LP, and decided to vent his spleen by pouring a pint of beer over my head. I too had drink taken and this emboldened me to retaliate, not least because I wasn't the author of the review that had so inflamed him. So I bought a pint and went over to where Pegg was sitting and poured it over his head. He was restrained from thumping me by others in his party. I think we made up later.

The Fairports appeared on the first evening of the festival, a Friday, and were followed on stage by John Cale who was billed to appear with Nico. In the event Nico elected to perform solo later in the evening, but I liked Cale whose acquaintance I'd made in America. I also felt that he, and not moody Lou Reed, was the key musician in the Velvet Underground. Idiosyncratic to a tee, Cale wore what today would be called a onesie, loose and unbuttoned to the waist, and after his set he walked straight off stage and carried on walking, striding purposefully past everyone backstage, out of the arena, up a hill and on into the town. I alone decided to follow him, maybe 20 or 30 yards or so behind, curious as to his intentions. When he reached the town centre he went into a bar, ordered a drink and sat down. He was still dressed in his distinctive stage wear but no one gave him a second thought, so I went into the same bar, ordered a beer and sat down alongside him.

"Hello Chris. What are you doing here?"

"Hello John. Taking a break from New York. I enjoyed your set."

"Thanks."

"Er, what's with leaving the arena and heading straight for this bar."

"I didn't like the crowds backstage."

"Fair enough. I didn't like them much either. I have to go back though. I'm supposed to be covering the show for *MM*."

"Rather you than me. You don't have any money, do you? I forgot to grab some on my way out."

I handed John a few francs. "Thanks. Bye."

"Bye John."

I walked back to the arena, which wasn't far, but was refused entry by the guardian of the backstage door who didn't believe I was from *MM*. Fortunately my plight was noticed by Patsy Collins, who worked for Artists Services, bodyguards to the stars, who knew me from past encounters, and he eased my entry in a manner that comes naturally to straight-talking Cockneys built like brick shithouses. That night he was working for Bad Company, the headliners, whose customary professional but rather predictable set was sadly diminished by a surfeit of the local speciality, full-bodied red wine. I heard later that some of their entourage were involved in a bust-up in a restaurant in the town. No doubt Patsy sorted it out.

Back at the festival the following morning I was wondering what the day would bring after yesterday's adventures. I wasn't to know it but I was to be knocked sideways by an act I hadn't seen before, Dr Feelgood. "They were an absolute knock-out," I reported, "providing an object lesson to bands who flounder in complexity for complexity's sake. The Feelgoods were so damn simple you just had to prick up your ears and listen as three-minute songs were punched out with fire and drive and a certain amount of self-parody. Their guitarist, Wilko, was electric, strutting the stage as if 5,000 volts shot through his system to power his Fender Telecaster. The crowd erupted as they thundered along, never hesitating for a second, like an express train on a quick inter-city route. 'Doctor Feelgood' itself brought the audience to their feet, and they stayed up for the closing sequence of 'I'm A Hog For You Baby', 'There's A Riot Goin' On' and the closer, 'Route 66'.

"For five minutes they cheered, but the Feelgoods never returned, and when the crew began to dismantle their equipment the cheers turned to hostile jeers and whistles. Procol Harum had the unenviable task of following, but the immediate danger was forestalled with a seemingly interminable pause between the two acts."

The next day, the Sunday, Lou Reed failed to appear which was a shame as I'd like to have contrasted his set with John Cale's. Even better would have been them appearing together, but I'd have to wait until 1993 for that.

*

Melody Maker kept me reasonably busy during my stay in England. For a few weeks in October I did the singles reviews. I went to Greece to interview Graeme Edge, the drummer with The Moody Blues, who was spending his year as a tax exile on his 70-foot yacht, *The Delia*, which he planned to skipper across the Atlantic, up the Panama Canal and on to California. In order to promote an LP he'd recorded with Paul and Adrian Gurvitz, he'd moored up on the coast of Corfu where I and two other journalists chatted with him over retsina in a restaurant. I reported on a concert in Hyde Park promoted by Virgin Records that was a bit of a flop as only 6,000 people turned up. I saw Wings again, this time at the Hammersmith Odeon, and noted that Paul McCartney had come to the belated realisation that the songs he wrote for The Beatles were what people wanted to hear. I saw and interviewed Santana in London, and watched Tangerine Dream in York Minster of all places and to round out my story interviewed a senior cleric about the wisdom of allowing pop music – if you can call Tangerine Dream pop – to be performed in cathedrals.

I attended an Art Garfunkel press conference at the Savoy Hotel where *NME* wag Charlie Murray asked him in all seriousness whether or not he might consider a collaboration with the Ramones for his next LP. Art, rapidly ascending the charts with his dreamy cover of 'I Only Have Eyes For You', an oldie originally written in 1934, didn't seem to know who the Ramones were.

Those looking after his PR had decided Art would do only one music press interview during his stay in London and this turned out to be with *MM*, conducted by me. At his request it took place in a car, a Daimler limousine, while a chauffeur drove us around West London, stopping briefly in Holland Park. When I asked him why his former partner was more active than he was, he replied: "Paul's heartbeat is a lot faster than mine. He is more neurotic than I am and needs to achieve new things more than I do. I can just sit back and eat a peach."

Alongside Art in the back of this spacious car was his girlfriend, the actress Laurie Bird, with whom he snuggled up close during the ride, making it pretty obvious that he'd prefer it if the interview was brief so they could return to their hotel, perhaps to listen to *The Dark Side Of The Moon*. "Their mutual affection was obvious," I wrote diplomatically in *MM*.

Then, much to my delight, along came The Who again.

*

The Who's seventh studio album, *The Who By Numbers*, was released in the first week of October and given to me to review. Recognising immediately that here was a record on which the group's guitarist and principal songwriter had elected to air his many frustrations, I wrote: "Unpredictable as always, Pete Townshend has chosen to bare his soul with nine songs that often reveal him as a bitter, frustrated and disillusioned man, weary of the task of running the band he created and generally dissatisfied with his lot. He can neither equate his financial success with his artistic achievements nor get over the fact that many feel he said it all with 'My Generation'."

The album was the precursor to a tour that lasted, with breaks, for over a year, visiting the UK, continental Europe and America three times. It opened with two shows at the New Bingley Hall near Stoke-on-Trent on October 3 and 4, both of which I attended, staying overnight at the same hotel as the group, all bar Pete who opted to stay elsewhere. Largely because it was the opening night of a tour and they were a bit rusty, and also playing a newly sequenced set, the first show had its faults but, as ever, The Who's vast experience enabled them to power through and the crowd went away happy. There were some adjustments to the set list for the second night, which was well-nigh perfect.

After the opening night's show Keith behaved quite shamelessly in a successful bid to gain the favours of a spectacularly beautiful young lady lingering backstage. She was just his type, blonde and dressed to kill in a short white dress and stiletto heels, and when he clocked her, post-gig adrenalin rushing through his veins, his libido went into overdrive. Within minutes he'd skilfully separated her from the bloke she was with, her fiancé as it turned out, by inviting them both back to the hotel for a drink and asking her if she'd like a ride in his white Rolls-Royce convertible, which she most certainly would. Calculating that her bloke couldn't join them in the Roller as he would have to drive their own car, Keith said they'd meet him back at the hotel and summoned his driver Dougal to take the wheel without delay. I watched all this play out with experienced eyes, knowing the likely outcome and, sure enough, when I got back to the hotel the Roller was parked outside but Keith and Miss Stoke-on-Trent were nowhere to be seen. The bloke, meanwhile, was pacing the lobby looking a bit peeved.

Eventually, after about half an hour, Keith came down to the hotel bar with the lady. She looked a bit unsteady on her feet, slightly sheepish, and was a bit giggly too, and was doing her best to appear as if nothing unseemly had occurred. In truth she was glowing, pink-faced, still lovely, and looking for all the world as if she'd just enjoyed the best half-hour of her entire life. I probably wasn't the only one who noticed that Keith was wearing different clothes from those he'd had on when he left the gig. As ever he was full of charm, especially to the bloke, even if there was a touch of the cat that's got the cream about him.

"What a delightful lady you're engaged to dear boy, absolutely charming," he said to her fiancé as she sat down next to him with as much modesty as she could muster. "You're a very lucky man. We've been watching television, and discussing gardening and foreign travel. I love gardening and we travel a lot with the group you know, especially to America. Have you been there? Fine country, most welcoming. Let me buy you both another drink, more champagne."

Keith was hilarious, prattling on, talking rubbish – I doubt he knew a rake from a hoe – to them both. In a gesture of reconciliation, she had sought out her boyfriend's hand and was gripping it tightly but his face was set in the kind of uneasy, fixed smile that people adopt when tact is an effort. Of course, he couldn't say what might have been on his mind because he was surrounded by people who worked for The Who, who were paid to protect them, so there was no way he could accuse Keith of anything or, heaven forbid, cause any trouble. So he had no choice but to go along with the charade, as did his now slightly tipsy girlfriend, albeit more enthusiastically. It was side-splittingly funny but somehow cruel at the same time.

In the end they left together, opting to take a taxi since both were a bit worse the wear for drink. As they were leaving Keith shook the man's hand vigorously, sincerely, and gave his girl a chaste kiss on the cheek. "Delighted to have met you both, absolute pleasure. Do come and see us again if we're ever in these parts. Ask for me personally," he said, but I couldn't help but wonder what might have been said between them the following morning when they'd sobered up, and if their relationship survived this brutal intrusion from the whirlwind that was Moon The Loon.

Of course, I didn't write about this kind of thing for *Melody Maker*, though my story about The Who's comeback stretched over three pages. "Like mountaineers tottering on the brink of some huge ravine, The Who crashed into their first tour in over two years at the weekend and, in the insanely mad tradition of this extraordinary little band from Shepherd's Bush, they survived one night of relative chaos before another night of absolute triumph."

I noted that on the opening night they came unstuck during 'The Punk And The Godfather', a song from *Quadrophenia*, and began it again, an unprecedented lapse for a band of The Who's stature. It was Keith who screwed up, and Pete looked annoyed. "An angry Townshend stopped playing, turned to Moon and told him, in no uncertain terms, to belt up," I reported. "Then he recommenced the song at the beginning of the solo. There was a short discussion after the song and Townshend apologised to the audience, who didn't seem to mind at all. The incident was forgotten after Moon walked across the stage, embraced Townshend, and apparently made up for the blunder."

For the first time ever, Keith had played his drums from a raised podium, built at a cost of £6,000 especially for this tour. The siting of the podium had apparently meant that his monitor speakers were placed further away from him than normal and throughout most of the show he was only vaguely aware what the rest of the band was playing. The podium was promptly scrapped.

"That wasn't so bad for an opening concert," Roger told me back at the hotel, nursing a vodka and smoking a cigar. "We haven't played for over a year so there's bound to be a problem or two. It wouldn't be the 'Oo without a problem, would it? Just wait till tomorrow. It'll be better."

He was right. The act was revamped and the concert flowed with far more purpose, finishing on 'Won't Get Fooled Again', which, like the previous night, was full of crazy power. Pete leaped the full length of the stage after the taped synthesiser sequence towards the end, bringing matters to a deafening, extended climax.

"What did I tell yer," said Roger, grinning insanely after the show and buttoning up a long, fur-lined leather coat. "We'll be OK now."

*

Then, unexpectedly but to my utmost delight, Ray Coleman told me to pack my bags for New York, this time for an uninterrupted spell lasting almost a year and a half.

27

*"Chris has left the room to use the bathroom. I hope he hasn't
eaten anything that's disagreed with his stomach."*
Paul Simon, New York City, November 1975

As the plane circled the illuminated towers of Manhattan it felt as if I was
returning to paradise. A taxi took me from JFK across the Queensborough
Bridge, the same one on which Simon & Garfunkel felt groovy. I dropped off
my case at the apartment on 78th Street and, without delay, hailed another cab
downtown to Ashley's where the proprietor hugged me like a long-lost child. I
was home again.

The first order of business next morning was to call Bob Gruen. "What's
happening, man?" I asked.

"Bob Dylan's *Rolling Thunder Revue*," he replied, and off we went, chasing Bob
and his friends in New England. With him at the wheel, we drove to Springfield,
Massachusetts, a four-hour journey from New York in a car I rented. In today's
world, when tickets for concerts by major rock stars go on sale anything up to a
year beforehand, it beggars belief that on Thursday, November 6, 1975, two hours
before it commenced, I was able to buy two tickets for a Bob Dylan concert at face
value ($7.50) for a 5pm show from the box office at the 10,000-seat Civic Centre,
and two tickets from a tout outside for an 8pm show for $10 each, opting to pay
the extra $2.50 for seats closer to the stage.

This was the fifth stop of the *Rolling Thunder* tour, the dates of which were
advertised only locally and not in advance. Springfield was actually the tour's
biggest venue and the second ticket was for Gruen who, before both shows,
stripped down to his briefs in our rented car and taped his camera equipment
to himself, then dressed again in loose fitting dungarees and a sweater so the
bulges wouldn't show. Photographers weren't allowed in but this was never going
to stop a man as determined as Gruen who, once inside, went to the bathroom
and retrieved his camera, lenses and film. He disappeared once the shows
started, edging his way towards the front, and six of his pictures accompanied
my lengthy report on the shows, stretched across three pages of *Melody Maker* of
November 15, 1975.

During the break between the first and second shows we went to a nearby
diner that was packed full of Dylan fans and in there met Larry Sloman, a writer

from New York, who ended up writing a book about the tour. He was following the tour everywhere it went and, because Bob knew him, I was able to pick Larry's brain. Some of the tour's road crew were in there grabbing a bite too, and I chatted with them as well.

"You need more than a weatherman to know which way Bob Dylan blows," was my opening line in a review that, sentence for sentence, was the longest show review I ever wrote for *MM*. The concerts were, after all, "revues" in the accepted sense of the term which meant everyone got a go, and the bill also featured Joan Baez, Roger McGuinn, Mick Ronson, Ramblin' Jack Elliott, Arlo Guthrie and others, all of whom played at least one song of their own alongside the band that accompanied Dylan who, naturally enough, grabbed the lion's share of stage time, both solo and in combinations with the others.

He was magnificent too, playing and singing not for profit or even to promote a new record but simply because he felt like it. After the hullabaloo surrounding the previous year's tour with The Band, which was Big Corporate Rock, Dylan had opted for something else entirely, a folksy down-home feel, almost like a Hootenanny, and he was happy to chime along with everyone else though there was no doubt who was the star of the show. Some of the songs he sang would appear on *Desire*, not yet released, and I was spellbound by 'Sara', his homage to his wife. The shows ended with the ensemble gathered round several microphones for 'This Land Is Your Land', Woody Guthrie's alternative American National Anthem, a fitting finale to an evening of music in which Dylan explored his roots, mused on his past and offered a glimpse into the future.

The tour wound up at Madison Square Garden on December 8, a benefit show for Rubin "Hurricane" Carter, a boxer wrongly imprisoned on a murder charge who was eventually freed. Dylan had recorded a single protesting Carter's innocence, and I was at this show too, way up in the seats behind the stage, but it wasn't anywhere near as enjoyable as the smaller shows in New England. The revue format didn't suit a big arena and the audience was unsympathetic to the other musicians. Nevertheless, the two *Rolling Thunder* shows at Springfield were among the best concerts I ever saw during my stint as *MM*'s man in America.

*

Back in New York, I interviewed Paul Simon, a nice symmetry after spending an afternoon with Art Garfunkel two months ago in London. He'd just released his *Still Crazy After All These Years* LP, on which he introduced a more sophisticated jazz ambience to his music while at the same time emphasising the delicacy of his lyrics and, as ever, wrapping up the whole package in pristine, state-of-the-art production. For the time being, he dropped the stylistic variety of his two previous LPs in order to accentuate a theme of nostalgia for times and lovers past, a subject that his maturing audience might readily appreciate as they left their twenties behind them.

I thought the result was his most mature sounding record to date, as far removed from the folk-singer of old as, in time, *Graceland*, would be from this collection. The public agreed, sending *Still Crazy After All These Years* to number one in the US on release, which called for an audience with *MM*. We met in his lawyer's office and talked for two hours, and as an interviewee he was as unhurried and painstaking as his public image suggests, considering his answers carefully and with discretion. "I tend not to be sloppy," he told me when I touched on this aspect of his personality, a characteristically understated response to my suggestion that he was popular music's greatest perfectionist.

We talked about the wide variety of musicians with whom he collaborated on his first two solo records, and how he wanted to broaden his musical palette, but on the thorny question of whether or not he might realign himself with Garfunkel he was ambiguous. I broached the subject by inquiring whether or not Columbia, his record label, had pressurised him to record with Art again for commercial reasons. "I think at the time of the split they were upset but there had never been a serious mention of us getting back together again, and there's certainly never been any pressure. That doesn't mean they wouldn't be very happy if we got back together again" he said, adding, "I don't think you can ever bring something back together. Again. I don't think if The Beatles got back together again it would be what it was. Ideally, I'd like to be able to sing a song with Artie now and then but not rejoin as a permanent partnership. We're certainly not going to go back to doing an act together."

For all his measured responses Paul Simon had a sense of humour. Halfway through the interview I excused myself to use the bathroom, switching off my tape recorder before I did so. Unbeknownst to me Paul switched it back on while I was out of the room and left me a message that I didn't hear until I was transcribing the conversation later. "Chris has left the room to use the bathroom," he said. "I hope he hasn't eaten anything that's disagreed with his stomach."

*

Patti Smith, impulsive and outspoken, was the polar opposite of Paul Simon.

After watching her at the Bottom Line, I knew she was treading a path of her own making, mixing her strident poetry with impromptu, three-chord rock, backed up by a band led by guitar-playing Lenny Kaye, a friend of mine who was the nearest thing to a degree-level rockologist – my own term – I would ever meet. Lenny had impeccable taste and wrote for *Rolling Stone* and fringe music magazines, penned sleeve notes, compiled the fabulous *Nuggets* collection of garage classics, and sometimes even worked behind the counter in Village Oldies, the collectors' shop in Greenwich Village run by a tight-fisted man called Robert Plotnik whom everyone knew as Bleecker Bob. I think Patti worked there on and off as well before her recording career took off.

I met Patti and her band in a rehearsal space on the West Side and we talked about *Horses*, her influential debut LP, produced by John Cale and just about to be released. "It's a live album," she told me, squatting amidst the guitars and cables on the floor. "We just went in and did the songs straight away. In the studio we went through hell. I begged John to do it for me and we had nothing but friction but it was a love-hate relationship and it worked. Even words were improvised in the studio. I'm not into writings songs. I find that real boring."

I liked Patti a lot and we got on well for a while, bumping into each other in the places where those from New York's rock world gathered after hours. Unfortunately, I earned her wrath after an underground newspaper called *The Planet* printed several topless photographs of her with cheesy captions written in the style of girly mags. Predictably, she was livid and the whole lurid business was the talk of the town in rock circles. As *Melody Maker*'s man in New York I felt duty bound to mention the vexed issue of Patti and the topless pictures in the news column I sent to London every week. Patti saw it and wasn't amused. The next time we collided with one another she let me have it with both barrels. In vain did I try to explain that I wasn't endorsing the actions of *The Planet* but that it was my job to report everything, good and bad, that occurred in the NY music world. Patti wasn't having it and she never spoke to me again.

Something similar had happened with Ian Hunter earlier in the year. Hunter and I were on fairly friendly terms and I'd interviewed him at least twice, once at the home he shared with his American wife Trudi in Connecticut, and written complimentary reviews of several Mott The Hoople concerts. Shortly after he formed the Hunter-Ronson Band in the spring on 1975 many dates on their first US tour were cancelled "because of Ian Hunter's illness", according to a press statement from their PR.

It was Ian Hunter's misfortune that at the time of these cancellations I was in the midst of a casual but nevertheless pleasant between-the-sheets relationship with a girl named Karen who worked for ABC, Hunter's US booking agency. One night at my flat she spotted the press release relating to Hunter's "illness" on my desk, read it and scoffed, telling me that the real reason several shows on their tour were cancelled was because Hunter-Ronson hadn't sold enough tickets.

The next day I confirmed what Karen had told me by calling a few box offices, inquiring about ticket availability as if I was a punter. Feeling indignant that the PR had lied, I duly reported the real reason for the cancellation of the Hunter-Ronson shows in my next *MM* New York news column, and also mentioned the poor ticket sales in an otherwise flattering HR Band concert review. Hunter evidently read one or both. Two or three weeks later I bumped into him at the Bottom Line. Quivering with rage, he accosted me, implying that I had somehow betrayed our friendship. I thought for a moment that he was going to hit me. I pointed out that I tried to report the truth in *MM*, not recycle PR bullshit. Hunter didn't deny that the dates had been cancelled through lack of ticket sales but he seemed to think that I, and by extension *Melody Maker* and the rest of the music press, existed simply to further his career and that we should ignore anything that reflected unfavourably on him. The argument raged but remained unresolved.

Ian Hunter and I never spoke to one another again after that night. If we had I'd have told him that the reason I relayed the real cause of the cancellations in *MM* was not out of malice but because I felt he'd betrayed his man-of-the-people image by lying, or at least condoning the lies perpetrated by his PR.

*

I ended 1975 by interviewing John Hammond, the legendary Columbia A&R man who'd signed many jazz greats to the label, then moved into the rock era by signing Bob Dylan – "Hammond's Folly", as he was known at first – and later Bruce Springsteen, among a score of others. A man of wealth and taste, he was a scion of the fabulously wealthy Vanderbilt family that built America's railroads, and he was as well known for his support of African Americans as he was for his work in music. Back in the 1930s he'd contributed a New York news column to *Melody Maker*, writing about Duke Ellington and Count Basie. I felt privileged to have followed in his footsteps.

For the first time in my life I was alone on a Christmas Day, spending most of it in bed recovering from a seriously late party the night before at Ashley's apartment where among the guests was Harry Nilsson who was swigging heartily from a bottle of sake, the Japanese rice wine usually drank warm. On Boxing Day, which Americans don't celebrate, I was up bright and early and decided that since no one had bought me any Christmas presents I'd buy one for myself.

I walked through Central Park, past the Latinos selling loose joints, all the way down to West 48th Street which, like Denmark Street in London, was wall-to-wall guitar shops. I'd already visited Manny's, the famous music shop where the big acts bought their gear, and even done an *MM* feature on the place, but I found what I was looking for a few doors down in a shop called We Buy Guitars: a used small-scale Gibson LG2 acoustic, circa 1960, so I paid the asking price of $165 + $13 tax and slipped the receipt into the accessory compartment in its case where it has stayed ever since. Elvis played one just like it in *Loving You*, his second movie. Two weeks later I enrolled at the Guitar Study Centre, a Manhattan music school run by Eddie Simon, Paul's younger brother, and over the next few months painstakingly learned how to finger pick. I wrote an *MM* feature about Eddie's music school too.

As 1975 became 1976 there was a nagging doubt in my mind as to what I would do after *Melody Maker*. This life I was leading wouldn't last forever. I was still checking out CBGBs, heading down to the Bowery in the scruffiest clothes I had lest someone mug me for the few dollars I had with me. I saw many of the bands that played there, reviewing most of them, the hits and the misses. I saw The Voidoids with Richard Hell in his torn t-shirt before Malcolm McLaren dressed some London lads the same way and that original punk 'Handsome' Dick Manitoba with The Dictators. The first time I saw the Ramones I thought they were a novelty act, but I loved them all the same. I somehow knew Talking Heads were destined for great things, as were Television.

I also saw Tom Petty & The Heartbreakers at CBGBs but thought they were out of place there. They weren't a punk band like the Ramones, or a power pop outfit like Blondie, or new wavers like Talking Heads. But they weren't hard rock either, more a traditional rock band whose music was built on the blues and fifties rock 'n' roll, like the early Beatles, Stones and Who. Also, there was none of the slightly under-rehearsed amateurishness about them that – not necessarily in a bad way – characterised groups like The Voidoids, Television and the Patti Smith Group, and they didn't dress or wear their hair in ways that knowingly contrasted with established rock performers. Equally importantly, they knew their chops, especially guitarist Mike Campbell, and had plenty of drive. I thought they were from the same disciplined domain as Bruce Springsteen's E Street Band or Bob Seger's crew from Detroit. Then again, Tom's high voice sounded a bit like Roger McGuinn of The Byrds which, coupled with his Rickenbacker guitar, gave them an added string to their bow. Nowadays it's called "heartland" music which implies a common bond with the blue-collar American working man and a tendency not to stray too far away from their rudimentary roots.

One night in early 1976 Debbie Harry called and asked me to meet her and Chris Stein in the upstairs bar at Max's Kansas City. They told me they needed a manager for their new group Blondie. Would I be up for it? I was astounded, incredibly flattered, but declined. I didn't think I knew enough about managing groups and wasn't up to the job. In any case, there would have been a conflict of interest and, besides, my presence in New York was contingent on my working for *MM*. My visa precluded doing anything else. Also, there was the same dilemma that discouraged me from forming steady relationships: I could be called back to London at short notice.

I wish now I'd said yes. I wish I'd thrown myself in at the deep end and taken the chance. I think Debbie and Chris thought it would be cool to have a British music writer as their manager, and they were probably right, but I wasn't ready to make this jump, not yet anyway. Still, Debbie and Chris had given me an idea about life after *MM*.

*

Since my early fondness for Sherlock Holmes, I've always loved a mystery and when time traveller Leon Redbone beamed down to the Bottom Line from earlier in the century I was determined to crack the enigma that surrounded him. He was certainly eccentric, performing American songs from the twenties and thirties, his identity as perplexing as his demeanour. Accompanied only by a tuba player, he played ragtime guitar, blues, and melodies from turn-of-the-century America with such authenticity that if you listened carefully enough you could hear the surface noise on scratchy 78s. He also looked the part, in a Panama hat, collar and tie and bushy moustache. He walked with a cane and sometimes wore a monocle. Among his admirers was Bob Dylan.

Redbone's repertoire, or at least the repertoire he had so far revealed, consisted of songs like 'The Sheik Of Araby', 'Any Old Time', 'Big Time Woman', 'Champagne Charley' and 'Polly-Wolly-Doodle', all vaudeville-type tunes, as well as some black blues from Chicago and the South. "Redbone has the deepest of deep voices and is extraordinarily proficient at 'mouth trumpeting'," I wrote. "He speaks very little, just shambles up to his chair, hanging his cane on a stand, murmuring inaudibly and suddenly coming to life as he picks the strings on his elderly Martin guitar. He sings Robert Johnson material in such a deep voice you could swear he was black, but he actually looks very Jewish. The humour of his appearance is not lost on him, of course. Occasionally he doffs his hat or twitches his eyebrows with deadpan, expressionless gestures worthy of Chaplin. Then he'll start picking again, faster and faster, and completely blow everyone's mind not only with his speed but also his accuracy."

I was determined to get to bottom of the Leon Redbone business and to this end approached a writer friend whom I knew was on speaking terms with him. With his introduction, I crept backstage into the tiny Bottom Line dressing room where he was sat on a chair idly picking on his guitar and drinking a Heineken beer. Also present was his tuba player and a lady called Beryl Handler, his manager and, apparently, his girlfriend.

Conversation was stunted, to say the least, but the upshot of our meeting was a vague promise to do an interview in the near future. Leon actually smiled once or twice, twinkling his eyes like Groucho Marx and expressing an interest in *Melody Maker*'s history which, of course, goes back to the period of his own particular interest.

Three weeks later we met again. Leon and his girlfriend were coming into New York – he lived somewhere between NY and Boston – to see Joe Turner, the great stride piano player, who was appearing for a three-month season at the Cookery, a Greenwich Village restaurant. The same writer friend arranged for me to join their party. First, however, we took in a pool hall on 14th Street where, perhaps unsurprisingly, Redbone demonstrated a keen mastery of the cue, and then we moved on to the Cookery, and a table with a good view of Joe Turner's keyboard technique. There was a good half hour to wait, so, with Leon's defences at their lowest, I attempted an interview, beginning with a question about how long he had been performing.

"Seriously I can't er... offhand... ha ha ha, and furthermore... how can I answer that? Not long... what I consider long."

But nobody heard of you until three years ago?

"Quite possibly. It could be longer, too. I guess it depends on how long it was doesn't it?"

Have you always performed the repertoire you are performing now?

"The same type of music? Yes."

Can you tell me how long you've been interested in this type of music?

"Well, in order to answer that you have to define the kind of music. You see,

I don't look at it as being any different than something by Chopin, for instance. To me it's the same feeling. My interest in music lies within a period of 1830 or so to 1930."

You look as if you've stepped out of a history book.

"Ahhh... I do?"

Is this for effect?

"Yes and no. That's a most difficult question to answer, but it could be taken that way, yes."

He mentioned that Caruso was probably his favourite singer, and that he liked Lonnie Johnson, Blind Lemon Jefferson and Jelly Roll Morton. He claimed the air of mystery that surrounded him was because he was misunderstood. "You've claimed to be several hundred years old," I said.

"In many ways that's true," he replied.

When Leon died in 2019 his website claimed he was 127. Only later did I discover, to my astonishment, that he was two years younger than myself.

*

I spent a pleasant afternoon with Bonnie Raitt later in the month. This was when she expressed her admiration for Little Feat's Lowell George and told me somewhat suggestively that she and her friend Linda Ronstadt would do "anything" to get him to play on their albums. I reviewed a concert by Linda at the Beacon Theatre that month too and, coincidentally, remarked that the best song in her set was Lowell's 'Willin''. "A trucking song of immense character, it enabled Linda to tone down the hoedown atmosphere," I wrote. "She did the same with 'Heart Like A Wheel' her encore. But the audience preferred the familiar stuff: 'Silver Threads And Golden Needles', 'It Doesn't Matter Anymore' and 'Heatwave' were attacked with a zest that belied the fact that she probably sings them every night and has done for years."

I saw the new look Deep Purple with Tommy Bolin on guitar at the Radio City Music Hall and commented on how the changing personnel in the group put them in a similar situation to various black vocal groups with permanently fluctuating line-ups that cast doubts on their authenticity. This was quite perceptive of me as, in 1980, their original singer Rod Evans, who was shown the door in 1969, would put together a group of unknown musicians that performed as Deep Purple until lawyers put a stop to his scam.

Back in 1976 I noted that it was the material from the Lord-Blackmore-Paice-Gillan-Glover edition of Purple that went down best with the audience, though I had a good word to say about Glenn Hughes who now shared vocal duties with David Coverdale. My only complaint was the volume. "They played too damn loud for comfort," I wrote. "A good proportion of the crowd spent long periods of the concert in the large Radio City lobby, seeking relief from the volume before returning to the inferno that caused smoke to drift across the water."

*

Stories and interviews that I wrote for *MM* were occasionally sold to other magazines around the world, some to one in Australia called *Go-Set*, others to one in Sweden for which they were translated. The longest interview I ever did with Robert Plant, conducted in February, was reproduced later in the year in *Creem*, one of the best American rock mags, so I wasn't about to complain about it, even if whatever fees were paid ended up in IPC's bank account and not my own.

Still, I couldn't help but feel it was thanks to my persistence that this interview took place. I'd seen Robert about town, at one or two gigs and in Ashley's bar, and knew all about the serious car crash on the Greek island of Rhodes that had brought a temporary halt to Led Zeppelin's touring plans, and suggested to him that we sit down with a tape machine. He said he'd think about and I gave him my phone number. "Give me a call if you decide to do it," I said. Which is precisely what he did a couple of weeks later.

I liked Robert, always the most genial member of Led Zeppelin, and we met up outside his hotel, the Park Lane, on the south side of Central Park. He was raving about an Indian restaurant that he'd discovered in the city, and in those days Indian restaurants were a bit of a rarity in NY. Robert's wife was Asian, so he was gagging for a chicken madras. He was still hobbling a bit, on crutches, a legacy of the motoring accident the previous August. Bob Gruen accompanied me to the interview in his hotel room, taking photographs as we talked.

"The fractured foot has stymied Plant's usual punk arrogance," I wrote. "Temporarily, at any rate, he can't run with the pack and this compulsory moderation to the pace of his life seems to have brought about a certain sympathy that wasn't always apparent in his personality. He might look like the proverbial Greek god rock vocalist as he struts magnificently across stages with the stud-like hauteur of the rock idiom, but he's human just like the rest of us, broken bones and all.

"Plant has always seemed rather divorced from reality, often giving the impression of being a leftover from the days of flower power, with his golden curls and brightly-coloured stage tops. That image has been perpetrated by interviews that are both vague and filled with scattered references to peace, love and world understanding – topics that have tarnished considerably in the reality of the seventies. It was something of a relief then, that the Robert Plant of 1976, with his crutch and newly curled hair, seemed to have come to terms with his public image on a more evenly-balanced level. Goddammit – *he* phoned me to arrange the time of the following interview, and if that isn't a turn up for the book, then I don't know what is."

We talked about the accident and its impact on Led Zeppelin's plans, his travels in Northern Africa, the soon-to-be-released *Presence* LP and his thoughts on the eight-year career of the group. Was there a chance, I asked, that you might have been crippled forever?

"Yes," he replied. "I had to, not so much grow up very quickly, as be prepared to face odds that I never thought I would come up against. I haven't come out of it too scarred, either physically and mentally, and, in fact, once I knew Maureen [Plant's wife] and the kids were OK I really threw myself back into my work. By engrossing myself more and more in the work we had on hand, the time passed by quicker. If I stop and brood, which is a very bad thing to do, then time moves with a lead weight around it, but the time between August 4 [the date of the accident] and now has gone by quickly because I applied myself to what I do best. I mean... I can do 99 per cent of what I could do before, so we sat down and had a meeting. We obviously couldn't tour, so we decided to make an album."

Robert became uncharacteristically serious when I asked when Zeppelin might tour again. "Already I've surprised the doctors by recovering as much as I have in such a short time. They've called me a model patient and that surprises me because hospitals are really not my cup of tea. I mean, I was faced with a situation that dented every single thing I had going for me. My usual, er, sort of leonine arrogance was instantly punctured by having to hobble around, so I'm having to take my time. I don't want to rush. Every day I walk more and more without the stick and I'm going to need physiotherapy so I should think it'll be the beginning of the next soccer season before I'm running about again."

After more chat about the accident and new LP, I asked Robert to look back at the highlights of eight years with Zeppelin. "There have been so many amazing things, things that were once beyond my wildest dreams. I mean, basically I wanted to sing, and sing and sing. Heavens, how could I ever have envisaged anything like this? Me and Bonzo had just come down from the

Midlands to join a band. Jimmy was the experienced man and he'd been over here on *The Dick Clark Show* or whatever, so he knew we would end up at least on that level. I don't think Jonesy had been to the States before, but Bonzo and I had no idea. We even got lost in London.

"I remember when we played the Fillmore West in San Francisco, Bonzo and I looked at each other during the set and thought 'Christ, we've got something'. That was the first time we realised that Led Zeppelin might mean something; there was so much intimacy with the audience, and if you could crack San Francisco at the height of the Airplane, Grateful Dead period then it meant something. Mind you, we went on with Country Joe & The Fish so we didn't have that much of a problem... how could we fail? But we knew the chemistry was there when we recorded the first album."

After a bit of chat about their forthcoming film and his travels in North Africa with Jimmy, Robert told me about how he woke up in the Greek hospital with a drunken soldier in the next bed. "He had fallen over and banged his head and as he was coming around he kept focusing on me, uttering my name. I was lying there in some pain trying to get cockroaches off the bed and he started singing 'The Ocean' from *Houses Of The Holy*."

*

As ever I was rattling off interviews thick and fast, Billy Swan, Andrew Gold, Wishbone Ash, CW McCall, Neil Sedaka and Dobie Gray. The next really big one though was John Denver, talking to me on the phone from his Rocky Mountain hideout for at least two hours. For three years his LPs had rarely been off the American charts, selling by the bucketload, and he was starting to make inroads into the UK too. Ray Coleman had been on at me for 18 months to get an interview with him but my requests to his record label, RCA, were stonewalled. I even offered to fly to Aspen, Colorado, where he lived, at *MM*'s expense, but this was greeted with robust disapproval. Mr and Mrs Denver – she being the Annie in 'Annie's Song' – guarded their privacy jealously, I was told.

Denver's image was as wholesome as a Disney character, an all-American Mr Nice Guy in check shirts and dungarees, playing his guitar for friends by the campfire and saying things like "aw gee", "shucks" and "far out". I thought he looked like a character in a Norman Rockwell painting, perhaps of a farm boy holding a pitchfork, with straw behind his ears, blonder than blond hair and a lopsided grin.

Melody Maker trailered my interview with him on its front page. "DENVER

SPEAKS" read the bold headline as if he'd broken a lifelong silence espoused by monks entering a cloistered monastery. Reading between the lines, however, it seemed he'd chosen to speak to me because he was about to undertake a UK tour. His manager, Jerry Weintraub, a wily wheeler and dealer who promoted concerts by Sinatra, Elvis and Led Zep, never missed a trick. I was told he had a Xerox of one of Denver's royalty cheques – for $6 million – framed on his office wall.

"With the sunshine on his shoulders and the mountain water in his veins, John Denver is an enigma surrounded by moonbeams, a friendly postman who delivers blissful music to millions of Americans," I wrote. "He looks like a haystack with hair of flaxen straw and a permanent smile to lighten darkness and gloom. Untouched by, but nonetheless concerned with, the problem of modern civilisation, Denver floats over the airwaves of America on a cloud of endless joy, gathering disciples like a musical Billy Graham."

To prepare for this interview I attended a Denver concert at Madison Square Garden and asked RCA to send me his entire catalogue of LPs, which they did, all 11 of them, including a hits collection and live set recorded at the Universal Theatre in Los Angeles. Duty bound, I listened to them all. "I've saturated myself in his music," I wrote. "I sing 'Country Roads' in the bathtub, hum 'Rocky Mountain High' as I inhale New York's polluted air and immediately recognise the opening bars of 'Sweet Surrender' whenever it's played on TV as the soundtrack to Walt Disney's wildlife movies. The next time I take a plane it'll be a miracle if I don't warble 'Leaving On A Jet Plane' as I exchange my ticket for a boarding pass."

At great and, I have to say, entertaining length, Denver told me his life story, beginning in New Mexico, through his stint with the Chad Mitchell Trio – who retained the name long after Mitchell left, with Denver as the senior member – right up to going solo, becoming managed by Weintraub and the present day. He called me sir, just like the young Elvis called his elders and betters, and after recording this lengthy biography in his own words I touched upon his clean-living image and how he reacted to those of a cynical disposition who might scoff at it. "It doesn't make any difference to me," he said. "My whole intention is to live my life as honestly as I can in reflecting what I know to be the truth. I want to do that in music, in my personal life at home and in every situation that I find myself. What people make of it is what they make of it and I can do nothing about that.

"You know, Chris," he continued, on a roll now, "I have a definition of success and what success is to me is when an individual finds that thing that fulfils himself, when he finds that thing that completes him and when, in doing it, he finds a way to serve his fellow man. When he finds that he is a successful person. It doesn't make any difference whether you are a ditch-digger or a librarian or someone who works at the filling station or the President of the United States or whatever, if you're doing what you want to do and, in some way, bringing value to the life of others, then you're a successful human being.

"It so happens that in my area, which is entertainment, that success brings with it a lot of other things, but all of those things, the money, the fame, the conveniences, the ability to travel and see the rest of the world, all of those are just icing on the cake and the cake is the same for everybody. For me, I love doing what I do more than anything else in the world and that is being able to sing for people, and the acknowledgement I get from the people who write to me and people who use my songs in their wedding or something that means I am doing something of value. That more than fulfils me."

Amen.

28

"I'm just doing this tour for the money."
David Bowie, Detroit, March 1976

We didn't talk about money with those we interviewed for *Melody Maker*. It was uncool to be a rock 'n' roll breadhead. The only strategic mistake that Led Zeppelin made early in their career was to authorise the mail out of a press release revealing that Atlantic Records had advanced them $200,000, unusually high for the time. Clearly they thought this would boost their launch but in an era when breadheads were despised by the alternative culture that was their market, it was both imprudent and unnecessary. They should have kept it to themselves. The consequence was that a number of US music writers immediately assumed they were in it only for the money, which explains the terrible relationship they had early on with *Rolling Stone* magazine, the American counterculture's biggest flag waver.

As it happened, Led Zeppelin became enormously wealthy very quickly because, unlike antecedents in his position, manager Peter Grant saw his role as supportive rather than predatory. To enrich the group, as well as himself, he set his sights on middlemen who in his view were creaming off funds that rightfully belonged to the boys in the band, and with this in mind he negotiated record and concert deals that saw the members of Led Zeppelin move into large houses and drive expensive cars within two years of their inception. In 1972 Jimmy Page was able to buy Tower House in Holland Park from the actor Richard Harris for £350,000, outbidding David Bowie who also had his eye on the distinctive Grade I listed building.

Perhaps the press release faux-pas explains why Page henceforth kept mum about his money. Rival bidder David Bowie, on the other hand, had no such qualms, telling me the sole reason for touring in 1976 was to shore up his bank account. "I'm just doing this tour for the money," he said. "I never earned any money before, but this time I'm going to make some. I think I deserve it, don't you?"

We were in his suite at the Pontchartrain Hotel in Detroit and David was 19 concerts into the *Isolar* tour on the back of his *Station To Station* LP. On stage he portrayed the Thin White Duke of the title track, an Ayran character of severe countenance who throws darts into his lover's eyes, as referenced in *Un Chien*

Andalou, the 1929 surrealist film by Salvador Dali and Luis Buñuel that preceded his arrival on stage. A woman's eye slashed by a razor blade is not the sort of thing US fans expect at a rock show.

Having long ago realised that absolute truth was of less significance than the effect his words might carry, David was among the most skilled interviewees I ever encountered. It wasn't often that he spoke to the press but when he did he invariably made headlines, not least in January 1972 when he announced to my *MM* colleague Michael Watts that he was gay, or at least bisexual, in what was perhaps the most significant interview he ever gave in terms of furthering his career. No one seemed to notice that he had a wife and son. Similarly, his comment to me about being strapped for cash didn't ring true either: he and I were in an expansive suite with trays of food and beverages discarded casually on pristine surfaces; the wardrobe contained designer suits and freshly laundered linen; he was waited on hand and foot by a team of support staff; a Mercedes 600 Pullman limousine waited downstairs for when he required transport. But the admission that David Bowie was broke screamed headline to me and I wasn't about to question it. So instead of saying, "Pull the other leg Dave, you're a rich rock star, everybody knows that," I urged him on.

"The other tours were misery, so painful. I had amazing amounts of people on the road with me. I had a management system that had no idea what it was doing and which was totally self-interested and pompous...".

And so it went on, another candid Bowie interview and I barely needed to interrupt the flow of remarkable quotes, almost all of them worthy of headlines in themselves.

"David Bowie is balanced delicately in an armchair in suite 1604 in the Pontchartrain Hotel in Detroit, his legs bent and hunched up, gazing absently at his bare feet which, like the rest of him, look remarkably clean," I wrote. "In his blue tracksuit he looks astonishingly healthy and although he could add a few pounds in weight his brain is as trim as his figure. His hair, blond at the front and red at the back, has been groomed by his personal hairdresser, and is swept up in a quiff. His classic, Aryan features alternate between expressions of genuine warmth and cold contempt whenever he senses troubled waters. His left eye is still strangely immobile, a legacy from the childhood injury he received, and it adds an incongruous touch to his rather aristocratic bearing. Even if David Bowie never opened his mouth, he would have found some niche in life purely on the strength of his looks."

I followed this bit of scene setting with what today reads like one of those caveats we find on advertisements for financial services. "The views and opinions of David Bowie as quoted below represent his statements made between 6.30pm and 7.30pm US Eastern Standard time on Monday, March 1, 1976. What he's said before that date and what he might say afterwards may vary considerably."

We began by talking about the current tour, the staging of which was a massive departure from the elaborate *Diamond Dogs* presentation I saw two years ago. Simplicity was the keynote this time around, right down to the white lighting effect designed by Scottish tour manager Eric Barrett. As I saw for myself later that same evening, it was wonderfully effective; quite stunning in fact. "It's more theatrical than *Diamond Dogs* ever was," said David, toying with an unlit Gitane and a glass of Heineken. "It's by suggestion rather than by over-propping. It relies on modern 20th Century theatre concepts of lighting, and I think it comes over as being very theatrical. Whether the audiences are aware of it, I don't know. It doesn't look like a theatrical production, but it certainly is."

Was it getting out of hand before? "No, it was just boring after a while. Once I got to Los Angeles and did the shows in the Amphitheatre there, I'd already done 30 of them and it was terrible. There's nothing more boring than a stylised show, because there was no spontaneity and no freedom of movement. Everything was totally choreographed and it was very stiff. It didn't look it if you went and saw the show once. The first time it was probably a gas, but there's nothing much in it if you are doing it every night. It just becomes repetition. I can't speak as an audience but certainly, as a performer, it was hard to keep it up, trekking all over the country doing the same thing night after night. This one changes almost every night. It's a lot looser. The only thing we have is a running-order, but I even change that around. The lighting guys have lighting cues, but that's on spec as well."

After a bit of chat about his changing image and the musicians in his current band I asked David whether John Lennon was an important contributor to 'Fame', the hit song from his LP *Young Americans*. "No, not really," he replied bluntly. "I think he appreciates that. It was more the influence of having him in the studio that helped. There's always a lot of adrenalin flowing when John is around, but his chief addition to it all was the high-pitched singing of 'Fame'. The riff came from Carlos [Alomar], and the melody and most of the lyrics came from me, but it wouldn't have happened if John hadn't been there. He was the energy, and that's why he's got a credit for writing it; he was the inspiration."

Bowie hadn't set foot in England for three years. Any particular reason? "I just haven't got around to it," he confessed. "Most of my affairs have been messed up so badly that I just hadn't time. There were plans at one time to take the *Diamond Dogs* tour to England, but I doubt if ever that show will see the light of day again. I've still got the scenery stored away in New York, so there's always a chance."

That tour must have been extraordinarily expensive to stage. "Apparently so. I never saw any money from that tour. I'm only making money now. That's why I wanted to simplify things this time around, to make money. I'm managing myself now, simply because I've got fed up with managers that I've known."

How were relations between himself and Tony Defries? "I haven't seen him since the day I left him. I wouldn't know. Is he still in the business? I honestly don't know."

David seemed a little reluctant to enlarge on this point, so I mentioned that Defries was still managing Mick Ronson and asked whether Bowie had any opinions on Ronson's role in Bob Dylan's *Rolling Thunder Revue*. He seemed indifferent. "I don't have any opinions. I honestly can't remember Mick that well nowadays. It's a long time ago. He's just like any other band member that I've had. Maybe I should react more than I should react. Anyway, I'm not a great Dylan fan. I think he's a prick, so I'm not that interested."

We talked about other musicians, films and the roles he adopted on stage. "I was never a rock and roll singer. I was clumsy as a rock and roll singer, but I do have a certain penchant for fabricating a character and portraying a cold, unemotional feeling. I'm still giving them a persona, but that persona out there is possibly an exaggeration of all the things I feel about me. Maybe it's some aspect of me as a person blown-up to life-size. A lot of the other characters were blow-ups of other rock and rollers that I saw around. I'm more approachable onstage this time around, unlike the last time when the character I played was a paranoid refugee of New York City. That was about the collapse of a major city and I think I was right to be remote, don't you?"

I agreed. But was it necessary to not even acknowledge the presence of the audience or his group? "Oh yes. That character was in a world of his own. This time I at least say 'good evening' to the people. Now you know that I'm not the warmest performer onstage, and I never have been, but that's because I feel too shy about talking to people onstage. I've never felt comfortable talking on stage. With *Diamond Dogs* I even wanted to have the band in an orchestra pit.

"If ever I have the audacity to do a *Diamond Dogs* tour again, I think I know how I would do it, and I will do it properly because of everything I've learned over the past few years. You know, unless you make some big mistakes you are never going to grow, you've got to make mistakes. I've made one a week, and if you don't make them then you won't become a self-invented man. I've got to learn to make mistakes to understand the character that I am clawing the air for. People like watching people who make mistakes, but they prefer watching a man who survives his mistakes. To make a mistake in life, and survive it, is the biggest kick of all."

It wasn't long ago, I mentioned, that David stated he wasn't going to tour again. He shrugged. "Oh yes, I did, but I don't feel that way now. I love it. The other tours were misery, so painful. I was getting all the problems every night. Ten or 15 people would be coming to see me and laying their problems on me because the management couldn't or wouldn't deal with it. For me touring was no fun, no fun at all. They were little problems, but to each individual they were important. I understood all their problems but I couldn't cope with them all, so the two major tours I did were horrendous experiences. I hated every minute of them, so I used to say I'd never tour again. Then I would be talked into doing it again to make somebody some money.

"If I'm in charge, I'll tour again, whereas before I always thought there was somebody better at doing this kind of thing. It wasn't until John [Lennon] pointed it out to me that I realised maybe the artist is as good at managing as anybody else. It was John that sorted me out all the way down the line. He took me on one side, sat me down, and told me what it was all about, and I realised I was very naive. I still thought you had to have somebody else who dealt with these things called contracts, but now I have a better understanding of show-business business."

And the right-wing politics I had read about? "Oh, that was just bullshit, something I said off the cuff. Some paper wanted me to say something and I didn't have much to say so I made things up. They took it all in."

At that point David wanted me gone so he could prepare for the evening's show, but as a parting shot I asked him whether he still professed to be bisexual. Momentary shock. "Oh lord, no. Positively not. That was just a lie. They gave me that image so I stuck to it pretty well for a few years. I never adopted that stance. It was given to me. I've never done a bisexual action in my life, onstage, record or anywhere else. I don't think I even had a gay following much, a few glitter queens, maybe.

"You know the funniest thing of all," he continued, talking to me like a conspirator, "I'd never heard of Lou Reed until somebody said my stuff was influenced by him. So when I heard that, I started saying it myself, that my songs were influenced by Lou Reed. It seemed the obvious thing to say, and that's when I started getting interested in Lou. The same with Iggy. It wasn't until people told me my music was very sort of Detroity that I happened to discover Iggy Pop & The Stooges. I thought 'what a great name', and although I'd never heard them, I used to tell everybody who asked that I liked them a lot. Then I got around to meeting Iggy, but it wasn't until months later that I actually heard anything he'd written.

"It's marvellous. A lot of people provide me with quotes. They suggest all kinds of things to say and I do, because, really, I'm not very hip at all. Then I go away and spout it all out and that makes it easier for people to classify me. People dissect the songs and say that's influenced by someone or other, but I don't know whether I'm influenced. All I know is I'm drinking a beer and enjoying myself."

I went to David's show that night and like everyone else at the Cobo Arena cringed when the eye was slashed. Many years later I read an interview with Madonna in which she stated that she too was there, and that it was the first rock concert she ever attended. "It was a major event in my life," she told the interviewer. "I was wearing my highest platform shoes and a long black silk cape. We arrived at Cobo Hall and the place was packed and the show began. And I don't think that I breathed for two hours. I came home a changed woman."

She would have been 17 at the time and for all I know I could have sat next to her.

*

The following month I was reporting that David had appeared in court in Rochester in upstate New York, accused of possessing marijuana in his hotel suite following a concert there. Also charged was James Osterberg, aka Iggy Pop. The bust occurred during a party in David's room when two female narcotics agents in attendance revealed their identity and arrested them and one other man. They were freed after posting bail of $2,000 each, and David looked shocked when asked if there was any truth in the rumour that a former business associate had planted the dope on him.

The *Isolar* tour reached Madison Square Garden in New York that week and I attended a small party at the Penn Plaza Club within the Garden complex afterwards but David was unwilling to comment on the case. Indeed, I thought I might get slung out on my ear by mentioning it but David calmed down and I chatted with Iggy who remembered me from the beach in southern LA.

Coincidentally, I happened to be in Rochester myself the same month that

David was up before the judge, not amongst the fans who mobbed him as he left the court but to interview Peter Frampton whose *Frampton Comes Alive* LP was number one in the album charts where it stayed for weeks on end, eventually selling over eight million copies. Its success was vindication of manager Dee Anthony's theory that if you tour endlessly for long enough, you'll hit the jackpot. Anthony, rumoured to have mob connections, looked after the American affairs of several British acts and, curiously, a fair few of them ended up damn near broke.

Peter Frampton, a sweet, guileless, unassuming fellow, was one of them though this wouldn't become apparent until much later. He and his gorgeous girlfriend Penny, whose similar blond curls made them look like twins, were often to be seen around the NY nightspots. "It's all quite unbelievable really," he told me in a modest hotel room. "I don't want to think about it too much. I know it's great and it's made me really happy but I've got to try and keep on the ground. I'd like to believe I haven't made it, because I haven't in my own head. If I start believing too much I'll go silly. It's not as if it hasn't happened before so I know to what to expect but this is more intense than all the others put together."

Peter was like a kid on Christmas morning. Not long after this interview I saw him and Penny at JPs, a music biz hangout on the Upper East Side, and they came over for a chat as they were leaving. When I left about an hour later, I was told he'd paid my bill.

*

I was at the opening night of Monty Python's three-week season at the New York City Centre West on 55th Street in May, and the party afterwards was attended by their pal George Harrison who had joined them on stage for 'The Lumberjack Song'. I sidled up to George at the party, introduced myself and said hello, thus completing my full house at Beatle poker, but I realised I was intruding on him and backed away almost immediately.

More fun was to be had with John Cleese, to whom I was introduced by Nancy Lewis, then the PR for Buddha Records which distributed Charisma, Python's UK label, in the US. I'd gone along with a married girlfriend of mine, name of Kathy, also a fan, and I asked Nancy to introduce me to John.

"How do you do Mr Cleese, sir," I said, opting for courtesy as I shook his hand. "I'm a big fan. This is my friend Kathy."

Kathy extended her hand which Cleese shook and continued to hold for rather longer than might be expected. "Hello Kathy," he said, peering down at her from his great height and completely ignoring me. "Have you known Chris long?"

"About a year," she said.

"I see you wear a wedding ring. Are you married to Chris?"

"No."

"I see. I understand. Does your husband know you're out with him?"

Kathy hesitated, wondering no doubt where this conversation was going.

Cleese finally let go of Kathy's hand and turned his attention to me. "Mind you get this woman home without any hanky-panky," he said sternly. "There's far too much of this sort of thing going on today. Ought to be a law against it."

And with that he turned and walked purposefully away.

*

Seeing Wings in Detroit was another adventure involving Bob Gruen. We flew to the Motor City together and rented a car which, as usual, he drove but we were running late and got clogged up in traffic on a freeway into the city. Bob, being Bob, wasn't having it and to my horror reversed up on an on-ramp to reach the gig through back streets. With my name on the rental agreement, I was fortunate they didn't have CCTV cameras everywhere in those days.

Backstage Paul gave an impromptu press conference. Asked about The Beatles, he almost lost his cool. "Look mate, it's 1976 and I don't think most people here care about what happened ten years ago," he muttered. "All they're interested in is what I'm doing now. The past is gone and it won't come back."

He was only half right. The biggest cheer of the night came when he performed 'Yesterday' solo. Afterwards I asked him whether John might turn up for his forthcoming Madison Square Garden show in New York. "Well, I know he wants to come to the show but I don't know whether he wants to play," he told me. "You'll just have to wait and see."

Wings' brass section included saxophonist Howie Casey, an old pal of Paul's from his Liverpool days, and Casey's girlfriend happened to be friendly with Maureen who'd eased my troubled mind back in London the previous year. Both came to New York for Paul's Madison Square Garden concert and Maureen stayed with me for two weeks at the apartment, the longest period during my NY posting that I had the pleasure of live-in female company.

That same May issue of *Melody Maker* contained the first feature on Kiss who'd become impossible to ignore. Whatever I thought of their music, regurgitated heavy metal riffs that made Black Sabbath look like maestros, I had to admire their dedication and work ethic. Leader Gene Simmons put the band through a rigorous rehearsal schedule before hiring the Diplomat Hotel for their earliest New York gigs and, at first, I wrongly pigeonholed them with the bands that appeared at CBGBs.

I interviewed them during a photo shoot at photographer Finn Costello's studio. They were costumed as they would for the stage, with massive stack-heeled boots, shoulder pads and made up to look like characters from a DC comic. The shoot also involved big motorbikes and a model, a tiny blonde girl in a skimpy white dress, the concept to contrast her purity with Kiss' evil ways. Political correctness never troubled Gene Simmons.

I also interviewed their manager Bill Aucoin, a very clever man with a background in sales. Hanging from a wooden frame in his office were beautifully crafted metre-high marionettes of the four Kiss guys, possibly a subliminal message to visitors about who pulled the strings in their manager-client relationship. After the interview I suggested to him that because the group was never seen (or photographed) out of character he could have more than one Kiss group operating at the same time, in different parts of the world, like a franchise, assuming he could recruit musicians of similar build, and no one would know the difference. He thought about this idea for a while then dismissed it – but I think I'd inadvertently invented the concept of tribute bands.

The members of Kiss were often seen out of make-up in clubs in downtown Manhattan but there seems to have been a tacit understanding on the part of photographers not to take their pictures.

*

After reviewing concerts by Dr Feelgood, Paul Simon, Bob Marley and Joe Cocker I was flown to San Francisco, courtesy of Peter Grant, to see Bad Company at Winterland. We stayed in the Miyako, a Japanese-themed hotel and in my room was the most enormous brick bath I'd ever seen. I bought myself a couple of happi coats in the shop by the reception, and wore them all that summer in the New York apartment.

From San Francisco the Bad Co party flew down to LA in their own plane. On the flight a roadie tapped me on the shoulder. "Peter wants to see you," he said ominously. I made my way to the private room at the rear of the plane and opened the door. Peter was sat at a table with Paul Rodgers. On a table in front of them was a gigantic mound of cocaine. Peter beckoned me to sit opposite him.

"Want some blow?" he said.

"Yes. Thanks."

He gave me a rolled-up bill and I snorted a line into each nostril.

"Did you enjoy the show Chris?"

"Er, yes Peter."

Under the circumstances, I felt it unwise to open a discussion on the merits or shortcomings of Bad Company.

"Well, mind you say so in that paper of yours. You can go now."

We flew into Burbank airport from where limousines took us straight to the Rainbow Bar & Grill. Members of Led Zeppelin awaited us there, Jimmy, Robert and Bonzo already enjoying the ambience, lapping up the waves of reverence that came their way in an establishment that catered to the rock trade. Crowds surrounded them as they left at around 2.30am and headed for the Beverly Hilton where a Swan Song Records sales convention was being held, attended by musicians and staff, led by Peter, that coincided with Bad Co playing the Forum. The following morning, we inspected an array of Native American turquoise jewellery offered for sale by a dealer who'd been invited to the hotel, such ornamentation having long been favoured by Led Zep and their entourage. Some bought belts, bracelets and necklaces. Not wishing to appear aloof, I bought a small ring.

Robert Plant was his usual talkative self when we encountered one another in the hotel lobby, and was particularly keen to discuss Ian Anderson of Jethro Tull who two weeks ago in *MM* had berated Led Zeppelin for spending a year out of the UK for tax reasons. "So Ian Anderson only earns as much as a well-paid bricklayer does he?" he remarked. "Well, as far as I'm concerned, he writes songs like a bricklayer too."

In the evening Bad Co played the Forum and I arrived there in the same limousine as Robert. As we inched into the car park, surrounded by fans, he was overcome with emotion. "Plant tensed visibly as the Forum came into view," I wrote in a lengthy report of the proceedings. "'Look at it,' he said. 'Just look at it. It's beautiful, isn't it?' he added, pointing to the huge oval arena designed on the lines of a Roman amphitheatre, complete with pillars. The white building was illuminated in the dusk. 'Oh my, what would I give for us to be playing here tonight. I want it so much. See all the people. I can feel it here... now.' Plant thumped his chest and grunted in frustration. The Los Angeles Forum is to Led Zeppelin what Anfield is to Liverpool FC.

"As our limousine slowed to a crawl in a line surrounded by slow moving traffic on either side, Plant gazed out of the window and smiled at the occupants of other cars. He was soon recognised and returned waves. 'This is too much for me! I mean… this is LA and I'm outside the Forum and I'm not going on stage. Driver, open the roof!'

"In a flash Plant was out of his seat, poking his curly hair out of the opening. Like a politician greeting voters he waved cheerfully to fans walking in the vicinity of the car. The effect was startling. Most couldn't believe their eyes."

Richard Cole, in the car with us, sensed trouble. "Get down yer dickhead," he yelled. "There'll be a fuckin' riot."

Plant slipped back down into his seat. "I can't believe I actually did that but I couldn't help it," he said to me, pulling on a Park Drive cigarette, "but I want to get back on stage so bloody much. I suppose you'll write about this won't you?" I nodded. "Well, who cares? Just say that I wish Bad Co all the luck in the world but that I'm fuckin' jealous, really fuckin' jealous."

As it happened Robert did get a chance to strut his stuff that night. For their encore of Willie Dixon's 'I Just Want To Make Love To You', Bad Co were joined on stage by Robert and Jimmy, much to the delight of the Forum crowd. It was the first time Robert had appeared on stage since his car crash the previous year.

The evening ended with a party thrown by Atlantic Records boss Ahmet Ertegun at a house he owned in Beverly Hills attended by dozens of beautiful people, among them Ringo. I left with Bad Co guitarist Mick Ralphs, who I interviewed at great length the following day. All in all, the weekend's fun and games filled three whole pages of *MM*.

*

Back in New York, I interviewed Boz Scaggs, Brass Construction, Andrea True, The Bellamy Brothers, John Sebastian, Melba Moore, Russ Ballard and Gary Wright before jetting off to Detroit to watch Aerosmith at the gigantic Pontiac Silverdome, close to the Canadian border. "Only a small proportion of the 80,000 Aerosmith fans were able to see and hear the band and, in order to join this small proportion, it was necessary to suffer the extreme discomfort of being among those pressed close to the front of the stage," I wrote. "Elsewhere in the stadium it was necessary to use binoculars or imagination to watch the act. At the very back a telescope from Jodrell Bank might have helped.

"From where I was sitting Aerosmith sounded like a permanent drone, a rhythmic thumping punctuated by vocal squeals. It was noticeable too that although I was halfway up the arena, I could talk to my neighbours and be heard without raising my voice unduly, and that's rare for a hard rock gig."

When you could hear it, Aerosmith's music seemed to me to be a judicious mix of Rolling Stones and Led Zeppelin, a bit like Queen except that they added a touch of Yes to the mix. They had found their market through the long absences from American shores of the Stones and Zep, who now toured every two years or so, if that, and then only in two-months spells. Aerosmith, on the other hand, toured all the time. Their song 'Dream On' was in heavy rotation on the radio, and singer Steve Tyler and I had been introduced at Ashley's.

The second time I met him, however, was in very different circumstances.

*

It was a Saturday morning in the spring of 1976. I awoke in the studio apartment on New York's Westside that belonged to my friend Karen, the same girlfriend who had tipped me off about the poor ticket sales on the Hunter-Ronson tour. The booking agency where she worked also represented Aerosmith. We'd been out together the night before and wound up back at her place, and in the morning were woken by the doorbell, so Karen climbed out of bed, slipped into her bathrobe and spoke to whoever was outside on the street. A moment later she put down the entry-phone and turned to me.

"It's Steven," she said. "He's coming up."

"Steven who?" I asked, sitting up in bed and fumbling for my glasses. I hadn't a stitch on. My clothes were strewn around the floor, as were hers.

"Tyler. He's been recording all night and needs a bed."

"Doesn't he have a hotel?"

"Yes, but he'd rather sleep here, with me."

"I don't blame him. Are you and him er…?"

"Not really. He just stays here sometimes."

Indeed, I thought. Well, so do I.

There was a knock on the door and Karen let Steven Tyler in. He was very eye-catching in a stylish, Jaggeresque, rock-star sort of way, all mouth and hair, sunglasses and silk scarves, and pencil-thin in tight black jeans, yellow t-shirt and velvet jacket the colour of claret. He looked like he was about to kiss her on the lips and pull open her robe, but then he noticed me in the bed on the other side of the apartment and thought better of it. Before he could say anything, Karen said, "Hi Steve. This is Chris. He works for *Melody Maker*, the English music paper."

"Hello Steve," I called from across the apartment. I tried to sound cheery. "We've met before, with Laura who works for Leber-Krebs." This was true. Laura Kauffman was the PR at Aerosmith's management company, and it was she who'd introduced me to Tyler at Ashley's.

"Oh yeah," he said, stepping into the apartment. "How'yr doin'?"

Steven looked quizzically at Karen and then at me in her bed, and seemed stuck for words. Eventually he said: "Karen, I need to use your bathroom."

He went into Karen's bathroom – can't think why – and locked the door. This enabled me to get out of bed and step into my jeans, very quickly. Equally quickly Karen shed her robe and pulled on her knickers and an XL sweat-shirt. "Do you want me to go?" I asked, quietly, so that Steven wouldn't hear.

"Not really," she replied. "It's up to you."

Karen was making coffee when Steven came out of the bathroom, rubbing his nose – can't think why. He took in that we were both now half-dressed and sat down at the dining table opposite me. We grinned at one another but didn't speak. It was pretty obvious he wasn't too delighted to find me here, any more than I was delighted at his arrival. I also got the impression that Karen wasn't really in the mood to entertain him either, not at 9am on a Saturday anyway. It was a bright, sunny morning and since Karen had no curtains daylight flooded into the apartment.

We drank our coffee and made small talk. Karen joined us around the table, keeping an even distance from us both so as not to appear to be taking sides. We all smiled at each other. I can't remember contributing much to the conversation, only that I was determined to sit it out and not abandon my position, not in these circumstances.

As lead singer with Aerosmith, Steve Tyler was obviously more than a match for me in the pulling stakes, but I was here first and was unwilling to relinquish Karen to him, especially as she seemed fairly indifferent to his charms. Also, it seemed to me that Tyler had a bit of a nerve turning up unannounced at this time of day, expecting her to leap back into bed with him with all that that might entail, but in my experience rock stars become accustomed to girls behaving submissively around them and he was evidently no exception. I was pretty sure that he expected me to leave, that his position entitled him to a sort of rock star *droit de seigneur* but I decided I wasn't having it, not least because Karen seemed to be enjoying this little encounter. Also, she looked gorgeous this morning. Her mid-length blonde hair was charmingly dishevelled, her open smile and bright eyes darted playfully between us, and her lean white legs stretched out alluringly from beneath the oversized top. But I liked Karen because she was smart too, fun to be around and straightforward, and seemed largely unaffected by the close proximity to rock stars afforded by her job at the booking agency. I was tempted to reach out and squeeze her hand, an affectionate gesture that might communicate "she's mine now mate", but thought it unnecessary. About 20 minutes went by before Steve realised I was definitely staying put and lost his patience, so he rose to his feet, a bit reluctantly I think, thanked Karen for the coffee and headed for the door.

"See you 'round man," he said in my direction.

"Bye Steve," I murmured, probably a bit smugly.

Karen walked across the room with him. At the door he pecked her on the cheek, opened it and stepped out. She closed it quietly behind him.

"Thank you for staying," she said, turning around and walking back towards where I was sat.

I stood up and put my arms around her. "There's no need to thank me Karen," I said, kissing her lightly on her forehead. "I didn't want to leave. I wanted to stay here with you."

She put her arms round my neck. "Thank you anyway," she said.

I never met Steve Tyler again.

29

"There's a great woman behind every idiot."
John Lennon, New York, July 1976

Befriending Elton John and writing supportively about him early on came
in useful after he broke into the big time. When *Captain Fantastic And The Dirt
Brown Cowboy* was released in 1975 his record label in New York invited me to
a luncheon for him but it was on a Thursday, my deadline day. As usual, I was
panicking to get my copy ready for the courier to pick it up, probably banging
out another NY news column at the last minute. "Dylan seen checking out
someone or other at the Bottom Line last Friday…".

My phone rang at about 1.30pm. It was someone from Elton's staff who
told me he'd noticed I wasn't at his luncheon and wanted to know why. I told
them to tell Elton I'd be along in a while but I was busy. The assistant said Elton
was worried that I didn't like him anymore! When I finally arrived, a good hour
late, he came running over and gave me a big hug and said he thought I wasn't
coming. I said I was sorry but I had a lot to do that morning and explained why
Thursdays were difficult for me.

"I have to write about people other than you, you know," I told him.

"I know. I'm sorry to be a pain about it."

Still, it was gratifying to know that Elton John cared that I still liked him.

A year later, in the summer of 1976, he was big time several times over but
when Ray asked me to cover his massive tour and interview him, I got short
shrift from his swanky New York PR. "We'll put your name on the list," I was
told rather condescendingly. "But there's a long queue."

"Just mention my name to Elton or someone close to him," I replied.

Something about the tone of my English accent must have set bells ringing
because about half an hour later the big chief of the PR company rang back,
grovelling unctuously. "How about tomorrow? We can fly you to Cincinnati to
join the tour for a few days, travelling with Elton on his own plane. We'll send a
limo to pick you up." Guess I jumped the queue. Thanks, EJ.

In Cincinnati we stayed at Swingos, a hotel favoured by touring rock 'n'
rollers whose management turned a blind eye to boisterous guests. A party was
held in guitarist Davey Johnstone's room and I became aware that he and Kiki
Dee were an item, but later that night I also became aware that an indiscrete

tryst on my part in New York the previous week had left me with a souvenir similar to the one I picked up in Paris five years ago. I decided not to drink to excess, unlike everyone else, as going to the loo would be painful and figured that with a bit of luck, I'd be able to fix the problem in Chicago, our next stop.

I was right. The helpful concierge at the Hyatt Regency steered me in the direction of a clinic not far from the hotel and for $25 I was cured, though one or two of those in Elton's entourage thought it odd that a music writer wasn't drinking alcohol and put two and two together.

I hung around backstage. In Elton's dressing room were huge portable wardrobes for his sparkling outfits, 30 pairs of shoes, 200 jackets, hats galore and drawers and drawers of spectacles. He was very good natured about it all, knowing full well it was wildly over the top and was self-mocking about the extravagance, all a big laugh really. I always thought Elton was like a kid let loose in a sweetshop, pitched into excesses that might spiral out of control.

It was the same plane, the Starship, that Led Zeppelin used, and I was a bit surprised that before we boarded in Cincinnati Elton insisted that the catering crew stocked up on Kentucky Fried Chicken, buckets of it, for everyone. I did my interview on the plane after the finger lickin' good feast and, good natured as always, he told me he was retiring, a genuine scoop at the time. He said it was all getting too much for him and that he was going to run Watford FC instead. It wasn't strictly true but he did slow down on the touring for a while. Around this time he admitted – if that's the right word – to a *Rolling Stone* writer that he was gay but this was no secret to those who'd known him for a while. I read that and thought, "Why are they making such a big deal of it? I've known that for years." Among the entourage was a very good-looking lad, slim with long blond hair, who didn't seem to have any fixed role. I put two and two together.

In Cleveland the backstage guests included Eric Carmen, who'd just had a big hit with 'All By Myself'. He introduced himself to Elton who responded, quick as a flash, with: "On your own, are you?"

*

I liked Elton and I'd like to be able to say the same thing about Neil Diamond, the writer of 'Sweet Caroline', nowadays our alternative national anthem, at least at sporting events, but he was one of the most disagreeable interviewees I ever faced. My meeting with him took place that summer in a luxury air-conditioned caravan that served as his dressing room backstage at the Forest Hills Tennis Stadium in Queens, and in order to impress a blonde woman hovering in the background Diamond spent most of the time ignoring my questions and bragging about his accomplishments. He was, he told me, far more popular and talented than Bruce Springsteen or any of "those long-haired British musicians and noisy groups who come over here and encourage our kids to take drugs." He seemed to have a taken a particular dislike to his Columbia label-mate Springsteen and was unable to understand why music papers were making such a fuss of him when he, Neil Diamond, deserved similar if not greater accolades.

Diamond went on at great length about his many achievements. He was, he said, about to direct his talents into acting where he fully expected to be as successful as he was in the field of music. He emphasised the depth of his career, pointing out that he'd paid his dues, unlike so many other pop singers, and was now reaping rewards that were fully justified. The rant veered worryingly towards right-wing political opinions he evidently espoused. He held strong opinions on drugs and drug culture, too, and I was left in no doubt that he vehemently disapproved of all recreational drugs and had no time for those who used them. He had no time for anti-war protesters either, and thought John Lennon should be deported, sent back to England where he came from.

I felt a growing sense of unease, not just because I disagreed with almost everything he stood for, but because he obviously wanted me out of the way so he could be alone with his female guest. It was almost as if my arrival had interrupted something between them and Neil was impatient to get back to it. She was nodding vigorously at almost everything he said, flirtatiously indicating her approval of his views. I noticed that she was drinking white wine, quite a lot of it too, and that the top buttons of her blouse were undone so as to draw attention to her ample cleavage. She wore an abundance of gold jewellery and tight black stretch pants that emphasised her curvy backside.

Diamond, well-tanned, was wearing tight white jeans and an unbuttoned white shirt with the collar turned up, and he had an ostentatious gold medallion around his neck. I'd done my research on him but he soon became impatient with my questions about his early years as a writer in the era of the Brill Building. He answered my questions about his recent association with Robbie Robertson of The Band, an unlikely pairing I thought, but made a point of mentioning all the gold and platinum albums he'd amassed and the vast crowds that were attending his concerts at Forest Hills, two shows no less. Even more he wanted me out of the way, and when the rising sharpness of his tone indicated that the meeting was over, I was summarily dismissed. I'd been promised an hour with him but the interview had lasted just over half an hour. In truth I was glad to leave.

Back at my apartment I somehow scraped together what I could from the interview tape without dwelling on the displeasing aspects of the encounter. It wasn't the sort of thing *Melody Maker* readers were accustomed to in those days and, in any case, I have no doubt the subs would have edited it out had I mentioned the frosty atmosphere.

A few weeks later I read in the newspapers that during a police raid on his house in Holmby Hills, a suburb of Los Angeles, marijuana had been found. So Neil Diamond was a hypocrite as well.

*

John Lennon would not be deported, which may have displeased Neil Diamond but was welcomed by everyone else in the music world. Before John was awarded his green card, however, I spent a hilarious evening in his company at Ashley's. On the night in question I went upstairs to find John with his friend Peter Boyle, the actor, and Boyle's companion Lorraine Alterman, whom I knew well as she wrote for *Rolling Stone* and had been *Melody Maker*'s New York correspondent before Roy, Michael and myself. Evidently Yoko had just left. John invited me to join their table and was on good form, cracking jokes and graciously signing autographs for anyone who asked. At one point in the evening he turned to me: "Have you noticed it's always men with moustaches and beards that ask me for my autograph?"

"No, but I'll watch out."

Sure enough, it seemed he was right. Only men with moustaches and beards asked John for his autograph.

"It was always the same," said John. "Me and George got the guys with beards wanting to know the meaning of life, while Paul and Ringo got the girls!"

Inevitably, perhaps, a short while later a girl came to ask John for his autograph. Much to our amusement, though doubtless to her amazement, John grabbed her around the waist and sat her down on his knee. "Where are you now McCartney?" he shouted. "I've got a girl at last."

The poor girl had no idea why we were all laughing so much.

It was a long night. John and I discussed reggae music and the emergence of Bob Marley as a world superstar. He insisted that The Beatles had recorded reggae music long before 'Ob-La-Di, Ob-La-Da' on the "White Album", citing the middle-eight in 'I Call Your Name' on the *Long Tall Sally* EP as an example. When I listened to it later I realised he was dead right.

We stayed until closing time and, because John took a fancy to a waitress who'd been serving us, stayed for an after-hours drink which turned into several. She joined us, as did Ashley. Peter Boyle did some wonderful impersonations, including absolutely stunning impressions of Marlon Brando and Al Pacino in *The Godfather*. We even persuaded John to sing a Beatles song – unaccompanied – and he chose 'You Can't Do That'. Eventually we all left together in John's silver limousine and headed for the waitress' apartment in Greenwich Village. While John remained closeted with her in the bedroom the rest of us helped ourselves to her coffee and gradually filtered away. It was 6am when I left, daylight outside, and John was still there.

It wasn't long after this night, on July 27, 1976, that John finally won his five-year battle against the immigration authorities, when his American application for a green card was approved. Effectively, this allowed him to remain permanently in the US and, most importantly, leave and re-enter the country unchallenged. John would have been able to apply for full American citizenship in 1981.

I attended the 90-minute hearing at the downtown New York offices of the US Immigration and Naturalisation Service, presided over by Judge Ira Fieldsteel. Ironically, it was Fieldsteel who had handed down the decision ordering John to leave America on March 23, 1973. When the verdict was announced, John embraced Yoko and the packed courthouse burst into spontaneous applause. The celebrities present who testified for John included the American news reporter Geraldo Rivera, the actress Gloria Swanson, the sculptor Isamu Noguchi and the writer Norman Mailer, who described John as "one of the great artists of the Western world". Close friends of the Lennons, Peter Boyle and John Cage were also in the courthouse.

This momentous day in the life of John Lennon began with the judge reading a brief resume of the history of the case, which had begun on August 31, 1971, when John last entered America. He had remained in the country ever since, refusing to leave in case he was not permitted to return.

In a white shirt, black suit and tie, cowboy boots and sporting a short-cropped haircut, John was called to give evidence, answering questions from his attorney Leon Wildes.

"Have you ever been convicted of any crime anywhere in the US?"
John: "No."

"Have you ever been a member of the Communist Party or any other organisation that may seek to overthrow the US Government by force?"
John: "No."

"Do you intend to make the US your home?"

John: "I do."

"Will you continue your work here?"

John: "Yes. I wish to continue to live here with my family and continue making music."

Wildes then asked John if there was anything he had to add in connection with his request to be granted permanent residency.

John: "I'd like to publicly thank Yoko, my wife, for looking after me and pulling me together for four years, and giving birth to our son at the same time. There are many times that I wanted to quit, but she stopped me. I'd also like to thank a cast of thousands, famous and unknown, who have been helping me publicly and privately for the last four years. And last, but not least, I'd like to thank you, my attorney, Leon Wildes, for doing a good job well, and I hope this is the end of it."

Wildes then called the witnesses to speak on behalf of John, and read a letter from the Bishop of New York, the Rt Rev Paul Moore, that emphasised Lennon's contribution to the culture of New York and praised him as being a "gentleman of integrity". The final witness was Gloria Swanson who, despite her advancing years, took the stand in perfect mental and physical health and spoke about John's fondness for healthy food, taking a swipe at junk food in the process. "We must educate the country in this sphere and the Lennons will help to do something about it," she added.

After a short deliberation, the Judge returned to enquire whether or not John was likely to become a state charge – US vernacular for drawing welfare benefit – which inspired a subdued round of sniggers in the packed courthouse. John's attorney rose from his seat: "On the contrary, your Honor. Mr. Lennon was a member of The Beatles, and has substantial earnings every year. It is therefore *most* unlikely. He is also the owner of several valuable copyrights, properties and such like."

Wildes sat down and, almost immediately, the Judge spoke again to deliver this short sentence: "I find him statutorily eligible for permanent residence."

John's five-year fight was over.

Following the hearing, John, Yoko, their friends and an army of reporters and cameramen were ushered into another room where an immigration official handed John his green card. It had already been prepared, which suggested that John's fate had been decided prior to today's hearing.

Outside the building, surrounded by the large crowd, a happy and relieved looking John said: "It's great to be legal again. I'll tell my baby. I thank Yoko and the Immigration Service who have finally seen the light of day. It's been a long and slow road, but I am not bitter. I can't get into that. On the contrary, now I can go and see my relations in Japan and elsewhere. Again, I thank Yoko, I've always thought there's a great woman behind every idiot."

As the Lennons continued to pose for the army of photographers and television crews, his green card proudly held aloft, I pushed through the crowd, shook John's hand and mentioned to him that his green card was actually blue. He laughed. I wasn't to know it but these were the last words I would ever speak to him.

Not long after the hearing, I sent another telegram to John requesting an interview. This time he responded by sending me a postcard, declining the request. He wrote: "No comment, was the stern reply. Am invisible," and signed it, as he almost always did, with a tiny self-portrait. I still have that postcard but I never communicated with John Lennon again.

*

Like many people in Britain, I was in bed when I first heard that John Lennon had been murdered. I was living in Shepherd's Bush in London with my girlfriend Jenny who'd risen before me on the morning of Tuesday, December 9, 1980. She was listening to the radio when she heard the news and came rushing into the bedroom to wake me. At first I didn't believe her, then when I heard the radio it sunk in. Jenny went off to work but I didn't go out all morning. I just sat there listening to the radio. At lunchtime I went to the Anglesea Arms pub across the road for lunch and sat on my own. Two men at the bar were discussing John and I almost told them that I knew him once. Then I didn't. I figured they wouldn't believe me.

43 years later the killing of John Lennon seems to me to be the single most tragic event in the history of rock 'n' roll. It is a cruel irony that John, essentially a man of peace, died in the manner he did. I have become both angry and cynical about America's gun culture, amazed and appalled at the immorality of a nation whose government sanctions, even encourages, the manufacture and sale of implements with which its citizens routinely slaughter each other. Nothing exposes the institutionalised corruption of American politics more than the ease with which arms manufacturers, through their stooges the National Rifle Association, can bribe the country's legislators to block measures designed to control the sale of their lethal products. Although I sympathise with all the

victims of America's gun madness, especially the families of those children in schools mowed down by lunatics with guns, these strong feelings of mine really stem from what happened to John, a man whom I liked to think of as a friend, at least for those few years in New York.

I have read a great deal of rubbish about John in the years since his death, not least that which emanated from the mendacious pen of the late Albert Goldman, but none of it in any way alters my firm conviction that the John Lennon I knew was a good-natured man of wit, integrity and talent who tried to use his exalted position to right a few wrongs and spread what he believed to be a gospel beneficial to mankind. He was no saint, it's true, but he never pretended to be either.

30

"We were playing for the people who weren't there."
Pete Townshend, Jacksonville, Florida, August 1976

I would see The Who on three more occasions in America. At the Philadelphia
Spectrum in late December 1975, they were magnificent, so much so that
New York Times rock critic John Rockwell and I exchanged glances as 'Sparks'
reached its second crescendo, sharing a moment that we both recognised as
transcendental. At the end of the song the crowd rose as they would at the end
of a show, acknowledging the group's flair in a spontaneous ovation.

The Madison Square Garden show in March 1976 was postponed for 24
hours due to Keith having collapsed midway through the previous evening's
show in Boston, causing it to be abandoned and rescheduled. It was another
triumph, albeit not quite reaching the magnitude of Philadelphia, and afterwards
I went to the Navarro to check in with the band. There was no sign of Keith.
John told me he'd been confined to his room by Bill Curbishley, now and
henceforth the dominant figure in The Who's management. They didn't want
him misbehaving and collapsing at any more shows.

But it was the third show, at Jacksonville in Florida on Saturday, August 7,
1976, that will remain etched on my memory until my dying breath. It was the
last time I would see Keith play drums with The Who, though this wasn't the
only reason it was memorable. I'd been invited there by Atlantic Records to write
about Black Oak Arkansas, another act appearing on an all-day bill at the Gator
Bowl, headlined by The Who. I wasn't particularly interested in BOA but I was
always keen to see The Who, whom I hadn't seen since the March show in New
York, so I accepted the invitation and flew down on Atlantic's ticket. I arrived at
Jacksonville Airport around lunchtime and rented a car to drive to my beachside
hotel, the Sea Turtle on Ocean Boulevard, then headed for the stadium, arriving
around 3pm.

I interviewed Jim Dandy, BOA's singer, and watched their set. Afterwards
I hung around in the backstage area waiting for The Who to arrive and in the
bar fell into conversation with a friendly girl called Andrea who was dressed in a
halter neck and cut-off jeans, well-tanned too. She had a nice smile and seemed
glad of my company, and before long I thought I'd found an ideal overnight
companion. All seemed to be going swimmingly until her elder sister's husband

arrived with the news that their babysitter had cancelled on them at the last minute, and since they were going out to some event with a bunch of friends in the evening they now needed Andrea to babysit instead. So Andrea did the decent thing and opted to leave with him instead of seeing The Who – but she did offer to meet me at my hotel later.

"You know the Sea Turtle by the beach?"

"Oh yes," she said, skipping off with her brother-in-law. "I'll try and be there before midnight."

This open-air all-day event was in a big stadium in muggy, unpleasant weather, a greedy promoter had overcharged and Florida was never really Who territory, so the crowd numbered about 35,000 instead of a potential 60,000. This hurt their pride and when they arrived they were angry, furious in fact, and having watched The Who at close quarters many times by now, I knew all too well that anger could bring out the best or the worst in them. Sharp words were exchanged backstage and I kept my distance; only Keith, fuelled as ever by brandy and cocaine, seemed sociable.

I settled down to watch The Who from the photographers' pit just in front of the stage and come show time an extraordinary transformation came over them. All the fury, all the frustration and pent-up rage was channelled into the music, and The Who at their almighty best came flooding over the crowd in that stadium that night; loud, precise and utterly compelling, every song played beyond perfection, with Pete careering around the stage, windmilling and jumping all over the place, his guitar leading the onslaught; Roger chucking the mic everywhere, bare-chested, singing his heart out; Keith animated like 10,000 volts was surging through his arms, legs and eye-sockets, battering his drums into submission; and John po-faced and cool as hell, holding everything together, his fingers dancing with his bass. The crowd exploded with endless ovations because they'd never seen or heard anything like it before, nor would they ever again.

Afterwards, backstage, in the calm of the caravan that served as The Who's dressing room, I sat down on the floor next to Pete and remarked to him how good this show had been. Exhausted, slumped in a corner, his fingers shredded and covered in blood, his skinny, loose-limbed body wrapped in a towel, he knocked back a huge plastic beaker of brandy in one gulp. There was a strange, faraway look in those deep blue eyes of his as he looked up at me. He thought for a minute, fingered the Meher Baba pendant that hung from his neck, then managed a wry smile. "We were playing for the people who weren't there," he said.

The Who had their own plane and were flying on to Miami that night so I didn't linger long. Pete's words were ringing in my ears as I drove back to the Sea Turtle. In truth the show had been so great and the aftermath so profound that I had completely forgotten about Andrea. She wasn't waiting for me anyway.

It was a warm night and there was no way I could turn in after the excitement of The Who's set, so I took a moonlit stroll along the deserted beach, gazing out across the sand towards the sea. Then I heard rock music, and followed the sound until I came across a bar by the boardwalk, a wooden shack, and approached the door. It was opened by a guy in jeans and t-shirt with long hair who seemed friendly, especially when he spotted the Access All Areas pass to the Who show that was still stuck to my shirt.

"You work for The Who?" he asked.

"No, but they're friends of mine."

He acknowledged my accent. "You're English?"

"Yes."

"Step right in."

I walked in and he followed. A band was playing but there weren't many inside, no more than a dozen. The night was drawing to a close. He tapped me on the shoulder.

"Can I have that pass you've got? I want to stick it on the wall behind the bar."

I looked towards the bar. A gorgeous looking girl in a skimpy yellow summer dress, a ribbon in her short blonde hair, was sitting on a stool nursing a beer.

"Do you know that girl on the stool?" I asked, nodding towards her.

"Sure, that's Melanie."

"Is she with anyone?"

"No, not tonight."

"If you introduce me to Melanie, you can have my pass. My name's Chris."

So it was that the manager of the bar introduced me to Melanie and we got talking. The band closed their set and I bought her another beer. She seemed happy to chat with a Brit who knew The Who and before long we were flirting. After about 20 minutes she asked if I wanted to go back to her apartment to smoke some grass. Her place was five minutes away in a car. The guy behind the bar grinned at me as we left together.

Melanie lived on the ground floor of a house in a one-bedroom apartment and no sooner had we closed the door behind us than we were at it like rabbits on the floor of her living room. When we'd got our breath back she produced a couple of bathrobes for us to wear while we smoked a joint on her balcony overlooking the ocean. We had a whisky each then retired to her bedroom for a more leisurely round two, after which she offered to drive me back to the Sea Turtle as she had to get up early in the morning. Melanie dropped me off outside the hotel at about 1.30am.

I walked through the lobby and asked at reception for my room key.

"Chris?"

It was Andrea. She was sat there waiting for me.

"Hi… er sorry, I've been for a walk along the beach."

"Can I come up?"

"It's a bit late."

"I've been waiting…"

"Of course."

Up we went. I had a quick shower. Andrea got undressed and was in bed waiting for me. She stayed the night. Keith Moon, a connoisseur in this line of behaviour, would have been proud of me I thought when I finally closed my eyes.

The next day, on a whim, Andrea collected a few clothes and flew up to New York with me, hanging out at my apartment for the best part of a week. It turned out her dad ran a pool hall in Jacksonville where she worked on the counter serving food and drink, and she played like a demon. I took her to the pool hall on 14th Street, the same one where I'd hung out with Leon Redbone, and she hustled about $30 in an hour, so we had a slap-up dinner that night. Brazen as they come, she knew exactly how to draw in marks so she did the same thing the next day, and the next, paying her way in NY by hustling pool until she decided to head back down to Jacksonville.

Andrea came back to stay with me in NY again a few weeks later. The next time I saw her in New York she was on the arm of Jimmy Bain, bassist with Ritchie Blackmore's Rainbow.

But what did I care after that night in Jacksonville, the last time I saw Keith Moon drum for The Who.

*

In September I had my second close encounter with the Bay City Rollers, in Philadelphia and then Boston, where the havoc at Logan Airport was exacerbated by the police grossly underestimating the threat to order posed by the group's arrival. They refused to allow the Rollers' limousine to pull up alongside their plane and as a consequence they had to make their way through the airport, me alongside them, where over 1,000 fans were waiting.

"We have the situation under control," a State Trooper told us. In reality it was anything but. "Just walk towards the exit and you will be surrounded by other Troopers like myself. There will also be a number of airport security men surrounding you. If any of you fall over in the rush, it will be taken care of. We will drag you out."

This didn't sound promising, I thought, glad that I didn't look like a Roller. The fans did, though, and the police couldn't tell them from the real thing in the melee. A fan might end up in the group's limousine while a Roller might be torn limb from limb. The cops, of course, were livid, not just because they'd misjudged the threat – which made them look foolish – but because they disapproved strongly of the effect the Rollers had on American girlhood.

"What followed," I wrote, "was the nearest thing to a nightmare I have experienced while fully awake. On leaving the plane, the tightly-knit group that comprised the five Rollers and their immediate entourage came up against over 1,000 screaming fans who had waited for their arrival since radio stations announced the time earlier in the morning. The majority were held back by barricades, but it seemed only too obvious that these would soon collapse.

"They screamed as if in terrible pain, as if red-hot needles were being driven into their bodies. They pushed and they broke through. They crushed against the Rollers and fury erupted, suddenly but not without warning. The route to the limousine was, perhaps, just over 100 yards. By the time the party had travelled half this distance, it was surrounded. They fell down and tumbled over one another. The State Troopers, who didn't know Rollers from fans, yelled angrily at each other at the same moment, confusing everyone.

"Glass doors blocked the way and, in the time taken to open them, the mob engulfed the Rollers, who stood their ground while security people shoved off attacks from all quarters. Fans were waiting by cars and police threw them aside, vainly trying to create a pathway. Ian Mitchell, the newest Roller, was thrown aside too. Some cop didn't know the genuine article from the ranks of tartan that blurred before his eyes. Mitchell clawed his way back to the car, while Paddy Callaghan, the Rollers' full-time bodyguard, spread his arms wide so that his charges could slip inside. They climbed on the car as it moved slowly away, they fell off as it accelerated and the scare was past. Only [US tour manager] Gary McPike had been left behind in the melee. He came along later in the luggage van."

I'd been sceptical about the Rollers' US prospects until I arrived in

Boston. The truth was that what their US fans lacked in numbers they made up in enthusiasm, all stoked by *16* magazine which specialised in promoting toothsome young pop bands to adolescent girls. I'd seen Marc Bolan's T. Rex die a death in New York when the group's on-stage deficiencies were brutally exposed before an audience that sat and listened instead of screaming, but no such fate befell the Rollers who inspired the same pandemonium they had in the UK. They had a more powerful PA system than before, however, and I tried my best to review their shows objectively, as I would acts whose audiences were more discerning: "The Rollers have improved beyond measure since [I last saw them], probably through the experience of playing together as a band more often," I wrote. "They've developed into a tight, harmony-conscious group, with few pretentions, though their limited repertoire still leaves little or no chance for individual instrumental talent to shine."

As in the UK, the group was strictly controlled by manager Tam Paton. "At their hotels on the road, the group are prisoners," I noted. "Outside, a constant vigil is maintained by parties of fans who, as elsewhere, dress up in those rather ungainly short/long trousers with a side stripe of tartan, tartan scarves and badges that denote their allegiance to one particular member of the group. Obtaining tartan material is not as easy in the US as it is in Britain and, as the uniforms are home-made, one can only marvel at their needlework and determination to acquire the raw materials."

Meanwhile, inside, the Rollers "lead a strangely celibate and temperate life-style, at odds with just about every other band that's travelled the Holiday Inn circuit. They drink milk or Coke and girls are chased away by muscular bodyguards before they pick up the scent of their tartan heroes. Even the road crew are obliged to follow the same regulations – no booze on room service and no girls in their rooms. The Rollers, too, exist on a diet of room service and television, though most of them smoke constantly."

Manager Tam Paton talked to me about the group's forthcoming plans, their potential earnings and the likelihood that they might become tax exiles, all of which was ironic considering the dreadful financial position in which the group would eventually find themselves. That is another story altogether and it would be 40 years until I learned the truth about it, or that in later life Paton ballooned to 26 stone and became a major-league Edinburgh slum landlord and drug dealer.

*

Back in New York I talked to Jeff Beck whose concert I attended at Nassau Coliseum on Long Island. "You know... I've no idea what I do on guitar when I get up there," he told me after the show. "I don't have a clue musically what it is when I'm working the fretboard, it's all totally by ear. I don't even watch my fingers which is good because if someone ever poked my eyes out, I'd still be able to get a job."

Autumn was as busy as ever. I reviewed shows by Joan Armatrading, Crosby & Nash, Roger McGuinn, and interviewed Norman Petty, Buddy Holly's record producer, boyish Jonathan Richman & The Modern Lovers and Emmylou Harris. Emmylou was also playing out on Long Island and I chatted with Albert Lee, her guitarist, too. I'd wanted to meet Albert, the UK's greatest ever country rock guitarist, but never had the chance, not until after I interviewed Emmylou in the dining room of the hotel where she was staying with her Hot Band. Albert was the band's newest recruit, replacing James Burton who'd gone off to play in Elvis' band, so he was following in the footsteps of his idol, hot on his tail in fact.

Emmylou told me Albert hadn't even rehearsed with her band before their first show together. "It came to a stage where we needed a firm commitment from James [Burton] but an Elvis tour came up right at the time we needed him to do some dates with us, so we needed a new guitar player real fast." Emory Gordy, the Hot Band's bass player had seen Albert playing with a latter-day line-up of The Crickets and he introduced Lee to the fold. "He came down to see us at a place in San Bernardino and joined in to play every song," said Emmylou. "He didn't miss a lick all night."

The Hot Band were sat at an adjacent table, polishing off a very late breakfast. Emmylou beckoned Albert over to join us. "I was supposed to go along to two or three gigs and watch James playing, but actually I'd listened to the records so I knew most of the things they were playing anyway," he said, with the calm ease of someone who knows his business. "I'd been living in California for about a year after having worked with Joe Cocker but that had finished so I was looking for a new gig. I was asked to go down to some gigs and if I'd like to do it and I knew even before I saw the band that I would love to. Actually, James got the flu so I was rushed into the band faster than I expected. I went down to a gig to watch and thought I'd bring my guitar just in case. I ended up playing all night."

"Someday this band is going to have a rehearsal," added Emmylou. "Just to see what it's like."

*

In my travels around the city I'd encountered Nik Cohn, the brilliant British writer with Irish roots who wrote a music column for *New York* magazine. Irreverent, provocative and fearless, Nik cared not one jot about whom he might offend in what he wrote, and in his dress affected the image of an English country squire, loud check suits, a cravat and a hat invariably worn at a rakish angle. I was at some bash thrown by Atlantic Records from which Nik was unceremoniously ejected for having suggested in his *New York* column that The Rolling Stones were past it, and I walked out with him in sympathy.

He and I were among a party of writers invited by Motown Records to fly to a state-of-the-art recording studio in Massachusetts to listen to *Songs In The Key Of Life*, the new LP by Stevie Wonder. We sat next to one another on the private plane that took off from La Guardia fairly early in the morning, which didn't suit Nik, and once airborne he demanded vodka in the orange juice that was served with breakfast. I smelled trouble and, sure enough, as we were going into the listening room Nik spotted a pool table. In a break between sides he dragged me out of the listening area for a game. We'd just started to play when a Motown flunky caught us and pointed out that the reason for our presence was to listen to Stevie's new album, not to play pool.

Nik protested. "We can hear it perfectly well in here," he said. "It's loud enough."

This was true. The record, excellent as it was, was being played at a high volume.

"We'd prefer it if you came and listened with all the others," said Mr Motown.

"And I'd prefer to listen while my friend and I play pool. There's speakers in here. Surely you can pipe it through?"

Not wishing to upset the reviewer from prestigious *New York* magazine, we got our own way but Messrs Cohn and Charlesworth were unlikely to be on Motown's Christmas card list that year.

*

My sister Anne visited me in October and, being a perfect host, I did all the tourist stuff that I never bothered with on my own: up to the top of the Empire State Building and World Centre Center, Central Park, Times Square and a boat trip around Manhattan. I also took her to see The Band at the Palladium on the same day that I interviewed Rick Danko, their bass player.

Although they looked and dressed like a bunch of lumberjacks from northern Canada, The Band blended so many influences – blues, country, R&B, folk, Cajun, rock 'n' roll, jazz, gospel, ragtime, hillbilly, you name it – that what emerged was a distillation of musical Americana that always sounds to me as if it could have been written at any time in the past 100 years. All five of them seemed to play everything, including the drums, four of the five had superb voices – each could have been lead singer – and their instrumental capacity went way beyond the usual guitars, keyboards and drums to include tubas, mandolins, accordions, violins, saxes – again, you name it – so much so that they had an infinite variety of combinations to play with in their music.

Rick had just signed a solo contract, the first member of this most distinguished group to do so, and like the rest of the group was a multi-instrumentalist who seemed to have music running through his veins. "He shares the vocal spotlight with Levon Helm and Richard Manuel but it is on the group's emotional songs that he comes into his own," I wrote. "His slightly croaky, lonesome voice with its overtones of breathless exhaustion lend just the right flavour to those Band tunes that echo the hard times of the pioneers of North America."

The Palladium show was superb and afterwards there was a party at the hotel where they were staying. I took Anne and when Rick came over for a chat I introduced her to him, then momentarily left them talking while I went to get her and I another drink. When I returned there was no sign of Rick.

Evidently as soon as my back was turned Rick tried to put the make on Anne but she was having none of it. "He wanted me to go to his room with him," she explained. "What did he think I was?"

"Welcome to my world," I said.

*

In October I had what turned out to be my final encounter with Led Zeppelin, at least while I was a staff writer for *MM*. I was having dinner with a girlfriend at Ashley's, minding my own business, when Robert Plant and an entourage of Led Zeppelin crew arrived, among them Richard Cole who was very drunk. He approached my table, glared menacingly and proposed to my companion that she abandon her meal and accompany him without delay to his hotel to spend the night in his arms. She declined, whereupon he issued the invitation for a second time, implying that she would have a better time in bed with him than with me. She again declined. This time I intervened, suggesting he make love elsewhere, at which point he aimed a punch at my head. Richard, as befitting the man Led Zeppelin had appointed to look after them on the road, was a big, strong bloke so it was fortunate for me that his intoxication was such that not only did his punch miss but that he lost his balance and had to grab a nearby table to stay upright. Plates and cutlery fell to the floor.

The confrontation had not gone unnoticed by fellow diners or the staff who at this point intervened. The doorman, a huge fellow nicknamed Tiny who knew me well, ordered Richard off the premises. He was reluctant to go but with a bit of effort on Tiny's part, Richard was turfed out.

Calm restored, Robert approached our table and apologised profusely. He explained that the whole group was in town for the premiere of *The Song Remains The Same*, the Zep movie, the following night and that much drink had been consumed in the first-class cabin on the flight from London to NY, so much so that an in-flight incident involving Telly Savalas, the bald-headed *Kojak* actor, who was on the receiving end of a plate of food, resulted in threats of arrest at JFK when the plane landed.

The following night I attended the premiere and an after-show party at the Pierre Hotel Cafe, and all seemed to have been forgotten. Richard kept a low profile around me and someone in their entourage told me that word of our altercation had reached Peter Grant, who gave him a good bollocking. I was a friendly journalist after all, and in America they were thin on the ground as far as Zep were concerned.

I reviewed the movie in the following week's *MM* and, in hindsight, think I was unduly kind about a film that even Robert described as "a load of bollocks" and Peter described as "the most expensive home movie ever made". The sequence in the movie that stood out was a scene in which Peter is seen berating the concessions manager at a Baltimore concert who had failed to prevent pirate photos of Zep being sold in the arena. "The verbal battle that ensues offers a unique glimpse into the heart of the rock industry," I wrote. "All smiles on the outside it may be but underneath the veneer lies big money and Peter Grant's responsibility as manager of Led Zeppelin is to make sure that as much of that money as possible heads in his and his band's direction."

One night the following week I was at home when the phone rang. It was none other than Robert, once again apologising for Richard's behaviour and, ever the diplomat, thanking me for not allowing the incident at Ashley's to cloud my judgement of the film or the group for which he sang. The whole affair confirmed my belief that Robert was the nicest bloke in and around Led Zep, an opinion that remains unchanged to this day, though Jimmy Page and John Paul Jones were pleasant enough when I bumped into them on the odd occasion after leaving *MM*.

*

In the autumn of 1976 my friend Glen Colson, the PR for Charisma Records who'd been knocking around the music business doing this and that for whoever slipped him a few quid, arrived in town at the behest of Charisma boss Tony Stratton Smith to promote a forthcoming concert by Van Der Graaf Generator. Glen, moored for a month at the City Squire Hotel in midtown Manhattan, proposed a deal to me. In exchange for eating there as often as I wanted on Charisma's account he could come and stay in my flat, kipping on the sofa bed in the living room for a couple of weeks when the VDGG business was over. He had two pairs of jeans, three t-shirts, a toothbrush and a bit of money he'd picked up from Strat for doing a good job but the two weeks became two months and then some. I didn't care. I was glad of the company apart from when it interfered with my sex life, which it rarely did as he knew when to make himself scarce.

Glen accompanied me to many a gig during the next few months and actually kept a tally which was more than I ever did. The pages of *MM* were my tally. In a subsequent memoir Glen wrote he listed the acts we went to see together, beginning with the time we saw three in one night: Johnny Cash & The Carter Family at the Felt Forum, Chicago at Madison Square Garden and Patti Smith at the Bottom Line.

These were followed by Peter Frampton, Earth, Wind & Fire, Jackson Browne, Orleans, Ry Cooder, Bruce Springsteen, Stephen Stills, Lynyrd Skynyrd, Peter Tosh, Van Der Graaf Generator, Southside Johnny, Vicky Sue Robinson, Neil Young, Cate Bros, Jimmy Cliff, Modern Lovers, Lou Reed, Beach Boys, Graham Parker, Tavares, Bee Gees, Daryl Hall & John Oates, Ted Nugent, Black Sabbath, Robert Palmer, Bob Neuwirth, Guy Clarke, Melba Moore, Al Kooper, Uncle Vinty, Laughing Dogs, Shirts, Tom Petty, Frank Zappa, Joan Armatrading, Bay City Rollers, Stanky Brown Group, Average White Band, Atlanta Rhythm Section, Sanford Townsend Band, The Kinks, Sutherland Bros, Talking Heads, Television, Toys, Blondie, Genesis, Peter Gabriel, Bad Boys, Manfred Mann's Earth Band, Gary Wright, Planets, Phil Rambow, John Cale, The Damned, Dead Boys, .38 Special, Nils Lofgren, Steve Gibbons, Babys, Asleep At The Wheel, Posset Dart

Band, Jessie Colin Young, Robin Lane, Little Feat, Dolly Parton and Alex Harvey.

I might not have reviewed every one of these bands but we certainly saw them all together, which in some ways demonstrates just how much music – this was a four-month period remember – I absorbed during my spell in America. The highlights were Little Feat at the Bottom Line, Bruce at the Palladium and, especially, Neil Young at the same venue.

"There was magic in the air," I wrote of Neil whose stage set featured a backdrop of enormous Fender amps. "Although the band [Crazy Horse] was hard pressed to keep up with him, he was on fire for 60 minutes. It was his guitar work rather than his vocals that shone. He pumped out effortless solos, making the best possible use of open string harmonics, maximum reverb and occasional feedback. The highlight was a new song, 'Like A Hurricane', which combined a strong melody line with an ascending chord sequence that reached climax after climax. While it was played, a wind machine at stage right blew across the musicians, creating an eerie, outdoor effect that harmonised perfectly with the music."

*

In November I spent an alarming afternoon in a hotel room with one-time Wailer Peter Tosh and his entourage. Deeply intimidating and stoned out of his skull, he talked in rhymes, mumbling in Jamaican patois that I found difficult to understand, and when I came to transcribe the tape later, I had to play it back time and time again to faithfully report what he had to say.

Tosh was tall and thin, black as ebony, with a mass of dreadlocks, and he wore very dark sunglasses with leather sides so I couldn't see his eyes. "He eased forward in an armchair, took a massive pull on a newly rolled joint and allowed the smoke to drift upwards across his features until he was almost totally obscured by clouds," I wrote.

Alongside him in the room were five or six other Rastas, one of them a white guy with dreads who kept nodding off and throughout my interview they passed round massive joints rolled from crinkly paper and a big bag of herb on a coffee table. Not once while I was there was there a moment when at least two spliffs weren't on the go. All of Peter's friends mumbled in agreement at what he was telling me, things like, "You gotta go through some humiliation to reach tribulation" or "communication is justification" or "exploitation is the manifestation of subordination" – there were lots of -ations – and the more he warmed to his subjects, the more it seemed to me as if I was participating in some sort of Jamaican religious ritual, with Peter as the preacher, his friends as the congregation and me taking communion for the first time. I couldn't help but wonder whether or not I was being taken for a ride.

Peter had strong feelings about legalising marijuana. "Yes mon. Dat is de message mon. I see no reason why man should be incriminated for a thing dat man cannot make. Dis was created de same de trees was created, de same de birds and de bees was created. Dis," he continued, waving his gigantic joint in the air, "is a part of the creation. Man is trying to show man dat dis thing is a part of dangerous drugs and poison. What am I? If I use dangerous drugs and poison 24 hours a day, what am I?"

"A dangerous person?" I suggested. Then I wrote: "Tosh let out a huge laugh, coughing dangerous and poisonous fumes into the air that smelled infinitely preferable to the exhaust from the cars that droned by on 57th Street below."

I asked Peter why he had left Marley and The Wailers, and he responded by telling me my question was back to front. Marley left him, he said. "You wanna aska why Marley leave me... well, dere was some spiritual vibration between de group. Bob is a leader, he is a singer and writer. All de years it is Bob dat de people has been hearing about and in all dat time we have been writing and making de music and haven't had the opportunity of putting it out to de people. De inspiration and ideas dat I got faded and it is a sin to get talent and hide it, just totally a sin. We can't go on living in sin all de days of our life, mon, and it was de same father who inspired Bob go sing who inspired I and Bunny, so we have to go out and put de message dere. And dere were other causes that come between us but we couldn't go through dat bullshit because I had de message and de message is to play music. Bunny and I had messages and dey were getting wasted, mon. We are strong together because unity is strength but the unity between de three minds have to be coordinated together. If two minds are together and one mind is somewhere else it fails to function, mon."

Make of that what you will.

*

Peter Tosh may have talked in riddles but the issue he talked about that made perfect sense to me was legalising marijuana. By now, like almost everyone I knew in the music industry, especially musicians, I had become a fairly regular consumer of cannabis-based drugs. I say 'fairly' because there were times of drought when my connections in either London or New York were unable to supply what I wanted, so a week or two might go by in which I couldn't get stoned but it wasn't that big a deal. I likened it to being unable to buy raspberries out of season.

Throughout this time my experience of cannabis was 100 per cent positive. Cannabis-based drugs heighten the senses, enrich experiences – they were great for sex, of course – and there was no hangover afterwards. After a couple of hours or so the effect wears off, and there was no craving for more, not for me anyway. Spliffs enhanced my music listening pleasure immensely, especially records played loudly through earphones, particularly if I'd just acquired a new album that I liked a lot. It also enhanced the emotional kick from movies if I was able to grab a toke on the way to the cinema. If a film was sad, I wept buckets and if it was funny, I split my sides. It even enriched my reading pleasure, though it did tend to make you read more slowly and maybe even lose the thread, but this was compensated by the pleasure I took in the beauty of the words by masters like Fitzgerald, Hemingway or Steinbeck, or the reproductions in art books by the likes of Magritte, Picasso or Edward Hopper whose narrative paintings I discovered in New York. Nicely stoned, I would gaze at the *Nighthawks* and imagine the conversation between the busboy and the man in the hat.

Almost all my cannabis consumption occurred where I lived. I might have had the odd joint during a rock concert and at parties, but it seemed to me that the drug was best enjoyed, whether alone or with others, within the security of your own fortress. This had nothing to do with 'security' from the point of view of illegality. The fact that I was breaking the law was irrelevant, of no concern to me whatsoever. I knew that if I was careful and took suitable precautions I'd never get busted, and those who were busted were either unlucky or careless or both. The bartering for loose joints that went on in Central Park and in queues outside rock concerts in New York was done in the open and coppers must have been aware of it. No one took any notice.

During my time on *MM* I tried other drugs – acid, speed, cocaine and even, on two occasions in New York, heroin – but they didn't appeal to me. The acid freaked me out and I decided not to do it again. Cocaine was widely available in NY and on just about every occasion I indulged I was offered a line by better-off folk in the music industry. It turned you into a blabbermouth and sobered you up if you'd had a skinful but that only exacerbated the hangover next morning. My first snort of heroin was accidental – I'd been told it was coke – but the second was in more controlled circumstances and it kept me awake for hours. I felt like Superman until it wore off. The next day, I felt like a dying rat.

The reality is that I preferred the lazy, contemplative sort of drug, not the type that energised you needlessly. I didn't talk about drugs with the rock stars I interviewed but, like an elephant in the room, we all knew what was going on. Nudge, nudge, wink, wink.

*

The Bee Gees were everywhere that November. They threw a party at the Waldorf Astoria and on my arm that night was Lisa Stolley, the elfin model with beautiful Bambi eyes who played 'Fanny (Be Tender With My Love)' repeatedly on the juke box at Ashley's where we both hung out until late. I was still besotted with her. We spent a night together only once, at her studio apartment on 14th Street, but nothing sexual occurred. Before we went to bed, however, Lisa demonstrated her agility by standing on her head. She was wearing a nightgown that fell to the floor, offering me a glimpse of her near naked body, but I was simply too overawed to embrace her, concerned that an unwelcome advance might destroy our friendship.

Lisa occasionally accompanied me to events where I wanted to make other men jealous, among them this swanky reception hosted by The Bee Gees at the Waldorf to celebrate the success of *Saturday Night Fever* whose origins lay in a *New York* magazine article by my friend Nik Cohn. Off we went, dressed to the nines, but at the bar I made the foolish mistake of introducing her to my friend Mick Rock, the photographer, who asked her to dance. She accepted and I never saw either of them again that night. A few weeks later they moved in together and stayed that way for about eight years.

That same month I had another encounter with The Bee Gees. Still riding high with the soundtrack to *Saturday Night Fever*, they had opened their own shop on 57th Street that sold BG merchandise, posing for the cameras on launch day. Later that day I interviewed them in a hotel room where their manager, Robert Stigwood, invited me to a party he was throwing that night at Chez Robert, a penthouse on the corner of one of those huge mansion blocks on Central Park West, actually the building next to the Dakota where John Lennon lived. Like many gay men, Robert was famous for hosting good parties and I'd been to one before, at his massive house in Stanmore in North London, back in 1971.

The apartment, once occupied by the Duke and Duchess of Windsor, was crowded. The Gibbs were there, along with many who worked for RSO Records, Robert's label that was distributed through Atlantic. Champagne corks popped and the pleasing smell of marijuana lingered in the air. Cocaine was being snorted by record company men with open-necked shirts and small spoons around their necks. Beautiful girls danced to loud disco music in a spacious living room furnished with huge leather sofas. It wasn't long before I was as high as a kite, and in search of a loo I wandered down a long corridor, its walls adorned with original artworks.

It was then that I realised the host had crept up behind me and was being rather too friendly. I explained to Robert as nicely as I could that I preferred girls, whereupon he led me into a room where a statuesque redhead from among his staff – or so he said – was sat on a bed reading a magazine. "This is…" he said, and though I cannot remember her name, the implication was that she and I might become enjoined while he watched or perhaps joined in with me as the target of his lust. She didn't demur and in different circumstances I might have done just that but something in my Yorkshire upbringing told me this was unwise and that was the end of the matter. Robert smiled graciously and the three of us returned to where the action was.

*

Since the day it opened Ashley's had been my New York local. I often went there after a show, sometimes in company, sometimes alone. Friends old and new could be found inside. I signed for my food and bar tab. Its proprietor and his wife Terry were my best friends, and I joined in the hunt when they lost Barnaby, their pet beagle, which to everyone's relief was eventually found wandering the neighbourhood streets. On the menu was pâté Hearst, commemorating the kidnap of the heiress, and other delicacies with names concocted from the fertile imagination of mine host.

One night at Ashley's, Glen and I got talking to Lou Reed. I mentioned that I'd reviewed his show at the Palladium, and Glen offered to drop off a copy of that week's *MM* at his apartment. At Lou's flat on the East Side he was greeted by Rachel, Lou's 'friend' whose gender was always in doubt. Sat in a room full to the brim with old black and white RCA TV sets, Lou explained that they were from the backdrop to the Palladium show and offered him one. Glen called me and when I gave him the thumbs up he relieved Lou of three TVs which we linked up in the front room. They didn't work that well but I wasn't bothered. I never felt the need to watch TV while I lived in New York.

It was Ashley who introduced me to Joy. One night that fall she and I were both seeking company so we had a beer or two before I suggested dinner at a restaurant with a nautical theme a couple of blocks away, and by the main course we somehow knew we were going to spend the night together. After the meal, we headed uptown and crept into my apartment on East 78th Street lest we awaken Glen on the sofa bed. Dawn was breaking by the time we closed our eyes.

Joy's name suited her. When she smiled she lit up the room; a New York free spirit with a strain of Irish blood, blonde, beautiful and well read, she knew her own mind, was bright as a button and did not suffer fools. The mother of a four-year-old boy, her marriage to a professional musician was failing but our courtship was nevertheless reckless, conducted with a certain degree of subterfuge, not least when I visited her apartment on 23rd Street where after caresses we discussed books we'd read and played darts on the board in her living room.

We also played chess. An accomplished player, at any one time Joy had several correspondence games on the go with other skilled players in various parts of the world. She beat me easily, switching the board around so that halfway through the game she would take on my losing position and me her winning pieces. She still beat me easily. Another of her interests was basketball and through her I obtained tickets to NY Knicks games at Madison Square Garden for Glen and myself, the only time I visited the Garden for anything other than a rock show.

That Christmas, with Joy elsewhere, Glen and I went out to a cheap diner for a turkey lunch. I didn't know it but my time as *MM*'s man in America was coming to an end. This had nothing to do with the amount of work I was doing. On the contrary, during the final three months of 1976 and into January of the following year I wrote stories on Southside Johnny, Stephen Stills, Orleans, Chicago, Hall & Oates, Ry Cooder, the Eagles, Dr Hook, Frank Zappa (who read me a prepared statement about his dispute with Warner Bros Records and declined to answer further questions), Sparks, John Cale, Dennis Wilson and George Benson whom I met in Electric Ladyland, the downtown studio built by Jimi Hendrix. I wrote my third big feature on the bands that played in CBGBs, interviewing its owner Hilly Kristal, and reported on another Bay City Rollers riot, this time at the New York Palladium.

It was the devaluation of sterling that sank me, and brought my New York posting to an end. The cost of the operation – the rent on the apartment, the utilities, the living allowance – had reached an unacceptable level. *Melody Maker* was no longer the best-selling weekly music paper in the UK. Change was in the air musically too. No one cared much about the American acts I was writing about after the Sex Pistols led the UK punk charge, so in January Ray Coleman called to tell me my time was up. There was a job waiting for me in London if I wanted it but I didn't. I loved New York too much and didn't want to leave, not least because of Joy, though she would draw the curtain on our affair early in the New Year. Moreover, I knew that working for *MM* in London again would be a monumental comedown after almost four years in America. Either way, I resigned.

The last issue of *MM* with my name on the staff list was published on February 19, 1977, and in it was my final interview, with Tom Scholz, whose group Boston was riding high in the charts with 'More Than A Feeling'. Elsewhere in that issue *Rumours*, the multi-million selling LP by Fleetwood Mac that would define the era, an album celebrating its 1,026th week in the charts as I write this, was given a scathing review. I read it and laughed. Perhaps my departure was for the best.

Ray sent me a nice letter thanking me for my "good work" and that was that.

EPILOGUE

New York City, September 2021

It was a day laced with nostalgia going back almost half a century. We left Brooklyn at 10am and headed via the subway to 86th Street and Lexington, then walked a few blocks across to Park Avenue and down to 78th Street, to number 51. Our appointment was at 11.

The current occupiers of apartment 3D were expecting us. I'd written to them in August, addressing my letter to "The Occupants" and enclosing a scan of the postcard that John had sent me. It was the only proof I had that I once lived there. The reply, via email, was prompt. Intrigued no doubt by the postcard, the young couple would be delighted to welcome me to my former home. We exchanged more emails and at the appointed time, my wife Lisa, daughter Olivia and I entered the doorway of number 51. The lobby looked exactly the same, the same mosaic tiles on the floor, the same big gilded mirror over the black marble fireplace, the same faded elegance common to 100-year-old buildings on the Upper East Side of Manhattan. We ascended to the second floor in the same creaky old elevator with its collapsible door that I remembered from years gone by.

I already knew that my old apartment had been combined with the one next door to create a much bigger living space, but I was unprepared for its chic, modern appearance. Polished wood floors had replaced the shag pile carpet, the walls were tastefully wallpapered where once there had been creamy yellow paint, the fixtures, fittings and furniture looked brand new. The current owners hadn't lived there long and they had improved on top of other improvements that had been done over the years by a stream of other occupiers. The rooms where I lived and worked were still where they used to be, the bedroom that saw so many intimacies was now their young daughter's room, and it was spotless, and the tiny bathroom, my private sauna, had a new tub and basin. Indeed, so much had changed that had I not known the address I could have been anywhere in the world.

Our hosts were gracious and accommodating. They showed us around, made us coffee and we chatted for almost 90 minutes. They were intrigued by my occupation and way of life in New York, especially the John Lennon connection, not least because the husband's father was a Beatles fan. They mentioned that a priest had been invited to somehow spiritually cleanse the bedroom that had been mine. Good job too, I thought.

It was clear to me they were interested in the history of the building, which was built around 1920 and was once a private residence. They told us that Madonna lived nearby in two similar buildings she had combined into one and surrounded with a security fence. Before we left we went up onto the roof, as I occasionally did when I lived there. As ever, the view over the rooftops where at night the stars put on a show for free, was magnificent. When we walked back down the five storeys they all looked the same as they did 45 years ago. The common areas had hardly been altered at all.

We walked around the neighbourhood which, like the apartment, was barely recognisable. No shops, bars or eateries had survived the 45 years, not one that I could see, and after lunch we walked through Central Park, past the model boating lake and statue of Alice In Wonderland where I often lingered in days done by. Further along, a jazz quintet, guitar, upright bass, mouth harp, horn and drums, played 'Take The A Train' and 'Sir Duke', so we sat and listened for a while and then moved on to Strawberry Fields, stopping at the Imagine stone. A boy with a guitar was playing 'I Saw Her Standing There' which segued into 'Let It Be', two songs by Paul, but I didn't feel the need to point this out.

I almost lost it when we crossed over Central Park West and walked alongside the Dakota. Standing in the exact spot where it happened, that most brutal, senseless and unforgivable atrocity, brought a momentary tear. Then we walked back into the park and sat down by the Bethesda Fountain. No one offered us loose joints.

The past is a foreign country, wrote LP Hartley in the opening line of *The Go-Between*. He was right. Two nights after vising my old apartment on 78th Street the three of us walked up Fifth Avenue from Washington Square. The neighbourhood around Fifth & 13th Street is gentrified now, almost all the buildings seemingly rebuilt in the last two or three decades. But one remained the same, the one I wanted to see, the one at 59 Fifth Avenue, Ashley's bar and restaurant.

How many times had I hailed a cab and told the driver to drop me at 13th and Fifth, almost as many times as 78th between Park and Madison? The wall that fronted Ashley's was still intact, though on either side the buildings looked new to me. Most recently it had been a deli called Merci Market but the sign on the barred door said "Permanently Closed" which suggested it had gone out of business, and above that was another sign advertising the premises for lease. It's a prime location so it won't be long before someone new opens a business there, someone unaware of how many famous faces once crossed its threshold.

Peering through the glass, it looked like the ground floor that housed Ashley's bar and restaurant had been the food shop, but the first floor – Upstairs At Ashley's, a semi-private space where I once spent a memorable evening with John – looked to me as if it was now separate, accessed from another door. There was a blue light in the windows upstairs, just like there was back when there was a DJ spinning records, a dance floor and a bar, and a private office where favoured customers did whatever they wanted behind locked doors.

I know it's only bricks and mortar and that it's the people that make what happens inside a building great, but it was sad to see how time had erased Ashley's. No more limousines pulling up outside to disgorge rock stars, no more beautiful waitresses bustling around the tables, no more New York Dolls on the juke box, no more unmade-up member of Kiss hiding from photographers, no more Lou Reed holding court at a corner table with his manager Jonny Podell – "A marriage made in the emergency ward," quipped Ashley – no more framed Art Deco pictures on the walls, no more Richard Cole aiming a punch at me, no more Gail, Lisa or Joy or any of the other girls I loved, and worst of all no more Ashley greeting his friends at their tables, hopping around with a beaming smile that never failed to light up the room, the room I peered into on my last visit to New York and realised the past is a foreign country.

ACKNOWLEDGEMENTS

I wouldn't have been able to write this memoir had not Ray Coleman offered me a job on *Melody Maker* in 1970. Ray died in 1996 but I remain forever grateful to him for how my seven years on *MM* radically altered and immeasurably enriched the life I have led ever since.

Working for *MM* during the first half of the seventies forged a bond between some of its staff that lasts to this day. My former colleagues Michael Watts, Richard Williams, Chris and Marilyne Welch, Geoff Brown and myself meet for lunch about twice a year to relive old times, and most of us have been amongst the mourners at the funerals of those we have lost: Ray, Roy Hollingworth, Carole Clerk, Rob Partridge and Alan Lewis. I liken it to having once played together on a football team that long ago won the league title, and I'm grateful to them all simply for having known them, and especially to Michael for advice with this memoir, and to Richard and Chris for enlightening me about *MM*'s perilous circumstances at the time I joined..

I'm also grateful for the website *Rock's Back Pages*, the world's largest online music library, on which can be found almost 350 articles written by me, the vast majority for *Melody Maker*. I wrote many more than that for *MM* but when I skim through them it's still like reading my own diary.

Two great friends who appear in this memoir, Chris Whincup and Ashley Pandel, have passed on. Both enhanced my life and I miss them enormously; also the music writer Johnny Rogan, from whom I learned more about literacy than any English teacher. My thanks are also due to Simon Goddard, Andy Neill, Glen Colson, Mike Tremaglio, Richard Houghton, Terry Donaldson, Joy Danaher, Lisa Stolley, Bob Gruen, Barrie Wentzell and many more whose names appear in this book. Thanks also to my daughter Olivia for designing the cover.

My dad taught me the difference between right and wrong, my mum the joy of reading, and my sister Anne Meehan did her best to keep me on the straight and narrow, not always successfully.

Finally, I might have slipped off this mortal coil before now had it not been for the love and support of the family I found 15 years after the events described in this book. Thanks Lisa, Olivia and Sam.

INDEX

SPECIAL THANKS

Special thanks to:
Horace Austin
Patrick Thomas
Mark Wilkerson
Neil & Christine Witten
Marc Starcke
Chris Ody
Ian Jones
Andre Boyer
Steve Knight
Jan Ertesvåg
John Martin
Ronald Shepcar
David Mortimer
Paul Voller
Charlie Shillibeer
Rex Patton
Tadhg Coughlan

Milton Keynes UK
Ingram Content Group UK Ltd.
UKHW040627181124
2908UKWH00058B/695

9 781915 858252